NOWELL'S CATECHISM.

The Parker Society.

Instituted A.D. M.DCCC.XL.

For the Publication of the Works of the Fathers
and Early Writers of the Reformed
English Church.

A CATECHISM

WRITTEN IN LATIN

BY

ALEXANDER NOWELL,

DEAN OF ST PAUL'S:

TOGETHER WITH

THE SAME CATECHISM

TRANSLATED INTO ENGLISH

BY

THOMAS NORTON.

APPENDED IS A SERMON PREACHED BY DEAN NOWELL BEFORE
QUEEN ELIZABETH AT THE OPENING OF THE PARLIAMENT
WHICH MET JANUARY 11, 1563.

EDITED FOR

The Parker Society,

BY

G. E. CORRIE, D.D.

MASTER OF JESUS COLLEGE, CAMBRIDGE.

Wipf & Stock
PUBLISHERS
Eugene, Oregon

Wipf and Stock Publishers
199 W 8th Ave, Suite 3
Eugene, OR 97401

A Catechism Written in Latin
Together with the Same Catechism Translated into English
By Nowell, Alexander
ISBN: 1-59752-208-2
Publication date 5/18/2005
Previously published by Cambridge, 1853

CONTENTS.

	PAGE
MEMOIR	i
Fac simile of the Title of the first Edition of Nowell's Catechism	i*
NOELLI CATECHISMUS	1
Prima Pars. De Lege et Obedientia	7
Secunda Pars. De Evangelio et Fide	26
Tertia Pars. De Oratione, et gratiarum Actione	64
Quarta Pars. De Sacramentis	83
Vocabula nostratia, et loquendi formæ Christianorum propriæ, etc.	99
Fac simile of the Title of the first Edition of Norton's Translation of the Catechism	105
NOWELL'S CATECHISM	113
The First Part. Of the Law and Obedience	120
The Second Part. Of the Gospel and Faith	141
The Third Part. Of Prayer and Thanksgiving	183
The Fourth Part. Of Sacraments	205
APPENDIX	221
INDEX	231

MEMOIR.

ALEXANDER NOWELL, the son of John Nowell, Esq., of Whalley, in the county of Lancaster, was born in that parish sometime in the year 1507 or 1508: educated at Middleton in the same county, and at the early age of thirteen, was admitted of Brasen-Nose College, Oxford. Of that society he afterwards became fellow; and very late in life (1595) was for a few months President of the College. In 1543 he was appointed Master of Westminster School[1]; and in November, 1551, was made prebendary of Westminster on the death and in the room of Dr Redmayn, Master of Trinity College, Cambridge.

On the accession of Queen Mary, Nowell was returned (probably through the influence of the Earl of Devon) as one of the burgesses to represent the borough of Loo in the parliament which met in October 1553. A committee of the House of Commons, however, declared him to be ineligible to be a member of that house, because of his "being a prebendary of Westminster, and thereby having a voice in the Convocation House." But unless Nowell were the Proctor elected to represent the Chapter of Westminster in Convocation, he would not have "a voice in the Convocation House" merely because he happened to be a prebendary of Westminster. Considering, therefore, that Dr Tregonwell, a zealous papist, who was also a prebendary of Westminster, was allowed to retain his seat in parliament, the ejection of Nowell from that assembly may be ascribed to his known attachment to the Reformation[2].

Of this attachment Nowell gave decisive evidence in the following year: for when the persecuting spirit of Queen Mary

---

[1] Carlisle Grammar Schools, II. 114.
[2] Carte, Hist. of Engl. III. 295.

had begun to shew itself, we find him at Strasburgh among those eminent persons who were exiles for their religion. It appears that from Strasburgh Nowell removed to Frankfort, and when the "troubles" arose there, that he at first adhered to the party who advocated the "new discipline," against Horn and the strictly episcopalian party. He was, however, afterwards found among those who enforced the importance of unity in essentials, and who expressed their willingness to submit to authority as regarded matters ceremonial. Yet when the question of rites and ceremonies came to be discussed in the Convocation of 1562, Nowell, with others, proposed some relaxation in the rubrics of King Edward Sixth's Service-book, as regarded the wearing of the surplice, the cross in baptism, and other like matters, respecting which some ministers had scruples[1]. Afterwards, also, we find him acting as a pacificator in the proceedings which were taken against Sampson, Dean of Christ's Church, and Humphry, President of Magdalen College, Oxford, for refusing the habits[2].

When, on the death of Queen Mary, the exiles returned to England, Nowell was among those who were employed to carry out Queen Elizabeth's plans for the reformation of religion. One of the most efficacious of those plans was the appointing of visitors for different parts of the country, whose duty it should be to see that such injunctions and ordinances as were issued by authority respecting religion and ecclesiastical affairs were complied with. To Nowell and others were assigned, in 1559, the visitation of the diocese of Lincoln, Peterborough, Oxford, and Lichfield[3]. Early in the following year Bishop Grindal collated Nowell to the archdeaconry of Middlesex, to the rectory of Saltwood (which however he very soon resigned), and to a stall in the church of Canter-

[1] Troubles at Frankfort, pp. 65, 115—135, 189, 190. Lond. 1846. Strype, Ann. I. i. 1591. Oxf.
[2] Strype, Life of Parker, I. 343. Oxf.
[3] Strype, Ann. I. i. 247.

bury. In the same year he was appointed to a stall in St Peter's, Westminster, which from being a monastery had been erected into a collegiate church; and at the close of the year, Nowell was preferred to the deanery of St Paul's[4], which he held till his death.

During the earlier periods of the Reformation licences to preach were but very sparingly granted. The persons selected for that privilege were always men of eminent abilities and of settled principles. It was to be expected therefore that Nowell would be very often employed in so important a service. Accordingly we find him among those appointed to preach at St Paul's Cross; in the Cathedral; before the Queen during Lent; and on other occasions. A specimen of his preaching is given in the Appendix to this Volume.

In the Convocation which revised the "Articles of Religion" agreed upon in the reign of King Edward VI., Nowell was chosen prolocutor, and took an active part in the proceedings of that assembly. He was soon after employed to compose a Homily[5] to be added to the Form of Prayer which was put forth in consequence of the plague which was raging.

Early in the year 1565 we find Nowell engaged in a controversy with Thomas Dorman, who had been fellow of All Souls' College, Oxford, during the reign of Edward VI., but went over to popery when Queen Mary came to the throne. This Dorman had put forth an attack on certain portions of Bp Jewell's Apology, under the title of "A Proof of certain Articles in Religion denied by Mr Jewell." He undertook in his book to prove that the supremacy of the bishop of Rome; transubstantiation; the sacrifice of the mass and communion under one kind; were severally held and professed by the Church of Christ within the first six centuries. It was, however, to establish his proposition respecting the universal supremacy of the bishop of Rome that Dorman chiefly laboured;

[4] Strype, Ann. I. i. 306.
[5] See Grindal's Remains, pp. 95, et seq. Park. Soc. Edit.

and to the refutation of that fable, therefore, "A Reproofe written by Alexander Nowell of a Booke entituled 'A Proofe of Certain Articles in Religion denied by M. Juell,'" &c., is directed. Nowell gives as a reason for proceeding no further in answering Dorman, "because the Bp of Sarum in the Answer he was preparing to Harding's would sufficiently confute the rest of Dorman's book, for that the latter had written little or nothing that was not taken from Harding[1]." Before the end of the year Dorman put forth "A Disproofe of M. Nowell's Reproofe," which was followed in 1567 by Nowell's "Confutation as well of M. Dorman's last Boke, entituled 'A Disproufe,' &c. as well as of D. Sander his Causes of Transubstantiation;" Nowell having, during 1566, been employed in writing and publishing the continuation of his Reproof, in which his object chiefly was to vindicate the supreme authothority of Christian princes in causes ecclesiastical as well as civil within their own dominions, " by M. Dorman maliciously oppugned." Nowell's controversy with Saunders arose out of an attack which the latter had made on an assertion in the "Reproof of Dorman's Proof," to the effect that "all the papists put together would never be able to shew cause why the words 'I am the true Vine' did not prove a transubstantiation as well as 'This is my body[2].'"

The work, however, which has identified the name of Nowell with the Church of England, is the Catechism reprinted in the present Volume. Among the important business to be brought under the consideration of the Convocation which met in 1562, it was advised that "there should be authorised one perfect Catechism for the bringing up of the youth in godliness, in the schools of the whole realm; which book," it is added, "is well nigh finished by the industry of the Dean of St Paul's:" and that "the said Catechism being once approved by the learned in the Convo-

---

[1] Nowell's Confutation, pp. 26, 27.
[2] Reproof, &c. p. 103. 2nd Edit.

cation-house, may be authorised to be taught also by the Universities, and to the youth wheresoever they be taught their grammar in any private men's houses[3]." Accordingly, 5 Feb., a committee of the upper house, consisting of Jewell and three other bishops, was appointed to examine a book called " The Catechism." On the 3rd March, the prolocutor of the lower house of Convocation returned to the upper the *Catechismus Puerorum*, as having been unanimously approved. Moreover, in a letter dated June 22, 1563, Nowell writes to Sir W. Cecil, to the effect that ' whereas the copy of the Catechism which he had caused to be written out for his Honor, to whom the book was dedicated, came to the hands of the bishops and clergy assembled in the late Convocation (that of 1562), and by reason that certain places were by their judgments altered, was interlined and blotted, he (Nowell) had caused it to be copied out again, and had sent it to his honor, not now in his own name, *as afore, but in the name of the clergy of the Convocation, as their book, seeing it is by them approved and allowed*[4].'

It will be observed, however, that there is a want of definiteness in the terms by which the book submitted to Convocation is described. It is called " The Catechism," when referred to a committee of the upper house; whilst the book approved unanimously by the lower house is " *Catechismus Puerorum*." It is remarkable, too, that when Nowell put forth, in 1570, the Catechism which is here reprinted, he did not claim for it any synodal authority. He dedicated it indeed to the Archbishops and Bishops of England, and submitted it to their judgments; but it was merely in the hope that the book, when known to be sanctioned by their high authority, would become more extensively useful. For these, and other reasons which might be mentioned, it has not unreasonably been doubted whether the Catechism approved and allowed by Convocation were the Catechism contained in the present volume. The

[3] Strype, Ann. 1562, I. i. 473.   [4] Strype, Ann. I. i. 526.

following letter, however, from Nowell to Sir W. Cecil, dated on the day on which this Catechism was first put forth in print, sets that question at rest:—

After my humble commendations unto your honour. Thes are to certifie the same that the Latine Catechisme, which aboute seaven yeres agoo I dyd write and dedicate unto your honour in the fyrst writen copie, is now at the laste putt in printe, by my lords of Canterburie and Yorkes appoynctment, and with your honours consent, as my lord of Canterburie informed me. The occasion of the dedicating of it now unto the byshopps, as men most mete to judge and allow, or disallow of such matiers, was inforced that about syxe yeres agoo, it was offred unto them, beinge assembled in Convocation, and by them allowed, and by the whole cleargie of the Lower Convocation-Howse subscribed unto, as is to be sene in the coopie remaininge with me.

Notwithstandinge I sent a copie of it, beinge fare writen ageine, unto your honour, with whom it remayned above one yeare, and then was delyvered me ageine by your honour, and withall certen notes of some lerned man uppon it. Wheruppon it hath ever synse remayned with me, untyll my lord of Canterburie his grace called for it, after that I had altered manie places in it, acordinge to the notes which your honour delyvered unto me, as your honour shall well perceyve, had yow leysure to compare the saide notes (which I have sent ageine to your honour, even the verie copie it selfe which your honour delyvered me) with the printed booke, which I have alsoo sent unto your honour. And after the coopie had remayned a while with my lord of Canterburie, he demaunded of me whie I dyd not put it in printe. I tolde his grace that without your honours consent, to whom I had in the fyrste writen copie dedicated it, I wold not printe it: and within a fewe dayes after he sending for me ageine, tolde me that your honour had consented that it shuld be printed, and that it was to your honour no matier were it dedicated unto the byshopps; and soo hym selfe allowinge it to the printe, by the subscription of his name and my lorde of Yorke doing the like, it came to the printe at the laste, syx yeres and more after it was fyrst wryten. Wherof in case your honour shall have good liking, I shall be verie gladde. And thus I commend your honour unto Allmightie Godde, who have yow and all yours in his blessed kepinge. 16 Junii, 1570.

Your honors to commande,
ALEXANDER NOWELL.

*To the right honorable and my singlare
good frend Sir Wyllyam Cecill,
knight, principall secretarie to the
Queene's ma^{tie}.*[1]

[1] State Paper Office (Domestic Cor.).

Of this Catechism there were two editions[2], or impressions, printed in 1570; and reprints of it appeared in 1571, 1574, 1576: and perhaps in other intermediate years. An abridgment of the Catechism was also made by Nowell, probably as early as 1570; and shortly after he put forth a still more condensed Catechism. We may judge of the high estimation in which these works were held, when we learn from the various injunctions, &c. put forth at that time by public authorities, that no Catechisms were allowed to be used by clergymen and schoolmasters except one or other of Nowell's[3].

With regard to the Catechisms and catechetical documents that appeared at and about the time of the Reformation, it is well known that they mainly consisted of an exposition of the Creed, the Lord's Prayer, and the Ten Commandments. Although, therefore, the arrangement of the matter was not always the same, there was, as might be expected, a great similarity as regarded doctrinal statements, and oftentimes a verbal agreement between one catechism and another. In drawing up his Catechism, therefore, Nowell informs the bishops that he had not scrupled to avail himself of the labours of others who had preceded him in this department of theology, both as regarded arrangement and matter. Yet a cursory comparison of Nowell's Catechism with any other of those referred to will shew the great superiority of his work. The Catechisms of Poinet and Calvin are, perhaps, those with which Nowell's is most frequently and verbally coincident, yet his will be found to excel both, not less in the full and lucid exposition of doctrine than in Latinity.

Four years after the publication of his Catechism, Nowell was one of the Divines appointed to confer with Campion, in consequence of a challenge which that Jesuit had given in his "Ten Reasons in favour of the Roman Church." A Report of that Conference was afterwards (1583) published.

[2] A Copy of each Edition is in the Bodleian.
[3] Cardwell, Synodalia, I. 128. Grindal's Remains, pp. 142, 152.

From that time until his death, which took place on 13 Feb. 1602, the Dean was frequently occupied in preaching on great public occasions, and at the funerals of the nobility; and of some of his sermons notes taken by contemporaries are still in existence.

Besides the Catechisms, the only works of importance left by Nowell are those which have been already mentioned. Among his acts of public beneficence may be recorded the founding of a Free Grammar School at Middleton, in Lancashire, and of several scholarships in Brasen-Nose College, Oxford. Of these and other interesting particulars connected with this great man, a full account is given in his Life, written in the early part of the present century, by the Rev. Ralph Churton.

Thomas Norton, the translator of Nowell's Catechism, is generally considered to have been of the profession of the law, and in later life to have been solicitor to the city of London. If he be the same person who wrote the letter to Calvin, which appears among the "Original Letters" published by the Parker Society, he had been tutor to the children of the Protector Somerset. He is said to have been a contributor to the Earl of Dorset's "Mirror of Magistrates;" and to have assisted that nobleman in the composition of the tragedy of Gorboduc. Warton, however, is of opinion that the identity of style to be observed throughout the whole of that play renders it improbable that Norton had any hand in it. Norton, also, is said to have versified twenty-seven of the Psalms in the version of Sternhold and Hopkins. In a copy of that version, printed in 1581, the rendering of Psalms li. and liii. certainly bears the initials T. N.; but to twenty-six others the letter N. only is attached. Strype speaks of a *minister* named Thomas Norton, who gave his advice about the Conference with Campion; who took notes of that Conference; and furthermore advised with Whitgift respecting the "Admonition to Parliament:" but it is much more probable that the party thus mentioned by Strype was the translator of Nowell's Catechism.

Norton is said to have died about 1584.

It remains to be stated that Norton translated from the second edition of the Latin which appeared in 1570: for his translation which bears that date omits a passage[1], the Latin of which is found in the edition which appeared June 16, 1570, but is not found in the other Latin edition of that year. In the reprints of the translation which appeared in 1571, and subsequently, the passage in question occurs.

Aug. 1854.

[1] See p. 170, line 2 from the bottom.

CATECHISMVS,

fiue prima Inſtitutio, Diſci=
PLINA'QVE PIETATIS
Chriſtianæ, Latinè explicata.

Qui ſimul eloquio linguam formare Latino,
Et vera mentem Relligione cupis:
Hic liber, atque labor votum dabit vnus vtrunque,
Commoda ſic vno bina labore feres.

Londini,
IN OFFICINA REGINALDI
Wolfij, Regiæ Maiest. in Latinis
Typographi.

ANNO DOM. M.D.LXX.
XVI. CALEND. IVL.

Reverendissimis in Chri-
STO PATRIBUS, AC DO-
minis, D. Archiepiscopis, Cantuariensi,
et Eboracensi, aliisque reverendis patribus, Episcopis
Ecclesiæ Anglicanæ, vigilantissimis fide-
lissimisque pastoribus.

Quum mente tota in hanc curam incumbendum, omnemque adeo operam in primis adhibendam esse existimem, ut pietatis doctrina, quanta fieri potest sinceritate, pueris, qui sunt Reipublicæ quasi seminaria, tradatur, ne vel teneri ipsorum animi pravis opinionibus imbuantur, vel ab iis, quæ recta sunt, discendis eorum mentes obscuritate nimia avertantur, aut retardentur: pro ea qua patriam juventutem benevolentia prosequor, statui omni ope atque opera mihi enitendum esse, ut illius pia studia promoverem, et Christianæ religionis summam ratione, atque compendio ad puerilem captum non incommodo, dilucide atque explicate proponerem. In quo Catechismo (sic enim nostri vocant) non putavi minutis interrogatiunculis, brevibusque responsis, quasi punctis quibusdam, quod proposui, efficiendum esse: neque satis esse, nudis tantum assertionibus, asseverationibusque universa breviter simpliciterque affirmare: nisi causas etiam aliquas, rationesque rerum afferrem, atque subjicerem. Et quo major fides atque authoritas rebus adjungeretur, testimonia Divina ex sacris literis in margine libri passim notavi, quibus sibi quisque, vel aliis cum hærent, satisfacere possit. In hoc etiam Catechismo curam et diligentiam adhibui, ut incorrupta latini sermonis integritas, quoad ejus fieri posset, ubique servaretur: ut latinitatem pariter, atque pietatem uno eodem labore pueri nostri addiscere possent. In paucis tantum quibusdam, vel singulis, vel continuatis, atque conjunctis verbis, quæ nostra sunt propria, et Christianæ religioni peculiaria, tametsi Ciceronis, et proxima illi ætate latinis hominibus inaudita, sinceræ nostræ potius pietatis, quam emendatæ loquutionis rationem habendam esse existimavi:

itaque in contextu quidem orationis ea non mutavi. Verum ne qui latine et pure loqui volunt, quicquam vel hac in parte desiderarent, ubi a communi more verborum latinorum discessum fuerit, et quibus ea vocabulis, atque loquendi formis posse explicari putem, in fine libri commonstravi. Quod autem orationis genere fuso, atque profluente potius, quam exili atque jejuno utor in hoc Catechismo, doctissimorum ex veteribus judicium, consiliumque in eo sum sequutus: qui quum ubertatem quidem orationis ætate, styloque facile depasci posse putent, siccitatem ejus puerilibus ingeniis, non minus quam teneris plantis soli sterilitatem, noxiam esse arbitrantur. Quam etiam ob causam lectissimos verborum, sententiarumque flosculos undique decerptos, maxime ex Ciceronis hortulis, transtuli atque inserui in hunc Catechismum, illis tanquam stellis quibusdam orationem notans atque illuminans. Nam ut de tota religione pure et emendate, ita de quibusdam etiam capitibus copiose splendideque putavi dicendum esse: ut permagni res momenti atque ponderis, verborum, sententiarumque floribus conspersæ, puerilibus sensibus blandientes, et quasi odorum suavitates afflantes, illorum animos illaberentur jucundius, facilius perciperentur, ac semel memoriis, pectoribusque juventutis insidentes, hærentesque penitus, et quasi infixæ perpetuo retinerentur atque custodirentur. Non defuturos ergo arbitror, qui lenitatem et æquabilitatem orationis alicubi requiret, et desiderabunt: ut quibus unus orationis sonus, idemque perpetuo stylus placebit. Quod si querentur etiam libellum, dum ea quæ paucis cognosci possent, pluribus sunt verbis amplificata, justum modum magnitudinemque excessisse: cogitent omnia pueris quam apertissime planissimeque esse explicanda: qui quum in scholis tam multos annos sedere soliti sint, fere ut latine tantum loqui discerent, id eos consequi ex pietatis Christianæ libris ne invideant, quod ex poetarum profanis, fictisque, et interdum impiis, atque impuris fabulis doceri antea solebant. Sed et ipsis brevitatis amatoribus statui morem gerere, eundemque hunc Catechismum edere exiguo libello, quam potest fieri brevissime, ita arctatum, ut arctius fere astringi non poterit, in quo magna parvis, longa brevibus, lata angustis, multa paucis permutata reperient: ut quibus hic liber, ut productione longior, non placebit, libellus ille ut contractione brevior, non displiceat. Verum cum in Catechismis fere omnibus ea Christianæ religionis capita explicentur, quæ Symbolo Apostolorum, Decalogo, et Oratione

Dominica continentur, non est in illis, ut sane nec esse potest, usque adeo magna in tradendi ratione varietas. Quid enim pie et utiliter de præcipuis nostræ religionis capitibus excogitari potest, quod ab aliquibus, ac sæpe quidem a multis illorum, qui eadem antea tractarunt, dictum jam non fuerit. Et qui Decalogum, Symbolum Apostolorum, et Orationem Dominicam interpretandum sumserit, eundem, quem in ipsis rebus invenerit ordinem, nisi perturbare permiscereque omnia velit, necessario sequi oportet. Alii quidem primo loco de lege, secundo de fide tractarunt: alii, ne similes per omnia viderentur, contrarium in his ordinem, quod sane pertenue discrimen est, sunt sequuti. Nam de Oratione, et Sacramentis post legem, atque fidem omnes fere tractarunt. Alium ergo ordinem instituere, qui non sit jam ab aliquo præoccupatus, nemo certe, nisi omnem omnino ordinem velit invertere, ullo modo potest. Hæc mihi hoc loco putavi esse commemoranda, quod existimem non defuturos, qui et eadem me, et eodem etiam ordine multa, quæ sunt ab aliis quibusdam antea perscripta, tradidisse in hoc Catechismo, conquerentur. In quo sane injurii æquis omnibus videri possunt, quum quod immutari recte non queat, non esse mutatum causabuntur. Hunc Catechismum Reverendissimi patres, viri omni doctrina, et virtute ornatissimi, qui summum dignitatis gradum in Ecclesia tenentes, sacris præestis, et rebus præsidetis Ecclesiasticis, vestro judicio permitto: quem si amplissimi ordinis vestri authoritate comprobatum, juventus nostra in manus sumserit,
summo id Reipublicæ Christianæ commodo futurum esse, in spem maximam, et quemadmodum confido, certissimam, verissimamque adducemur.

Vestri studiosissimus, observantissimusque,

A. N.

NOELLI CATECHISMUS.

MAGISTER. AUDITOR.

Magister. Quum præceptorem discipulis suis alterum patrem, parentemque, non corporum, sed animorum esse oporteat; ad officii mei rationem pertinere video, charissime Fili, non tam literis te atque moribus liberaliter instituere, quam mentem tuam animumque tenerum bonis opinionibus et vera Religione imbuere. [a]Puerilis enim ista ætas non minus præceptis sanctis ad pietatem, imo multo etiam magis, quam ingenuis artibus ad humanitatem est informanda. Quamobrem consentaneum putavi, quæstiunculis quibusdam tecum agere, ut certo sciam num recte an secus in ea re studium operamque posueris. Præceptoris officium.
Pietatis puerilis.
a Deut. iv. 9, 10. et xxxi. 12, 13. Psal. lxxviii. 3, 4, &c. Matt. xix. 13. 2 Tim. iii. 15.

Auditor. Et ego, Præceptor venerande, quantum ea, quæ me ex sacris literis edocuisti, animo percipere, et memoria custodire potui, quantumque audita reminisci et recordari in præsenti possum, quæsitis a te libenter respondebo.

M. Age igitur, dic mihi, mi Fili, quænam ea sit Religio quam profiteris.

A. Eam, Præceptor venerande, Religionem profiteor cujus author magisterque est Christus Dominus, quæque ob eam ipsam causam proprio et vero nomine, Christiana appellata est; ut et qui eam profitentur, [b]Christiani nuncupati sunt. Christiana Religio.
Nomen ab authore.
b Act. xi. 26.

M. Agnoscis igitur te Christianæ pietatis et Religionis cultorem, ac Christi Domini nostri atque Præceptoris discipulum?

A. Id equidem agnosco, atque [c]ingenue et libere profiteor; quin et universæ [d]fœlicitatis meæ summam in eo pono, tanquam in summo hominis bono, ut sine quo conditio nostra quam quorumvis brutorum multo esset infœlicior futura. c Rom. x. 9, 10.
d Psal. i. et xxxiii. 12. Joan. iii. 18, 36.

M. Religionis ergo atque pietatis Christianæ, cujus est gravissimum sanctissimumque nomen, vim et naturam mihi definitione aliqua breviter explicari velim. Definitio.

A. Religio Christiana est ᵉverus piusque Dei cultus, et observatio præceptorum illius.

M. Unde eam discendam esse putas?

A. Non aliunde profecto quam ex cœlesti Dei ipsius ᶠverbo, quod nobis sacris literis descriptum tradidit.

M. Quænam sunt ea scripta, quæ verbum Dei, et sacras literas nuncupas?

A. Non alia quam quæ per ᵍMosen et Prophetas sanctos, Dei optimi maximi amicos, divini Spiritus instinctu, in Veteri Testamento primum, deinde clarius in Novo Testamento, per ʰDominum nostrum Jesum Christum Dei Filium, atque sanctos ejus ⁱApostolos numine Dei afflatos divulgata sunt, et ad nostram usque ætatem integra ᵏconservata atque illæsa.

M. Cur verbum suum Deus ita nobis Scripturis manifestare voluit?

A. Quoniam Dei optimi maximi voluntatem, in cujus ˡcognitione atque erga eum obedientia vera pietas sita est, ipsi ex nobis, quæ cordium nostrorum sunt ᵐtenebræ, intelligere non possumus; misertus nostri Deus eam nobis ⁿpatefecit, atque illustravit, illustratamque in utriusque ᵒTestamenti volumine, quæ Sacræ ᵖScripturæ dicuntur, reliquit; ne ᑫincerti huc illuc ferremur, sed per cœlestem ejus doctrinam veluti aditus quidam nobis in cœlum daretur.

M. Cur Dei verbum Testamenti appellatione nuncupas?

A. Quia in Religione suscipienda caput esse constat, intelligere quæ sit ʳvoluntas Dei immortalis, testamenti vero nomine non voluntas solum, sed et ˢsuprema etiam, atque immutabilis voluntas significatur; monemur ne aliud in ᵗReligione sequamur aut quæramus amplius quam a Deo ibi docemur; sed ut unus est verus Deus, ita unus sit unius Dei pius cultus puraque Religio. Alioqui novas nobis quotidieque ᵘcommentitias Religiones fingeremus, et sua cuique genti, sua cuique civitati, sua cuique homini esset Religio. Imo non Religionem et veram pietatem, virtutum omnium initium atque fundamentum, sed superstitionem mendacem pietatis umbram, ducem ad res gerendas haberemus; id quod ex priscarum ˣgentium in rebus alioqui humanis sapientium variis innumerisque non Religionibus, sed superstitionibus plusquam anilibus ipsa est luce clarius.

M. Omnia ergo ad pietatem salutemque necessaria in verbo Dei scripto contineri affirmas?

A. ʸCerte: esset enim intolerabilis impietatis atque dementiæ existimare, vel Deum imperfectam doctrinam reliquisse; vel homines, quod ille non perfecerit, absolvere potuisse. Itaque Dominus severissime interdixit, ᶻne verbo suo quicquam adderent vel subtraherent; neve ab eo ad dexteram vel sinistram deflecterent.

M. Si hoc verum sit quod asseris, quorsum tam multa in Conciliis et conventibus Ecclesiasticis sæpius decernuntur, et a doctis hominibus in concionibus docentur, vel scriptis traduntur?

A. Hæc omnia, vel ad obscuros verbi Dei locos interpretandos, et ad emergentes controversias tollendas; vel ad externam Ecclesiæ gubernationem constituendam pertinent; non ut nova de Religione dogmata prodantur. ᵃOmnia enim ad salutem necessaria, quomodo videlicet pietas, sanctitas, Religio, pure et caste Dei numini tribuendæ sint; quæ præstanda sit Deo obedientia, ad quam solam piæ vitæ ratio instituenda est; quæ collocanda in Deo fiducia; quomodo item invocandus sit Deus, illique accepta referenda bona omnia; quæ in mysteriis Divinis peragendis observanda ratio; hujusmodi, inquam, ex verbo Dei discenda sunt, sine cujus cognitione ista vel ignorantur prorsus, vel absurdissime fiunt, ita ut infecta esse præstiterit. Sicut et Dominus ipse alicubi testatur, ᵇScripturarum ignorationem errorum omnium esse matrem; ipseque etiam docens, verbum Dei ᶜScriptum fere allegat, et nos ad discendum ex illo relagat. Ob hanc igitur causam, et antiquitus in templis verbum ᵈDei publice legebatur, adhibitis etiam, si quando illorum copia erat, interpretibus, sicuti ex sacris historiis liquet; et Dominus ipse in cœlum mox ascensurus, Apostolis, quos selegerat, in mandatis præcipue dedit, ᵉut universos orbis terrarum mortales verbo suo instituerent; et ejus exemplum insequutus Paulus, ᶠin Ecclesiis constituendos esse decrevit, qui populum docerent; quod intelligeret fidem, et quæ ad pietatem pertinent omnia, ex lectione ᵍet auditione verbi Dei pendere: Itaque ʰApostolos, Doctores, Prophetas, et Interpretes, in Ecclesia Dei maxime esse necessarios.

M. Hos ergo Doctores atque Interpretes audiendos esse censes?

A. Non minus quam ipsum Dominum si præsens adesset, quoad ea tantum tradant, quæ a Domino acceperunt. Quod

ʸ Deut. xiii. 4, 18. Psal. xii. 6. et xviii. 28. et xix. 6, &c. Joan. iv. 25. 1 Cor. i. 19. et ii. 6. Gal. i. 8, 9. Col. i. 25.
ᶻ Deut. iv. 2, 40. Prov. xxx. 6. Esai. xxx. 21.

ᵃ Deut. xxxii. 4. Psal. xix. 6, 7, &c. Psal. cxix. toto. 2 Tim. iii. 15, 16, 17.

ᵇ Matt. xxii. 29. Joan. xx. 9. Act. xiii. 27.
ᶜ Matt. xix. 4. et xxi. 13. Marc. vii. 6. Luc. x. 26. Joan. v. 39.
ᵈ Act. xiii.15, 27. et xv. 21.

ᵉ Matt.xxviii. 20. Marc.xvi. 15. Joan. xxi. 15.
ᶠ Act. xiv. 23.

ᵍ Rom. x. 14, 17.
ʰ 1 Cor. xii. 28. Eph. iv. 11, 12.

et ipse testatur dicens, ¹Qui vos audit, me audit; qui vos spernit, me spernit. Imo et his verbi sui præconibus ᵏligandi atque solvendi potestatem dedit, ut quorum peccata in terris illi per Dei verbum condonarint, vel detinuerint, ea vel condonata, vel detenta essent in cœlo.

M. An istos satis est semel de Religione disserentes audivisse?

A. ¹Christi nos discipulos usque ad finem, vel potius sine fine esse oportet. Parum est ergo incœpisse, nisi perseveres. Et quæ nostra est ᵐtarditas atque oblivio, sæpe docendi atque admonendi sumus, extimulandi sæpe, et quasi auribus vellicandi; semel enim, aut raro audita, facile excidere solent. Et eam ob causam (ut ante dictum est) ⁿsingulis sabbatis (sicut ex historiis sacris apparet) confluente simul multitudine, legebatur publice verbum Dei, et ejus interpretes, si qui adessent, audiebantur. Quæ consuetudo et in nostris hodie Ecclesiis ex Apostolica adeoque divina ordinatione est recepta.

M. An ergo verbum Dei peregrina lingua, et populo ignota legendum esse censes?

A. Id vero esset Deum pariter, atque ejus populum crasse irridere, atque utroque impudenter abuti. Nam cum Deus verbum suum omni ætati ᵒatque sexui clare legi mandet, ut omnes videlicet intelligant, et discant timere Dominum Deum suum, sicuti ipse in verbo suo diserte testatur; ridiculum cum primis esset, verbum Dei ad ejus populum docendum ab ipso Deo destinatum, populo lingua ipsi incognita, unde nihil discere possint, prælegere. Sed et divus Paulus de ea re clare disserit; ᵖitaque concludit, indoctum populum non posse respondere Amen, ad eam gratiarum actionem, quam non intelligat; sed legentem audientesque mutuo sibi ᑫbarbaros futuros, si quid in cœtu sit dictum, quod non ab his qui intersunt percipiatur; ʳseque adeo malle in Ecclesia Dei quinque verba intellecta loqui, quam decem millia non intellecta.

M. Satisne ergo munere nostro defuncti erimus, si operam dederimus, ut audiamus, intelligamusque verbum Dei?

A. Minime; verbum siquidem Dei non audire modo et intelligere, sed ˢfirma animi assensione, ut veritatem Dei de cœlo delapsam, amplecti, et ex animo amare, ᵗdociles item nos eidem præbere, mentesque nostras in ejus obsequium formare oportet; ut cordibus semel infixum, altas illic radices agat, fructumque piæ vitæ ad ejus regulam institutæ proferat; ut ita in salutem nobis, sicuti destinatum est, cedat. ᵘConstat ergo omni studio enitendum esse, ut in eo legendo, meditando, audiendo, tum privatim, tum publice, proficiamus; proficere autem nullo modo possumus, si ignota nobis lingua proponatur.

<small>ᵘ Deut. xvii. 19. Jos. i. 9. Psal. i. 2.</small>

M. Verum an legendo tantum Dei verbum illudque et ejus doctores sedulo audiendo, ad eam, quam dicis, perfectionem perveniemus?

A. Quia Dei sapientia est, frustra in ea, vel docenda, vel discenda, homines operam ponerent, nisi ˣDeus magisterio Spiritus sui corda nostra instituere dignaretur; sicuti Paulus docet, ʸfrustra vel plantari, vel irrigari, nisi Deus incrementum dederit. Itaque ut sapientiam Dei, in ejus verbo absconditam, intelligamus, ᶻardenti precatione a Deo petendum est, ut Spiritu suo mentes nostras, tenebris ᵃplusquam Cimmeriis offusas, illustret; hunc enim cœlitus demissum ᵇDoctorem in omnem nos veritatem perducturum Dominus ante promisit.

<small>ˣ Deut. xxix. 4. Luc. xxiv. 25, 27. 45, 46. Act. xvi. 14. 2 Cor. iv. 6. ʸ 1 Cor. iii. 7. ᶻ Psal. lxxxvi. 11. et cxix. 33, 34, 35. ᵃ Marc. vi. 52. Joan. i. 5. 1 Cor. ii. 14. ᵇ Joan. xvi. 13.</small>

M. Universum illud Dei verbum in quas præcipue partes distribuis?

A. In Legem, et Evangelium.

<small>Partitio verbi Dei.</small>

M. Hæc duo quomodo distinguuntur?

A. Lex, officia tum pietatis erga Deum, id est, verum Dei cultum, tum ᶜcharitatis erga proximum, describit; exactamque nostram ᵈobedientiam severe requirit, atque exigit; et obsequentibus vitam æternam pollicetur; minus vero obsequentibus, minas proponit, et pœnas, adeoque mortem perpetuam denunciat. Evangelium ᵉDei promissiones continet, et violatoribus Legis, modo eos admissi pœniteat, propitium fore Deum, per Fidem in Christum, pollicetur.

<small>ᶜ Matt. xxii. 36. Marc. xii. 30, 31. 1 Joan. iii. 23. ᵈ Lev. xxvi. toto. Deut. v. 32. et xxviii. toto. Joan. xiv. 15, 21, 23. ᵉ Marc. i. 15. et xvi. 16. Luc. v. 32. et xxiv. 47. Joan. i. 17. Act. ii. 38. et xiii. 38. Rom. i. 16. Gal. iii. 13.</small>

M. Verbum ergo Dei, voluntatem nos ejus docere, et omnia ad salutem necessaria continere, in eoque meditandum esse diligenter, ejusque Doctores atque Interpretes sedulo audiendos, super omnia vero Doctorem nobis cœlitus precatione esse impetrandum, quid item sit illud, et ex quibus constet partibus, hactenus a te est explicatum.

<small>Rerum divinarum summa.</small>

A. Ita est.

M. Quoniam igitur ex verbo Dei, tanquam ex fonte quodam dimanat Religio Christiana, ut antea verbum Dei, ita nunc et Religionem ipsam, quæ ex verbo Dei haurienda est, mihi in suas Partes, et veluti membra, distribue; ut, quo referenda sint singula, et ad certas quasi metas dirigenda, liquido statuamus.

<small>Religionis partitio.
f Lev. xxvi. 3, 14. Deut. xi. 26. Joan. xiv. 15, 21, 23, 24.
g Marc. i. 15. et xvi. 15, 16. Rom. i. 5, 16. et iii. 22. et iv. toto.</small>

A. Ut verbi Dei, ita et Religionis duæ præcipuæ sunt partes: ᶠObedientia, quam Lex, perfecta justitiæ regula, exigit; et Fides, ᵍquam Evangelium, quod promissiones de Dei misericordia complectitur, postulat.

M. Videntur tamen aut plures, aut non eædem esse Religionis Partes; aliis enim interdum nominibus in partiendo utuntur Sacræ literæ.

<small>h Gal. v. 6. 1 Joan. iii. 23.
i Marc. i. 15.
k Matt. xxii. 37, 39. Marc. xii. 30, 31, 33.
l Psal. xiv. 2. Rom. iii. 9.
m Matt. iv. 17. Marc. i. 15. Act. ii. 38.
n Rom. iii. 20. et vii. 7.
o Rom. iii. 21. Gal. ii. 16.
p Psal. xxxii. 5, 6. Rom. x. 12.
q 2 Cor. i. 11. et ii. 14. Eph. v. 4, 20. Phil. iv. 6. Col. iii. 17.</small>

A. Verum id quidem est; nam alicubi in Fidem ʰet Charitatem, alicubi in ⁱPœnitentiam et Fidem Religionem totam partiuntur; pro Obedientia enim aliquando ᵏCharitatem, quæ per Legem in Deum atque homines perfecta requiritur; aliquando vero, quia neque obedientiam, ˡneque charitatem, quam debemus, præstamus, ᵐPœnitentiam, peccatoribus ad Dei misericordiam consequendam maxime necessariam, substituunt. Quibusdam, qui plures partes volunt, prima est, ⁿCognitio debiti officii ex Lege, et damnatio per Legem ob desertum repudiatumque officium; secunda, ᵒCognitio fiduciaque liberationis ex Evangelio; tertia, ᵖPrecatio imploratioque Divinæ clementiæ atque auxilii; quarta, ᵠGratiarum actio pro liberatione cæterisque beneficiis Divinis. Sed utcunque nominibus varient, res eædem sunt, et ad duas illas præcipuas partes, Obedientiam et Fidem, in quibus omnis Religionis Nostræ vis et natura continetur, cætera omnia referuntur. Quum enim invocationem et gratiarum actionem, et istis conjunctissima mysteria Divina, quæ Sacramenta dicuntur, plerique ut partes adjungant, hæc quidem prioribus illis duabus continentur. Nemo enim vel fiduciæ vel obedientiæ officio erga Deum defungi recte potest, qui non premente eum aliqua necessitate, ad ipsum confugere, et omnia illi bona accepta referre, cumque usus et tempus postulat, mysteriis ejus sacris rite uti velit.

M. Assentior quidem tibi, quod omnia ad has duas partes referri possint, si quis accuratius ista, et paulo subtilius pertractare cupiat. Verum quoniam accuratissima partiendi ratio a pueris non est exigenda, malim ut in plures partes, pingui quadam Minerva, Religionem distribuas, quo dilucidior res tota sit. Crassius ergo, modo apertius, ista tractemus.

A. Quando ita visum est pingui (ut dicis) Minerva mecum agere, possem non incommode ex duabus quatuor partes efficere, Religionemque totam in Obedientiam, Fidem, Invocationem, et Sacramenta distribuere.

M. Age ergo, quum nostram hanc Religionis tractationem quam explicatissimam esse cupiam, huic ordini insistamus; ut primo loco de Obedientia, quam Lex requirit; secundo, de Fide, quæ Evangelii promissiones respicit et amplectitur; tertio, de Invocatione, et gratiarum actione, quæ sunt conjunctissimæ; quarto et ultimo loco, de Sacramentis mysteriisque Divinis percontemur.

A. Et ego, Præceptor venerande, sicuti ex te audivi, et studiose, ut est puerorum captus atque memoriola, didici, interroganti tibi libenter respondebo.

Prima pars, de Lege et Obedientia.

M. Quum ergo ʳObedientia nostra, de qua primum nobis dicendum est, ad normam Legis Divinæ sit revocanda, necesse est ut Legis vim atque naturam universam prius excutiamus; qua cognita et explorata, quæ, et qualis nostra debeat esse Obedientia, ignorari non potest. De Lege itaque quid sentias, dicere ordire.

A. Legem Dei justitiæ, quæ ab homine exigitur, ˢperfectam et omnibus numeris absolutam regulam esse sentio, quæ ᵗjubet ea quæ facienda sunt, prohibetque contraria. In hac Lege Deus omnia ad voluntatem ᵘet arbitrium suum revocavit, ut nulla ipsi neque erga se, neque erga homines pietas probari possit, nisi ea sola, quæ ad hujus regulæ amussim per omnia quadret. Frustra ergo mortales, suo sibi ᵛarbitratu, pietatis rationes confingunt. Legem enim suam Deus, ut certissimam, tum cultus Divini, ˣtum officiorum erga homines regulam, duabus ʸdescriptam tabulis nobis proposuit; simulque ᶻObedientia nostra nihil, quod quidem in terris fiat, sibi gratius acceptiusve esse demonstravit.

M. Prior tabula quo est argumento?

A. De pietate nostra ᵃin Deum tractat, et prima quatuor Legis Præcepta complectitur.

M. Secunda vero?

A. De charitatis sive dilectionis ᵇmutuæ inter homines officiis; quæ sex præcepta continet. Ita in summa ᶜdecem

ʳ Lev. xxvi. 3, 14. Deut. x. 12. et xxviii. toto. Psal. cxix. 4. Luc. x. 25. Joan. xiv. 15, 21, 23, 24. Jac. ii. 10.
ˢ Deut. iv. 2. et v. 32. et xxxii. 4. Psal. xix. 6, 7.
ᵗ Exod. xx. toto. et Deut. v. Esai. xxx. 21.
ᵘ Deut. vi. 17, 18. et xiii. 18. Rom. xii. 2. Eph. v. 17. et vi. 7. Col. i. 9.
ʷ 1 Reg. xv. 22. Esai. xxix. 13. Matt. xv. 3, 9.
ˣ Matt. xxii. 36, 40. 1 Joan. iii. 23.
ʸ Exod. xxxi. 18. et xxxiv. 28, 29. Deut. iv. 13.
ᶻ Deut. v. 32. et x. 12. et xi. 26. Matt. xix. 16. 1 Joan. iii. 24.
ᵃ Deut. vi. 5. Matt. xxii. 36, 37.
ᵇ Matt. xxii. 39. Rom. xiii. 8, 9. Gal. v. 14.
ᶜ Exod. xxxiv. 28. Deut. iv. 13.

omnino præceptis tota Lex absolvitur; cujus rei gratia, Decalogi nomen Legi inditum est.

M. Recita mihi primæ tabulæ primum præceptum.

A. DEUS AD HUNC MODUM EFFATUS EST. [d]AUDI ISRAEL; EGO SUM DOMINUS DEUS TUUS, QUI TE EDUXI EX DOMICILIO SERVITUTIS ÆGYPTIÆ. NON HABEBIS DEOS ALIENOS CORAM ME.

M. Cur de se, atque beneficio suo, quædam primum Deus commemorat?

A. In primis illi curæ fuit, ne legum a se latarum [e]existimatio mox per contemptum imminueretur; ideoque quo major authoritas accederet, isto veluti exordio utitur: Ego sum Dominus Deus tuus; quibus verbis [f]conditorem se, Dominum ac servatorem nostrum, omnisque boni authorem esse docet; jubendique authoritatem jure optimo ex legislatoris dignitate sibi vendicat; et Legi suæ ex bonitate gratiam conciliat; atque ex utroque pariter necessitatem nobis obsequendi summam imponit, nisi et in potentissimum [g]rebelles, et in optimum ingrati esse velimus.

M. At cum Israelem nominatim appellet, ac de rupto servitutis Ægyptiæ jugo diserte mentionem faciat, an non ad populum Israeliticum proprie pertinet?

A. Israelitas quidem corporali [h]servitute, per servum suum Mosen exemit Deus; at suos omnes ex spirituali peccati [i]servitute et diaboli tyrannide, qua alioqui pressi oppressique jacuerant, per Filium suum Jesum Christum asseruit. Hoc liberationis genus ad omnes [j]peræque homines pertinet, qui in Deo liberatore fiduciam omnem collocant, illiusque legibus [k]pro virili parent; Quod ni faciant, summæ eos ingratitudinis [l]reos fore, hac beneficii summi commemoratione denunciat. Cogitet enim quisque [m]Satanam, infernum illum Pharaonem suo capiti imminentem; [n]peccatum item fœdissimum esse lutum illud in quo turpissime volutatur; et [o]gehennam, Ægyptiam servitutem teterrimam, sibi ob animi oculos proponat; et libertatem hanc quam dixi, unice sibi [p]expetendam esse, ut quæ sua maxime intersit, facile intelliget; qua tamen indignissimus erit, ni libertatis [q]authorem omni obsequio atque obedientia colat.

M. Perge.

A. Confirmata jam Legis suæ authoritate, sequitur ipsum præceptum: NON HABEBIS DEOS ALIENOS CORAM ME.

M. Hoc quid sibi velit, dicito.

A. Idololatriam, ʳquam penitus odit Deus, vetat atque prohibet. ʳ Lev. xxvi. 1, 13. Deut. xii. 3. Jud. xi. 6, 16.

M. Idololatria, aut Deos alienos habere quid est?

A. Est in locum unius ˢveri Dei, qui se palam nobis manifestoque in sacris literis ostendit atque patefecit, alias vel personas vel res constituere, et ut Deos ᵗquosdam nobis fingere et comminisci, quas ut Deos colamus, et in quibus spem nostram ponamus atque collocemus. Jubet enim ut ᵘunum se tantum Deum agnoscamus; id est, ut quæ ad ejus majestatem spectant universa, ˣquæque soli illi debemus, eorum ne vel minimam quidem partem transferamus alio; sed suum illi honorem cultumque soli atque in solidum exhibeamus; cujus quicquam ad alterum deferre summum esset nefas.
ˢ Deut. vi. 4, 5. Marc. xii. 29, 32.
ᵗ Esai. xliv. 17. Dan. iii. 5, 7, 12, 15.
ᵘ Deut. iv. 35, 39. et vi. 4, 5. Marc. xii. 29, 32.
ˣ Deut. x. 20. Luc. iv. 8. Act. x. 25, 26. Apoc. xix. 10.

M. Quæ sunt illa, quæ Deo peculiariter debemus, in quibus cultum illi proprium et peculiarem situm esse dicis?

A. Deo quidem innumera debemus, verum universa ad quatuor capita non inepte referri possunt.

M. Quæ sunt ea?

A. Ut ipsius majestati ʸsummam venerationem, summum ejus ᶻbonitati amorem atque fiduciam præstemus, ad illum confugiamus, ᵃet ipsius imploremus opem, illique nos et ᵇnostra omnia accepta referamus. Hæc ut nulli alii, ita illi soli exhibenda sunt omnia; si illum solum Deum ᶜnostrum habere, illiusque populus peculiaris esse volumus.
ʸ Deut. x. 12. 1 Par. xvi. 28. Psal. xxix. 2, &c. et xcvi. 6, 7.
ᶻ Matt. xxii. 37. 1 Joan. iv. 17. et v. 10.
ᵃ Psal. l. 16. Matt. vi. 9.
ᵇ Psal. xxxiv. lxvi. cxlv. et toto libro Psal.

M. Ultima illa verba, CORAM ME, quid significant?

A. Non posse nos vel semel ad defectionem spectare, nisi Deum ᵈtestem habeamus; nihil enim tam abditum atque reconditum esse, ut eum latere possit. Præterea non apertæ solum ᵉconfessionis honorem, sed et cordis intimam ac sinceram pietatem requirere sese Deus indicat; ut qui occultarum sit cogitationum cognitor atque judex.
ᶜ Lev. xxvi. 12. Deut. vii. 6. Psal. xcv. 6, 7. et xxxiii. 12. Tit. ii. 14. Heb. viii. 10.
ᵈ Psal. xxxiii. 14. Esai. xxix. 15. Jer. xvii. 9, 10. Heb. iv. 13.
ᵉ Esai. i. 16. et xxix. 13, 15. Matt. v. 8. et xv. 8, 18.

M. Satis ergo dictum esto de primo præcepto; jam ad secundum pergamus.

A. ᶠSIMULACHRUM ULLIUS REI, QUÆ AUT SUPRA IN CŒLO, AUT INFRA IN TERRA, AUT IN AQUIS INFRA TERRAM SIT, NON EFFINGES; EA NON VENERABERIS NEQUE COLES. NAM EGO SUM DOMINUS DEUS TUUS, ᵍZELOTYPUS, QUI PARENTUM INIQUITATEM ETIAM IN LIBERIS VINDICO, AD TERTIAM USQUE QUARTAMQUE PROGENIEM OSORUM MEI; CLEMENTIAQUE UTOR
ᶠ Exod. xx. 4. Lev. xxvi. 1. Deut. iv. 15. et v. 8, 9, 10. et xxvii. 15. Psal. xcvii. 7. Esai. xlii. 8.
ᵍ Exod. xxxiv. 7, 14. Deut. vii. 9.
Id est, impatiens socii.

AD MILLESIMAM USQUE PROGENIEM, ERGA MEI AMANTES, MEA-
QUE PRÆCEPTA CONSERVANTES.

M. Horum verborum quis est sensus?

A. Sicuti primo præcepto solum se coli adorarique jubet, ita isto ab omni superstitione vitiosisque et corporeis figmentis avocat, quandoquidem ipsius cultus [h]spiritualis purusque esse debet; maxime vero ab externa [i]idolatria crassissimo vitio nos deterret.

[h] Esai. ii. 18.
Joan. iv. 23, 24.
[i] Psal. lxxviii. 64.
Esai. xlii. 8, 17. et xliv. 9.
Jer. x. 14.

M. Pingendi itaque fingendique artes in totum damnat hæc lex, ut videtur, ita ut nullas omnino imagines fieri liceat.

A. Minime; verum primo ne vel Dei [k]exprimendi, vel adorandi causa, imagines ullas formemus, vetat: Deinde ne imagines [l]ipsas adoremus edicit.

[k] Lev. xxvi. 1. Deut. iv. 15. Esai. xl. 18. 12; et xlvi. 5. 6. Psal. lxxviii. 64. Act. xvii. 29.
[l] Deut. v. 8, 9. Psal. xcvii. 7. et cvi. 34. Esai. xliv. 17, 19.
[m] Psal. cxv. 3, 4. Esai. xl. 10, &c. Joan. iv. 24. Rom. 1. 20, 23.
[n] Esai. ii. 18, 19. xl. 18, 19. et xlvi. 5, 6. Jer. x. 14. Act. xvii. 29.

M. Cur Deum non licet corporea et aspectabili figura exprimere?

A. Quia inter Deum, qui [m]spiritus est, æternus, immensus, infinitus, incomprehensibilis, et ab omni concretione mortali segregatus, et inter caducam et corpoream, exilem et inanimem, inanemque [n]figuram, nihil potest esse simile aut commune. Itaque per summam injuriam Dei optimi maximi majestatem minuunt, quum eam in hunc modum repræsentare conantur.

M. Non ergo recte dixerunt hi, qui imagines esse idiotarum libros contendunt?

A. Quales libri sint nescio; de Deo certe nihil nisi errores docere possunt.

M. Quænam est illa adorationis forma, quæ hic damnatur?

[o] Psal. xcvii. 7. et cvi. 34. Esai. xliv. 17, 19. Dan. iii. 5, 7. Osee xi. 2. Mich. v. 12. Act. vii. 41.

A. Quum precaturi, [o]ad statuas aut imagines convertimur, coram illis prosternimur, genibus inflexis, aperto capite, aut aliis signis honorem illis exhibentes, ac si Deus nobis illis repræsentaretur. In summa, in imaginibus, ne vel Deum quæramus vel colamus; vel quod idem est, ne imagines ipsas in Dei honorem veneremur, aut illis quoquo modo, ad majestatis suæ injuriam, per idololatriam, aut superstitionem abutamur, hac Lege prohibemur. Alioqui vero [p]statuariæ picturæque usus legitimus minime interdicitur.

[p] 3 Reg. vii. 24, 25. Ezech. xli. 19. Matt. xxii. 20.
[q] Deut. vii. 5. et xxvii. 15. 2 Par. xxxi. 1. Esai. x. 10, 11. et xxx. 22. Ezech. vi. 4. Matt. xxi. 13.

M. Ex his quæ mihi commemoras, colligi facile potest, in templis, [q]quæ Dei cultui proprie dicantur, statuas aut imagines ullas collocare, valde periculosum esse.

A. Id verum esse, totius pene Religionis interitu, jam nimium profecto experti sumus.

M. At adhuc superest hujus Legis quasi appendix quædam.

A. Nam ego, inquit, sum Dominus Deus tuus, [r]socii impatiens, qui vindico iniquitatem parentum in Filiis, usque in tertiam, et quartam progeniem eorum qui me oderint.

[r] Exod. xx. 5. Deut. v 9. et vi. 15. Psal. lxxviii. 58. Nah. i. 2.

M. Quorsum tandem, aut cur ista dicuntur?

A. Hæc eo pertinent, ut Legem hanc, adhibita veluti sanctione, statuat et confirmet. Nam Dominum se, ac Deum nostrum nominans duplici ratione, [s]authoritatis videlicet, et beneficentiæ, nos ad sibi per omnia parendum urget; [t]zelotypiæ vocabulo indicat, se socium aut æqualem ferre non posse.

[s] Deut. x. 12. 3 Reg. xviii. 39. 1 Tim. vi. 15.
[t] Exod. xxxiv. 14. Jos. xxiv. 19. Esai. xlii. 8.

M. Quæ subest hujus quam dicis, zelotypiæ ratio?

A. Æquissima profecto. Postquam enim nobis nihil [u]promeritis, tantum pro infinita sua bonitate se donavit, optimo jure nos [x]totos omnino, atque in solidum vult esse suos. Hoc enim est illud veluti sancti conjugii [y]vinculum, quo fideli illi marito Deo, animæ nostræ, tanquam castæ sponsæ, copulantur. Quarum castitas est, Deo soli dicatas esse, et illi penitus adhærere; sicuti rursum, [z]adulterio pollui dicuntur animæ nostræ, cum a Deo, ad idololatriam aut superstitionem deflectunt. Quo vero sponsæ amantior est maritus, quoque castior ipse, eo est sponsæ fidem violanti infensior.

[u] Psal. xliv. 4, 5. Esai. xlviii. 9. Rom. v. 8. et xi. 35. 2 Tim. i. 9.
[x] Matt. iv. 10. et xxii. 37.
[y] Jer. ii. 2. 2 Cor. xi. 2. Eph. v. 24.
[z] Jer. ii. 20. et iii. 1, &c. Ezech. vi. 9. et xvi. 15.

M. Prosequere.

A. Jam quo impendio magis odisse se idololatriam ostendat, et graviore nos formidine a peccando coerceat, non de iis modo qui ipsi offenderint, sed et de eorum [a]quoque liberis ac posteris pœnas se sumturum minatur.

[a] Exod. xxxiv. 7. Deut. v. 9, 10. et vii. 9, 10. Esai. xiv. 20, 21.

M. Verum quo tandem modo istuc Dei justitiæ est consentaneum, quenquam propter alterius admissum pœnas dare?

A. Ipsa humani generis conditio hanc questionem satis explicat. [b]Natura enim exitio obnoxii sumus omnes; in qua nos conditione si Deus relinquat, nihil est quod de eo conqueramur. Et sicut suam erga pios dilectionem et misericordiam, eorum posteritatem [c]tuendo, fovendoque, et illis salutem quam non debuit impertiendo, demonstrat; ita suam in impios vindictam, ipsorum [d]filios hac beneficentia privando, exequitur; neque tamen injuria interim ulla eos afficit, quod

[b] Esai. i. 4, &c. Rom. iii. 9, 10. Eph. ii. 3.
[c] Deut. iv. 37. Psal. xxxvii. 25. et lxix. 36. et cxii. 2.
[d] Esai. xiv. 20. et xlviii. 18.

gratiam quam illis ᵉnon debuit, non sit impertitus, sed quales invenit, tales ingenio naturæque suæ relinquit.

M. Perge ad cætera.

A. Ne solis nos minis urgere videatur, jam sequitur altera pars, qua Deus benigne et liberaliter pollicendo, nos ad obsequium invitat atque allectat. ᶠClementia enim se summa usurum promittit, tum erga omnes qui se diligunt, suisque mandatis obtemperant, tum erga ipsorum etiam posteros.

M. Qua ratione istuc æquum esse tibi videtur?

A. Ratio quidem aliqua est propter piam educationem, ᵍin qua suos liberos pii parentes sic instituunt, ut illis in vero Domini timore et dilectione quasi hæredes succedere soleant. Sed et ʰnatura ipsa nos ad benevolentiam erga amicorum liberos invitat; certissima tamen ratio est, quod Deus ita promittit, ⁱqui neque a justitia aberrare, neque fidem fallere potest unquam.

M. Atqui istud constans et perpetuum esse non apparet; quia pii aliquando parentes ᵏliberos progignunt impios, et a parentum virtute degeneres, in quos Deus non obstante hac promissione, graviter animadvertit.

A. Hoc quidem negari non potest. Nam Deus ut propitium se (cum visum fuerit) ˡimpiorum liberis exhibet; ita nulla hujusmodi necessitate piorum liberis devinctus tenetur, ᵐquin ipsi liberum sit, ex illis quos velit, repudiare. Verum in eo hujusmodi moderationem adhibet, ut certa promissioni suæ fides semper constet.

M. Quum ante in vindicta tres, aut quatuor ad summum progenies nominet, cur hic in misericordia mille complectitur?

A. Ut ostendat ad mansuetudinem ⁿet beneficentiam, quam ad severitatem, se multo esse procliviorem; sicut et ipse alibi profitetur, se ad iram tardum esse, ad ignoscendum vero propensissimum.

M. Ex his quæ commemorasti omnibus, videris mihi intelligere, Deum, ne ipsius cultus, qui spiritualis et purissimus esse debeat, crassa ulla idolatria aut superstitione pollueretur, magnam adhibuisse cautionem?

A. Maximam profecto. Nam non aperte ᵒsolum et prolixe enumeratis omnibus simulachrorum formis, in prima fere legis suæ parte, ut rem ad suam majestatem maxime spectantem edixit; sed et horrendis ᵖminis violatori, maximis rursum observatori propositis præmiis hanc legem sancivit.

Ita ut, aut non intellectum fuisse hoc mandatum, ut obscurum, aut non animadversum, ut in turba delitescens, aut non curatum, ut leve et minimum; sed ut nullum potius mandatum, nullis minis, nullis promissionibus adjunctis, neglectum prorsus ab omnibus jacuisse, plusquam stupendum videri possit.

M. Sic est profecto ut dicis; verum recita mihi jam preceptum tertium.

A. ^qNomen Domini Dei tui inaniter non usurpabis; neque enim sinet impunitum Jehova, qui ejus nomen inaniter adhibuerit. _{q Exod. xx.7. Lev. xix. 12. Deut. v. 11.}

M. Quid est inaniter usurpare nomen Dei?

A. Eo vel ^rpejerando, vel temere, et incogitanter, ac præter ^snecessitatem jurando, aut vel semel præter gravem causam nominando, abuti. Quum enim sit Divini ^tnominis majestas sacrosancta, omnibus modis cavere debemus, ne aut ipsi contemsisse, aut aliis contemnendi ejus occasionem præbuisse videamur; adeoque nomen Dei, nisi cum summa ejus ^ureverentia, nunquam proferamus, ut venerandum et gloriosum cum nobis ipsis, tum aliis omnibus appareat. De ^xDeo enim ejusque operibus, ne cogitare quidem, nedum loqui aliter quam in ejus honorem fas est. In summa, qui Dei nomine, nisi gravissimis de causis, et sanctissimis negotiis utitur, eo abutitur. _{r Lev. xix.12. Psal. xv. 4. 1 Tim. i. 10. s Eccles. xxiii. 9. Matt. v. 33. t Deut. xxviii. 58. Psal. viii. 1. Jer. x. 6. u 1 Par. xxix. 13. Psal. xlviii. 9, et cxi. 1, &c. x Sap. i. 1. et xiv. 30. Eccles. xxiii. 9. et xxxix. 33.}

M. Quid ergo de iis qui Deo convitium faciunt, de Magis item, atque aliis ejus generis hominibus impiis, censes?

A. Si qui tantum ex consuetudine ^yprava, et importuna solum quadam facilitate Dei nomine utuntur, summa eum injuria afficiunt; multo magis illi, qui in diris ^zexecrationibus, incantationibus, imprecationibus, aut ulla superstitione alia, Dei nomine abutuntur, atroci atque nefario scelere sese astringunt. _{y Eccles. xxiii. 9. Matt. v. 34. z Deut. xviii. 11. Esai. viii. 19. et xlvii. 9. et lii. 5. Mal. iii. 5. Act. xix. 13. Gal. v. 20.}

M. Ecquis ergo est divini nominis usus in jurejurando legitimus?

A. Sane; cum justa ^ade causa datur jusjurandum, vel ad asserendam veritatem, maxime si id requirat jubeatve magistratus; vel ob aliud magni momenti negotium, quo videlicet suum Deo honorem integrum servemus, aut mutuam inter homines concordiam charitatemque tueamur. _{a Exod. xxii. 11. Jos. ii. 12; ix. 15. Psal. xv. 4, et lxiii. 12. 2 Cor. xi. 31. Gal. i. 20.}

M. An ergo quoties vera loquimur, adhibere juramentum licebit?

A. Hoc minime licere jam ante dictum est; sic enim

existimatio atque authoritas nominis Divini imminueretur, vileque illud et vulgare redderetur. Sed cum in [b]gravi negotio veritati fides alioqui non haberetur, eam sacramento confirmare licebit.

M. Quid deinde sequitur?

A. Neque enim impunitum, inquit, sinet Jehova, qui nomen ejus inaniter adhibuerit.

M. Quum in universum se in Legis suæ violatores animadversurum, [c]alibi Deus denuntiet, quid est quod hic nomine suo abutentibus peculiariter minatur?

A. Indicare voluit, quanti nominis [d]sui gloriam faciat, ut paratam ultionem videntes, majori studio ab eo profanando caveremus.

M. An divorum, aut aliorum hominum, rerumve nomine in jurejurando adhibere fas esse putas?

A. Nequaquam. Cum enim legitimum jusjurandum nihil sit aliud, quam religiosa affirmatio, se Deum omnium conscium cognitoremque, [e]testem citare, atque adhibere, jusjurandum se verum jurare, eundemque si falsum juravit, mendacii scelerisque sui vindicem atque ultorem invocare atque imprecari; hunc divinæ sapientiæ atque majestatis honorem, qui suus est proprius [f]atque peculiaris, partiri, et cum aliis vel personis vel rebus communicare, summum esset nefas.

M. Superest quartum præceptum, primæ tabulæ ultimum?

A. DIEM SABBATI [g]SANCTE AGERE MEMENTO. SEX DIEBUS OPERABERIS, ET FACIES OMNIA OPERA TUA; SEPTIMO VERO DIE, QUOD EST DOMINI DEI TUI SABBATUM, NULLUM OPUS FACIES; NEC TU, NEC FILIUS TUUS, NEC FILIA TUA, NEC SERVUS TUUS, NEC ANCILLA TUA, NEQUE JUMENTUM TUUM, NEQUE APUD TE DEGENS PEREGRINUS. NAM SEX DIEBUS [h]PERFECIT DEUS CŒLUM ET TERRAM, ET MARE, ET QUICQUID IN ILLIS CONTINETUR. SEPTIMO QUIEVIT. ITAQUE DIEM SABBATI SACRUM, SIBIQUE DICATUM ESSE VOLUIT.

M. Sabbati nomen quid significat?

A. Sabbatum si interpreteris, [i]requiem significat. Eo die, ut qui ad cultum [k]Dei solummodo sit institutus, profana negotia omnia a piis longe semovenda sunt, quo religioni, et pietati sedulo vacare queant.

M. Cur suum nobis exemplum ad imitandum proposuit Dominus?

A. Quod clara, atque illustria ¹exempla animos hominum acrius excitent atque acuant. Nam et dominum servi, et filii parentem libenter imitantur; et nihil magis est expetendum, quam ut homines ad Dei ᵐexemplar et imitationem se forment.

M. Septimo ergo quoque die ab omni nobis labore abstinendum prorsus esse dicis?

A. Duplex est hujus præcepti ratio; quatenus enim cæremoniam complectitur, externam tantum quietem exigens, ad Judæos ⁿproprie spectabat, nec perpetuæ æternæque legis vim habet: sed Christi jam °adventu, ut cæteræ Judaicarum cæremoniarum umbræ abrogatæ sunt, ita et de ista lege ex hac parte est derogatum.

M. Quid ergo præter cæremoniam subesse putas, quo perpetuo astringamur?

A. Tres ob causas hæc lex est instituta; ut disciplina ᵖEcclesiastica, et Reipub. Christianæ status aliquis constituatur, atque retineatur; ut servorum ᑫconditioni, quo tolerabilis ea fiat, provideatur; et ut spiritualis illius quietis forma ʳatque figura quædam exprimatur.

M. Quæ est illa quam dicis Ecclesiastica disciplina?

A. Ut populus Christianus ad Christi ˢdoctrinam audiendam, ad conficiendam fidei ᵗsuæ professionem, ad preces ᵘDeo publice adhibendas, ad divinorum ˣoperum, atque beneficiorum memoriam celebrandam atque retinendam, traditaque ab eo mysteria ʸperagenda, in unum conveniat.

M. An ista septimo quoque die præstitisse satis erit?

A. Sunt hæc quidem privatim ᶻcuique assidue recordanda, et cogitanda; nostræ tamen negligentiæ atque imbecillitatis causa, status dies peculiariter huic negotio publice destinatur.

M. Jam de servis sublevandis, quare hoc mandato cautum est?

A. Æquum fuit illos, ᵃqui sub aliena potestate sunt, aliquod tempus a labore intermittere; alioqui enim illorum conditio nimium dura difficilisque toleratu futura esset. Et sane par erat, servos communi nostro ᵇpariter atque ipsorum Domino, adeoque patri etiam, quum eos sibi per Christum æque adoptarit, una nobiscum aliquando inservire: Sed et dominis ipsis præterea utile est, ut servi interdum ᶜinterquiescant, quo videlicet ad intermissum paululum laborem alacriores validioresque revertantur.

M. Superest jam ut de spirituali quiete dicas.

A. Ea est, dum a mundanis negotiis, ^dpropriisque operibus atque studiis feriati, et quasi sanctum quoddam otium agentes, nos totos in Dei potestatem permittimus, quo ille sua in nobis opera peragat; et dum carnem nostram, ^eut Scriptura loquitur, crucifigimus, hoc est, appetitus et motus animi pravos frænamus, ingenio nostro temperantes, ut Dei spiritui obtemperemus; ita enim externæ quietis figuram atque imaginem, ad rem veritatemque optime revocabimus atque traducemus.

M. An ergo reliquis diebus hanc curam abjicere licebit?

A. Nequaquam: Postquam enim semel cœperimus, pergendum ^fest per totum vitæ curriculum; et numerus ^gseptenarius, quum perfectionem in Scripturis designet, omni ope atque opera assidue eniti, atque ad eam ^hcontendere oportere nos admonet. Una tamen ostenditur, nos quoad in hoc mundo vivimus, a spiritualis hujus quietis perfectione atque absolutione ⁱlonge abesse, gustumque tantum quendam hic nobis præberi quietis illius, quam in regno Dei sumus perfecte ^kabsolutam fœlicissimamque habituri.

M. Recte recitatæ jam mihi a te sunt Leges primæ tabulæ, qua verus Dei cultus, qui est bonorum omnium fons, summatim comprehenditur. Jam vero quæ sint amoris charitatisque nostræ erga homines officia, quæ ex isto fonte scaturiunt et derivantur, quæque secunda tabula continentur, mihi dicas velim.

A. Secundæ tabulæ initium est, ^lHonora patrem et matrem; ut sis longævus super terram, quam daturus est tibi Dominus Deus tuus.

M. Honoris nomine hoc loco quid significatur?

A. Honor parentum, amorem, ^mtimorem, et reverentiam complectitur; et in obediendo illis, in salute atque auxilio ferendo, eos defendendo, atque etiam, si quando rerum inopia laborent, fovendo, ut in proprio suo munere atque officio versatur.

M. An de iis tantum qui natura parentes sunt, Lex præcipit?

A. Tametsi ipsa verba aliud sonare non videntur, intelligendi tamen sunt omnes, quibus aliqua attributa est authoritas; ut ⁿMagistratus, Ecclesiæ ^oMinistri, ^pPræceptores; denique ornamento aliquo vel honoratæ ^qætatis, vel ingenii sapientiæque, vel doctrinæ, vel gloriæ, vel fortunæ præditi, vel cæteris rebus superiores, parentum nomine continentur; quando ex eodem fonte ipsorum pariter atque parentum authoritas derivatur.

M. Quonam?

A. Ex sacrosancta Legum [r]divinarum sanctione, qua illi æque ac parentes dignitate atque honore afficiuntur, et decorantur. Inde enim omnes vel Parentes, vel Principes, vel Magistratus, vel alii superiores, quicunque tandem sint, vim suam atque authoritatem omnem habent, atque obtinent; quod per hos Deo mundum hunc regere atque administrare visum fuerit.

[r] Deut. xvii. 10. Tit. iii. 1. 1 Pet. ii. 18.

M. Hoc quale tandem est, quod Parentum nomine Magistratus, cæterosque superiores appellat?

A. Ut intelligamus eos a Deo nobis nostro [s]publicoque bono datos esse; simulque ingenium [t]humanum superbia elatum, et celsitudinis appetens, atque ab alterius imperio perferendo refugiens, authoritatis illius, [u]quæ minime omnium est invidiosa, exemplo, ad officium obsequiumque in Magistratum perduceret, atque assuefaceret. Parentum enim nomine, non solum ut obtemperemus obediamusque magistratibus, sed etiam ut eos colamus et diligamus; vicissimque ut superiores imperent inferioribus, ut justus parens probis filiis solet, præscribitur.

[s] Rom. xiii. 4. Heb. xiii. 17.
[t] Exod. xxxii. 9. Luc. xix. 14.
[u] Prov. iii. 12. Matt. vii. 9. Luc. xi. 11. 1 Thess. ii. 11.

M. Promissio illa mandato addita quid sibi vult?

A. Longa [x]fruituros vita, et in certa ac stabili bonorum possessione diu permansuros esse, qui meritos debitosque Parentibus, et Magistratibus honores habuerint.

[x] Exod. xx. 12. Deut. v. 16. Eph. vi. 2, 3.

M. At hæc promissio peculiariter ad Judæos, qui pii in Parentes fuerint, spectare videtur.

A. Non est dubium, quin quod de terra [y]Chanaan nominatim dictum sit, ad Judæos proprie pertineat; verum cum Deus totius orbis sit [z]Dominus, quascunque nobis sedes incolendas dederit, eas in possessione nos nostra esse retenturos, hac Lege promittit et confirmat.

[y] Gen. xii. 7. et xiii. 15. et xxvi. 3. Deut. xxiv. 4.
[z] Gen. i. 1. Psal. xxiv. 1. et cxv. 16. Dan. iv. 22.

M. Verum in tam ærumnosa pariter ac flagitiosa vita, provectam ætatem cur Deus in beneficii loco ponit?

A. Quia dum suorum miseriis [a]et calamitatibus opem fert, vel eos in tot circumstantibus periculis tuetur, et a vitiis atque peccatis avocat; paternum in eos ut liberos suos animum, benevolentiamque declarat.

[a] 2 Reg. xxii. 1. Psal. xviii. 1, 2, 3. Jer. xiv. 8. Heb. ii. 15.

M. Quid, an ex contrario sequitur, eos quibus cito aut

[NOEL. CATEC.]

ante decursam ætatem vita adimitur, aut quos vitæ hujus miseriæ atque ærumnæ premunt, in odio apud Deum esse?

A. Nihil minus; imo quo quisque [b]fere Deo est charior, eo vel gravius malis oneratur, vel citius ex hac vita, quasi e carcere, a Deo evocatus atque emissus, migrare solet.

M. An non ista interim veritatem fidemque promissionis Divinæ infirmare videntur?

A. Minime. Quum enim terrena nobis bona Deus pollicetur, hac vel aperta [c]vel tacita exceptione semper utitur, modo ne ea animis interim nostris minus salutaria sint, aut perniciosa. Esset enim valde præposterum, atque perversum, nisi animæ semper [d]præcipua ratio haberetur, atque ita mundana commoda vel consequamur, [e]vel illis careamus, ut ævo sempiterno beati perpetuo fruamur.

M. Jam quid de illis, qui Parentibus Magistratibusve minus obsequentes fuerint, aut illos violarint, aut occiderint etiam, dicemus?

A. Hujusmodi fere omnes vel [f]fœdissimam miserrimamque vitam producunt, vel eam immaturo acerboque interitu, et infami morte de medio sublati, per summum dedecus amittunt: Neque in hac modo vita, sed et in futuro [g]sæculo æternas impietatis suæ pœnas perpetuo luent. Nam si homines a nobis alienissimos, vel inimicos [h]etiam adversariosque capitales lædere, nedum occidere, Dei mandato, quod proxime sequitur, prohibemur; quam sit nobis ab omni in parentes injuria, a quibus vita, patrimonium, libertas, civitas tradita est, abstinendum atque cavendum, facile profecto intelligimus. Et si præclare a sapientibus priscis dictum est, vultu lædi pietatem, parentesque verbo voceve violare, summum esse nefas, quod supplicium satis acre reperietur in eum, qui mortem obtulerit parenti, pro quo mori ipsum, si res postularet, jura Divina atque humana cogebant?

M. At multo est adhuc atrocius patriæ parentem, quam suum violare, aut occidere.

A. Profecto: Nam si singulos homines parentes suos privatim violare, flagitium; necare, parricidium sit; quid dicemus de illis, qui contra rempub. contra patriam antiquissimam sanctissimamque, et communem omnium parentem, quam nobis chariorem esse quam nosmetipsos decet, et pro qua nemo bonus dubitat mori, si ei sit profuturus; qui contra Principem, patrem patriæ ipsius, et reipub. parentem conjurarunt, atque impia arma tulerunt; et quos deserere vel destituere proditio sit, de illorum pernicie, exitio, interitu cogitare? Verbo satis digno tam nefaria appellari nullo modo potest.

M. Recita jam sextum mandatum.

A. ⁱNon occides. ^{i Exod. xx. 13. Matt. v. 21. Jac. ii. 11.}

M. Satisne huic Legi obtemperabimus, si manus a cæde et sanguine puras habuerimus?

A. Deus non externis tantum operibus, sed animi etiam ᵏaffectibus, adeoque his potissimum legem tulit; ˡira enim et odium, et quævis nocendi cupiditas, cædes coram Deo censetur. Ab his ergo nos etiam Deus hac Lege prohibet. ^{k Deut. xxx. 6. Psal. xxiv. 4. Matt. ix. 4. Heb. iii. 12. l Matt. v. 21, 22, 23. Gal. v. 20. 1 Joan. ii. 11.}

M. Plene ergo Legi satisfaciemus, si odium in neminem concipiamus?

A. Imo odium damnando, Dominus amorem erga ᵐomnes homines, etiam inimicos exigit; adeoque ut illis qui nobis male precantur, et hostili in nos sunt odio atque crudelitate, non modo salutem et incolumitatem, omniaque bona precemur, sed de illis, quantum in nobis erit, bene etiam mereamur. ^{m Matt. v. 23, 24, 25. Luc. vi. 27. Rom. xii. 18.}

M. Jam præceptum septimum quodnam est?

A. ⁿNon adulteraberis. ^{n Exod. xx. 14. Deut. v. 18. Matt. xix. 18.}

M. Quid eo tibi contineri videtur?

A. Hoc præcepto omne fœdæ vagæque libidinis genus, omnisque quæ a libidine nascitur turpitudo, ut contrectandi petulantia, orationis ᵒobscœnitas, vultus gestusve lascivia omnis, atque impudicitiæ significatio quævis prohibetur. Nec verborum modo turpitudo, obscœnitasque rerum vetatur, sed, quoniam tum corpora, tum animæ nostræ ᵖtempla sunt Spiritus sancti, quo pura sit in utrisque castitas, pudor pariter, et pudicitia a Deo exiguntur; ne vel corpora ullis libidinis sordibus, vel animi obscœnis cogitationibus, ᑫaut cupiditatibus ullo modo polluantur; sed casti purique perpetuo serventur. ^{o Rom. xiii. 13. Eph. v. 3, 4. Jac. ii. 11. p 1 Cor. iii. 16, 17. et vi. 15, 19. 2 Cor. vi. 16. q Job. xxxi. 9. Prov. vi. 25. Matt. v. 27, 28.}

M. Perge ad cætera.

A. Octavum præceptum est, ʳNon furaberis. Quo præcepto non tantum furta illa quæ humanis legibus puniuntur, verum etiam omnes fraudes, ˢatque fallaciæ damnantur; nulli vero contra hanc legem flagitiosius committunt, quam qui per rationem fiduciæ, eos erga quos amicitiam simulant, maxime fraudare solent. Qui enim fidem lædunt, oppugnant omnium commune præsidium. Ne ergo cuipiam imponamus, ne circumveniamus quenquam, ne emendi aut vendendi quæstu et lucro duci nos ad injuriam sinamus, neque mercaturis faciendis injuste ^{r Exod. xx. 15. Matt. xix. 18. 1 Cor. vi. 8, 9, 10. s 1 Thess. iv. 6. Tit. ii. 10.}

rem quæramus, aut [t]mensuris vel ponderibus imparibus atque iniquis utentes, quæstum faciamus, aut fallaces, et fucosas merces vendentes, opes augeamus, prohibemur.

M. Quicquam amplius de hoc præcepto dicendum existimas?

A. Maxime: Nam non externa solum furta fraudesque prohibentur; nec ut mercatum tantum sine furto atque fallaciis instituamus, cæteraque omnia sine insidiis agamus, hac lege jubemur; verum etiam ut animo ita affecti simus, ut impunitate et ignoratione omnium proposita, ab injuria abstineamus tamen. Nam quod agere coram hominibus iniquum, id etiam velle coram Deo malum est. Omnia ergo consilia et studia, ipsaque in [u]primis cupiditas ex alienis incommodis nostra quærendi commoda, hac lege vetantur. Denique ut ad suum quisque quam primum perveniat, et quod quisque habeat sui ut cuique salvum maneat, omnibus modis operam dare, hac lege admonemur.

M. Nonum præceptum quod est?

A. NON ERIS [x]ADVERSUS PROXIMUM TUUM TESTIS MENDAX.

M. Quis est hujus præcepti sensus?

A. Ne jusjurandum aut fidem [y]violemus; nec publica tantum manifestaque perjuria, sed et omnia in universum mendacia, calumniæ, [z]obtrectationes, maledicta, quibus damnum vel detrimentum proximus faciat, vel famam et existimationem amittat, hac lege prohibentur; una enim forma generalem doctrinam continet. Adeoque falsa aut vana, nec ipsi unquam loqui, nec in aliis, vel verbis, vel scripto, vel silentio, vel præsentia adeo nostra, tacitoque assensu approbare debemus; sed simplicis veritatis [a]amicos perpetuos et cultores esse, in veritatis lucem, prout locus, tempus, aut necessitas postulabit, omnia studiose proferre, veritatis denique patrocinium ubique arripere, illamque modis omnibus tueri et defendere oportet.

M. Huic ergo legi ut satisfiat, linguæ et calamo temperare non est satis?

A. Secundum rationem ante adductam quum maledicentiam vetat, sinistras [b]etiam suspiciones et judicia iniqua vetat. Nam hic legislator animi affectiones semper maxime respicit. Hæc ergo lex vel ad male de proximis sentiendum, nedum ad eos [c]infamandos propensos nos esse prohibet: imo hoc nos esse candore atque æquitate jubet, ut et de illis, quantum veritas patitur, bene sentiamus, et suam ipsis existimationem, quantum in nobis erit, integram tueri studeamus.

M. Quæ subest ratio, quod Dominus in Lege sua animi vitiosos affectus gravissimorum scelerum nominibus appellat? Odium enim et iram, cædis appellatione; lasciviam omnem cogitationemque fœdam, adulterii; cupiditatem injustam, furti nomine complectitur.

A. Ne, ut est hominum ingenium, ad impios ᵈanimi affectus, ut ad levia quædam, conniveremus, eos Dominus justitiæ suæ regula metiens, veris nominibus designat. Ita enim Servator noster paternæ mentis interpres optimus, ita Divinus ille Spiritus recte intelligendi Magister summus, ista explicat: ᵉQui irascitur, inquit, fratri suo, homicida est; qui concupiscit mulierem, adulterium perpetravit. ᵈ Rom. vii. 7. 1 Cor. x. 6. Jac. iv. 1.
ᵉ Matt. v. 22, 28. et xv. 19. 1 Joan. iii. 15.

M. Verum cum vitia tantum et peccata his præceptis prohibeantur, cur tu interpretando virtutes etiam contrarias præcipi dicis? Nam prohibito adulterio, castitatem; cæde et furto vetitis, summam benevolentiam beneficentiamque præcipi dicis; atque ita in cæteris.

A. Quia idem Servator noster sic interpretatur, summam legis non in abstinentia tantum ab injuria maleficioque, sed in ᶠdilectione atque charitate constituens. Sicut et Regius Propheta ᵍantea monuerat: Declina (inquiens) a malo, et fac bonum. ᶠ Matt. xxii. 39. Rom. xiii. 8, 9. Gal. v. 14.
ᵍ Psal. xxxvii. 27.

M. Superest jam ultimum præceptum.

A. NON CONCUPISCES ʰCUJUSQUAM DOMUM, NON UXOREM, NON SERVUM, NON ANCILLAM, NON BOVEM, NON ASINUM, NEC QUICQUAM OMNINO ALIUD, QUOD ALTERIUS SIT. ʰ Exod. xx. 17. Mich. ii. 2. Rom. vii. 7. 1 Cor. x. 6.

M. Cum totam legem spiritualem esse, nec ad coercendum tantum externa maleficia, sed ad internos animi affectus frænandos institutam esse jam aliquoties commemoraris, quid hic amplies præcipitur, quod antea fuit omissum?

A. Actiones pravas, affectusque animi vitiosos Deus supra prohibuit; nunc vero ⁱexactissimam a nobis integritatem requirit, ut ne cupiditatem quidem ullam vel levissimam, aut cogitationem minimam a recto quoquo modo declinantem, in animum obrepere sinamus. ⁱ Esai. i. 16. Rom. xiii. 14. Gal. v. 14.

M. Quid ergo, improvisas et repentinas etiam cupiditates, momentaneasque cogitationes, quæ piis etiam sese ingerunt, peccata esse dicis, etiamsi illis obnitantur potius quam obtemperent?

A. Omnes certe pravas ᵏcogitationes, etiamsi non accedat consensus, ex natura nostra depravata prodire constat. Cupi- ᵏ Gen. vi. 5. et viii. 21. Psal. xciv. 11. Prov. xx. 9. Matt. xv. 18, 19.

ditates vero repentinas, quæ corda humana sollicitant, nec tamen firmam animi assensionem approbationemque eliciunt, non est dubium quin Deus hoc præcepto, ut peccata damnet. Par enim est, ut coram ¹Deo in cordibus etiam nostris, atque animis, sua atque ea summa integritas et mundities reluceat. Non enim illi potest innocentia justitiaque ᵐnisi summa placere; cujus et hanc suam Legem, perfectam nobis regulam proposuit.

^l Esai. i. 16. et xxix. 13, 15. Jer. iv. 14. Ezech. xviii. 31. Matt. v. 8.
^m Psal. v. 4, 5. 2 Cor. vi. 14.

M. Hactenus Decalogum breviter et dilucide explicuisti; verum hæc omnia sigillatim a te per partes tractata, an non possunt paucis in unam quasi summam colligi?

A. Quid ni? cum Christus cœlestis magister universam Legis vim ac naturam summatim brevissimoque compendio sit complexus, in hunc modum dicens: ⁿDiliges Dominum Deum tuum, ex toto corde tuo, ex tota anima tua, ex tota mente tua, et ex totis viribus tuis; et hoc maximum est præceptum in Lege. Secundum autem est huic simile, Diliges proximum sicut teipsum. Ad hæc enim duo mandata, universa Lex et Prophetæ referuntur.

ⁿ Matt. xxii. 37. Marc. xii. 30. Luc. x. 27.

M. Dei amorem qualem hic requiri intelligis?

A. Qui Deo videlicet conveniat; id est, ut simul et Dominum °eum potentissimum, et optimum ᵖPatrem, et Servatorem clementissimum agnoscamus. Huic proinde amori, et majestatis suæ ᵍreverentia, et obsequium erga ʳvoluntatem ejus, et in bonitatem ejus ˢfiducia adjungenda est.

^o Deut. x. 17. 3 Reg. xviii. 39. 1 Tim. vi. 15.
^p Esai. lxiii. 16. Matt. vi. 8. 1 Tim. i. 1.
^q Deut. x. 12. Psal. xcvi. 7. 1 Cor. x. 31.
^r Deut. vi. 17. Rom. xii. 2.
^s Psal. ii. 12. et xxv. 1. et xxxi. 1. et cxviii. 8.

M. Totum cor, anima tota, totæque vires quid significant?

A. Eum nimirum amoris ardorem, eamque sinceritatem, ut nullis omnino ᵗcogitationibus, desideriis nullis, nedum studiis et actionibus, quæ Dei amori adversentur, locus sit. Chari parentes, (inquit ille,) chari liberi, propinqui, familiares, charior adhuc patria; sed omnes omnium ᵘcharitates pietas erga Deum summusque in eum amor non complectitur solum, verum etiam longe multumque superat; pro quo quis bonus dubitet mortem oppetere? Deum enim non tantum suis omnibus, sed et seipso etiam chariorem habet homo vere pius.

^t Deut. xxx. 6. Jos. xxiii. 11. Matt. x. 37. Luc. xiv. 26.
^u Joan. xiv. 15, 21, 23, 24. et xv. 10.

M. Jam de proximi amore quid dicis?

A. Amoris vincula, Christus inter Christianos suos arctissima esse voluit. Quum vero natura ad nos ipsos ˣamandos simus propensissimi, nec apertior, nec brevior, denique nec efficacior, aut æquior fraternæ charitatis regula excogitari potest, quam quæ a Domino ex ipsa natura desumpta nobis proponitur;

^x 2 Cor. xiii. 5. Eph. v. 29. Phil. ii. 21.

ut eadem videlicet proximum benevolentia, qua seipsum, quisque prosequatur. Ex quo sequitur, ut nihil proximo ʸfaciamus, nihil de illo dicamus, aut sentiamus, quod non et alios nobis facere, vel de nobis loqui, aut sentire velimus. Qua unica lege si teneremur, quæ omnium aliarum legum est quasi anima, nihil opus esset profecto tot legum cancellis, quos ad cohibendas mutuas injurias, et civilem societatem tuendam, homines quotidie excogitant; idque pene frustra, si hujus unius legis nulla sit inter mortales observatio.

ʸ Matt. vii. 12. et xxii. 39. Luc. vi. 31. Rom. xiii. 9, 10.

M. Proximi nomen quam late se fundit?

A. Non cognatos modo, affines, aut amicos, qui aliqua nobiscum necessitudine sunt conjuncti; verum et eos etiam, qui nobis ᶻsunt incogniti, adeoque inimicos etiam nostros complectitur proximi appellatio.

ᶻ Matt. v. 43. Luc. x. 33, 36. Joan. xiii. 34. 1 Thess. iv. 9.

M. At quid isti nobiscum habent communionis?

A. Eo sane vinculo, quo Deus universum genus humanum colligavit, nobis sunt conjuncti; quod inviolabile ᵃac firmum esse voluit, et nullius proinde pravitate, odio, aut malevolentia aboleri potest. Quamvis enim nos quispiam oderit, manet nihilominus ipse nobis proximus, eoque loco semper habendus est, quod ordo ille, per quem hæc hominum inter homines societas, et conjunctio est conciliata, firmus atque inviolabilis semper manere debeat. Atque ex hoc facile intelligi potest, quare Scriptura Sacra charitatem, ᵇsive amorem inter primarias religionis christianæ partes esse voluerit.

ᵃ Matt. v. 44. Luc. vi. 27. 1 Joan. ii. 9. et iii. 10. et iv. 7.

ᵇ Gal. v. 6. 1 Joan. iii. 23.

M. Verum quid sibi vult quod in fine adjungitur, huc referri totam Legem et Prophetas?

A. Quod revera omnium summa illuc pertineat. Admonitiones enim, præcepta, cohortationes, promissiones, minæ, quibus passim ipsa Lex et Prophetæ, et Apostoli utuntur, ad nihil aliud quam hujus legis finem, quasi ad scopum collimant. Et ad charitatem ᶜomnia in sacris literis sic referuntur, ut eo nos quasi manu ducere videantur.

ᶜ Matt. vii. 12. Luc. vi. 31. Rom. xiii. 8, 10. Gal. v. 14. 1 Tim. i. 5.

M. Jam porro volo ut mihi dicas, quænam sit Lex hæc quam narras, eademne illa quam nos vocamus Legem naturæ, an præter eam etiam altera?

A. Id olim abs te me didicisse memini, præceptor, nempe Legem, ut rationem summam in natura humana a Deo insitam fuisse, cum ᵈintegra adhuc ea esset, et incorrupta (ut quæ scilicet ad Dei imaginem erat creata); itaque Lex naturæ et est, et dicitur. Post contractam vero peccati labem, tametsi

ᵈ Gen. i. 26, 27, 31. Eph. iv. 24. Col. iii. 10.

sapientum ᵉanimi utcunque hujus nativi luminis fulgore illustrati sint, in maxima tamen hominum parte ita restinctum est hoc lumen, ut ejus vix ullæ scintillulæ conspiciantur. Adeoque contra divini decreta atque edicta in hac conscripta Lege, quæ amorem in Deum atque homines summum jubent, Dei ᶠatque hominum odium acre penitus est multorum animis insitum; unde tanta in Deum impietas, tam hostilis crudelitas in homines.

M. Unde fit quod Deus voluerit eam in tabulis describi?

A. Dicam: Imago ᵍDei in homine post Adami lapsum, nativo malo, et consuetudine prava adeo obscurata est, et judicium naturale adeo vitiatum, ut homo non satis intelligat, honestum turpi quid intersit, nec justum injusto. Eam itaque imaginem volens benignus Deus in nobis renovare, per Legem in tabulis descriptam ʰperfectæ justitiæ regulam expressit; adeo quidem ad vivum, ut nihil a nobis aliud requirat Deus, nisi ut eam sequamur. Neque enim aliud ille sacrificium acceptum habet, quam ⁱobedientiam; et proinde exosum illi est, quicquid præter ejus prescriptum in Religione, aut pietatis negotio suscipimus.

M. Verum quum nihil de privata cujusque vocatione in hac Lege præcipiatur, quomodo potest hæc vitæ regula esse perfecta?

A. Ut nihil de singulorum officiis hic explicate præcipiatur, quum tamen quod suum est cuique ᵏreddere nos lex jubeat, in summa colligit, quæ sint cujusque in suo privatim ordine, ac vitæ genere partes atque officia. Hic vero Dominus breviter et summatim paucis complexus est, quæ extant passim in Scripturis, de singulorum officiis, singulisque præceptis explicatissima.

M. Quum ergo formam rite colendi Dei perfectam Lex ostendat, nonne omnino secundum ejus præscriptum vivendum est?

A. Adeo quidem, ut Deus ex Legis præscripto viventibus vitam ˡpolliceatur; contra vero, Legis suæ violatoribus ᵐmortem denuntiet, sicut ante dictum est. Atque hanc ob causam superius in partiendo, obedientiam, ut unam ex primariis Religionis veræ partibus, recensui.

M. Justos ergo esse censes eos, qui Legi Dei per omnia obediunt?

A. Sane, siqui id præstare possint, justi ex Lege essent;

verum ea imbecillitate [n]laboramus omnes, ut nemo quod debet omni ex parte impleat. Nam ut demus inveniri, qui Legi aliqua ex parte obtemperet, non tamen is ideo coram Deo justus erit; nam [o]execrandos et detestabiles pronuntiat omnes, qui non omnia impleverint, quæ in Lege continentur.

[n] Gen. vi. 5, 8, 11. Prov. xx. 9. Rom. vii. 14, 15. Gal. ii. 16.
[o] Gal. iii. 10. Jac. ii. 10.

M. Nullum ergo mortalem ex Lege coram Deo justum esse statuis?

A. Nullum omnino. Nam et [p]Scripturæ idem pronuntiant.

[p] Job. xxv. 4. Rom. iii. 28. et iv. 15. Gal. ii. 16, 21. et iii. 10.

M. Cur ergo Legem tulit Deus, quæ perfectionem exigat facultate nostra majorem?

A. In Lege ferenda Deus non tam quid nos præstare possemus, qui nostra culpa [q]imbecillitate laboramus, quam quid ipsius justitia dignum esset, spectavit. Quum vero Deo non nisi summa [r]justitia placere possit, eam vivendi normam quam ipse descripsit, omnino perfectam esse oportuit. Deinde nihil a nobis exigit Lex, cui præstando obstricti non simus. Quum vero longissime a debita [s]Legis obedientia absimus, nulla idonea aut justa excusatione homines coram Deo sese defendere possunt; adeoque universos coram Dei tribunali Lex et reos sistit, [t]et condemnat etiam. Atque id est quod Paulus, Legem ministerium mortis, et damnationis vocat.

[q] Luc. xvii. 10. Rom. iii. 20. Gal. vi. 3.
[r] Psal. v. 4, 5, 6. 2 Cor. vi. 14.
[s] Job. iv. 17. et xv. 14. 2 Par. vi. 36. Gal. ii. 16.
[t] Rom. iii. 19. et vii. 8, 10. Gal. iii. 10.

M. An Lex ergo universos simul in hoc deploratissimo statu collocat?

A. Incredulos [u]quidem atque impios, hoc, quo dixi, loco Lex et statuit et relinquit; qui ut ne minimum quidem Legis apicem implere possunt, ita nullam prorsus in Deo per Christum fiduciam habent. Inter pios tamen, alios præterea usus Lex habet.

[u] Deut. xxvii. 26. Rom. iii. 10. Jac. ii. 10.

M. Cedo quos?

A. Principio Lex tam [x]exactam vitæ perfectionem flagitans, quasi scopum piis, ad quem collimare, et metam, ad quam eniti conveniat, demonstrat, ut ad summam rectitudinem indies proficiendo magno conatu contendant; hanc enim mentem voluntatemque Deo immortali duce pii suscipiunt. Maxime vero cavent, quantum efficere et consequi possunt, ne quod in ipsis insigne vitium fuisse dicatur. Deinde cum multo majora [y]viribus humanis Lex exigat, cumque tanto oneri se impares esse sentiant, ad petendam a Domino virtutem eos excitat. Præterea cum Lex eos perpetuo [z]reos agat, salutari dolore animos eorum percellit, et ad pœnitentiam, de qua ante me-

[x] Deut. vi. 6, 7. Jos. i. 7, 8. Psal. i. 2.
[y] Psal. cxix. 5. Rom. vii. 14. 2 Cor. iii. 5.
[z] Deut. xxvii. 26. Rom. iii. 10, 11, 12. 2 Cor. iii. 9.

mini, veniamque a Deo per Christum petendam atque impetrandam adigit; simulque ne suæ innocentiæ confidant, aut superbire coram Deo audeant, coercet. Estque illis perpetuo fræni instar, quo in Dei timore retineantur. Postremo dum absolutam justitiam [a]per opera sua se consequi non posse ex Lege discunt, cum per eam animorum suorum maculas atque sordes [b]tanquam in speculo contueantur, ad humilitatem hoc pacto eruditos, ad quærendam in Christo justitiam eos et præparat et remittit.

[a] Prov. xx. 9. Rom. i. 20, 21. Gal. ii. 16.
[b] Rom. iii. 20. et vii. 7.
[c] Rom. x. 4. Gal. iii. 10, &c. 24.

M. Quantum ergo video, [c]Legem Dei, quasi pædagogum quendam ad Christum esse dicis, quæ nos per agnitionem nostri, pœnitentiam, et Fidem ad Christum recta deducat.

A. Ita est.

Secunda pars de Evangelio et Fide.

Transitio.

M. Quum ergo abunde, ut in compendio, toti huic de Lege atque obedientia quæstioni satisfactum sit, charissime Fili, jam de Evangelio, quod Dei promissiones continet, et juris divini violatoribus Dei clementiam per Christum pollicetur, quodque Fides maxime respicit, ut dicamus, ordo postulat; hoc enim in nostra partitione secundum fuit; atque huc etiam, ipsa rerum, de quibus jam egimus, series nos quasi manu perduxit. Evangelii ergo, simulque Fidei nostræ summa quænam est?

A. Ea nimirum ipsa, qua Fidei Christianæ præcipua capita, breviter olim perstricta, continentur; quæque vulgo Symbolum Apostolorum appellatur.

M. Fidei compendium cur Symbolum nominatur?

A. Symbolum, si interpreteris, est signum, nota, tessera, aut indicium, quo commilitones ab hostibus dignoscuntur; unde compendium Fidei, quo Christiani a non Christianis distinguuntur, Symboli nomen sibi recte ascivit.

M. Sed qua de causa Apostolorum Symbolum dicitur?

A. Quod vel ab ore Apostolorum exceptum, vel ex illorum scriptis summa fide collectum, ab initio usque Ecclesiæ receptum, perpetuo inter omnes pios firmum, ratum atque immotum, ut certa atque constituta christianæ Fidei regula, permanserit.

M. Age nunc, Symbolum ipsum mihi recites velim.

A. Fiet. CREDO IN DEUM PATREM OMNIPOTENTEM, CREATOREM CŒLI ET TERRÆ, ET IN JESUM CHRISTUM, FILIUM

EJUS UNICUM DOMINUM NOSTRUM, QUI CONCEPTUS EST DE SPIRITU SANCTO, NATUS EX MARIA VIRGINE; PASSUS SUB PONTIO PILATO, CRUCIFIXUS, MORTUUS, ET SEPULTUS EST; DESCENDIT AD INFEROS, TERTIA DIE RESURREXIT A MORTUIS; ASCENDIT AD CŒLUM, SEDET AD DEXTERAM DEI PATRIS OMNIPOTENTIS, UNDE VENTURUS EST AD JUDICANDUM VIVOS ET MORTUOS. CREDO IN SPIRITUM SANCTUM, SANCTAM ECCLESIAM CATHOLICAM, SANCTORUM COMMUNIONEM, REMISSIONEM PECCATORUM, CARNIS RESURRECTIONEM, ET VITAM ÆTERNAM.

M. Breviter ista a te, et strictim proposita sunt, mi Fili; quocirca operæ prætium est, ut de singulis quid credas, clarius dicas atque explicatius. Et primum, in quot partes totam hanc confessionem distribuis?

A. In quatuor præcipuas; quarum in prima de Deo Patre, et rerum omnium creatione; in secunda de ejus Filio Jesu Christo, quæ etiam totam redemptionis humanæ summam complectitur; in tertia de Spiritu sancto; in quarta de Ecclesia, et Divinis in ipsam beneficiis tractatur. *Partitio.*

M. Perges ergo ordine quatuor istas mihi partes explicare; et primum quid in ipso statim Symboli initio credendi nomine significas?

A. Me veram ac vivam, id est, ᵈchristiani hominis Fidem in Deum Patrem, Filium, et Spiritum sanctum habere, eamque hac confessionis formula ᵉtestari me, atque comprobare. ᵈ Matt. xxviii. 19. Rom. i. 17. Joan. i. 12, 13. Gal. iii. 26. ᵉ Matt. x. 32. Rom. x. 9. Heb. iv. 14.

M. Estne ergo Fides aliqua, quæ vera vivaque non sit?

A. Est certe Fides quædam generalis, ut ita loquar, est et Fides mortua. ᶠ Rom. i. 32. Tit. i. 16. Jac. ii. 26.

M. Quum ergo non levis momenti res sit, quam credendi, christianæque, id est, veræ ac vivæ Fidei nomine complecteris, age explica mihi quænam ea sit, quomodoque a Fide illa generali et mortua etiam distinguatur.

A. Fides in genere ea est, quæ veritati verbi Dei ᵍFidem habet; id est, quæ omnia in Scripturis de Deo, ejusque immensitate, potentia, justitia, sapientia, misericordia item in homines fideles ac pios, summaque severitate in incredulos atque impios, cæteraque in Scripturis tradita universa vera esse credit. ᵍ Matt. vii. 22. Luc. xii. 47. 1 Cor. xiii. 2.

M. Annon omnia hæc etiam et vera illa, quam dicis, Fides credit?

A. Maxime; verum ea ultra progreditur, sicuti mox dicemus. ʰNam hactenus non impii solum homines, sed et ʰ Rom. i. 32. Tit. i. 16. Jac. ii. 19.

dæmones etiam credunt; neque tamen ⁱfideles proinde sunt, aut dicuntur. At vera Fides, ut omnia in verbo Dei tradita certissima esse nihil dubitat, ᵏita promissiones de Dei Patris misericordia, et peccatorum remissione fidelibus omnibus per Christum factas, quæ proprie ˡEvangelium dicuntur, amplectitur; quam qui habent, non solum ᵐDeum ut potentissimum omnium Dominum, justissimumque judicem timent (quod et homines impios plerosque et ⁿdæmones etiam facere jam antea diximus) verum etiam ut ᵒpatrem suum optimum atque clementissimum amant; cui ut placere per omnia piis studiis operibusque, quæ Fidei fructus dicuntur, uti obsequentes filios decet, student, ita de ejus ᵖvenia, si quando ut homines ab ejus voluntate aberrarint, per Christum impetranda, bonam certamque spem concipiunt. Peccata enim sua, Christo, cui fidunt, ᑫiram Patris placante, non magis sibi unquam imputanda sciunt, quam si ea nunquam fuissent perpetrata. Et quamvis Legi, officioque erga Deum atque homines suo non satisfecerint ipsi, Christum tamen summa Legis observatione, Deo pro se cumulate satisfecisse credunt; et per hanc illius ʳjustitiam et divinæ Legis observationem, in numero locoque justorum, et Deo charos haberi se, haud aliter ac si Legem observassent ipsi, persuasum habent. Atque hæc ea est ˢjustitia, quam nos Fide consequi sacræ literæ declarant.

M. Annon ista etiam in dæmonibus, aut hominibus impiis esse possunt?

A. Nihil minus. Nam ᵗtametsi Deum ut potentissimum justissimumque timeant, aut horreant potius, quum suæ eum impietatis ultorem fore sciant, in ejus tamen in se bonitate et clementia, neque ullam Fiduciam, neque ad ejus gratiam receptum aliquem habere, neque ejus voluntati obsequendi studium ullum suscipere possunt. Itaque eorum Fides, tametsi de veritate verbi Dei non ambigant, mortua ᵘdicitur; ut quæ trunci instar aridi atque emortui, fructus nullos piæ vitæ, id est, amoris in Deum, charitatisque in homines, unquam ex se edat.

M. Ex his ergo, quæ hactenus commemorasti, definitionem mihi cedo vivæ illius et veræ christianæ Fidei.

A. ˣFides est certa cognitio, paternæ Dei erga nos per Christum benevolentiæ, fiduciaque in eadem, sicuti in Evangelio testatum est, quæ ʸstudium piæ vitæ, id est, Dei Patris voluntati obsequendi semper conjunctum habet.

M. Satis explicuisti, quid Fidei, credendique nominibus significes. Perge jam, quibus commodissime possis verbis mihi edissere, quid per Dei nomen, quod in Symbolo proxime sequitur, intelligas.

A. Annitar pro meo ingenio atque facultate, præceptor optime. Intelligo ^znaturam esse unam, vel ^asubstantiam, vel animum, vel mentem, vel ^bspiritum potius divinum (variis enim modis de Deo loquuti sunt sapientes, tum Ethnici, tum nostri, quum nihil de eo proprie dici possit) ^cæternum, absque principio et fine, ^dimmensum; ^eincorporeum, oculis humanis minime conspicuum, majestate ^faugustissima, quem vocamus Deum; quem oportet universos mundi populos ^grevereri, et summo honore colere, omnemque in eo, ut optimo maximo, spem ^hfiduciamque collocare.

<small>z Gal. iii. 20.
2 Pet. i. 4.
a Heb. i. 3.
b Joan. iv. 24.
c Rom. i. 20. et xvi. 26.
d Matt. vi. 13. et xix. 26.
e Joan. i. 18. Col. i. 15.
f Psal. civ. 31. Esai. ii. 10, 19. 1 Tim. i. 17. et vi. 16.
g 1 Cor. x. 31.
h Psal. xxxvi. 7.</small>

M. Quum unus sit Deus, edissere cur in Christianæ Fidei confessione tres commemores, Patrem, Filium, et Spiritum sanctum?

A. Non ⁱmultorum Deorum, sed trium distinctarum in una divinitate personarum hæc sunt nomina. In ^kuna enim Dei essentia, ^lPATREM, qui Filium ab æterno ex se genuit, intueri convenit, ut originem primumque rerum omnium authorem: ^mFILIUM, ex Patre ab æterno genitum, qui sit æterna Dei Patris sapientia; ⁿSPIRITUM SANCTUM, ab utroque procedentem, ut Dei virtutem, per omnia diffusam, sed ita, ut etiam perpetuo in ipso resideat: ^oneque dividi tamen propterea Deum. Ex his enim tribus personis nulla aliam, aut ^ptempore, aut magnitudine, aut dignitate anteit; sed Pater, Filius, et Spiritus Sanctus, tres distinctæ Personæ, ^qæternitate æquævæ, potentia æquales, dignitate pares, Deitate unum sunt. ^rUnus ergo æternus, immortalis, omnipotens, gloriosus, optimus Max. Deus Pater, Filius, et Spiritus Sanctus. Ita enim de Deo Patre, Filio, et Spiritu Sancto, a Christianorum universitate, quæ Catholica Ecclesia dicitur, ex Scripturis Sacris proditum est; quum alioquin hujus mysterii immensitas tanta sit, ut ne mente quidem concipi, nedum verbis explicari queat; in quo proinde simplicitas Fidei christianæ ad credendum parata, potius quam ingenii ^sacumen ad inquirendum, vel linguæ etiam officium ad explicandum mysterium tam arcanum, atque occultum requiratur.

<small>i Matt. xxviii. 19.
1 Joan. v. 7.
k Joan. x. 30. Gal. iii. 20.
l Gen. i. 1. 1 Cor. viii. 6.
m Joan. i. 1; xvii. 5. Col. i. 15. Heb. i. 2, 3, 5.
n Luc. i. 35. Joan. xiv. 26. Act. v. 3, 4. 1 Cor. xii. 4.
o Joan. x. 30. 1 Cor. viii. 6. Gal. iii. 20.
p Joan. i. 1 et v. 17, 18, 21, 23. Phil. ii. 6.
q 1 Joan. v. 7.
r Deut. iv. 35, 39. Psal. lxxxvi. 9, 10. et civ. 30, 31. 1 Tim. i. 17. In Symbolis, sive confessionibus Fidei Christ. Apost. Nicæn. et Athan.
s Prov. xxv. 26.</small>

M. Verissimum quidem est quod dicis. Perge ergo; cur Deum vocas Patrem?

A. Ejus rei præter eam, quam ante memoravi, præcipuam causam, quod videlicet ^tnaturalis sit Pater unici Filii sui ab æterno ex se geniti, duæ sunt aliæ causæ, ob quas noster etiam Pater et sit, et dicatur. ^uUna, quod nos omnes initio creavit, quodque vitam omnibus est largitus; de qua mox plura dicemus. ^xAltera vero majoris etiam momenti est, quod videlicet iterum divinitus per Spiritum Sanctum nos genuit, et ^yFide in verum, et naturalem Filium suum Jesum Christum, nos sibi Filios adoptavit, et regno suo, ac vitæ æternæ hæreditate per eundem donavit.

M. Quo sensu nomen illi omnipotentis tribuis?

A. Quod ^zmundum et universa, uti condidit, ita in potestate etiam habeat, providentia gubernet, arbitrio constituat, omnibusque, prout illi visum fuerit, imperet; sic ut nihil nisi ejus decreto permissuve fiat, nihil sit quod ille efficere non possit; neque enim otiosam quandam Dei potentiam, quam non exerceat, imaginor.

M. An impios etiam homines, spiritusque malignos Dei imperio subdis?

A. Quid ni? ^aMiserrime enim alioqui nobiscum ageretur, ut quibus nunquam securis esse liceret, si quid illis in nos, præter Dei voluntatem, permitteretur. Verum eos Deus quasi frœno suæ potentiæ ita coercet, ut ne movere quidem se, nisi ejus nutu aut permissu, possint unquam. Nos vero una hæc consolatio sustentat, ita nos in omnipotentis esse Patris potestate, ut ne unus ^bquidem capillus noster, nisi ex ejus voluntate, qui nobis tam bene vult, perire possit.

M. Perge.

A. ^cQuum Dei Opt. Max. bonitatem atque immensitatem mens humana per se capere nullo modo possit, cœli eum et terræ, et rerum, quæ in eis continentur, universitatis creatorem esse addimus; quibus verbis, Deum in operibus suis ^det mundi opificio, tanquam in speculo quodam contemplandum, et quoad nostra id refert, cognoscendum esse significamus. Quum enim magnitudinem illam immensam mundi videmus, ejusque partes omnes ita esse constitutas, ut neque ad speciem pulchriores, neque ad usum meliores esse potuerint; statim intelligimus Dei opificis atque ædificatoris infinitam potentiam, sapientiam, bonitatem. Quis enim est tam vecors, qui cum suspexit in cœlum, Deum esse non sentiat? Imo ob hanc maxime causam Deus homines primum humo excitatos, celsos et erectos constituisse videtur, ut superarum atque cœlestium rerum essent spectatores, et ipsius cognitionem, cœlum intuentes, capere possent.

M. Quomodo Deum omnia creasse dicis?

A. ^eDeum Patrem Opt. Max. initio, et ex nihilo, non solum cœlum, et universum hunc mundum aspectabilem, et res in eis omnes quæcunque continentur, ^fsed et Spiritus etiam incorporeos, quos Angelos appellamus, ^gper potentiam verbi sui, id est, Jesu Christi Filii sui, fabricasse et condidisse. ^e Gen. i. 1. Psal. xxxiii. 6. Act. xiv. 15. ^f Col. i. 16. ^g Joan. i. 3. 1 Cor. viii. 6. Heb. i. 2.

M. Verum an pium esse putas, affirmare Deum Opt. Max. spiritus universos, etiam malignos illos, quos diabolos vocamus, condidisse?

A. Deus quidem eos tales non ^hcondidit: sed ipsi ab origine sua, absque ulla spe recuperandæ salutis, sua ipsorum malitia exciderunt. Itaque non creatione et natura, sed naturæ corruptione mali effecti sunt. ^h Gen. i. 31. Joan. viii. 44. Col. i. 16. Jud. 6.

M. Quid; an satis habuit Deus semel universa condidisse, omni rerum cura in posterum abjecta?

A. Hoc quidem antea breviter attigeram; cum vero tueri et conservare res conditas multo sit præstantius, quam eas semel condidisse; ⁱcerto credendum est, ubi mundum et omnia sic fabricasset, ea deinceps et conservasse, et hactenus conservare. Ruerent enim universa, atque ad nihilum reciderent, nisi ejus virtute, et quasi manu sustinerentur. ^kA Deo etiam totum naturæ ordinem, et rerum mutationes, quæ fortunæ vicissitudines falso putantur, pendere: ^lDeum cœlum versare, terram tueri, maria moderari, omnem hunc mundum regere, ejus numini omnia parere, ejus numine omnia gubernari certo credimus; ^meum serenitatis et tempestatis, pluviæ et siccitatis, fœcunditatis et sterilitatis, sanitatis, ac morborum authorem esse; eum, ⁿquæcunque ad vitam nostram tuendam conservandamque pertinent, et vel ad usus necessarios, vel ad honestam voluptatem expetuntur, rerumque adeo omnium, quas natura desiderat, abundantiam et copiam munifica manu suppeditasse semper, atque etiam suppeditare largissime; ut nimirum illis perinde uteremur, ac memores et pios filios decet. ⁱ Psal. lxxv. 3. et civ. 10. et cxlv. 15. Heb. i. 3. ^k Matt. x. 29, 30. ^l Exod. xiv. 21. Psal. lxxxix. 10. et cxlvii. 8, 9. ^m Lev. xxvi. 4, &c. ⁿ Psal. cxliv. 13. et cxlv. 16. 17. Esai. li. 3. Matt. v. 45. Rom. xiv. 6. 1 Cor. x. 31. Eph. v. 4. 1 Tim. iv. 3, 4. 1 Pet. v. 7.

M. Quem ad finem, Deum Opt. Max. universa hæc condidisse existimas?

A. Mundus ipse hominum ^ocausa factus est, et quæcun- ^o Gen. i. 26, 29, 30. Psal. viii. 7, &c.

que in eo sunt, ad usum fructumque hominum parata sunt. Et ut res alias omnes Deus hominis gratia, ita hominem ipsum ad suam ipsius ^pgloriam condidit.

p Prov xvi. 4. Esai. xliii. 7. Rom. xi. 36. Col. i. 16.

M. Quid ergo habes, quod dicas de prima hominis origine et creatione?

A. Id quod scripsit Moses: Deum scilicet ex argilla primum ^qhominem finxisse, illique animam et vitam inspirasse; deinde de viri latere, somno sopiti, detractam mulierem in lucem produxisse, ut eam illi vitæ sociam adjungeret. Ac propterea homo Adamus vocatus est, quia ex ^rterra traxit originem: mulier autem, quia omnium ^sviventium mater erat futura, appellabatur Eva.

q Gen. ii. 7. et 21, 22.

r Gen. ii. 7. et iii. 19.
s Gen. iii. 20.

M. Cum tanta in utrisque, viris pariter atque fœminis, vitiositas, improbitas, perversitasque hodie conspiciatur, an eos Deus tales ab initio condidit?

A. Nihil minus. Deus enim summe bonus, nihil nisi ^tbonum potest efficere. Hominem ergo primum Deus ad ^uimaginem et similitudinem suam condidit.

t Gen. i. 31.
u Gen. i. 26. Col. iii. 10.

M. Imago autem illa, ad quam hominem ais formatum esse, quænam est?

A. Ea est absolutissima justitia, et perfectissima sanctimonia, quæ ad ipsam Dei naturam quam maxime pertinet; quæque in ^xChristo novo nostro Adamo, præclarissime est demonstrata; cujus in nobis quædam quasi scintillulæ vix jam compareant.

x Rom. viii. 29. 1 Cor. xv. 49. 2 Cor. iii. 18. et iv. 4. Col. i. 15. et iii. 10.

M. Itane vix comparent?

A. Profecto; neque jam ita splendent ut in initio ante hominis lapsum, quandoquidem homo peccatorum ^ztenebris, et caligine errorum imaginis hujus splendorem restinxit.

z Rom. i. 22. 1 Cor. i. 18, 23. et ii. 14. et iii. 19. Eph. iv. 17.

M. At quomodo hoc factum sit dicas, volo?

A. Dicam: Cum mundum hunc fabricatus esset Dominus Deus, ^ahortum ipse paravit cultissimum, plenissimumque oblectationis et jucunditatis, quæcunque expetibiles erant, deliciis undique affluentem. Hic Dominus Deus singularis cujusdam benevolentiæ gratia hominem collocavit, omniaque illius usui permisit; tantum illi fructu arboris ^bscientiæ boni et mali interdixit, morte, si illum gustaret, denunciata. Par enim erat, ut tot beneficiis ^caffectus homo, hactenus parendo, libenter se Dei imperio obtemperare ostenderet, utque sua contentus sorte, altius sese contra conditoris voluntatem conditus ipse non efferret.

a Gen. ii. 8.

b Gen. ii. 17.

c Gen. iii. 11. Psal. viii. 4, 5, 6, &c.

M. Quid deinde factum est?

A. Mulier ᵈa Diabolo illusa, viro persuasit, ut vetitum fructum gustaret; quæ res utrumque morti statim obnoxium effecit; deletaque illa cœlesti imagine, ad quam primum est conditus, in locum sapientiæ, virtutis, sanctitatis, veritatis, justitiæ, quibus eum ornamentis Deus induerat, teterrimæ successerunt pestes, ᵉcæcitas, impotentia, impietas, vanitas, injustitia, quibus etiam malis atque miseriis progeniem suam, atque adeo omnem posteritatem implicuit et cooperuit. <small>ᵈ Gen. iii. 1, 6, 7. ᵉ Act. xiv. 12, 13. et xvii. 21. Rom. i. 22. et viii. 7, 8. 1 Cor. ii. 14. Eph. iv. 17, 18, 22.</small>

M. Verum an non nimium severe unius pomi gustum ultus esse Deus videri possit?

A. Nequis hominis scelus gravissimum, ut parvum delictum elevet, neve ex pomo tantum, ᶠet immensa gula factum spectet. Nam ille una cum conjuge sua, dolosis ᵍSatanæ illecebris captus atque irretitus, a Dei veritate incredulus ad mendacium deflexit; serpentis calumniis, quibus Deum et mendacii, et invidiæ, et malignitatis insimulat, fidem habuit; tot ʰbeneficiis affectus, in authorem ingratissimus extitit; terræ filius, cui parum videbatur, quod ad Dei similitudinem factus esset, intolerabili ⁱambitione atque superbia, sese Dei majestati æquare affectavit; denique conditoris se imperio ᵏcontumaciter subduxit, imo jugum ejus petulanter excussit. Frustra ergo Adæ peccatum verbis extenuatur. <small>ᶠ Gen. iii. 6. ᵍ Gen. iii. 4, 5. ʰ Psal. viii. 4, 5, 6. ⁱ Gen. iii. 22. ᵏ Gen. iii. 11. Ose. vi. 7. Rom. v. 19.</small>

M. Atqui parentum culpa omnem posteritatem summa privari fœlicitate, ultimisque malis atque miseriis onerari, quomodo non iniquum videbitur?

A. Adamus generis humani primus parens extitit: ornamentis itaque illis eum Deus affecit, ut ea tam sibi quam suis, hoc est, universo hominum generi haberet simul ac perderet. Eo itaque spoliato, natura universa nuda inopsque ac bonis omnibus destituta deseritur; illoque peccati labe inquinato, quasi ˡa radice trunco vitiato, rami vitiosi enati sunt; qui vitium suum in alios ex se nascentes surculos transtulerunt. Inde autem tam breve, ᵐexiguum, atque incertum vitæ curriculum nobis circumscriptum; inde nata est carnis nostræ infirmitas, ⁿcorporum debilitas, imbecilitas, fragilitasque humani generis; inde horribilis mentium ᵒcæcitas, et animorum pravitas; inde ista distortio depravatioque affectionum, et cupiditatum omnium; hinc illud ᵖseminarium, et quasi sentina peccatorum omnium, cujus vitiis genus humanum inficitur et conflictatur; cujus mali proprium verumque nomen quærentes, nostri PECCATUM ORIGINIS appellarunt. <small>ˡ Rom. v. 12, 14, 17, 18, 19. 1 Cor. xv. 22, 48. ᵐ Psal. cii. 3, 6, 7, 9, 10, 11. et ciii. 15, 16. et cix. 23, &c. ⁿ Job. xiv. 1, &c. ᵒ Rom. i. 22. 1 Cor. iii. 18, 19. Eph. iv. 17, 18, 19. ᵖ Rom. v. 12, &c.</small>

M. An in hac tantum vita, peccati hujus pœnas luit humanum genus?

A. Imo hoc nativo malo ita corrupta est natura et perdita, ut nisi bonitas ^(q)et misericordia omnipotentis Dei, afflictis nobis, adhibita medicina, tulisset opem atque auxilium, quemadmodum fortunis in calamitates omnes, corporibus in universas ^(r)morborum mortisque miserias incidimus; ita necessario in ^(s)tenebras, atque sempiternam noctem, et ignem, qui extingui non potest, ibi omni supplicio perpetuo excruciandi, præcipites rueremus. Nec mirum alias etiam res ^(t)conditas, eam pœnam, quam commeruit homo, in cujus usum conditæ erant, subiisse; perturbatoque in cœlo ^(u)et terra toto naturæ ordine, noxias tempestates, sterilitatem, morbos, atque alia infinita mala in orbem invasisse; in quas ^(x)miserias atque ærumnas, præter nativum illud malum, multis nostris, magnisque peccatis meritissimo incidimus.

M. O funestam atque horrendam ex peccato cladem et calamitatem! At quænam tandem illa est, quam nobis fecisse Deum medicinam dicis, in qua primi nostri parentes, et reliqui deinceps eorum posteri spem posuerunt et defixerunt?

Secunda pars Symboli. Deus Filius.

A. Ad eam nimirum salutis spem erecti sunt, quam ex Fide in Jesum Christum liberatorem atque servatorem ipsis a Deo ^(y)promissum conceperunt. Hoc enim est quod jam proxime in Symbolo sequitur: Credo in Jesum Christum, &c.

M. An et primis parentibus nostris, Deus liberationis per Jesum Christum spem statim fecit?

A. Profecto: Nam ut Adamum ^(z)et Evam verbis primum graviter castigatos, de horto deturbavit, ita serpentem devovit, ^(a)et minatus est illi tempus olim fore, quo mulieris semen caput illi imminueret.

M. Quod vero est semen illud, de quo loquitur Deus?

A. Semen ^(b)illud est (uti clarissime nos docet Paulus) Jesus Christus Filius Dei, verus Deus, et filius virginis, verus homo, in quo nos fiduciam atque spem nostram collocare, secundo loco in Symbolo profitemur; qui conceptus est e Spiritu ^(c)sancto, et genitus ex sanctæ, castæ, atque incorruptæ virginis Mariæ natura; atque ea matre sic natus et enutritus est, ut reliqui infantes, nisi quod ab omnis peccati contagione ^(d)omnino purus esset atque alienus.

M. An satis ergo habuit Deus semel in Veteri Testamento de hoc semine promisisse?

A. Imo promissionem hanc humano generi optatissimam, Dominus Deus parentibus ͤnostris primum factam, identidem illorum posteris confirmavit, quo majore expectatione illius præstandi homines tenerentur. Nam fœdere per circumcisionem ᶠcum Abrahamo et ejus semine inito, ipsi primum, mox Isaaco ejus filio, deinde Jacobo nepoti promissum suum confirmavit. Postremo, clarissimis per Mosen ᵍcæterosque prophetas suos editis oraculis, promissi sui constantiam retinuit atque servavit.

M. Quid autem sibi volunt ista verba, Serpentis caput conterere?

A. In ʰSerpentis capite venenum ejus continetur, vitæque et virtutis summa consistit; caput ergo Serpentis universam vim atque potentiam, et regnum, aut, ut verius loquar, tyrannidem diaboli, serpentis antiqui significat; quam ⁱuniversam, Jesus Christus, semen illud mulieris, in quo promissi sui summam Deus complevit, virtute mortis suæ subegit. Itaque Serpentis caput conterens, omnes sibi fidentes ab ejus tyrannide in libertatem vindicavit. Hoc enim est, quod hic in Symbolo profitemur, nos IN JESUM CHRISTUM DEI FILIUM CREDERE; id est, Jesum Christum nobis, qui impietate et scelere obstricti atque obligati, et mortis æternæ laqueis irretiti tenebamur, et serpentis Diaboli fœda servitute premebamur, libertatis vindicem esse, atque servatorem.

M. Videris mihi interim, et ipsum nomen JESU, illustri admodum explicatione esse interpretatus.

A. Profecto; neque enim aliud Hebræis est JESUS, quam Σωτήρ Græcis, Latinis SERVATOR. Nam ut vim ejus exprimant, aliud magis aptum nomen non habent. Ex his autem quæ diximus obscurum jam esse non potest, quare hoc nomen sit adeptus; solus enim ille suos æterno exitio, cui alioqui erant destinati, exemit et servavit. Et alii quidem hoc nomen usurparunt, quod corporibus hominum salutem attulisse visi sint: At ᵏJesus Christus animas simul et corpora sibi fidentium solus servare potest.

M. A quo est illi hoc nomen inditum?

A. Ab ˡAngelo, Dei ipsius jussu. Nomini vero quod ipsi Deus imposuit, revera etiam eum respondere necesse fuit.

M. Jam CHRISTI nomen quid sibi velit dicito.

A. Idem est, ac si ᵐunctum diceres; quo significatur, eum summum Regem, Sacerdotem, ac Prophetam esse.

M. Unde hoc constabit?

A. Ex sacra Scriptura; quæ et ⁿunctionem ad tria hæc accommodat; et eadem sæpe Christo tribuit.

M. An ergo oleo, quali in priscis Regibus, Sacerdotibus, et Prophetis creandis usi sunt, unctus est CHRISTUS?

A. Nequaquam; verum multo præstantiore; uberrima videlicet °Spiritus Sancti gratia, qua repletus ᴾfuit, divinisque ejus opibus accumulatissime præditus; cujus cœlestis unctionis externa illa, umbra tantummodo fuit.

M. Sibine soli hæc adeptus est, an et nobis etiam aliquas inde utilitates præbet?

A. Imo a Patre ista Christus accepit, ut nobiscum eadem, modo atque ratione, quam convenire cuique maxime novit, communicet; ᑫex ejus enim plenitudine, ut ex unico, sancto, atque augusto fonte, haurimus omnes quicquid habemus cœlestium bonorum.

M. Non ergo mundanum dicis esse CHRISTI Regnum?

A. ʳMinime; sed spirituale et æternum, quod verbo et Spiritu Dei, quæ justitiam secum et vitam ferunt, regitur atque administratur.

M. Quem nos ex hoc regno fructum percipimus?

A. Virtute et spiritualibus ˢarmis, ad carnem, mundum, peccatum, Satanam, immanes et capitales animarum nostrarum hostes debellandos, nos instruit; beatam conscientiarum libertatem largitur; denique Divinis suis opibus præditos, ad pie sancteque vivendum juvat et confirmat.

M. Qualis sacerdos est CHRISTUS?

A. ᵗMaximus, et æternus; qui solus sese Deo sistere, solus sacrificium, quod ille gratum acceptumque habeat, facere, et solus Dei iram placare valet.

M. Quo ista nostro commodo facit?

A. Quia nobis a ᵘDeo pacem ac veniam petit et precatur, nobis iram Dei placat, nosque Patri reconciliat. Solus enim Christus Mediator noster est, per quem cum Deo redimus in gratiam. Sed et collegas nos quodammodo sibi ˣin sacerdotio suo facit, nobis quoque dans aditum ad Patrem, ut in ejus conspectum cum fiducia prodire, et nos ac nostra omnia Deo Patri in sacrificium per ipsum offerre audeamus.

M. Prophetia CHRISTI cujusmodi est?

A. Quum Prophetas Dei optimi maximi servos, ut voluntatem suam mortales edocerent, antea a se missos, homines ycontemnerent atque aspernarentur, verbumque ejus sacrosanctum suis somniis atque inventis jam plane obscurassent atque obruissent, ipse Dei Filius Prophetarum omnium Dominus in hunc mundum descendit, ut Patris voluntate quam plenissime declarata, prophetiis ac vaticinationibus omnibus finem imponeret. Patris ergo legatus zatque internuncius ad homines venit, ut ipso interprete, in rectam Dei cognitionem ac veritatem omnem adducerentur. Ita triplex illud officium et munus, quod Dei Filius a Patre coelesti susceptum explevit, ut nobiscum fructum ejus omnem communicaret, Christi nomine continetur.

y Matt. xv. 3, 8, 9. et xxi. 34, 37. Luc. xi. 47, 50. Act. vii. 51, 52. Heb. i. 1, 2.

z Joan. i. 4, 5. et viii. 26, 40. et xv. 15. et xvii. 6, &c.

M. Hoc ergo in summa dixisse videris, Filium Dei non modo dici, et esse JESUM CHRISTUM, id est, Servatorem, Regem, Sacerdotem, Prophetam, sed et nobis, et ad nostrum commodum atque salutem ita esse.

A. Omnino.

M. Verum quum piis aomnibus hic honor habeatur, ut Dei Filii nuncupentur, quomodo Christum Filium Dei unicum appellas?

a Joan. i. 12, 13. et xi. 52. Rom. ix. 26.

A. Solius Christi Deus bnaturalis est Pater, solus Christus natura Dei Filius est, ut qui ex substantia Patris genitus, uniusque cum Patre essentiæ est; nos vero Deus gratuito per Christum Filios sibi ascivit atque adoptavit. Itaque Christum unicum Dei Filium recte agnoscimus[1], quum hic illi honor suo summoque jure debeatur; Filiorum tamen nomen adoptionis cjure nobiscum etiam per Christum gratis communicatur.

b Matt. ii. 15. et iii. 17. Joan. i. 14, 49. et xiv. 10. Heb. i. 3. et v. 5.

M. Jam Dominum esse nostrum quomodo intelligis?

c Rom. viii. 15. Gal. iv. 5. Eph. i. 5. 1 Joan. iii. 1.

A. Quod Principatum illi Pater in dhomines, Angelos, atque universa detulerit; quodque Dei regnum in cœlo pariter ac in terra nutu atque potestate sua administret. Hinc vero admonentur pii omnes, non sui ese juris esse, sed totos tum corporibus, tum animis, tum in vita, tum in morte in Domini sui esse potestate, cui ut servos fidissimos obedire, et in omnibus obsecondare oportet.

d Deut. x. 17. Matt. ix. 6. et x. 1. et xxi. 9. [et xxviii. 18.] Luc. i. 32. Eph. i. 20.
e Deut. x. 12, 20. Mal. i. 6.

M. Quid deinde sequitur?

A. Quomodo naturam humanam assumpserit, necessariaque ad salutem nostram universa præstiterit, memoratur.

M. Itane Dei Filium hominem fieri oportuit?

A. Omnino; quod enim homo in Deum peccavit, fhominem quoque luere atque expiare necesse erat; quod onus longe gravissimum, gnullus nisi homo Jesus Christus tollere

f Matt. xvii. 22, 23. et xx. 18, 19. Joan. xi. 50. Rom. v. 15, &c. 1 Cor. xv. 21. Phil. ii. 6, 7. Heb. ii. 9.
g Esai. liii.

[1 agnoscamus.]

atque sustinere poterat. Sed neque ʰmediator esse alius poterat ad Deum hominibus conciliandum, pacemque inter eos conficiendam, nisi idem Deus pariter atque homo Christus. Itaque homo factus, nostram quasi personam induit, ut in ea salutis nostræ partes susciperet, sustineret, perageret, atque absolveret.

M. Verum cur e Spiritu Sancto conceptus est, natusque ex Maria Virgine, potius quam consueta, ac naturali ratione procreatus?

A. Qui aliorum scelera expiare, impiosque ac damnatos in integrum restituere debeat ac possit, nulla ipsum ⁱlabe aut macula peccati imbutum vel aspersum, sed singulari ac summa integritate, et innocentia præditum esse oportet. Quum ergo penitus ᵏcorruptum et contaminatum esset humanum semen, in cenceptione Filii Dei, mirificam atque arcanam Spiritus Sancti virtutem, ˡqua in utero castissimæ purissimæque Virginis, atque ex ejus substantia formaretur, intercedere oportuit, ne communi illa humani generis labe ac contagione pollueretur. Christus ergo purissimus ᵐille agnus a Spiritu Sancto, conceptu virginis sine crimine genitus editusque est, ut maculas nostras, qui ut in peccato et dedecore primum concepti natique sumus, ita deinde in turpi vita commoramur, lueret, elueret, atque deleret.

M. At cur nominatim Mariæ Virginis fit mentio, in hac confessione Christiana?

A. Ut agnoscatur esse verum illud ⁿAbrahæ ac Davidis semen, de quo divinitus vaticinationibus Prophetarum prædictum atque præmonstratum fuerat.

M. Ex his quæ jam sunt dicta, intelligo Jesum Christum Dei Filium, naturam humanam ad hominum salutem induisse; perge ergo, quid deinde factum est?

A. Doctrinam illam de salute per Christum restituenda, lætissimam, et modis omnibus divinam, quæ Græco vocabulo εὐαγγέλιον nominatur, a Prophetis ᵒsanctis Dei servis antiquitus proditam, ᵖipse tandem Prophetarum Dominus Jesus Christus, Dei, atque idem Virginis Filius, id est, illud ipsum promissum semen, omnes luculentissime docuit; eandemque ut per universum orbem terrarum docerent, Apostolis ᵠsuis, quos ad illud munus elegerat, mandata dedit.

M. An satis habuit doctrinam hanc simpliciter et clare verbis tradidisse?

A. Imo quo propensioribus eam animis mortales amplecterentur, ʳdepulsis morbis, fugatis ˢdæmonibus, atque aliis infinitis beneficiis, miraculis, et signis, quibus tota ᵗejus, atque Apostolorum suorum vita innocentissime sanctissimeque acta, refertissima erat, eandem confirmavit atque comprobavit.

ʳ Matt. iv. 24. et viii. 2,13,15.
ˢ Marc. ix. 18. Act. x. 38.
ᵗ Act. ii. 22, 43. et iii. 6. et v. 5,12,15,16, 19.

M. At quamobrem Symbolum, omissa ejus vitæ historia, a natalibus statim ad mortem transilit?

A. Quia ea tantum in Symbolo recensentur, quæ sunt in redemptione nostra ᵘpræcipua, quæque illius ita sunt propria, ut ejus quasi substantiam in se complectantur.

ᵘ Esai. liii. toto. Act. xiii. 23, 27, &c.

M. Jam mortis ejus ordinem et modum mihi edissere.

A. A suis nefarie ˣproditus, a Judæis per calumniam malitiamque accusatus, a Pontio Pilato judice damnatus, sævis verberibus crudeliter cæsus, et indignis modis acceptus atque illusus, in crucem sublatus, illi suffixus est; atque ita omni supplicio excruciatus, ignominiosa atque acerbissima morte affectus est.

ˣ Esai. liii. Matt. xxvi. 14, 59, 60, 61. et xxvii. 26, 28, 33, 34, &c. Marc. xv. toto. Luc. xxiii. toto. Joan. xviii. et xix. toto.

M. Hanccine gratiam pro cœlesti illa doctrina, et pro maximis illis atque infinitis meritis ipsi retulerunt?

A. Hæc quidem illi in eum crudeliter, malitiose, atque impie perpetrarunt; verum ipse sua sponte ʸac volens hæc omnia perpessus atque perfunctus est, ut iratum humano generi Patrem sacrificio hoc suavissimo placaret, utque pœnas ᶻnobis debitas dependeret ac persolveret, atque nos ex illis hoc modo eximeret. Neque enim inter homines inusitatum, ut alter pro altero spondeat, ᵃet fidejubeat, aut luat etiam. Cum Christo autem quasi sponsore, pro nobis sic passo, Deus summo quasi jure egit; in nos vero, quorum peccata, merita supplicia, pœnasque debitas in Christum transtulit, lenitate, mansuetudine, clementia, misericordia singulari usus est. Christus ergo mortem, quæ pœna hominum scleri a Deo immortali erat constituta, pertulit, ac perferendo vicit. Sed et morte sua victum et subactum fregit, ac domuit illum, qui mortis tenebat imperium, ᵇid est, diabolum, a cujus nos tyrannide atque servitute in libertatem vindicavit.

ʸ Matt. xx. 28. Marc. x. 45. Joan. x. 11, 15, 17, 18. Rom. iv. 25. Col. i. 20.
ᶻ Esai. liii. toto. 2 Cor. v. 21. Gal. i. 4. Eph. i. 7. Col. ii. 14.
ᵃ Gen. xlii.19, 24, 37. et xliii. 9, 23. et xliv. 16, 32, 33.

ᵇ Act. x. 38. Col. i. 13. Heb. ii.14.

M. Verum quum nos morte, quæ quotidie imminet atque impendet, nihilo minus mulctemur, et peccati nostri pœnas luimus, quem tandem ex hac victoria fructum percipimus?

A. Amplissimum profecto. Nam morte Christi effectum est, ut mors ᶜfidelibus jam non sit interitus, sed quædam quasi migratio commutatioque vitæ, brevisque adeo et certa

ᶜ Luc. xxiii. 43. Joan. xi. 25, 26.

in cœlum transmissio, quo ducem nostrum intrepide sequi debemus; qui sicuti morte non interiit, ita nec perire nos patietur. Quocirca pii ^dmortis metu, quæ laborum, solicitudinum, atque malorum hujus vitæ omnium perfugium illis et dux in cœlum sit, exhorrescere jam amplius, aut trepidare non debent.

^d Joan. xi. 11. 1 Cor. xv. 18. 1 Thess. iv. 13, 14.

M. Ecquod aliud commodum nobis ex Christi morte accedit?

A. Qui unius cum Christo per Fidem sunt corporis, ^ein his pravi affectus et appetitus vitiosi, quos Carnis concupiscentias vocamus, quasi una cum eo in crucem acti, emoriuntur, ne amplius in animis nostris dominentur.

^e Rom. vi. 4, 7, 11, 12, 13, 22. et viii. 1, 2, 3, 10, 11, 13. Col. ii. 13.

M. Romanus Præses sub quo passus est, cur diserte nominatur?

A. Primum, personarum et temporum designatio rebus fidem tribuit; deinde, Christum suo, atque a Deo assignato et constituto tempore, naturam nostram suscepisse, ac mortem oppetiisse res ipsa indicat: ^fquum sceptrum videlicet a Judæ posteris ad Romanos, ^gac alienigenas Reges, qui precarium sub Romanorum imperio Regnum obtinebant, translatum jam esset. Ad hæc, Christum gentibus ^had supplicium tradendum fore, et sententia judicis capite damnandum, divinitus olim fuerat præmonstratum.

^f Gen. xlix. 10. Dan. ix. 25.
^g Luc. ii. 1. et iii. 1.
^h Psal. ii. 2 Luc. xviii. 31, 32. et xxiv. 26.

M. Id quamobrem tandem?

A. Sententia judicis innocens damnatus est, ut sontes nos, quorum causa Divino judicio convicta atque damnata erat, pro cœlesti ⁱtribunali absolveret, et in integrum restitueret. Si enim a latronibus jugulatus, aut commota et concitata seditione, a privatis hominibus ferro trucidatus fuisset, nullam ea mors satisfactionis, compensationisque speciem habuisset.

ⁱ Esai. liii. 3, 8. Rom. v. 1, 6, 8. et viii. 1. 2 Cor. v. 18, 21. 1 Pet. iii. 18.

M. Atqui Pilatus de illius innocentia testimonium dixit.

A. Recte hoc illi testimonium tribuit ^kPilatus, cui de ejus innocentia plane constitit. Nam si ^lnocens extitisset, minime fuisset aptus atque idoneus, qui alieni peccati pœnas sufferret atque persolveret, Deumque placatum peccatoribus efficeret. Eum tamen postea, assiduo Judæorum clamore atque convitio jactatus, et improbissimis vocibus ^mfatigatus atque victus, idem ille Pilatus innocentem de sententia populi condemnavit. Unde liquet non sua ipsum peccata, quæ ⁿnulla in eo erant, nec pœnas ipsi debitas morte luisse, sed debitas

^k Matt. xxvii. 18, 23. Marc. xv. 10. Luc. xxiii. 14. Joan. xviii. 38.
^l Esai. liii. 5. Joan. i. 29, 36. 1 Pet. iii. 18.
^m Matt xxvii. 22. Luc. xxiii. 18, 21, 23, 24.
ⁿ Esai. liii. 4, 5. 1 Pet. ii. 24. et iii. 18.

hominum sceleri, sibi indebitas pœnas sua voluntate in se susceptas subisse, sustinuisse, atque dependisse; et nostrorum flagitiorum maculas morte voluntaria, et suo innocentis sanguine luisse atque eluisse.

M. At qua de causa populus summa et singulari integritate atque innocentia virum tam acerbe et penitus oderat?

A. Sacerdotes, Pharisæi, et Scribæ, invidiæ °incendio flagrantes, quum ᵖveritatis vim atque lucem ferre non possent, in ejus vindicem atque assertorem, imperitæ ᑫmultitudinis odium concitarunt.

° Matt. xxvii. 18. Marc. xv. 10.
ᵖ Matt. xv.12. Luc. xx. 19. Joan. viii. 40, 45 et xi. 47.
ᑫ Matt. xxvii. 20. Marc. xv. 11.

M. Quum judicio damnatus sit, quomodo sua ipsum sponte mortem obiisse dicis?

A. Si Pharisæi, aut Scribæ, aut Judæi alii, aut simul universi, vitæ necisque potestatem in Christum habuissent, jamdudum illi mortem maturassent; sæpe enim ʳantea illi perniciem necemque machinati fuerant. Sed et quum in aliud tempus supplicium ejus differre statuissent, ˢquod festus ille Azymorum dies, quem anniversarium summa religione cæremoniaque celebrare solebant, jam adesset: ne id quidem efficere potuerunt, quin sub ipsum diem festum, alieno ipsis tempore, sed divinitus huic rei constituto, pateretur. Unde satis constat, in ipsorum manu ac potestate nulla harum rerum aut temporum momenta sita fuisse, sed sua ipsum ᵗvoluntate, nulla vi coactum, hanc mortem pro nostra salute oppetiisse.

ʳ Luc. xi. 53. et xx. 19. Joan. viii. 59. et xi. 53, 57.
ˢ Matt. xxvi. 4. Marc. xiv. 1.
ᵗ Esai. liii. 7, 12. Matt. xx. 28. et xxvi. 53. Joan. x. 17.

M. Quare eum potissimum necis diem illi Deus destinavit?

A. Ut ex ipso etiam tempore intelligeretur, Christum esse illum ᵘPaschalem, id est, vere castum purumque agnum; qui morte mactatus, gratissimam se Patri victimam pro nobis præberet.

ᵘ Matt. xxvi. 2. Luc. xxii. 1, 7. Marc. xiv. 1. 1 Cor. v. 7. Heb. vii. 27.

M. Quum eligendæ mortis optio penes ipsum fuerit, cur in crucem agi voluit, potius quam alio quovis supplicio affici?

A. Primum quidem ex Patris sui voluntate, ad quam se ᵛconformavit, quæque tot vaticinationibus, oraculis, signis, atque indiciis divinitus olim prodita fuit atque declarata. Deinde, ultima omnia pati voluit pro nobis, qui ultima omnia eramus commeriti. Erat enim illud mortis genus præ cæteris omnibus ʷexecrandum et detestabile, quo potissimum tamen pro nobis occumbere voluit, ut diram execrationem, qua scelera nos nostra devinxerant, in se susciperet, eaque nos hoc pacto exolveret. ˣContumelias enim omnes, omnia probra atque supplicia, pro salute nostra levia omnino sibi esse, atque

ᵛ Esai.liii.12. Matt. xxvi. 39, 42. Marc. xv. 28. Luc. xxii. 37. Joan. iii. 14.
ʷ Deut. xxi. 23. Gal. iii. 13.
ˣ Esai. liii. toto. Psal. xxii. 6, 7, 12, 13, &c. Matt. xxvi. 67. et xxvii. 21, 26, 28, 34, 38, 44, 48. Phil. ii. 7, 8.

pro nihilo duxit; adeoque contemptus, abjectus, et omnium hominum infimus esse sustinuit, quo nos plane perditos ad amissæ salutis spem erigeret.

M. Ecquid amplius de Christi morte dicendum habes?

A. ʸChristum non communi modo morte in hominum conspectu mulctatum, sed et æternæ mortis horrore perfusum fuisse; cum universis Inferorum copiis quasi manum conseruisse, atque luctatum esse; pro summo Dei tribunali judicium triste, Divinæque animadversionis gravem severitatem subiisse; in summas angustias adductum fuisse; horribiles formidines, atque acerbissimos animi dolores, quo justo Dei judicio per omnia satisfaceret, iramque ejus plene placaret, pro nobis perpessum atque perfunctum esse. Peccatoribus enim, ᶻquorum hic quasi personam Christus sustinuit, non præsentis modo, sed et futuræ etiam æternæque mortis dolores atque cruciatus debentur. Quum vero humani generis perditi jam atque damnati culpam pariter, justamque poenam ita in se susciperet atque sustineret, tam gravi metu, tantoque animi motu ac dolore perturbatus est, ᵃut exclamaret, Deus meus, Deus meus, quare dereliquisti me?

M. An non ignominia interim hoc pacto Dei Filius afficitur, aut desperationis illi nota quædam inuritur?

A. Ille quidem hæc omnia absque omni omnino ᵇpeccato perpessus est; tantum abest, ut ulla animum ejus desperatio occuparet. Nunquam enim interea Patri ᶜconfidere, et bene de salute sperare desiit, nec circumfuso undique pavore obtorpuit unquam, aut dolore oppressus fuit; et cum universa ᵈinferorum potestate luctatus, adversam vim omnem, et furentes ac violentos impetus fregit, atque superavit; universaque hæc in se suscepta, funditus delevit; ipseque in primis beatus nihilominus permansit, beatitudinemque suam nobis, qui ipsi fidimus, impertivit. ᵉNisi enim hac ejus vere beata morte salutem vitamque essemus consequuti, sempiterna omnes morte perpetuo perieramus.

M. Verum in Christum, qui Deus sit, quomodo potuit tantus animi dolor atque trepidatio cadere?

A. Secundum humanæ ᶠnaturæ affectionem, Divinitate interim potestatis suæ vim non intendente, hoc effectum est.

M. Jam ergo mihi breviter summatimque amplissima illa commoda, quæ ex Christi morte cruciatuque longe maximo percipiunt fideles, recense.

A. In summa, ^gunico mortis suæ sacrificio, peccata nostra coram Deo expiavit, et placata Dei ira nos in gratiam cum eo reduxit; sanguine suo ut purissimo ^hlavacro, animarum nostrarum sordes atque maculas omnes eluit, atque delevit; et peccatorum nostrorum ⁱmemoriam, ne amplius unquam in Dei inspectum veniant, sempiterna oblivione obruens, ^kChirographum illud, quo tenebamur et convincebamur, decretumque, cujus sententia damnabamur, induxit, et inane factum abolevit. Hæc ille omnia vivis pariter atque mortuis, illi dum vixerunt ^lconfisis, morte sua præstitit. Postremo mortis suæ vi, cupiditates alioqui effrænatas atque indomitas, in iis, qui illi per fidem omnino adhærescunt, ita ^mfrænat ac frangit, et illarum ardorem ita restinguit, ut spiritui facilius obtemperent atque obsequantur.

^g Heb. vii. 27. et ix. 12. et x. 12, 14.
^h Heb. ix. 14. 1 Joan. i. 7. Apoc. i. 5.
ⁱ Psal. xxxii. 1, 2. Rom. iv. 7, 8. Heb. x. 17.
^k Col. ii. 14.
^l Joan. iii. 16. et xi. 25, 26.
^m Rom. vi. 4, 8, 11, &c. et viii. 1, 2, 3, 10, 11, &c. Col. ii. 13.

M. Cur sepultum fuisse etiam addis?

A. Exangue, atque ⁿexanimum corpus sepulchro conditum est, ut mors ejus testatior esset, utque de ea inter omnes constaret. Si enim statim revixisset, mortem ejus plerique in disceptationem et controversiam vocassent, atque ita in dubium ea ventura videretur.

ⁿ Esai. liii. 9. Matt. xii. 40. et xxvii. 59, 60. 1 Cor. xv. 4, 5.

M. Quid sibi vult quod sequitur de ejus ad Inferos descensu?

A. Christum ut corpore in terræ viscera, ita anima a corpore separata, ad inferos descendisse; simulque etiam mortis suæ virtutem atque efficacitatem ad mortuos, ^oatque inferos adeo ipsos ita penetrasse, ut et incredulorum animæ acerbissimam justissimamque ^pinfidelitatis suæ damnationem, ipseque inferorum princeps ^qSatanas, tyrannidis suæ, et tenebrarum potestatem omnem debilitatam, fractam, atque ruina collapsam esse persentiret; contra vero ^rmortui, Christo dum vixerunt fidentes, redemptionis suæ opus jam peractum esse, ejusque vim atque virtutem, cum suavissima certissimaque consolatione, intelligerent atque perciperent.

^o 1 Pet. iii. 19.
^p Joan. viii. 24.
^q 1 Cor. xv. 55. Col. i. 13, 14. Heb. ii. 14, 15.
^r Joan. v. 25. et xi. 25, 26. Rom. xiv. 9. Col. i. 19, 20.

M. Jam ad sequentia pergamus.

A. Tertio die post ^srevixit, et quadraginta dierum spatio, suis se vivum frequenter exhibuit, et inter discipulos versatus est, edens ac bibens cum illis.

^s Matt. xxviii. 6, 9. Marc. xvi. 6, 9. Luc. xxiv. 6, 7, 14, 15. Joan. xx. 14, 19, 20, 26. et xxi. 1, 4. Act. i. 3, 4. et ii. 24, 32.

M. Quid, an non satis erat, quod per mortem ejus peccatorum liberationem veniamque impetramus?

A. Id non satis erat, si vel ejus, vel nostri rationem habeas. Nisi enim revixisset, minime putaretur ^tFilius Dei;

^t Rom. i. 4.

quin et illud ipsi, dum in cruce penderet, ii qui viderant, exprobrabant atque objiciebant: "Alios, inquiunt, servavit, seipsum non potest servare; descendat nunc de cruce, et credemus ei. Jam autem excitatus a mortuis, ad vitæ perennitatem, ˣDivinitatis suæ potentiam declaravit majorem, quam si descendendo de cruce, mortis terrores refugisset. ʸMori quidem omnibus est commune; tametsi vero intentatæ morti quidam se ad tempus subduxerunt, mortis tamen semel oppetitæ vincula solvere, aut abrumpere, et virtute propria reviviscere, id unici Filii Dei Jesu Christi, authoris vitæ, proprium est; quo se ᶻpeccati, et mortis, ipsiusque adeo Diaboli victorem demonstravit.

M. Quam aliam ob causam excitatus est?

A. Ut ᵃDavidis, et aliorum sacrorum vatum implerentur oracula, qui prædixerunt fore, ut nec corpus ejus tentaretur corruptione, nec anima apud inferos relinqueretur.

M. At quas nobis utilitates præbet, quod revixit Christus?

A. Multiplices, et varias. Inde enim nobis ᵇjustitia, qua ante carebamus; inde innocentiæ ᶜstudium, quam Vitæ novitatem vocamus; inde vires, et ad pie sancteque vivendum virtus nobis, ac robur accedunt; inde nobis spes, et mortalia corpora nostra a morte in ᵈintegrum aliquando tandem restituenda. Si enim Christus ipse ᵉmorte absumptus fuisset, liberator noster minime extitisset; quæ enim nobis spes esset reliqua salutis per illum, qui seipsum non servarit? Fuit igitur et consentaneum illi personæ quam sustinebat Dominus, et necessarium nobis ad salutem adjumentum, ut primum Christus ᶠseipsum morte liberaret, post autem, ut nobis mortis claustra rumperet, atque revelleret; atque ita salutis nos nostræ spem in resurrectione ipsius collocaremus. Neque enim fieri potest, ut Christus ᵍcaput nostrum reviviscens, nos corporis sui membra, morte et interitu deleri omnino sinat.

M. Attigisti, mi Fili, principes causas resurrectionis Christi; nunc de ejus in cœlum ascensu quid censeas, libet audire.

A. In Apostolorum suorum conspectu, circumfusa velatus nube, in cœlum ʰascendit, aut potius supra omnes cœlos, ubi ad Dei Patris dexteram assidet.

M. Hoc quomodo sit intelligendum dicito.

A. Simplicissime quidem Christum [i]corpore in cœlum ascendisse, ubi prius corpore non fuerat; terramque, ubi prius corpore fuerat, reliquisse. Nam Divina natura, quæ omnia implet, et in cœlis semper extitit, et eadem, ac spiritu suo [k]Ecclesiæ suæ semper in terris præsens adest, aderitque usque ad mundi dissolutionem.

[i] Joan. xiv. 19. et xvi. 10, 16, 28.

[k] Matt. xviii. 20. et xxviii. 20.

M. Aliam ergo Divinitatis ejus rationem, humanitatis aliam esse dicis?

A. Dico, Præceptor; neque enim aut de ejus Divinitate corpus, aut de illius corpore Deum facimus. Hæc enim [l]creata est, illa minime; hanc in cœlum assumptam, in cœlo [m]manere; illam autem sic [n]ubique esse, ut cœlum et terram impleat, testantur sacræ Scripturæ.

[l] Esai. vii. 14. Matt. i. 2, 23. Luc. ii. 7, 40, 52. Joan. i. 3, 14. Gal. iv. 4.

[m] Marc. xvi. 19. Luc. xxiv. 51. Act. i. 9, 10. et iii. 21. Eph. iv. 10.

[n] Joan. i. 3. et xvi. 15.

M. Verum, an aliquo modo corpore præsentem nobis adesse Christum dicis?

A. Si magna parvis componere licet, sic Christi corpus præsens adest nostræ fidei, ut sol cum cernitur adest oculo; nulla enim res, quæ sub sensus cadit, ad similitudinem Christo propius accedit, quam sol; qui cum cœlum semper occupet, et proinde oculum revera non contingat, tamen corpus solis præsens aspectui adest, nihil id impediente tanta intervalli distantia. Sic Christi corpus, quod ejus ascensu nobis sublatum est, [o]quodque reliquit mundum, et ad Patrem abiit, sensibus quidem nostris abest; Fides tamen nostra [p]versatur in cœlo, atque intuetur solem illum justitiæ, ac præsens præsenti in cœlo vere adest, ut visus noster adest corpori solis in cœlo, aut sol in terris nostro visui. Præterea vero, quemadmodum Sol lumine suo rebus omnibus adest, sic etiam et Christus Divinitate, Spiritu, atque potentia sua [q]præsens adest omnibus, atque omnia complet.

[1] Cor. xv. 28. Eph. i. 23. Col. i. 16, 17.

[o] Joan. xiv. 19. et xvi. 10, 28.

[p] Act. vii. 55. Col. iii. 1. Heb. iv. 16. et x. 22. et xi. 1, 3.

[q] Matt. xxviii. 20. 1 Cor. xv. 28. Eph. i. 23. Col. i. 17, 18.

M. Jam quod ad Christum attinet, quid potissimum spectas in ejus ascensu, sessioneque ad dexteram Patris?

A. Par erat ut Christus, qui a [r]summo honoris atque dignitatis gradu, ad infimam servi conditionem, ad ignominiam damnationis atque probrosæ mortis descenderat, amplissimam rursum gloriam atque splendorem obtineret; eundem nimirum, quem ante habuerat, ut scilicet humilitati et ignominiæ gloria ejus atque majestas proportione quadam responderet. Quod et D. Paulus ad [s]Philippenses scribens clarissime docet: Factus est, inquit, obediens usque ad mortem, mortem autem crucis; propter quod et Deus illum Ecclesiæ caput constitutum, supra

[r] Phil. ii. 6, 7, 8.

[s] Phil. ii. 8, 9, 10. Eph. i. 20, 21, 22, 23. Col. i. 18. Heb. ii. 9.

omnes principatus evectum, cœli et terræ imperio, ut omnia gubernet, donatum, ad summam extulit sublimitatem, et dedit illi nomen, quod est supra omne nomen, ut in nomine JESU omne genu se flectat, cœlestium, terrestrium, et infernorum.

M. An quum Dei dexteram, et sessionem nominas, esse Deum humana specie, aut figura, animo et cogitatione fingis?

A. Nequaquam, Præceptor; sed quia nobis sermo est de Deo apud homines, humano more, quomodo delatum sibi a Patre regnum Christus acceperit, utcunque exprimimus. Solent enim Reges, quos ^tpræcipuo honore dignantur, suæque dominationis vicarios constituunt, sibi ad dexteram collocare. Istis ergo verbis significatur, Deum Patrem Filium suum Christum ^ucaput Ecclesiæ constituisse; per quem suos tueri, et rerum universitatem gubernare velit.

^t 1 Reg. ii. 19. Psal. cx. 1. Matt. xx. 21.

^u Eph. i. 22. et iv. 15, 16. et v. 23. Col. i. 18.

M. Recte; jam nos ex ejus ascensu in cœlum, sessioneque ad dexteram Patris, quid capimus commodi?

A. Primum, Christus ut in terram, quasi exilium, nostra causa descenderat, ita et cœlum, paternam hæreditatem adiens, nostro nomine ingressus est; ^xviam atque aditum illuc nobis patefaciens, januamque cœli, nobis antea propter peccatum clausam, aperiens. Nam cum Christus caput nostrum, humanam nostram carnem secum in cœlum vexerit, nos corporis sui membra, tam ^ypotens atque benevolum caput in terra perpetuo non relinquet. Præterea in conspectu ^zDei astans, et nos illi commendans, atque pro nobis intercedens, causæ nostræ patronus existit; quo advocato, causa non cademus.

^x Joan. xiv. 2. 2 Cor. v. 1. Eph. ii. 18. Heb. x. 19, 20, 22.

^y Eph. i. 22, 23. et iv. 15, 16. et v. 23. Col. i. 18.

^z Joan. xvi. 26. Rom. viii. 34. Heb. vii. 25. et ix. 24. 1 Joan. ii. 1.

M. At cur non potius in terris hic nobiscum mansit?

A. Rebus, quæ illi a ^aPatre fuerant mandatæ, quæque ad salutem nostram pertinerent, omnibus perfunctus cum esset, nihil illi opus fuit diutius in terris versari. Sed et quæ faceret, si corpore præsens adesset, ea omnia absens facit, tuetur, juvat, corroborat, corrigit, coercet, castigat. Præterea Sacrum Spiritum ^bsuum, uti promisit, cœlo in corda nostra demittit, ut certissimum benevolentiæ suæ pignus, per quem e tenebris nos atque caligine in lucem vocat, mentium cæcitatem illuminat, mœstitiam ex animis nostris pellit, et illorum vulneribus medetur; efficitque Divino ^cSpiritus sui instinctu, ut cœlum intuentes, mentes animosque nostros humo excitatos, ab affectionibus pravis, et terrenis rebus sursum, ubi Christus

^a Joan xiv. 31. et xvii. 4. et xix. 30.

^b Joan. xiv. 16, 26. et xvi. 7, 13. Rom. v. 5. et viii. 9, 16. 1 Cor. xii. 4, &c. 2 Cor. i. 22. Eph. i. 17.

^c Rom. viii. 4, &c. Col. iii. 1, 2. Eph. iv. 22, 30.

est ad dexteram Patris, erigamus; cogitantes, spectantesque supera atque cœlestia, celsi et erecti hæc nostra exigua contemnamus, vitam, mortem, divitias, paupertates, humanaque omnia excelso magnoque animo despicientes. Summa denique illa sit, Christum ad dexteram Dei assidentem, ^dpotentia, prudentia, providentia sua mundum universum regere atque administrare, movere, gubernare, et moderari omnia; eadem usque facturum, quoad mundi fabrica dissolvetur.

^d Matt.xxviii. 18. Luc. i. 33. Joan. xvii. 2. Eph. i. 20,21. Phil. ii. 9, 10.

M. Quum ergo corpore sublatus in cœlum, suos hic in terris Christus non destituat, crasse judicant qui præsentiam absentiamque illius solo corpore metiuntur.

A. Sane. Nam res quæ incorporeæ sunt, sub sensum cadere non possunt. Quis unquam suam ipsius animam viderit? Nullus. At quid nobis adest præsentius, quid propinquius, conjunctiusve, quam anima cuique sua? Quæ spiritualia sunt, non videntur nisi ^eoculo Spiritus. Christum igitur qui in terris videre vult, aperiat oculos non corporis, sed animi et Fidei, et videbit præsentem, quem oculus non videt.

^e Joan. viii. 47. et xiv. 21. Gal. iii. 1. Eph. i. 18.

M. At quibus peculiariter et efficacissime adesse eum præsentem agnoscit Fides?

A. Conspiciet eum Fidei acies præsentem, atque adeo in medio, ubicunque sunt duo vel tres congregati ^fin nomine ejus; videbit præsentem suis, id est, vere piis omnibus usque ad sæculorum omnium exitum. Quid dixi? Christum videbit præsentem? Imo et videbit, et sentiet in seipso habitantem quisque pius, haud aliter atque animum suum proprium. Habitat ^genim ac residet in animo ejus, qui suam fiduciam omnem atque spem in eo collocat.

^f Matt. xviii. 19, 20. et xxviii. 20. Joan. xiv. 18, 21.

^g Joan. xiv. 23. Eph. iii. 16, 17. Col. iii. 11.

M. Ecquid præterea habes adhuc dicendum?

A. Christus ascendendo assidendoque ad dexteram Patris, falsam ^hillam opinionem, quam aliquando Apostoli ⁱetiam ipsi acceperant, amovit atque ex hominum animis penitus evellit, quod scilicet Christus in terris nobis conspicuus regnaturus esset, haud aliter ac reliqui reges terræ, et principes mundani. Hunc ^kerrorem mentibus nostris eripere, ac de regno suo magis sublimia cogitare nos voluit Dominus; abesse ergo ab oculis, atque omni sensu corporeo voluit, ut ea ratione, Fides ^lnostra et excitata et exercitata sit, ad intuendum moderationem et providentiam ejus, qui corporeo aspectu non sentitur.

^h Luc. xvii. 20, 21. Joan. vi. 15.
ⁱ Matt.xx.21. Luc.xxiv. 21. Act. i. 6.
^k Joan. xviii. 36.
^l Eph. i. 18. Col. iii. 1,2.

M. Ecqua alia ratio est, quare e terris in cœlum se subduxerit?

A. Cum non unius alicujus regionis terræ, sed omnium [m]terrarum orbis pariter atque [n]cœli princeps sit, vivorum pariter atque mortuorum Dominus; par erat, ut clam sensibus nostris regnum suum administraret. Nam si sub aspectum veniret, locum atque sedem mutare, huc [o]et illuc identidem trahi, et nunc in hanc regionem, nunc in aliam migrare eum opus esset, ut suscepta negotia transigeret. Si enim eodem momento temporis ubique omnibus præsens adesset, jam non homo, sed spectrum potius esse, neque corpus habuisse verum, sed imaginarium videretur; aut certe quod Eutyches censuit, corpus ejus abiisse in Divinitatem, aut ubique esse putaretur. Unde mille continuo nascerentur opiniones falsæ, quas omnes, corpore integro in cœlum sublato, depulit, animosque hominum maximis erroribus liberavit. Mundum interim, tametsi nobis non conspicuus, summa [p]virtute, et sapientia admirabiliter regit atque administrat. Hominum est, humana quadam ratione respublicas suas gubernare et moderari; Christi autem, id est, Filii Dei, divina.

M. Attigisti præcipua quædam ex infinitis et immensis beneficiis, quorum fructum ex Christi morte, resurrectione, et ascensione, percipimus; nam universa ne mente quidem atque animo humano concipi, nedum verbis atque dicendo explicari ullo modo queunt. Hactenus tamen scientiam in hac re tuam experiar, ut mihi prima rerum capita, ad quæ reliqua omnia referuntur, breviter et summatim describas.

A. Dico igitur, cum ex his, tum etiam ex aliis Christi actionibus duplicem nos utilitatem capere. Unam, quod quæcunque fecit, ea omnia nostro commodo fecerit; adeo quidem, ut perinde [q]nostra sint, modo eisdem firma vivaque Fide inhæserimus, ac si nos ea fecissemus ipsi. Ipse quidem cruci suffixus est, et nos cum ipso in crucem sublati sumus, et nostra in eo peccata sunt punita. Ipse mortuus est et sepultus, nos itidem una cum peccatis nostris mortui sumus et sepulti; idque ita, ut omnis peccatorum nostrorum memoria, sempiterna oblivione penitus deleatur. Ipse a morte excitatus est, et nos cum eo reviximus, resurrectionis et vitæ ejus sic facti participes, ut nobis deinceps mors non dominetur; est enim idem in nobis [r]Spiritus, qui Jesum a mortuis excitavit. Postremo, præterquam quod ab ascensu ejus

Spiritus Sancti ᵃdona cumulatissime nobis accesserunt, nos secum etiam in coelum sublevatos, sublatosque tulit, ut ejus quasi possessionem, una cum capite nostro occuparemus. Ista quidem nondum apparent, ᵗtamen tum demum hæc omnia proferentur in lucem, cum Christus, qui est lux mundi, in quo spes nostræ omnes atque opes positæ sunt atque defixæ, immortali gloria clarus, sese palam omnibus ostendet.

ᵃ Eph. iv. 8.

ᵗ Joan. viii. 12. Rom. viii. 24. 1 Cor. i. 30. Col. i. 5. et ii. 3. et iii. 4, 11. 1 Pet. i. 4.

M. Alterum illud commodum, quod ex Christi actionibus consequimur, cujusmodi tandem est?

A. Quod Christus se nobis ᵘexemplar ad imitandum proposuit, ad quod vitam nostram omnem formemus. Christus si mortuus sit pro peccato, si sepultus, id semel perpessus est; si revixerit, si in coelum ascenderit, semel tantum revixit, semel ascendit; jam non amplius moritur, sed vita sempiterna fruitur, et in summa atque perenni gloria regnat. Sic ˣsi nos simus mortui, si sepulti peccato, quomodo posthac vivemus in eodem? Si excitati cum Christo simus, si per certam fidem atque spem firmam in coelo cum eo versemur, in coelestes res, divinas, æternas, non terrenas, mundanas, et caducas, curas omnes cogitationesque in posterum conferre debemus. Et quemadmodum ʸterrestris hominis hactenus gestavimus imaginem, coelestis deinceps imaginem induamus; dolores et injurias omnes ejus exemplo placide et sedate ferentes, cæterasque illius virtutes Divinas, quoad mortales possunt, imitantes atque exprimentes. Et cum Christus Dominus nunquam desistat nobis benefacere, Patris misericordiam perpetuo nobis exposcere, et implorare, Spiritum suum sanctum nobis largiri, Ecclesiam suam amplissimis donis mirabiliter et assidue exornare; par est nos simili ᶻratione proximum omni studio juvare, et arctissimis amoris, concordiæ, atque summæ conjunctionis vinculis, quantum in nobis erit, cum omnibus hominibus astringi; atque ita nos totos in Christi, velut unici ᵃexempli, mores formari.

ᵘ Joan. xiii. 15. 1 Pet. ii. 21. 1 Joan. ii. 6.

ˣ Rom. vi. 2, 3, 10. Gal. ii. 19. Col. ii. 20. et iii. 1. 2 Tim. ii. 11.

ʸ Rom. viii. 20. 1 Cor. xv. 47, 48, 49.

ᶻ Joan. xiii. 13, 14. et xv. 12. Eph. v. 2. Heb. xii. 14.

ᵃ Gal. ii. 20. 1 Pet. ii. 21. 1 Joan. ii. 6.

M. An non et nostri etiam erga Christum ipsum officii ex his admonemur?

A. Admonemur sane, ut voluntati ᵇChristi, cujus toti sumus, quemque Dominum esse nostrum profitemur, obediamus et pareamus; ut Christum servatorem, qui eam nobis, suis adhuc hostibus, charitatem præstitit, ut ad ejus summum erga nos amorem nihil posset accedere, ita ex animo, ita toto vicissim pectore amemus, diligamus, amplectamur, ut Christum

ᵇ Rom. v. 8, 10. 2 Cor. v. 15. 1 Thess. v. 10.

nobismet ipsis chariorem habeamus; Christo, qui ita se totum nobis dedit, ^cnos ipsos totos, omniaque nostra invicem tradamus; opes, honores, gloriam, patriam, parentes, liberos, conjuges, chara, grata, jucundaque omnia præ Christo vilia, pericula omnia pro Christo levia habeamus, atque despiciamus; vitam denique animamque ipsam amittamus potius, quam Christum, nostrumque in illum amorem atque officium deseramus. Fortunata enim mors, quæ naturæ debita, pro Christo est potissimum reddita; pro Christo, inquam, qui sese pro nobis voluntariæ morti obtulit atque objecit; quique vitæ author, mortuos nos eripere morti, ^dac vitæ restituere, et vult, et potest.

M. Perge.

A. Admonemur præterea, ut Christum Dominum in cœlo jam regnantem, non terrestri ^ealiquo cultu, impiis traditionibus, et frigidis hominum inventis, sed cultu cœlesti et ^frevera spirituali, qualis et nos qui demus, et illum qui accipiat, deceat maxime, pure et caste veneremur; haud aliter atque ille et honoravit, et honorat Patrem; cum eadem opera et Patrem pari honore prosequamur. Qui enim honore ^gChristum afficit, honorat et Patrem; cujus rei ipse certissimus est, et locupletissimus testis.

M. Jam de ultimo judicio, et mundi fine quid sentias, paucis audire cupio.

A. Veniet Christus in ^hnubibus cœli, cum summa gloria, et augustissima atque maxime verenda majestate, sanctorum Angelorum comitatu et frequentia stipatus atque circumfusus; et horribili tubæ sonitu, ac classico tremendo, mortui omnes, qui ab orbe condito ad eum usque diem vixerunt, animis atque corporibus integris excitabuntur; et pro ⁱtribunali illius judicio sistentur; vitæ suæ rationem, quæ ab incorrupto atque severo judice ad veritatem revocabitur, pro se quisque, reddituri.

M. Verum, cum in fine mundi judicii dies futurus sit, morsque omnibus sit definita atque constituta, quomodo in Symbolo quosdam tum vivos futuros dicis?

A. Divus Paulus docet eos, qui tunc erunt 'superstites, subito immutandos atque innovandos esse, ita ut deleta corporum ^mcorruptione, ac mortalitate abolita, immortalitatem induantur; atque hæc illis mutatio instar mortis erit, quum et corruptæ naturæ interitus, incorruptæ initium futurus sit.

M. An judicii hujus cogitatione pios percelli, atque horrore perfundi, illudque reformidare et refugere oporteat?

A. Minime; is enim sententiam feret, qui pro nobis sententia Judicis damnatus est, ne nos grave Dei judicium subeuntes condemnemur, sed judicio absolvamur; is, inquam, judicium pronunciabit, in cujus nos fide atque clientela sumus, quique causæ nostræ patrocinium suscepit. Imo singulari quadam ⁿconsolatione conscientiæ nostræ sustentantur, et inter medias hujus vitæ miserias et ærumnas, gaudiis exultant, quod Christus semel futurus sit mundi judex; hac enim maxime spe nitimur, quod tum demum regnum illud immortalitatis et æternæ vitæ, hactenus tantum ^oinchoatum, quod Dei filiis ante jacta mundi fundamenta constitutum atque definitum fuit, omni ex parte plene et cumulate perfectum, immutabili æternitate possidebimus. ^pImpii vero, qui vel Dei justitiam atque iram non formidarunt, vel ejus per Christum clementia, misericordiaque non sunt confisi, quique pios, terra marique persequentes, omnibus injuriis affecerunt, summisque suppliciis et mortibus crudelissimis mactarunt, cum Satana atque Cacodæmonibus universis in destinatum ipsis inferorum carcerem, impietatis et scelerum vindicem, et tenebras perpetuas conjicientur; ubi scelerum suorum conscientia, et sempiterno igne, atque omni summoque supplicio excruciati, æternas pœnas dabunt, atque dependent. Nam quod a mortalibus in Dei immortalis immensam, infinitamque Majestatem peccatum est, infinito etiam perpetuoque supplicio dignum est.

n Rom. viii. 9, 23, 38, 39. 1 Cor. i. 7. Phil. iii. 20. Tit. ii. 13. 2 Pet. iii. 12.

o Matt. xxv. 34. 1 Cor. xiii. 9, 10. et xv. 42, 43, 53, 54.

p Matt. viii. 12. et xxii. 13. et xxv. 30, 41. Heb. x. 26, 27. Jud. 6, 7, 8. Apoc. xiv. 10, 11. et xix. 20. et xx. 10, 14. et xxi. 8.

M. Ultimo judicio mundi finis conjunctus est, de quo apertius adhuc explicare te velim.

A. Mundi finem hujusmodi futurum esse ^qApostolus commemorat. Cœlum procellæ in morem transibit, elementa æstuantia solventur, terra et quæ in ea sunt universa, flamma conflagrabunt; quasi diceret fore aliquando, ut hic mundus ardore deflagrans, omni suo vitio per ignem (uti in auro fieri videmus) excocto, totus repurgetur, atque in absolutam summamque perfectionem renovetur, faciemque induat longe pulcherrimam, quæ sempiternis seculorum ætatibus non immutabitur. Hoc enim est quod Divus ^rPetrus ait: Cœlum novum, et terram novam, in quibus justitia inhabitabit, secundum promissionem Dei expectamus. Neque vero a fide abhorret, ut peccatum, ita et corruptionem ^srerum, atque mutabilitatem, cæteraque ex peccato enata mala, aliquando tandem finem esse habitura. Atque hæc est summa secundæ

q Matt. xxiv. 29, 30, 32. 2 Pet. iii. 10, 11, &c.

r 2 Pet. iii. 13.

s Rom. viii. 19, 22, &c. 2 Pet. iii. 13. Apoc. xxi. 1.

4—2

partis Fidei Christianæ, qua tota redemptionis nostræ per Jesum Christum historia continetur.

M. Quum ergo de Deo Patre conditore, deque ejus Filio Jesu Christo servatore jam dixeris, id est, duas confessionis Christianæ partes absolveris; jam de tertia libet audire, quid de Spiritu Sancto credas.

A. Illum tertiam ^tpersonam sanctissimæ Trinitatis esse confiteor, a Patre et Filio ab æterno procedentem, utrique æqualem, atque ejusdem prorsus naturæ, unaque cum utroque adorandum atque invocandum.

M. Cur Sanctus appellatur?

A. Non tantum ob suam ipsius sanctitatem, quæ utique summa est, sed quod per eum electi Dei, et membra Christi sancta ^uefficiantur. Qua de causa Divinæ literæ illum Spiritum sanctificationis vocarunt.

M. Quibus in rebus hanc sanctificationem constituis?

A. Primum quidem ejus instinctu afflatuque Divino ^xregeneramur; et idcirco dixit Christus oportere nos ex aqua et spiritu renasci. Cœlesti itidem ejus afflatu, Deus Pater nos sibi Filios ^yadoptat; unde non immerito Spiritus adoptionis est dictus. Illo interprete, ^zDivina nobis mysteria aperiuntur; ejus lumine, animorum nostrorum oculi, ad ea intelligenda illustrantur; ejus judicio, ^avel condonantur, vel reservantur peccata; ejus vi, reprimitur et ^bdomatur vitiosa caro, et cupiditates pravæ coercentur atque restringuntur; ejus arbitrio, multiplicia ^cdona in pios distribuuntur. Is in hujus vitæ multis variisque incommodis, molestiis, atque miseriis, ægritudinem luctumque piorum, qui fere sunt in hoc mundo gravissime afflicti, et quorum dolores omnem humanam consolationem vincunt, arcano solatio suo, et bona spe sedat, lenit, et consolatur; unde et ^dParacleti, id est, consolatoris verum propriumque nomen sibi ascivit. Ejus denique virtute, corpora nostra mortalia ^ereviviscent; breviter, quæcunque nobis deferuntur in Christo beneficia, ea omnia Spiritus Sancti ^fopera intelligimus, sentimus, accipimus. In tantorum ergo donorum authore, non immerito fiduciam atque spem collocamus, eumque colimus, atque invocamus.

M. Superest jam quarta pars de Sancta Ecclesia Catholica, de qua quid sentias audire velim?

A. In pauca conferam, quæ Scripturæ sacræ fuse explicant et copiose. Antequam cœlum et terras fabricatus est

Dominus Deus, regnum quoddam sibi pulcherrimum, et rempub. sanctissimam habere decrevit; eam Apostoli, qui Græce scripserunt, [g]ἐκκλησίαν appellarunt, quæ, ut verbum verbo exprimam, congregatio dici non inepte potest. In hanc quasi civitatem suam adscripsit Deus infinitam [h]hominum multitudinem, qui omnes unico suo Regi Christo pareant, et dicto audientes sint atque obedientes, qui ipsius sese tutelæ commendarunt, et quorum ipse patrocinium suscepit, eosque perpetuo tuetur et conservat. Ad hanc Rempub. proprie pertinent, quotquot [i]vere timent, honorant, et invocant Deum, prorsus applicantes animos ad sancte pieque vivendum; quique fiduciam atque spem omnem in Deo constituentes, vitæ æternæ beatitudinem certissime expectant. Qui autem sunt in hac Fide firmi, stabiles, atque constantes, hi [k]electi atque designati, et (ut nos loquimur) prædestinati erant ad hanc tantam fœlicitatem, ante posita mundi fundamenta; cujus rei testem [l]ipsi intus in animis habent spiritum Christi, fiduciæ hujus authorem pariter et pignus certissimum. Cujus Divini Spiritus instinctu, mihi etiam certissime persuadeo, meipsum quoque beata hac civitate, Dei per Christum beneficio, gratuito donatum esse.

[g] Matt. xvi. 18.
[h] Matt. xxviii. 19. Act. ii. 5, 9. 1 Cor. xii. 13. Eph. v. 23, 24.
[i] Act. x. 34, 35. Rom. ii. 11. Gal. vi. 15, 16. Col. iii. 11, 12, &c.
[k] Matt. xvi. 18. Rom. viii. 29, 30. Eph. i. 4, 5. Col. iii. 12. Tit. i. 1.
[l] Rom. viii. 9, 15, 16. 2 Cor. i. 22. et v. 5. Eph. i. 13, 14. et v. 30.

M. Pia sane et plane necessaria persuasio. Ecclesiæ ergo quam dicis, definitionem mihi cedo.

A. Brevissime verissimeque dixerim, ECCLESIAM ESSE CORPUS [m]CHRISTI.

M. At paulo adhuc explicatius velim.

A. Ecclesia est [n]corpus Reipub. Christianæ, id est, universitas societasque fidelium omnium, quos Deus per Christum ad [o]vitam perpetuam ab æterno tempore destinavit.

M. Quorsum hoc caput in Symbolum inseritur?

A. Quia nisi Ecclesia esset, sine causa tum Christus fuisset mortuus, tum ea, quæ usque adhuc relata sunt, omnia frustra essent, atque ad nihilum reciderent.

M. Quid ita?

A. Quia hactenus salutis causas tractavimus, ejusque fundamenta contemplati sumus, quomodo videlicet, Christi merito nos amet Deus, charosque habeat; quomodo item, hanc Dei gratiam, in quam sumus restituti, Spiritus sancti opera retineamus. At horum hic unus effectus est, ut sit [p]Ecclesia, id est, cœtus piorum apud quos hæc Dei beneficia collocentur; ut sit Civitas et Respub. quædam beata, in qua nostra omnia

[m] 1 Cor. xii. 27. Eph. i. 23. et v. 23. Col. i. 18, 24.
[n] Rom. xii. 5. 1 Cor. xii. 12, &c. 20, 26. 2 Cor. i. 22. Eph. iii. 9.
[o] Matt. xxv. 34. Eph. i. 4, 5. 2 Thess. iii. 18.
[p] Matt. xvi. 18. Act. xx. 28. 1 Cor. xii. 12, &c. et xiv. 12. 2 Cor. xi. 28. Eph. iii. 10, 11, 21. et v. 25. 1 Tim. iii. 15.

ponere et quasi consecrare, et cui nos totos dedere debeamus, et pro qua mori non dubitemus.

M. Ecclesiam hanc cur Sanctam appellas?

A. Ut hac notione ab impiorum ^qnefario cœtu discernatur. Quoscunque enim Deus elegit, in vitæ eos sanctitatem atque innocentiam restituit.

<small>q Rom. viii. 29. 1 Cor. xiv. 33. Eph. i. 4, 5, 11.</small>

M. Estne hæc, quam Ecclesiæ tribuis, sanctimonia integra jam, atque omni ex parte perfecta?

A. Nondum. Quoad enim mortalem in hoc mundo vitam agimus, quæ est imbecillitas ^rfragilitasque humani generis, infirmis viribus sumus ad omnia omnino vitia declinanda. Est ergo Ecclesiæ sanctitas nondum quidem expleta et perfecte absoluta, præclare inchoata tamen. Verum quum Christo, a quo illi omnis accedit ^smundities, atque puritas, plene conjuncta fuerit, tum demum innocentiam et sanctitatem omnibus suis partibus expletam, et perfecte absolutam, ut vestem quandam niveam purissimamque, induetur.

<small>r Rom. viii. 26. 1 Cor. xiii. 9, 11, 12. 2 Cor. xii. 5, 9.</small>

<small>s 1 Cor. xiii. 10. et xv. 53. Eph. v. 26. Apoc. xix. 8. et xxi. 2, 10, &c. 27.</small>

M. Quorsum tandem Ecclesiam hanc Catholicam nominas?

A. Perinde est, ac si universalem dicerem; non est enim hic cœtus conciliumque piorum, certo quopiam uno loco, aut tempore astrictum; ^tsed fidelium, qui ab orbe condito, omnibus locis, atque sæculis vixerunt, victurique sunt, universitatem continet atque complectitur; ut unum sit Ecclesiæ corpus, ^usicuti unus est Christus, unicum corporis caput. Cum enim Judæi Ecclesiam Dei, ut populo suo peculiarem, et quasi gentilitiam sibi assumerent, et vendicarent, et suam tantum esse confirmarent; Christiana fides profitetur ^xingentem piorum hominum numerum multitudinemque infinitam, ex omnibus terrarum orbis regionibus, ex omnibus omnium ubique gentium partibus, ætatibusque sæculorum, sacri verbi, vocisque suæ vi et potestate, atque cœlestis Spiritus divino instinctu collectam, in hanc Ecclesiam, quasi civitatem suam, a Deo ascriptam esse; qui omnes una ^yvera Fide, una mente, voceque consentientes, unico suo regi Christo, ut membra ^zcapiti, per omnia pareant.

<small>t Matt. xxviii. 19. Act. ii. 5, 9. et x. 34, 35. 1 Cor. xii. 13, 14.</small>

<small>u Matt. viii. 11. Eph. ii. 13, 14, &c. et iv. 4, 5, &c.</small>

<small>x Act. i. 8. et ii. 5, 8, 9. et x. 35. Col. iii. 11, &c.</small>

<small>y Eph. iv. 4, 5. et v. 23.</small>
<small>z 1 Cor. vi. 15. Eph. iv. 15, 16. et v. 30. Col. i. 18.</small>

M. An ergo recte quosdam huic Christianæ Fidei parti adjungere existimas, se credere sanctam Catholicam Romanam Ecclesiam?

A. Eos non solum alienum huic loco sensum affingere arbitror, dum nullum in Ecclesia Christi nisi qui Romani pontificis decreta edictaque omnia sacrosancta habeat, censeri velint; verum etiam, dum universitatem Ecclesiæ, quam ipsi ubique terrarum et gentium longe lateque diffusam esse primum confitentur, postea nomine unius gentis apposito, contrahunt, et in angustum adducunt, haud paulo amplius, quam Judæos insanire judico; ut qui contraria, et inter se pugnantia uno spiritu volvant, et pronuncient. Verum ad hanc eos insaniam adegit cœca cupiditas, studiumque Romanum Pontificem Ecclesiæ in terris caput in locum Christi supponendi atque substituendi.

M. Jam id ex te audire velim, cur Sanctæ Ecclesiæ Catholicæ statim adjungas, nos CREDERE SANCTORUM COMMUNIONEM?

A. Quia hæc duo eodem pertinent, et sunt inter se apta admodum atque convenientia. Hæc enim pars eam, quæ est inter Ecclesiæ membra, conjunctionem societatemque, qua nulla propior esse potest, clarius adhuc exprimit. Nam quum Deus per universas terrarum regiones atque oras, ut et per omnes ætates atque sæcula, habeat, qui se pure casteque venerentur; hi [a] omnes, licet diversis, et longinquis temporibus, atque locis separati sint atque distracti, ubicunque gentium, ubicunque terrarum fuerint, unius tamen sunt ejusdemque corporis, cujus caput Christus est, membra inter se quam maxime connexa atque cohærentia. Ea est piis hominibus et cum Deo, et inter se communitas. Spiritus [b] enim, Fidei, Sacramentorum, precum, remissionis peccatorum, et æternæ fœlicitatis, omniumque adeo beneficiorum, quæ Deus Ecclesiæ per Christum largitur, communitate sunt inter se conjunctissimi. Quin et concordiæ, [c] atque amoris inter se vinculis arctissimis ita sunt astricti, ita unum est omnibus propositum, ut eadem sit utilitas uniuscujusque et universorum; et in id maxime studium incumbant, quomodo beneficiis ultro citroque datis, atque acceptis, sese mutuo cum ad alia omnia, tum præcipue ad beatam illam æternamque vitam, consilio atque auxilio juvent. Verum quia hæc sanctorum communio neque sensibus nostris, neque [d] naturali atque insita in nobis notione, aut intelligentiæ vi aliqua, ut aliæ civiles communitates, societatesque hominum, percipiatur; merito inter ea, quæ creduntur, hoc loco posita est.

[a] 1 Cor. xii. 12, 13, &c. 20, 26. Eph. iv. 15, 16. et v. 30. Col. i. 18. et ii. 19.

[b] Eph. iv. 3, 4, 5, &c. 15, 16. Col. ii. 19.

[c] Matt. vii. 12. et xix. 14. et xxii. 39. Rom. xii. 5. 1 Cor. x. 24. et xiii. 5. 2 Cor. xi. 28. Gal. vi. 2. Phil. ii. 1, 2, 3, 4, 5.

[d] 1 Cor. ii. 14, 15.

M. Brevis hæc tractatio de Ecclesia, collocatisque apud eam Dei per Christum beneficiis, vehementer mihi placet;

eadem enim clarissime in Sacris Scripturis docentur. Verum potestne Ecclesia aliter cognosci, quam quum Fide creditur?

A. Hic quidem in Symbolo proprie agitur de eorum congregatione, quos Deus arcana [e]electione per Christum sibi adoptavit; quæ Ecclesia nec oculis cerni, neque ex signis cognosci perpetuo potest. Est tamen et visibilis seu spectabilis Dei Ecclesia, cujus nobis indicia notasque ostendit atque patefacit.

M. Quo ergo tota hæc Ecclesiæ tractatio clarior fiat, visibilem illam Ecclesiam, ita mihi suis notis signisque describe, et quasi depinge, ut ab alia quavis hominum societate discernatur.

A. Experiar quomodo quam optime id possim præstare. Visibilis Ecclesia non est aliud, quam certa quædam multitudo hominum, qui in quocunque loco sint, puram et sinceram [f]profitentur doctrinam Christi; illam ipsam videlicet, quam Evangelistæ atque Apostoli Sacrarum literarum sempiternis monumentis fideliter memoriæ prodiderunt: quique Deum Patrem [g]Christi nomine vere invocant; utuntur præterea ejus mysteriis, quæ usitato nobis vocabulo [h]Sacramenta appellantur, eadem puritate, et simplicitate (quod ad ipsorum naturam attinet) qua usi sunt, et literis consignarunt Apostoli Christi.

M. Visibilis ergo Ecclesiæ notas esse dicis Evangelii, id est beneficiorum Christi, prædicationem, invocationem, et Sacramentorum administrationem sinceram.

A. Sunt hæ quidem Ecclesiæ visibilis notæ præcipuæ et plane necessariæ; ut sine quibus ne Ecclesia quidem Christi esse, dicive recte possit. Sed et in eadem Ecclesia, si probe instituta fuerit, certus gubernationis [i]ordo et modus, disciplinæque Ecclesiasticæ ea ratio observabitur, ne impune liceat cuiquam, qui in illo grege versatur, publice quicquam impie, flagitioseve vel dicere, vel facere; adeoque ut omnes prorsus offensiones, in illa hominum congregatione, quoad ejus fieri potest, omnino vitentur. Verum labente paulatim jam olim hac disciplina, ut sunt hodie corrupti, depravatique omnium mores, maxime vero divitum atque potentum, qui peccatorum, adeoque scelerum omnium impunitatem, atque summam licentiam habere volunt, censoria animadversio, et castigatio teneri in Ecclesiis vix jam potest. In quocunque cœtu tamen verbum Dei, ejusque invocatio, et Sacramenta pure et sincere retinentur, non est dubium, quin ibi etiam sit Ecclesia Christi.

M. An non omnes ergo in hac visibili Ecclesia sunt ex electorum ad vitam æternam numero?

A. Multi per hypocrisin, et simulationem pietatis, in hanc se societatem adjungunt, qui nihil minus quam vera Ecclesiæ membra sunt. Verum, quia ubicunque verbum Dei sincere docetur, et Sacramenta rite administrantur, ibi perpetuo sunt aliqui ad [k]salutem per Christum designati, totum illum coetum Ecclesiam esse Dei censemus; quum et Christus sese, vel duobus [l]aut tribus, qui suo nomine congregati fuerint, adfuturum polliceatur.

[k] Esai. lv. 11. Act. xiii. 48.
[l] Matt. xviii. 20.

M. Cur Ecclesiæ REMISSIONEM PECCATORUM subjungis?

A. Primum, quia [m]claves, quibus coelum et claudendum est, et reserandum, id est, potestas illa ligandi et solvendi, reservandi atque remittendi peccata, quæ in verbi Divini ministerio sita est, Ecclesiæ per Christum delata, atque permissa, ad eam proprie pertinet; deinde quia nemo remissionem peccatorum consequitur, qui non sit verum corporis [n]Christi membrum; id est, qui communem Ecclesiæ consociationem studiose, pie, sancteque, perseveranter etiam, [o]atque ad ultimum non colat, et tueatur.

[m] Matt. xvi. 19. et xviii. 18. Luc. xxiv. 47. Joan. xx. 23.
[n] Joan. xv. 4. Col. ii. 19.
[o] Matt. xxiv. 13.

M. Nullane ergo salutis spes extra Ecclesiam?

A. Extra eam nihil nisi damnatio, exitium, atque interitus esse potest. Quæ enim potest [p]membris a capite corporeque avulsis, abscissisve, vitæ spes superesse? Qui ergo discordiam [q]in Ecclesia Dei seditiose concitant, dissidiumque, et dissentionem in ea faciunt, factionibusque eam perturbant, iis donec in concordiam atque gratiam cum Ecclesia redeant et revertantur, spes omnis salutis per peccatorum remissionem præciditur.

[p] Joan. xv. 4, 6. Col. ii. 19. 1 Tim. iii. 15.
[q] Rom. ii. 8, 9. 1 Cor. i. 11. et iii. 3. 1 Tim. i. 4, 6. 2 Tim. ii. 16, 23. Tit. iii. 9, 10, 11.

M. REMISSIONIS nomine quid significas?

A. Liberationem culpæ, erratique veniam fideles a Deo impetrare. Deum enim gratuito [r]propter Christum peccata ipsis condonare, eosque judicio et damnatione, justisque, et sceleri debitis suppliciis eripere et liberare.

[r] Psal. xxxii 1, 2. Act. xiii. 38. et xxvi. 18. Rom. iii. 24. Eph. i. 7. Col. i. 13, 14.

M. An non ergo piis officiis atque operibus Deo satisfacere, et peccatorum veniam ipsi mereri possumus?

A. Nulla meritis nostris debetur misericordia; sed Deus animadversionem suam et supplicium, quo in nos usurus erat, Christo remittit et condonat. Solus enim Christus perpessione dolorum, [s]et morte sua, qua poenam scelerum nostrorum dependit atque persolvit, Deo satisfecit; per solum ergo Chris-

[s] Esai. liii. 4, 5, 8, 12. Rom. v. 8, 10. Col. i. 20, 21. 2 Tim. i. 10. Heb. ix. 14, 15.

tum receptum ad Dei gratiam habemus. Nos ex gratuita ^tejus liberalitate atque benignitate beneficium hoc accipientes, nihil habemus, quod præmii aut compensationis nomine, ipsi vicissim offeramus aut reddamus.

^t Rom. iii. 24, 25, 27, 28. Gal. ii. 16.

M. Nihilne omnino pro nostra parte faciendum, ut veniam peccatorum impetremus?

A. Tametsi inter homines concesso peccato, difficile est ab eo, qui peccatorum vindex esse debet, ut ignoscat impetrare; confessionem tamen erranti medicinam quandam esse, ne a pietate quidem nostra ^ualieni ignorarunt. Et Pœnitentia, quam Resipiscentiam quidam malunt appellare, atque consilii mutatione peccatoribus opus esse ad veniam impetrandam, jam ante dictum est; et peccatoribus se veniam daturum, Dominus promittit, si eos pœniteat, ^xsi resipiscant, animosque a vitæ pravitate ad ipsum convertant.

^u Cic.

^x Jer. xviii. 8. Ezec. xviii. 21, 30, 31, 32. et xxxiii. 14. Matt. iv. 17. Luc. v. 32.

M. Quot sunt Pœnitentiæ partes?

A. Duæ præcipuæ. Veteris hominis, sive carnis mortificatio; et Novi hominis, sive Spiritus vivificatio.

M. Apertius ista planiusque explicari velim.

A. Veteris hominis mortificatio, est agnitio, ^yconfessioque peccati ingenua atque sincera, tum animi pudor atque dolor, cujus sensu, quod a justitia aberrarit, et Dei voluntati minus obsequens fuerit, graviter afficitur. Debet enim unusquisque anteactæ vitæ peccata recordans, sibi totus ^zdisplicere, sibi succensere, acrem se vitiorum suorum judicem præbere, et ipse de se sententiam ferre, et judicium pronuntiare, ne irati Dei grave judicium subeat. Hunc dolorem quidam Contritionem appellarunt, cui peccati odium acre, amissæque justitiæ amor et desiderium, propinquitate atque natura conjuncta sunt.

^y Psal. xxxii. 4, 5. li. 3, 4. Prov. xxviii. 13. 1 Joan. i. 8, 9.

^z Psal. vi. 6, 7. xxxi. 9, 10. et xxxviii. 3, 4, 6, 8, 9, 10, 17, 18. et li. 17. et cii. 4, 5. 1 Cor. xi. 31. 2 Cor. vii. 9, 10, 11.

M. At tanta esse potest scelerum conscientia, et pœnitendi vis, ut circumfuso undique pavore, hominis animum salutis desperatio occupet.

A. Verum ^aid quidem est, nisi doloris magnitudini consolationem Deus adhibeat. Sed piis superest adhuc altera illa pars resipiscentiæ, quæ ^bSpiritus renovatio sive novi hominis vivificatio dicitur. Ea est, cum Fides accedens animum ita affectum ^crecreat sublevatque, dolorem levat, et consolatur, a desperatione ad spem veniæ, a Deo per Christum impetrandæ, et a limine mortis, atque ab inferis adeo ipsis, ad vitam revocat, atque erigit. Atque hoc est, quod REMISSIONEM PECCATORUM nos credere profitemur.

^a Gen. iv. 13. Matt. xxvii. 3, 4. 2 Cor. ii. 7, 8.
^b Eph. iv. 23, 24. 1 Pet. iv. 6.
^c Matt. iv. 17. Luc. vii. 38, 47, 48, 50. et xv. 18, 21. xviii. 13. et xxiv. 47. Act. ii. 37. iii. 19. et xvi. 30, 32. 1 Tim. i. 15.

M. An homo hoc metu, atque his difficultatibus, suis se viribus liberare potest?

A. Nihil minus. Solus enim Deus est, ^dqui diffidentem rebus suis confirmat, afflictam erigit, perditum recreat, et quo duce hanc quam dixi spem, mentem, voluntatemque peccator suscipit.

^d Matt. xviii. 12. Luc. xv. 22. 2 Cor. i. 3, 4. 2 Thess. ii. 16, 17.

M. Jam quod superest in Symbolo, recita.

A. CREDO RESURRECTIONEM CARNIS, ^eET VITAM ÆTERNAM.

^e Matt. xxii. 31, 32. Joan. xi. 25. 1 Cor. xv. toto.

M. De his, quoniam in explicando ultimo judicio antea nonnihil attigisti, pauca tantum a te percontabor. Quorsum tandem, aut cur ista credimus?

A. Tametsi animos hominum immortales, sempiternosque esse credamus, tamen si corpora nostra interitu omnino delenda fore putaremus, ^fconcideremus prorsus, ut qui solido gaudio et ævo sempiterno integri, altera nostri parte desiderata, nunquam frueremur. Non animas ergo solum nostras, quum ex hac vita migramus, admistione corporum liberatas, puras et integras statim ^gin cœlum ad Christum evolare, certo credimus, verum etiam corpora nostra ^hin meliorem vitæ statum restituta, suis tandem animis rursum conjungenda, totosque nos perfecte atque absolute beatos efficiendos; hoc est, tam corporibus, quam animis nostris, æternitate, immortalitate, vitaque longe beatissima, quæ perpetuis sæculorum ætatibus non immutabitur, fruituros esse, nihil profecto dubitamus. Hæc spes nos in miseriis ⁱconsolatur, hac spe præditi, non solum incommoda et difficultates, quibus in hac vita afficimur, sed vitæ commutationem, ac mortis dolores toleranter patimur et sustinemus. Mortem enim, non interitum omnia tollentem, atque delentem, sed ducem nobis in cœlum esse, quæ nos in viam placatæ, tranquillæ, beatæ, sempiternæ vitæ deducat, persuasissimum habemus. Et proinde ex corporum vinculis tanquam ex carcere, ad ^kcœlum quasi communem urbem et civitatem Dei atque hominum, alacres lætique excurrimus atque evolamus.

^f 1 Cor. xv. 14, 17, 18, 19.

^g Luc. xvi. 22. et xxiii. 43.
^h Rom. viii. 11. 1 Cor. xv. 42, 43, 44, 53, 54. Phil. iii. 21. 1 Thess. iv. 13, 14, 15, 16, 17.

ⁱ Joan. xi. 25. 1 Cor. xv. 58. 1 Thess. iv. 13, 14, 18. Apoc. xiii. 18.

^k 2 Cor. v. 1, 2. Eph. ii. 19.

M. Ecquid præterea conducit ista credidisse?

A. Admonemur ne rebus incertis, fluxis, et caducis nos impediamus, aut implicemus; ne ad terrenam gloriam aut fœlicitatem spectemus; sed mundum hunc ^lut inquilini, et de migratione perpetuo cogitantes, incolamus; ad cœlum et cœlestia aspiremus; ubi beati ævo sempiterno fruemur.

^l Heb. xiii. 13, 14. 1 Pet. ii. 11.

M. Cum impios conditione a piis longissime ᵐdiversa, ad miseriam æternam videlicet, sempiternamque mortem resuscitandos esse antea docueris, cur Symbolum vitæ duntaxat æternæ, inferorum vero mentionem nullam facit?

A. Fidei hæc est Christianæ confessio, quæ non nisi ad pios pertinet; et proinde ea tantum recenset, quæ sunt ad consolandum ⁿaccommodata, amplissima nimirum præmia, quibus suos Deus donabit. Impios ergo a regno Dei alienos quæ maneant supplicia, non commemoratur.

M. Explicato jam Symbolo, id est, summa Fidei Christianæ, dic mihi quid commodi ex hac Fide comparamus?

A. Justitiam °coram Deo, per quam hæredes vitæ æternæ instituimur.

M. An non ergo pietas erga Deum nostra, ac vita inter homines honeste sancteque acta justos coram Deo nos efficit?

A. De hoc quædam superius post explicatam Legem, et alibi etiam, in hanc fere sententiam diximus. Si quisquam ad præscriptam normam ᵖjuris divini integre vivere posset, is merito justus ex operibus bonis censeretur; verum cum ab ea vitæ perfectione longissime absimus ᑫomnes, adeoque peccatorum nostrorum conscientia opprimamur; ʳalia nobis ineunda ratio, et via reperienda est, qua nos Deus in gratiam recipiat, quam nostro merito.

M. Quæ tandem quæso?

A. Ad Dei ˢmisericordiam confugiendum est, qua gratis nos in Christo, nullo nostro merito, nec operum respectu, amore, et benevolentia complectitur; tum peccata nobis nostra condonans, tum justitia Christi per Fidem in ipsum ita nos donans, ut ob eam, perinde ac si nostra esset, ipsi accepti simus. Divinæ ergo per Christum clementiæ, justitiam nostram omnem acceptam ferre debemus.

M. Unde ista ita esse intelligimus?

A. Ex Evangelio, quod Dei per Christum promissiones continet, ᵗquibus dum Fidem, id est, certam animi persuasionem, et stabilem benevolentiæ Divinæ fiduciam, qualis jam per totum Symbolum est descripta, adjungimus, in hujus, quam dico justitiæ possessionem, pedem quodammodo ponimus.

M. Non ergo inter hujus justitiæ causas Fidem principem locum tenere dicis, ut ejus merito nos ex nobis justi coram Deo habeamur?

A. Nequaquam; id enim esset Fidem in Christi locum substituere. Verum hujus justitiæ fons ˣest Dei misericordia, quæ in nos per Christum derivatur; per Evangelium vero nobis offertur, ʸet a nobis Fide, quasi manu prehenditur.

M. Fidem igitur non causam, sed instrumentum esse justitiæ dicis, quod scilicet Christum, ᶻqui est justitia nostra, amplectitur, tam arcta nos conjunctione cum illo copulans, ut omnium ejus bonorum participes faciat.

A. Sic est.

M. Verum an a bonis operibus ita separari hæc justitia potest, ut qui hanc habet, illis careat?

A. Nequaquam; Fide enim Christum, qualem se nobis offert, accipimus; ipse vero non modo a peccatis et morte nos liberat, et cum Deo in gratiam reducit, sed et Spiritus ᵃsancti divino afflatu et virtute, ad studium innocentiæ atque sanctitatis, quam vitæ ᵇnovitatem appellamus, regenerat, atque reformat.

M. ᶜJustitiam ergo, Fidem, ac bona opera, natura cohærentia esse dicis, quæ proinde non magis distrahi debeant, quam Christus illorum in nobis author, a seipso divelli possit?

A. Omnino.

M. Hæc igitur Fidei doctrina, hominum voluntates ab operibus officiisque piis nequaquam alienat?

A. Nihil minus. Nam opera bona Fide, ᵈut radice sua nituntur; tantum ergo abest, ut a vita integre agenda animos nostros Fides retardet, ut contra ad ejus studium maxime incitet; adeoque vere fidelis non sit, qui non et vitia pro virili ᵉdeclinet, et virtutes studiose amplexetur; ita semper vivens, ut rationem sibi reddendam arbitretur.

M. Ergo explicate mihi, quomodo opera nostra Deo accepta sint, et quibus donentur præmiis edissere?

A. ᶠIn operibus bonis duo præcipue requiruntur. Primum, ut ea opera, ᵍquæ Lege Divina præscripta sunt, deinde ut ea mente atque ʰFide, quam Deus exigit, a nobis suscipiantur. Nullæ enim vel actiones, vel cogitationes sine Fide susceptæ, Deo placere possunt.

M. Perge.

A. Constat ergo omnia opera quæcunque facimus antequam renati ⁱsumus, Deique Spiritu renovati, quæ proprie nostra dici possunt, vitiosa esse. Qualemcunque enim speciem splendoris et dignitatis præ se ferant, præbeantque oculis hominum; quum e pravo corruptoque ^kcorde, quod Deus maxime spectat, manent et proficiscantur, non nisi inquinata contaminataque esse, et Deum proinde graviter offendere possunt. Hujusmodi igitur opera ut malos fructus, ¹ex arbore mala editos, aspernatur Deus, atque a se rejicit.

M. Nullis ergo operibus, aut meritis Deum antevertere possumus, quibus illum ad benevolentiam, beneficentiamque priores provocemus?

A. Nullis plane. Nam nos Deus non solum quum inimici ejus essemus, ^mid est, peccatores, sed et ante mundi jacta fundamenta in Christo dilexit, atque elegit. Et hic est ille, quem dixi, justitiæ nostræ fons atque origo.

M. De illis vero operibus, quæ jam in gratiam apud Deum positi, Spiritusque sacri instinctu facimus, quid censes?

A. Debita pietatis officia, quæ ex Fide, ⁿper charitatem operante proficiscuntur, Deo quidem grata sunt, non tamen ipsorum merito, ^osed quod ille suo favore ea liberaliter dignetur. Nam tametsi a Divino afflatu, ut a fonte rivuli deducantur, ex ^pcarnis tamen nostræ, quæ sese in agendo admiscet, quasi contagione vitium concipiunt; haud secus, ac rivus alioqui purus et limpidus, cœno, limoque, per quod fluit, turbatur atque inficitur.

M. Quomodo ergo ea Deo placere affirmas?

A. Fides ^qest, quæ Dei gratiam operibus nostris conciliat, dum pro certo habet, eum summo nobiscum ^rjure acturum non esse, neque facta nostra quasi ad calculos vocaturum, aut exacturum ad perpendiculum; id est, in illis æstimandis expendendisque non adhibiturum severitatem; sed omni eorum vitiositate Christo ejusque meritis remissa atque condonata, pro perfecte absolutis esse habiturum.

M. Persistis ergo in eo, non posse nos operum merito consequi, ut justi coram Deo habeamur, quum actiones humanas vel perfectissimas venia indigere existimes.

A. Deus ipse in verbo suo ita statuit; ejusque sacer Spiritus nos instituit, ut precemur, ne ^sin judicium nos adducat. Nam quum justitia Deo judici probanda, perfecte ^tabsoluta atque expleta omnibus suis partibus et numeris esse debeat, ut quæ ad acerrimam Divinæ legis judiciique normam, et quasi ad perpendiculum dirigenda simul atque exigenda sit; opera vero nostra vel ^uoptima, quum a Divini juris justitiæque regula, ^xatque præscripto longissime aberrent, ʸatque absint, multisque modis et culpanda sint et damnanda, operibus justificari coram Deo nulla omnino ratione possumus.

M. Annon hæc doctrina hominum animos ab officiis pietatis abducit, et ad bona opera segniores atque tardiores efficit, aut minus certe alacres promptosque ad pia studia reddit?

A. Nequaquam; neque enim proinde inutilia esse, et frustra, aut sine causa fieri bona opera dicemus, quod justitiam per illa non consequamur. Nam et in proximi commodum, ᶻet in Dei gloriam cedunt; et de Divina erga nos benevolentia, nostraque vicissim in Deum charitate et fide, atque ita de salute nos nostra, quasi testimoniis quibusdam ᵃcertiores faciunt. Et æquum omnino est, ut Christi Filii Dei sanguine redempti, et innumeris præterea atque immensis Divinis beneficiis affecti, ad redemptoris ᵇarbitrium atque nutum viventes, et nos totos accommodantes, memores nos, gratosque erga salutis nostræ authorem præbeamus, aliosque illi ᶜexemplo nostro acquiramus atque lucrifaciamus. Ista recogitans aliquis, piis suis studiis operibusque satis lætari potest.

M. At præmiis tamen tum in hac vita, tum in futura nos ad bene agendum invitat Deus, et quasi mercede quadam nobiscum paciscitur.

A. ᵈMerces illa non pro dignitate, ut dixi, operibus tribuitur, et illis quasi gratia pro meritis refertur, sed Dei benignitate gratis præter meritum, in nos confertur. Justitiam vero Deus nobis pro sua in nos charitate, et liberalitate per ᵉChristum dono dat. Dei donum liberalitatemque quum dico, ᶠgratuitam, et sine mercede, aut merito nostro benignam intelligo; ut sit mera sinceraque Dei liberalitas, quam ad nostram modo, quos diligit, quique illi fidimus, salutem referat, non conducta, aut mercenaria, quasi quædam commodorum utilitatumque suarum mercatura, quam ad fructum aliquem suum exerceat, aliquod vicissim præmium, aut pretium a nobis repetens; qua sola vel cogitatione Dei benignitas, simul et majestas minueretur.

M. Quum ergo Deus, et justitiam nobis per Fidem tribuat, et opera nostra per eandem grata acceptaque habeat; dic mihi, Fidem hanc, naturæne dotem, an Dei donum esse putas?

A. Donum ᵍDivinum, et quidem singulare, atque eximium,

ʸ Job. xv. 14, 15, 16. et xxv. 6. Esai. lxiv. 6. 1 Cor. vi. 4.

ᶻ Matt. v. 16. 1 Pet. ii. 12.

ᵃ Matt. xii. 33. Phil. ii. 12. 1 Pet. i. 10.

ᵇ Rom. xiv. 7, 8. 1 Cor. vi. 19. 2 Cor. v. 15. 1 Thess. v. 10.

ᶜ Matt. v. 16. 1 Pet. ii. 12.

ᵈ Matt. v. 12. et x. 41, 42. et xxv. 34, 35. Eph. iii. 20. 2 Tim. i. 9.

ᵉ Rom. iii. 24. 1 Cor. i. 1.

ᶠ Rom. iii. 24. et xi. 6. Gal. v. 4. 2 Tim. i. 9. Tit. iii. 4, 5. Apoc. xxi. 6.

ᵍ Marc. ix. 23, 24. Joan. ix. 39. 1 Pet. i. 20, 21.

<small>ʰ Matt. xvi.
7, 8, 9, 11.
Luc. xviii. 34.
Rom. viii. 6,
7. 1 Cor. ii.
14.
ⁱ Matt. vi. 30.
et viii. 26. et
xvi. 8. et
xiv. 31.

ᵏ Matt. xvi.
17. Luc.
xxiv. 45.
Col. i. 9.
2 Tim. ii. 7.

ˡ Luc. xvii. 5.</small>

Fides est. Nam hebetiora ʰtardioraque sunt ingenia nostra, quam ut Dei sapientiam, cujus fontes Fide aperiuntur, concipere, et animo comprehendere possint; et corda nostra, vel ad ⁱdiffidentiam, vel ad pravam perversamque in nobis, vel aliis creaturis confidentiam, quam ad veram in Deo fiduciam, sunt propensiora. Verum Deus verbo suo nos instruens, simulque ᵏmentes nostras Spiritu suo sancto illustrans, ad ea, quæ alioqui obtusam ingeniorum nostrorum aciem longe fugerent, dociles nos reddit, et salutis promissiones in animis nostris consignans, nos ita format, ut de illarum fide nobis sit persuasissimum. Hæc intelligentes Apostoli, Dominum orant, ut ˡFidem ipsorum augeat.

Tertia pars de Oratione, et gratiarum actione.

M. Opportune de oratione mentionem fecisti. Absoluta enim juris Divini, et Symboli, id est, confessionis Christianæ explicatione, proximum est ut de precatione, et quæ illi finitima est, gratiarum actione, jam dicamus; est enim horum cum superioribus implicita, et apte cohærens ratio.

A. Aptissime profecto; ut quæ ad priorem legis Divinæ <small>ᵐ Psal. l. 15, 23. Act ix. 21. Rom. x. 12. et xv. 6. 2 Cor. i. 2, 4. 2 Tim. ii. 22. 1 Pet. i. 17.</small> tabulam referuntur, officiaque ᵐpietatis in Deum præcipua complectuntur.

M. In explicanda oratione, quem ordinem sequemur?

A. Hunc, si ita tibi videbitur, Præceptor, ut primo loco, quis sit orandus; secundo, qua fiducia; tertio, qua animi affectione; quarto, quid orandum sit explicemus.

M. Primum igitur dic mihi quem invocandum esse censeas?

A. Nullum profecto, nisi Deum solum.

M. Quid ita?

<small>ⁿ Psal. xvii. 7, 8. et xxvi. 1. et xxxviii. 8. et lxxviii. et civ. toto.</small>

A. Quia in Dei unius manu, ⁿvita salusque nostra posita est, in cujus potestate sita sunt omnia; quum ergo omne quod bonum est, quodque hominem Christianum optare et expetere oporteat, Deus nobis largiatur; quumque is solus in quovis <small>ᵒ Psal. xviii. 1, &c. 26, 27, 28, &c. et xci. 1, 2, &c.</small> ᵒdiscrimine opem atque auxilium ferre, periculaque omnia depellere possit, ab eo rem omnem petere, atque ad ipsum solum in quavis difficultate confugere, et ipsius opem implorare nos convenit. Hoc enim ipse in ᵖverbo suo tanquam <small>ᵖ Psal. l. 15, 23. et lxxxi. 7. et lxxxix. 26, 27.</small> peculiarem, propriumque numinis sui cultum exigit, atque deposcit.

M. Annon ergo recte sanctos homines, qui ex hac vita abierunt, aut Angelos etiam invocabimus?

A. Minime; id enim esset, vel infinitatem illis, ut ubique praesentes sint, vel absentibus abditarum voluntatum nostrarum intelligentiam, hoc est, Divinitatem quandam tribuere; simulque fiduciam atque spem nostram, ᑫquae tota in solo Deo collocanda esset, partim in ipsos transferre, atque ita in idololatriam prolabi. Sed et quum Deus ad se unum nos vocet, ʳse nos et auditurum et adjuturum, interposito etiam jurejurando, promittat, ad aliorum opem confugere diffidentiae esset, atque infidelitatis certum argumentum. Et quod ad sanctos homines, qui ex hac vita excesserunt, attinet; quale quaeso hoc esset, relicto Deo ˢvivente, audiente ᵗpreces nostras, potentissimo, ᵘpropensissimo ad juvandum, qui nos ad se ˣvocet, suo numine atque auxilio nos defensurum in verbo veritatis promittat, ʸatque juret; illo inquam relicto, ad homines mortuos, surdos, imbecilles confugere; qui neque opem promiserint, neque auxilium ferre possint, quibus juvandi nostri partes Deus nusquam tribuerit, ad quos nullis Scripturis, quibus ᶻFides certo nitatur, dirigamur, sed capitis tantum nostri somniis, aut deliriis potius fidentes, temere agamur?

ᑫ Psal. ii. 12. et xxv. 1. 2. et cxviii. 8, 9.
ʳ Psal. l. 15. et lxxxix. 26, 27. Joan. xvi. 23, 24.
ˢ Psal. cii. 21, 23, 24.
ᵗ Psal. l. 15.
ᵘ Eph. iii. 20.
ˣ Matt. xi. 28.
ʸ Joan. xvi. 23, 24.
ᶻ Rom. x. 8, 14, 17.

M. At Angelorum, qui nos circumstant, et nos proinde audiunt, opera Deus ad salutem nostram utitur.

A. Verum id ᵃquidem est; nusquam tamen in verbo Dei apparet, Deum velle nos vel Angelis, vel hominibus piis jam mortuis, preces adhibere. Quum vero Fides ᵇverbo Dei nitatur, et quod non est ex Fide ᶜpeccatum sit, recte dixi certum esse infidelitatis signum, relicto Deo, ᵈad quem solum nos Scripturae remittunt, Angelos, aut pios homines, hac vita carentes, de quibus invocandis nullum in sacris literis verbum extet, precari atque implorare.

ᵃ Psal. xci. 11, 12. Heb. i. 14.
ᵇ Rom. x. 17.
ᶜ Rom. xiv. 23.
ᵈ Matt. vi. 6, 9.

M. Quum tamen charitas piorum animis nunquam ᵉexcidat, etiam in coelo versantes, soliciti sunt de nobis, et salutem nostram expetunt.

ᵉ 1 Cor. xv. 18.

A. Id vero negari non potest; non tamen sequitur a nobis proinde esse invocandos; nisi putemus amicorum, quamvis longe absentium, tantum quod nobis bene velint, opem atque auxilium esse implorandum.

M. Ab hominibus tamen vivis, praesentibusque quibuscum versamur, opem saepe petimus.

A. Fateor; homines enim, ut ᶠmutuae inter se opis in-

ᶠ 1 Cor. xii. 11, 21, 25. 1 Pet. iv. 10.

[NOEL. CATEC.]

digent, ita facultatem sese mutuo juvandi Deus illis concessit;
diserteque etiam præcepit, ut quisque proximum suum, quo
possit adjumento, ^gsublevet. Homines ergo, ut beneficentiæ
Divinæ ministros, ex voluntate Dei imploramus, opem atque
auxilium ab ipsis expectantes; at ita tamen, ut tota fiducia
nostra in solo Deo reponatur, illique quicquid ^hper manus
hominum traditur, ut omnis benignitatis fonti acceptum referamus. Recte ergo atque ordine ista fiunt, neque quicquam
impediunt, quo minus unum Deum invocemus, ita ut nihil
aliunde boni nos expectare, nec alibi totum nostrum præsidium
collocare testemur.

M. Prece igitur et obsecratione, ut et aliis omnibus pietatis officiis, ex præscripto verbi Dei nobis esse utendum,
alioqui Deo placere non posse statuis?

A. Omnino; ⁱin Religione enim ordinis atque rationis
a Deo institutæ perturbatione peccatur, quicquid peccatur.

M. Solum ergo Deum, collocata in eo omni fiducia,
invocandum esse, eique ut bonorum omnium fonti accepta
referenda esse omnia, hactenus dictum est. Jam proximum
est, ut qua fiducia miseri mortales, qui tot modis indigni
sumus, immortalem Deum appellare debeamus, declares.

A. Sumus quidem nos omnibus modis indignissimi, verum
non superbe atque arroganter, quasi digni irrumpimus, sed
Christi ^kmediatoris nomine, atque fiducia accedimus; a quo
janua nobis patefacta, quamvis vilissimi homunculi simus, ex
argilla et luto ficti, scelerumque nostrorum conscientia oppressi,
aditu non prohibebimur, neque difficiles accessus ad Divinam majestatem, ejusque gratiam nobis conciliandam sumus
habituri.

M. Non ergo ut ad Principem aliquem mundanum, ita
et ad Deum accessuris opus est homine aliquo internuntio,
aut interprete, qui nos illi commendet, causamque nostram
exponat.

A. Nihil minus; nisi et Deum hominum ^linstar, ut uni
loco inclusum, multa nisi per servos suos intelligere non
posse, vel dormitare interdum, vel non satis otii ad auscul-
tandum habere statuamus; nam quod ad indignitatem nostram
attinet, preces nostras nulla re nobis insita, sed unica ^mChristi,
cujus nomine precamur, dignitate niti jam diximus.

M. Ergo solius omnino Christi nomine, atque fiducia
Patrem Deum invocandum esse censes?

A. Certe, Præceptor; solus enim ille supra alios omnes singulari nos ⁿamore complectitur, ut omnia nostra causa velit; solus est apud Deum Patrem, cui ad dexteram assidet, °gratiosissimus, ut quidvis ab eo impetrare possit; solus ergo mediator Dei et hominum, homo Jesus Christus; solus inquam, ut redemptionis, sic et invocationis (ut ita loquar) mediator, cujus solius ᵖnomine Deum Patrem adire nos diserte Sacræ literæ jubent, additis etiam promissionibus, eum sua intercessione effecturum, ut, quæ oramus, exoremus. Alioqui ᑫsine Christo, Dei auris atque animus ab hominibus abhorret.

ⁿ Joan. xv. 9, 13. Rom. viii. 17, 18, 19. Eph. v. 2, 25.
° Matt. iii. 17. et xii. 18.
Rom. viii. 34.
ᵖ Joan. xiv. 13. et xvi. 23, 26.
ᑫ Joan. xv. 5. Eph. ii. 12, 13.

M. At mutuis ʳprecibus alios adjuvamus tamen, quoad in hoc mundo hæremus.

ʳ 1 Thess. i. 2. Col. iv 2, 3. Eph. vi. 18, 19.

A. Verûm id quidem est, non tamen ideo alios mediatores Christo substituimus, sed conjunctis animis et votis, ad charitatis atque verbi Dei præscriptum, uno ˢmediatore, communem Patrem invocamus.

ˢ 1 Tim. ii. 5. Heb. ix. 15.

M. Alios ergo mediatores ad Deum, aut causæ nostræ patronos, præter unum Christum constituere; et a Scripturis Sanctis, ac proinde a Fide alienum, et cum Christi ipsius summa injuria conjunctum esse dicis?

A. Dico, Præceptor.

M. Perge.

A. Summa rei illuc pertinet, ut promissionum ᵗnobis per Christum factarum fiducia nixi, ejusque freti patrocinio, omissa omni dignitatis nostræ ratione, precibus quasi ex ore ᵘChristi conceptis, ad Deum Patrem invocandum accedamus; quod ut veritati Scripturarum maxime consentaneum est, ita ab ˣarrogantiæ, temeritatisque culpa longissime utique abest.

ᵗ Rom. i. 2, 5. et iv. 21, 24 2 Cor. i. 20. et iii. 4, 5. Gal. iii. 22. Tit. i. 2.
ᵘ Matt. ix. 10. Job. xiv. 15, 16. et xv. 16, 21. et xvi. 20, 21, 22.
ˣ Psal. xxix. 1, 2. Act. iii. 12, 16.

M. Sic vero ut dicis, Deum precantes, quod petunt impetrandi spem bonam concipere debere existimas?

A. Et Dominus ipse certa nos ʸFide petere jubet, addita promissione, et jurejurando etiam interposito, nobis datum iri, quicquid credentes petierimus; et ejus item Apostoli rectam precationem ex Fide manare docent. Proinde firmissimum hoc orationis ponere fundamentum perpetuo oportet, ut in certa paternæ bonitatis ᶻfiducia acquiescentes, Deum preces votaque nostra exauditurum, et quod petierimus, quatenus quidem id nobis expediet, impetraturos nos esse statuamus. Proinde, qui temere ᵃatque inconsulte ad precandum

ʸ Matt. xxi. 21. Marc. xi. 22, 23, 24. Joan. xvi. 23. Jacob. i. 6. et v. 15, 16.
ᶻ Matt. vii. 10. Heb. iv. 6. et x. 22. 1 Joan. v. 14.
ᵃ Matt. xx. 22. et xxi 21. Joan. xvi. 24. Jacob. i. 6. et iv. 3.

accedunt, quique hæsitantes, et de successu incerti orant, vana irritaque verba incassum fundunt.

M. Intelligo qua fiducia Deum invocandum esse dicas; nunc qua animi affectione accedendum sit, explica.

A. [b]Indigentiæ, egestatisque nostræ, et ærumnarum, quæ nos premunt, sensu animos nostros graviter affici oportet; adeo quidem, ut liberationis ex ea molestia, atque opis Divinæ, quam expetimus, desiderio ingenti flagremus. Sic vero animis affecti, fieri non potest, quin attentissime, [c]ardentissimoque studio, quod cupimus, precibus omnibus votisque exposcamus.

M. Video ergo non satis esse lingua tantum, et voce precari.

A. Mente [d]atque attentione, sine qua preces nunquam efficaces esse possunt, non adhibita, precari non solum est laborem inutilem frustra suscipere; (quomodo enim nos Deus exaudiat, quum non attendimus [e]nec exaudimus nosmetipsos?) nec inanes solum sine fructu, sed et noxias [f]etiam, læsa majestate Divina, voces fundere; tantum abest, ut Divinum numen scelere violatum ejusmodi preces placare queant.

M. Unde ista ita esse intelligimus?

A. [g]Quum Deus sit Spiritus, (ut ita loquar) atque animus purissimus, animum mentemque, cum alias semper, tum vero in oratione, per quam homines cum Deo quasi colloquuntur et communicant, vel maxime requirit. Sed et iis tantum, qui ipsum [h]vere, id est, ex animo invocant, propinquum fore se, eorumque preces sibi cordi esse, testatur. Contra vero, qui [i]simulate, temereve in lingua promptum habent, quod animo et cogitatione non comprehendunt nec consequuntur, et cum immortali Deo [k]negligentius, quam cum mortali homine solent, agunt, horum preces Deus merito aversatur, atque detestatur. Mente ergo semper opus est, at lingua in precatione perpetuo non est necessaria.

M. Est tamen aliquis in precibus linguæ usus.

A. Maxime. Æquum enim est, ut [l]lingua etiam omnem vim atque facultatem suam ad amplificandum Dei gloriam, sedulo studioseque conferat; quum præ aliis corporis partibus in hunc usum proprie a Deo condita sit. Præterea ut animo cogitatione curaque vehementer intento, vox imprudentibus interdum nobis erumpit; ita nonnunquam ipse pronunciandi sonus, auditioque nostrorum verborum mentum excitat, atque acuit, ejusque intentionem juvat, et remissionem, qua assidue animus urgetur, arcet atque depellit.

M. Quum hæc ita se habeant, quid de illis censes, qui in precando peregrina atque ipsis incognita lingua utuntur?

A. Eos non operam modo (quod aiunt) sed Deum etiam ipsum pariter ludere. Si enim LOQUI est suo loco verbum quodque scienter ponere, qui ᵐnon intellecta verba pronuntiant, perstrepunt verius quam loquuntur; tantum abest, ut precentur. Psittacos enim potius quam homines, nedum Christianos agunt. Itaque facessat procul a piis hominibus talis hypocrisis, atque ineptia. Nam si ⁿD. Paulus absurdum putet, ut quis apud alios sermonem habeat, quem non intelligunt, quod verba neminem moveant nisi eum, qui ejusdem linguæ societate sit conjunctus, loquentemque atque audientes mutuo sibi barbaros fore affirmet; quanto est absurdius, nosmet nobis ipsis esse barbaros, dum eo sermone, qui nobis non est notus, utimur, illaque lingua, in qua ipsi surdi sumus, sensus nostros atque vota explicare conamur? Hujusmodi certe homines ut maxime ineptos optimo jure rideri, homines olim sapientissimi existimaverunt.

ᵐ 1 Cor.xiv.7, 9, 11.

ⁿ 1 Cor. xiv. 11.

Cic. de Offic. Tusc. Quæst. lib. v. et de Oratore.

M. Video quam attentus animus, studiumque ardens in oratione requiratur. Verum dic mihi, ardorem istum naturalemne, et animis nostris insitum, an Divinam hanc mentium nostrarum incitationem esse putas?

A. Sacræ literæ testantur Dei Spiritum °gemitus inenarrabiles, quibus preces nostræ efficaces redduntur, ciere. Is ergo sine dubio mentes nostras afflatu suo concitat, et ad orandum acuit atque adjuvat.

° Rom. viii. 26. Eph. ii. 18.

M. Quid ergo? cum hic animi ardor, qui semper adesse non potest, consederit, aut extinctus omnino fuerit, an pigritia torpentes, et quasi dormitantes, agitationem, motumque Spiritus oscitanter expectabimus?

A. Nihil minus; quin potius languentibus nobis atque animo remissis, Divinum ᵖprotinus auxilium expetendum est, ut is alacritatem nobis addat, animosque nostros ad precandum excitet; hanc enim mentem, voluntatemque Deo duce suscipimus.

ᵖ Psal. li. 17. Matt. xxvi. 40, 41.

M. Superest jam, ut quid precibus a Deo debeamus exposcere, ex te intelligam. Licetne, quicquid in mentem buccamve nobis venerit, a Deo petere?

A. Quum homines a vera pietate alieni, tam honestam

Cic. pro domo sua.

opinionem de Deorum suorum numine ac mente habuerint, ut expeti nihil ab iis, quod sit injustum, ac inhonestum debere arbitrarentur; absit ut homines Christiani quicquam, a quo divina mens atque voluntas ^qabhorreat, precibus a Deo petamus unquam. Hoc enim esset divinam majestatem injuria, atque ignominia etiam summa afficere; tantum abest, ut talis illi precatio placere, aut quicquam ab eo impetrare queat. Quum vero et hebetiora sint mortalium ^ringenia, quam ut quid ipsis expediat intelligere possint, et animorum cupiditates tam cœcæ atque indomitæ, ut non solum duce, quem sequantur, sed frænis etiam, quibus coerceantur, opus habeant, nimis absurdum esset, affectibus nos nostris temere præcipitesque in precando ferri. Ad certam ergo normam atque præscriptionem precationes nostræ omnino sunt dirigendæ.

M. Quam tandem quæso?

A. Eandem profecto illam, ^squam cœlestis magister discipulis suis, ac per eos nobis omnibus precandi formulam constituit; qua, quæ a Deo petere fas est, ac nostra impetrare interest, universa in pauca admodum contulit, quæ etiam ab ipso authore Precatio Dominica est appellata. Si ergo doctorem cœlestem divina voce nobis præeuntem sequemur, nunquam profecto a recta precandi regula aberrabimus.

M. Dominicam ergo precationem mihi recita.

A. Quum volueritis orare (inquit ^tDominus) sic dicite: PATER NOSTER QUI ES IN CŒLIS, SANCTIFICETUR NOMEN TUUM. VENIAT REGNUM TUUM, FIAT VOLUNTAS TUA, SICUT IN CŒLO, SIC ETIAM IN TERRA. PANEM NOSTRUM QUOTIDIANUM DA NOBIS HODIE. ET REMITTE NOBIS DEBITA NOSTRA, SICUT ET NOS REMITTIMUS DEBITORIBUS NOSTRIS. ET NE NOS INDUCAS IN TENTATIONEM, SED LIBERA NOS A MALO. QUIA TUUM EST REGNUM, ET POTENTIA, ET GLORIA IN SECULA. AMEN.

M. Arbitrarisne ista a nobis quasi dictata perpetuo reddenda esse, ita ut uno verbo ab ipsis discedere sit nefas?

A. Non est dubium, quin aliis in precando verbis uti liceat, modo ab hujus precationis sententia non aberremus. In ea enim certa quædam, et præcipua rerum capita Dominus proposuit, ad quæ nisi precationes nostræ omnes referantur, Deo placere non possunt; petat tamen quisque a Deo, ut præsens ^utempus atque necessitas flagitabunt; et cui volet parti hujus precationis, et quamdiu volet, immoretur, eamque prout visum fuerit, variis modis amplificet; nihil enim impediet, modo ea fiducia atque affectu, quo est ante dictum, in eam item sententiam, quæ hac oratione ostenditur, Deum precetur.

M. Precatio Dominica quot partes habet?

A. Postulationes quidem sex continet, partes tamen in summa duæ sunt; quarum prior ad solam Dei gloriam attinet, et tres priores petitiones complectitur; posterior, quæ reliqua tria postulata continet, ad nostrum commodum proprie pertinet.

M. Itane utilitatem nostram a divina gloria divellis, atque distrahis, ut æqualiter etiam inter ea partiaris?

A. Cohærentia non distraho, sed quo tota tractatio perspicua fiat, secernenda distinguo; ut quorsum quidque pertineat intelligatur. Alioqui, quæ proprie ad Dei gloriam spectant, ea nobis quoque summas utilitates præbent; quæ rursum utilitati nostræ serviunt, omnia ad divinam gloriam revocantur. ˣIs enim finis, ad quem referenda sunt universa, hic esse nobis scopus debet, ut Dei gloria quam maxime amplificetur. Partitionem tamen hanc in tractando interim non incommodam fore, nec temere, sed ex rerum ipsarum proprietate fieri arbitror; quia dum illa, quæ ad Dei gloriam amplificandum proprie pertinent, petimus, utilitates interim nostras omittere oportet, quum tamen in posterioribus illis petitionibus commodis nostris recte serviamus.

M. Jam verborum omnium pondera paulo diligentius examinemus. Cur Deum patrem nominas?

A. Permagna in unius hujus nominis usu vis inest. Duo enim, quæ supra in precando cum primis necessaria esse demonstravimus, complectitur.

M. Quæ sunt illa?

A. Primum, non quasi absenti, ʸaut surdo loquor, sed ut præsentem audientemque appello atque invoco, certo persuasum habens, eum precantem me exaudire; alioqui enim ejus auxilium frustra implorarem. Hoc ita de Angelorum aut hominum etiam mortuorum ᶻquoquam statuere, sine omni dubitatione profecto non possum. Deinde, fiduciam impetrandi ante diximus esse rectæ precationis fundamentum; charum vero ipsum verbum est Patris, ac paterni amoris, et spei bonæ atque fiduciæ plenissimum. ᵃNomine ergo, quo nullum in

ˣ 1 Cor. x. 30, 31. Col. iii. 17.

ʸ Psal. xxxiii. 13, 14. et xxxiv. 15. 17. et xciv. 9, 10, 11. et cxxxix. 1, 2, &c.

ᶻ Esai. lxiii. 16.

ᵃ Psal. ciii. 13. Luc. xv. 18.

terra dulcius, appellari Deus voluit, ita nos ad se invitans, ut eum, omni sublata de patrio ejus animo atque benevolentia dubitatione, intrepide adeamus. Cum enim Patrem eum nobis esse decernimus, [b]ejus spiritu animati, ut suum liberi parentem solent, accedimus. PATER ergo charitatis [c]atque amoris nomine, potius quam dignitatis, aut majestatis vocabulis, REX aut DOMINUS nuncupari hoc loco Deus voluit, et paterni nominis amplissimum patrimonium nobis interim quasi [d]liberis suis relinquere.

M. Eane igitur impetrandi fiducia, qua suos filii parentes adire solent, ad Deum accedemus?

A. Firmiorem multo stabilioremque esse Divinæ benevolentiæ quam humanæ fiduciam, [e]Christus naturalis Dei Filius, ingenii Patris optime gnarus, nobis confirmat dicens: [f]Si vos (inquit) cum mali sitis, filios vestros inanes voces fundere non sinitis, sed eorum postulationibus conceditis, quanto erit cœlestis Pater, qui ipsa est bonitas atque benignitas, in vos beneficentior? Verum omnem hanc fiduciam [g]Christus, ut est ante dictum, nobis affert; neque enim nos, qui natura iræ filii sumus, Deus sibi nisi per Christum adoptat, aut filios esse agnoscit.

M. Ecquid præterea nos docet Patris nomen?

A. Ut cum eo amore, [h]reverentia, atque obedientia, quæ Patri cœlesti a suis liberis debentur, ad precandum accedamus, utque eam mentem, quæ Filios Dei decet, habeamus.

M. Deum cur nostrum potius communiter Patrem appellas, quam tuum separatim?

A. Fas quidem est pio cuique Deum [i]suum nominare, verum eam oportet esse hominum Christianorum inter ipsos communitatem, atque societatem, eaque charitate atque benevolentia singuli universos complecti debent, ne aliis neglectis, quisquam unum se curet, sed publicam omnium utilitatem respiciat; unde privatim nihil in tota hac precatione, sed communi omnium nomine cuncta postulantur. Sed et cum illi, quorum infima est fortuna, ac vitæ conditio, communem [k]Patrem cœlestem, æque ac fœlices, et amplissimæ dignitatis gradus adepti, appellent, eos ne fratres dedignemur, qui filiorum honore apud Deum dignantur, admonemur. [l]Despicatissimi vero, et qui in hoc mundo sunt contemptissimi, hac interim consolatione lenire se, atque sustentare possunt, quod in cœlo potentissimum eundemque benignissimum Patrem habeant. Præterea qui Deo [m]fidimus, eum recte Patrem esse nostrum profitemur. Impii enim atque increduli, ut Dei potentiam justitiamque extimescant, paternæ tamen ejus erga se bonitati confidere non possunt.

M. Cur Deum in cœlo esse dicis?

A. Quemadmodum cœlum rotundo atque immenso ambitu omnia complectitur, circundat terram, circundat maria; nec res, aut locus est aliquis, qui cœli capacitate non cingitur atque concluditur, estque ex omni parte patens atque apertum, et rebus omnibus perpetuo sic adest, ut in ejus quasi conspectu locentur universa; ita Deum ⁿarcem cœli tenentem, rerum pariter omnium gubernacula tenere, ubique præsentem adesse, videre, audire, moderari universa intelligimus. ⁿ Psal. xi. 4, 5. et xx. 6. et xxxiii. 13. et cxiii. 4, 5, 6. et cxv. 3.

M. Perge.

A. In cœlo etiam, ob id Deus esse dicitur, quod suprema, atque °cœlestis illa regio, Divinis ejus atque præclaris operibus magnificentius collucet atque illustratur. ᵖDeum præterea in cœlo regnantem, in æterna et summa fœlicitate esse demonstratur, cum nos adhuc in terris patria pulsi, ut paternorum bonorum exhæredes filii misere et calamitose exulemus. Idem ergo valet, ᑫDeum in cœlo esse, ac si cœlestem et modis omnibus Divinum eum appellem, id est, incomprehensibilem, excelsissimum, potentissimum, beatissimum, optimum, maximum. ^o Psal. viii. 3. et xix. 1. ^p Psal. viii. 1, 2, 3, 4. et xi. 4, 5. ^q Psal. l. 3, 4, 6. et lvii. 5, 10, 11. et lxviii. 32, 33. et cxiii, 4, 5.

M. Quem ex istis fructum percipis?

A. Evellunt ista ex animis nostris vulgares atque corruptas de Deo opiniones, instituuntque mentes nostras, ut de cœlesti ʳPatre cogitationem longe aliam, quam de terrenis parentibus solemus, suscipiamus; ut reverentiam summam adversus sanctam ejus majestatem adhibeamus, eamque venerabundi suspiciamus et admiremur; cum attendere, precesque ac vota nostra ˢexaudire certo statuamus; in eo, qui cœli et terræ præses sit et custos, spem omnem collocemus; simul autem ne quid Deo indignum petamus, sed ut cœlestem Patrem appellantes, animos ᵗhumo excitatos, celsos et erectos, terrena despicientes, supera atque cœlestia cogitantes, habeamus, et ad beatissimam illam Patris nostri fœlicitatem, atque ad cœlum quasi ᵘhæreditatem paternam, perpetuo aspiremus, his verbis admonemur. ^r Psal. l. 4. 5. et lxxxix. 5, 6, 7. Matt. xxiii. 9. ^s Psal. xx. 6. cii. 15, 17. et cxiii. 4, 5. ^t Col. iii. 1. ^u Rom viii. 17. Eph. i. 14, 18. Heb. ix. 15. 1 Pet i. 3, 4.

M. Hoc ergo tam fœlici aditu, introituque precationis nobis jam patefacto, age primum mihi postulatum recita.

A. Precamur primum, ut Dei nomen sanctificetur.

M. Hoc quid sibi vult?

A. Non aliud, quam ut ejus gloria [x]ubique amplificetur.

M. Cur istuc primo postulamus?

A. Quia æquissimum est, ut filii patris, [y]servi domini, conditi conditoris gloriam augeri, maxime expetant atque exoptent.

M. An quicquam Dei gloriæ accrescere aut decedere potest?

A. Dei quidem gloria cum perpetuo fit [z]amplissima, in seipsa neque accessione major, neque decessione minor fieri potest; neque enim accretione, aut diminutione aliqua, ut hæc nostra solent, mutatur. Verum ut Dei nomen illustre [a]notumque mortalibus fiat, ejusque laus et gloria in terris, ita uti par est, celebretur, precamur. Et sicuti immensa Dei potentia, sapientia, justitia, bonitas, divinaque ejus opera omnia gloriam Dei atque amplitudinem revera illustrant, ita optamus ut [b]nobis etiam illustria et gloriosa appareant; quo authoris magnificentia, ut in sese est amplissima, sic et inter nos modis omnibus splendida, atque præclara reluceat, et laudibus atque honoribus privatim publiceque celebretur.

M. Perge adhuc.

A. Precamur præterea ne sanctissimum Dei nomen ab aliis propter nostra vitia [c]male audiat, et quasi ignominia afficiatur; sed ut potius ejus gloria per nostram erga Deum hominesque pietatem ubique gentium amplificetur. Optamus denique, ut aliorum omnium, qui cœlo, terra, marive, vel aliis uspiam locis [d]Deorum appellationes et honores adepti sunt, et in templis, variis figuris, atque cæremoniis coluntur; quibusve pectora sua, quasi delubra quædam, homines errore et vanis opinionibus imbuti consecrarunt; hujusmodi inquam commentitiorum, fictorumque Deorum nominibus funditus extinctis, et oblivione sempiterna obrutis, atque deletis, solum Dei cœlestis Patris divinum nomen atque numen, magnum clarumque sit, illudque mortales omnes ubique terrarum agnoscant, auguste sancteque colant atque venerentur, et puris votis atque animis precentur, invocent, implorent.

M. Recte quidem dixisti; perge quæso.

A. Secundo loco petimus, ut ADVENIAT REGNUM DEI, id est, ne verbi sui divinam [e]veritatem, quam et Evangelium regni Christus nuncupat, obscuram in tenebris sinat jacere, sed eam quotidie magis ac magis in lucem proferat, contra

Satanæ ᶠatque impiorum hominum ingenia, calliditatem, solertiam, contraque fictas omnium insidias, qui veritati tenebras offundere, eamque infirmare, aut mendacio contaminare nituntur; contraque tyrannorum violentiam, ᵍet crudelitatem, qui modis omnibus veritatem extinguere atque opprimere, adeoque funditus delere conantur, præsidio suo tueatur, et defendat; ut nihil esse, quod Divinæ veritatis invictæ virtuti resistere queat, manifestum atque testatum omnibus fiat.

ᶠ Matt. xiii. 25, 38, 39. et xv. 2, 3, 6. Luc. xvi. 8. Joan. iii. 19, 20.
ᵍ Luc. x. 3. et xx. 12, &c. 17, 18. Joan. xvi. 2, 3. et xvii. 14, 15.

M. Perge porro de regno Dei dicere.

A. Precamur ut quamplurimos ʰsacrosancti hujus verbi doctrina institutos, et veritate adductos e tenebris in lucem vocet, eosque in numerum sanctumque cœtum suum, id est, Ecclesiam suam, in qua præcipue regnat, aggregatos, ⁱSpiritu suo assidue gubernet, atque ut milites suos, ᵏcum hostili vitiorum agmine, quasi exercitu Satanæ, summa contentione perpetuo decertantes, auxilio suo juvet; ut in Divina ejus virtute firmitatem et robur tenentes, coercitis affectionibus pravis ˡatque distortis, fractis domitisque cupiditatibus, victis, fusis, fugatis, atque profligatis vitiis omnibus, cœlestem Rempublicam et Regnum augeant atque amplificent, Deo ᵐper Spiritum interim suum in ipsorum animis regnante atque imperante.

ʰ Marc. i. 14, 15. Luc. iv. 18, 19. Joan. xvii. 17, 19, 20, 21. 1 Pet. ii. 9, 10.
ⁱ Joan. xvi. 13.
ᵏ Luc. xxii. 31. Eph. vi. 10, 11, 17, 18. 1 Pet. v. 8, 9.
ˡ Rom. i. 11, 12. et viii. 1, 5, &c. 10, 12, &c.
ᵐ Rom. viii. 9, 10, 11. 1 Joan. iii. 24. et iv. 13.

M. Ista quotidie fieri videmus.

A. Fiunt quidem hæc quotidie, ita ut ⁿDeum piorum atque impiorum rationem habere satis intelligamus, utque Regnum Dei in hoc mundo præclare inchoatum videri possit; optamus tamen, ut assiduis incrementis eo usque augescat, ut reprobis omnibus, ᵒqui Satanæ instinctu contra divinam veritatem contumaciter, atque obstinate resistunt, et repugnant, et vitiis atque flagitiis omnibus sese contaminantes, Dei Regno atque imperio subjicere recusant, sub jugum missis, atque perditis; ᵖSatanæque ipsius tyrannide funditus deleta, hostibusque omnibus confectis, oppressis, atque obtritis, ita ut nihil contra Dei nutum atque ditionem respirare queat, ipse solus ubique gloriose regnet, imperet, triumphet. Et sicuti Deo ᑫper Spiritum suum in nobis regnante, communitas quædam hominibus cum Deo est in hoc mundo; ita fœlicissimi ʳetiam Regni sui gaudium, atque gloriam sempiternis seculorum ætatibus non immutandam in cœlo nobiscum per Christum ut communicet, quo cœlestis Patris nostri non filii modo, ˢsed et hæredes simus, precamur atque optamus; cujus voti Patrem

ⁿ Psal xxxiv. 15, 16. et xxxvii. 9, 10, &c. et lviii. 5, 6, 9, 10.
ᵒ Matt. xiii. 38, 41. et xxii. 6, 7, 13. Luc. xix. 14, 27. et xxii. 45, 46. et xx. 16.
ᵖ Matt. xxv. 41. Rom.xvi. 20. 1 Cor. xv. 24, 25, 26, &c. 54, 55, 56, 57.
ᑫ Rom. viii. 9, 10, 11. 1 Joan. iii. 24. et iv. 13.
ʳ Matt. xiii. 43. 1 Cor. ii. 9. Apoc. xxi. 10, 11, &c.
ˢ Matt. xxv. 34. Rom.viii. 15, 16, 17. Tit. iii. 7.

cœlestem nostrum aliquando tandem nos compotes facturum esse, nihil profecto quicquam ambigimus aut dubitamus.

M. Quid deinde sequitur ?

A. UT DEI VOLUNTAS FIAT ; [t]filiorum enim est, ut ex patrum voluntate vitam suam instituant. Non contra ut parentes ad filiorum voluntatem sese conforment.

M. An ergo homines quicquam invito Deo facere posse existimas ?

A. Multa certe scelera atque flagitia, illius voluntate pergraviter [u]offensa, quotidie a mortalibus fieri, atque admitti perspicuum est, planeque inter omnes constat; ita tamen ut nulla vi, aut necessitate cogi possit Deus, quin quod facere [x]destinavit, id facillime efficiat. Non tantum igitur precamur, ut quod illi decretum fuerit, eveniat; quod quum divina voluntas efficiendi necessitatem secum semper adferat, evenire necesse est; sed quum mentes nostræ [y]cupiditatibus flagrantes, plerumque ferantur ad eas res appetendas, atque peragendas, quæ Deo maxime displicent, petimus, ut omnes omnium voluntates, [z]Sacri Spiritus sui impulsu, ad sensum et voluntatem numinis sui ita commutet atque conformet, ut nihil velimus aut optemus, nedum faciamus unquam, a quo divina ejus voluntas abhorreat ; et quicquid ex ejus voluntate [a]evenire intelligimus, id non æquis solum sed et libentibus animis accipiamus, et patiamur.

M. Quorsum addis, ut IN TERRA FIAT ITIDEM AC IN CŒLO Dei voluntas ?

A. Nimirum ut, ad exemplar cœlestium illorum spirituum quos [b]Angelos vocamus, divinæ Majestati dicto audientes atque obedientes per omnia simus ; et quemadmodum in cœlo nulla est rebellio, ita neque in terra quisquam qui contra sanctam Dei voluntatem resistere et repugnare aut velit, aut audeat, usquam inveniatur. Sed et quum [c]solem ac lunam, reliquasque stellas in cœlo nobis conspicuas, assiduo motu et perenni agitatione ferri, et terram radiis suis ex divina voluntate perpetuo illustrare videmus, obedientiæ exemplum nobis ad imitandum propositum intuemur. Præterea vero quum in Sacris Scripturis voluntatem suam [d]Deus diserte explicuerit, id quod Testamenti [e]nomine illis indito aperte significavit, qui in Scripturarum sententia non manent, a Dei certe voluntate manifeste recedunt.

M. Satis jam a te tractata esse videtur prima pars precationis Dominicæ, quæ tria illa capita ad Dei solam gloriam pertinentia complectitur. Nunc ad secundam partem, quæ utilia et commodis nostris apta proprie spectat, tametsi eadem ad Dei quoque gloriam referantur, opportune pergemus.

A. Secundæ partis primum caput est: PANEM NOSTRUM QUOTIDIANUM DA NOBIS HODIE.

M. Quid panis quotidiani nomine significas?

A. Non ea modo, [f]quæ victum cultumque suppeditent, verum etiam res alias omnes in universum, quæ ad vitam tuendam, conservandam, et in tranquillitate, ac sine metu degendam sunt necessariæ.

[f] Psal. civ. 15, 27, &c. et cv. toto. et cxliv. 10, 11, 12, &c. et cxlv. 14, 15, 16, &c.

M. Ecquid est aliud, de quo hæc vox Panis nos admoneat?

A. [g]Ne res ad epulandum exquisitissimas, neve vestes pretiosas, aut magnificam supellectilem ad voluptatem studiose conquiramus, et comparemus; sed ut delicias atque luxum despicientibus nobis, et parvo contentis, tenuis salubrisque victus, et vestitus moderatus, atque necessarius satisfaciat.

[g] Psal. lxxviii. 18, 19, 20, 29, 30. et cvi. 14. Matt. vi. 25. Luc. xvi. 19. 1 Tim. v. 8, 9.

M. Quomodo vero panem appellas tuum, quem a Deo dari postulas?

A. Dei [h]munere noster fit, quum nobis ad quotidianos usus, tametsi jure minime debeatur, ab ipso benigne donetur.

[h] Psal. cxv. 16. Matt. vii. 7, 8. 1 Cor. iv. 7. Jacob. i. 17.

M. Num qua alia de causa tuum panem vocas?

A. Hoc verbo admonemur victum [i]labore nostro, aut legitima ratione parandum esse, ut eo contenti, de rebus alienis quicquam per avaritiam aut fraudem ne appetamus unquam.

[i] Gen. iii. 19. Eph. iv. 28. 2 Thess. iii. 8, 10, 12.

M. Quum nos Deus labore nostro victum jubeat quærere, cur ab eo panem postulas?

A. Unus est Deus, qui terris [j]fœcunditatem dat, qui uberes, fructuumque fertiles agros efficit; frustra ergo omnem nos vitæ cursum in labore corporis, atque animi contentione confecturos esse, atque consumpturos certum est, [k]nisi Deus conatus nostros velit prosperare. Par est ergo, ut a Deo Opt. Max. qui juxta Davidis oraculum, omnia ut condidit, [l]ita pascit etiam atque tuetur, ad victum vitamque necessaria, precibus quotidie exposcamus; eaque quasi dante porrigenteque Deo, et de illius manu in manus nostras tradita, gratis animis accipiamus.

[j] Psal. xxiv. 1. et lxv. 9. et lxviii. 9. et civ. 13. et lxxxv. 12. et cxlvii. 8, &c.

[k] Psal. cxxvii. 1, 2. 1 Cor. iii. 7.

[l] Psal. civ. et cxxxvi. 25. et cxlv. 15. et cxlvii. &c.

M. An divitibus etiam, qui rebus omnibus circumfluunt atque abundant, panem a Deo in diem petendum esse existimas?

A. Frustra ^mcongeremus, recondemusque copias, quæ vel ambitioni nostræ, vel quotidianis sumptibus, vel necessario usui, in multos etiam annos suppetent, nisi illarum usum salutarem nobis Deus ad vitam sua gratia effecerit. Imo frustra ⁿin stomachum cibum ingerimus, nisi divina virtus, qua potius quam ciborum nutrimentis alimur et sustentamur, et alendi vim cibis, et stomacho concoquendi facultatem tribuerit. Ob quam causam cœnati etiam diurnum cibum, quem jam accepimus, a Deo tamen nobis præberi, id est, vitalem atque salutarem fieri postulamus.

M. Quotidianum, et Hodie, quorsum adduntur?

A. Ut solicitudinum ^ocrastinarum aculeos, ne dies noctesque illis frustra excruciemur, ex animis nostris evellat; utque nimiarum opum inexplebili cupiditate, et quasi rabida fame, a mentibus nostris ^pdepulsa, officium nostrum sedulo facientes, a benignissimo Patre quotidie petamus, quod ille paratus est quotidie impartiri.

M. Perge ad cætera.

A. Sequitur quinta petitio, qua Patrem precamur, UT DELICTIS NOSTRIS IGNOSCAT.

M. Quem tandem ista venia fructum consequemur?

A. Amplissimum; nam quum Deus supplicum ^qmiseretur, eodem apud eum loco, atque in ea cum ipso gratia erimus, ac si innocentes, sancti, et in omnibus vitæ partibus integri essemus.

M. An hæc veniæ petitio omnibus est necessaria?

A. Maxime; quum nemo vivat mortalium qui in officio frequenter ^rnon labatur, et a quo non sit in Deum sæpe ac graviter peccatum; adeoque testimonium in nos dicente ^sScriptura, qui in uno aliquo offenderit, omnium manifestus tenetur; et qui de uno peccato se Deo ut purget contendit, mille facinorum reus arguetur. Ut ergo erratorum veniam impetremus, ^tuna spes est reliqua, unicum omnibus perfugium, Dei per Christum bonitas et misericordia. Qui vero se peccasse ^unon fatentur, neque delictorum veniam petunt, sed ^xcum Pharisæo illo, innocentia atque justitia sua apud Deum, vel contra Deum potius gloriantur, ii a societate fidelium, quibus hæc precandi formula, quam sequantur, est constituta, et a portu atque perfugio salutis sese excludunt. Hoc est enim quod ^yChristus dicit, se non ut justos, sed peccatores ad pœnitentiam vocaret, in hunc mundum venisse.

M. Gratuitone Deum peccatis nostris ignoscere statuis?

A. ^zOmnino. Alioqui non remissio, sed compensatio quædam videri posset; ad compensandum vero unum vel minimum vitium, facultate ulla nostra sufficere nullo modo possumus. ^aNon ergo præteritam culpam pariter, atque Dei pacem operibus nostris, quasi pretio quodam redimere, et paria paribus, quod aiunt, referre possumus; sed errati pariter atque supplicii ^bveniam a Deo per solum Christum impetrabilem precibus omnibus petere, atque ut ignoscat suppliciter postulare debemus.

z Rom. iii. 24, 25. et xi. 5, 6.
a 2 Tim. i. 9, 10. Tit. iii. 5.
b Psal. xxxii. 5,6. 1 Joan. l. 9. et ii. 1.

M. Verum ista, atque ea quæ mox nobis statuitur conditio, vix apte satis inter se cohærere videntur. Petimus enim, ut Deus ita nobis ignoscat, ut nos debitoribus nostris condonamus.

A. ^cÆquissima quidem conditione veniam nobis Deus offert; quæ tamen, in eam partem accipienda non est, quasi hominibus ignoscendo, veniam ita promereamur, ut ea quasi gratia quædam nobis a Deo referatur. ^dGratuita enim tum Divina remissio non foret, neque solus Christus, sicuti Scripturæ docent, et nos ante explicuimus, peccati pœnas nobis debitas, in cruce persolvisset. Verum, nisi alii nos ad sibi condonandum faciles habeant, atque ita clementiam et lenitatem Dei patris ^eimitando, ejus nos filios esse ostendamus, clare denuntiat, ut nihil a se aliud, quam summam animadversionis severitatem expectemus. Nostram ergo placabilitatem, non ut causam promerendæ a Deo veniæ proposuit, sed ut pignori foret, ad animos nostros certa Divinæ clementiæ fiducia confirmandos.

c Matt. xviii. 32, 33 Luc. vi. 36, 37, 38.
d Rom. iii.24, 25. et xi. 5, 6. Gal. v. 4.
e Matt. v. 7. Luc. vi. 36. Jacob. ii. 13.

M. Nullusne ergo veniæ locus apud Deum iis relinquitur, qui ad ignoscendum, et ad offensiones deponendas implacabiles sese, inexpiabilesque aliis præbent?

A. Nullus omnino; id quod cum ^faliis multis sacræ Scripturæ locis testatum est atque manifestum, tum parabola illa Evangelica de servo, qui cum Domino suo decies mille talenta deberet, ipse interim conservo debitori, centum quos illi crediderat denarios, condonare recusavit, præclare nos admonet; ^gad eandem enim severitatis regulam, atque idem exemplum, judicium sine misericordia in illum constituetur, qui ad lenitatem atque misericordiam erga alios mentem suam revocare nescit.

f Matt. vi. 14, 15. et xviii. 24, 28, 29, 33, 34.
g Matt. vii. 2, 3. Luc. vi. 37, 38. Jacob. ii. 13.

M. Litesne in foro, de jure et injuria, hic damnari existimas?

A. Animum [h]vindicem atque ultorem injuriarum verbum Dei certe condemnat; videant ergo litigatores, qua mente litem cuiquam intendant. [i]Leges tamen et Instituta juris publici; et illorum usus legitimus, id est, ad justitiæ et charitatis normam directus, Evangelio Christi minime aut tolluntur, aut damnantur. In hac vero precationis Dominicæ parte, ad Christianæ lenitatis, et dilectionis regulam mentes nostræ exiguntur, [k]ne scilicet a malo vinci, id est, aliorum culpa eo nos adduci sinamus, ut malum malo rependere velimus, sed ut bono malum vincamus potius; hoc est, maleficia benefactis pensemus, benevolentiamque erga inimicos atque hostes etiam immanes, et capitales habeamus atque conservemus.

M. Perge porro ad sextam petitionem.

A. Ea precamur, NE NOS INDUCAT IN TENTATIONEM, SED A MALO LIBERET. Nam ut ante præteritorum veniam petimus, ita nunc ne [l]amplius peccemus, oramus. Mille formidines opponuntur, [m]mille intenduntur pericula, mille nobis insidiæ comparantur, atque collocantur. Nos vero natura [n]imbecilles, ad præcavendum incauti, ad resistendum ita infirmi sumus, ut minimis momentis, atque occasionibus levissimis in fraudem impellamur, feramurque præcipites.

M. Perge.

A. Quum ergo et ab hominibus [o]astutis atque violentis, et a concupiscentia [p]atque appetitione propria, a carnis, mundi hujus, atque corruptelarum omnium illecebris; super omnia vero, a fallaci illo, vafro, et veteratore [q]serpente, id est Diabolo, qui, rabidi [r]leonis instar, quærens quem devoret, cum aliis infinitis malitiosis [s]spiritibus mille nocendi artibus ad perniciem instructis, perpetuo capitibus nostris imminet, vehementissime assidueque oppugnemur, adeoque, qua sumus ipsi infirmitate, statim concideremus, planeque de nobis actum foret; confugientes ad fidem [t]Opt. Max. patris, eum oramus ne nos in his difficultatibus et periculis deserat atque destituat, sed ut sua nos virtute [u]ita armet, ut contra carnis nostræ cupiditates, hujus mundi illecebras, et Satanæ vim atque impetum non resistere modo et repugnare, sed illos vincere etiam atque superare valeamus; itaque animas nostras a [x]vitiis atque flagitiis avocet, ne in illa delabamur, aut in officio labamur unquam, sed in optimi pariter atque potentissimi patris [y]tutela, et præsidio, tuto et sine metu perpetuo lateamus.

M. Satanæ igitur astutiam atque impetum, mundi hujus

insidias et præstigias, ac carnis nostræ corruptelas atque illecebras, quibus animi nostri ad peccatum solicitantur, atque irretiti tenentur, tentationis nomine significas?

A. Sane, Præceptor.

M. Quum tamen tentationum quasi laqueis homines captare atque implicare ᶻSatanæ proprium sit, cur, ne Deus te in tentationem inducat, precaris? <small>ᶻ Act. v. 3. 1 Cor. vii. 5.</small>

A. Deus ut ᵃsuos, ne Satanæ fraudibus illaqueati, in vitia atque flagitia delabantur, tutatur et conservat; ita impiis opem atque auxilium suum ᵇsubducit atque subtrahit; quo destituti, cupiditate cœci, ac præcipites omnibus insidiis circumveniuntur, et in omne feruntur nefas; tandemque consuetudine scelerum, quasi obducto ᶜcallo, animi illis obdurescunt, atque ita Satanæ tyranno mancipati, et in servitutem addicti, in perniciem atque interitum sempiternum ruunt. <small>ᵃ Luc. xxii. 31, 32. 1 Cor. xv. 10. 2 Cor. xii. 9. Eph. vi. 10, 11. 2 Tim. iv. 17, 18. ᵇ 1 Reg. xvi. 14. Gal. v. 4. 1 Pet. v. 5. Jud. 18, 19. ᶜ Esai. vi. 10. 2 Cor. iv. 3, 4. Eph. iv. 18, 19.</small>

M. Superest adhuc Dominicæ precationis appendix quædam.

A. QUONIAM TUUM EST REGNUM, ET POTENTIA, ET GLORIA IN SECULA. AMEN.

M. Cur Christus hanc conclusionem addi voluit?

A. Primum, ut certam nobis fiduciam impetrandi, quæ antea postulavimus omnia, in ejus bonitate, et potentia, ᵈnon in ullis nostris, aut aliorum meritis sitam esse intelligeremus. Nihil enim esse, quod is qui ᵉorbem terrarum regit et gubernat, in cujus ditione atque potestate sunt universa, qui amplissima atque immortali gloria clarissimus super alios omnes infinite excellit, ᶠpetentibus nobis dare vel non possit, vel nolit, modo recte, et certa fide rogetur, his verbis declaratur; ut nulla jam in animis nostris dubitatio relinquatur amplius; id quod etiam addita ad precationis finem vox ᵍAMEN declarat atque confirmat. Præterea vero, quum solus Deus quæcunque decrevit, pro sua voluntate ʰlargiri possit, ab uno illo universa hæc et peti debere, et impetrari posse clarissime apparet; ⁱnullumque periculum, aut malum nostrum usque adeo magnum esse, quod is incredibili potentia, sapientia, et bonitate sua vincere, et a nobis depellere, atque ad salutem etiam convertere facillime non possit. <small>ᵈ Psal. iii. 3, 8. Ose. xiii. 9. Joan. x. 28. ᵉ Psal. xxii. 28. et xxiv. 1, &c. 7, &c. et xxix. 1, 2, &c. et xlvii. toto. et xcv. 3, 4, &c. 1 Tim. vi. 15, 16. ᶠ Matt. vii. 11. et xxi. 22. Jacob. i. 6. ᵍ 2 Cor. i. 20. Psal. cxv. 3. ʰ 2 Cor. ix. 8. Eph. iii. 20. 1 Tim. vi. 15. ⁱ 2 Cor. i. 8, 9, 10. 2 Tim. iv. 17. Jud. 24.</small>

M. Gloriæ Divinæ qua de causa in extrema parte fit mentio?

A. Ut omnes precationes nostras Dei laudibus claudere instituamur; is enim est ᵏfinis ad quem referenda sunt universa; is exitus, ad quem ut non precationes solum, sed <small>ᵏ 1 Cor. x. 31. Eph. iii. 20, 21. Phil. i. 11. 1 Tim. i. 17. Jud. 25.</small>

et actiones nostræ, cogitationesque omnes perveniant, nobis hominibus Christianis semper propositus esse debet, ut Dei gloria quam maxime amplificetur, atque illustris reddatur; utcunque interim inter mortales, quorum animis Christiana religio non est infixa, vix inveniatur, qui laboribus susceptis, periculisque aditis, [1]non quasi mercedem rerum gestarum suarumque virtutum desideret gloriam; qua tamen, ut non vera solidaque gloria, sed inani venditatione atque ostentatione, vehementer suis graviterque interdicit Dominus.

[1] Matt. vi. 1, 2, 3, 4, 5, 6, &c. Gal. v. 26. Phil. ii. 3. et iii. 19.

M. Precationis ergo tractatui quædam de Dei laudibus, et gratiarum actione apte atque opportune subjungemus?

A. [m]Aptissime sane; neque enim in extremo tantum precationis Dominicæ fine, gloria Dei memoratur, sed ipsum etiam principium ejus a gloria laudibusque divinis ducitur. Quum enim optamus, ut Dei nomen sanctificetur, quid optamus aliud, quam ut ipsi ex omnibus ejus operibus sua constet gloria? Videlicet, ut peccatoribus condonans, [n]misericors; in impios [o]animadvertens, justus; præstans quod promisit, [p]verax; indignos beneficiis quotidianis cumulans, [q]optimus benignissimusque censeatur; ut quicquid [r]operum ejus vel cernimus, vel intelligimus, eo ad ejus gloriam laudibus amplificandam excitemur. Ita gloriam suam, cum sui invocatione Deus voluit esse conjunctissimam. Par enim est, ut sicuti [s]difficultatibus affecti atque afflicti, ad Dei opem atque misericordiam supplices confugimus, ita malorum atque molestiarum liberationem nos per eum consequi, eumque bonorum omnium unicum nobis authorem esse ingenue agnoscamus. Nam a quo veniam bonaque omnia precamur, danti illi gratiam non habere atque agere, summa profecto esset ingratitudo. [t]Meritam ergo Deo immortali gratiam memori mente, et justis honoribus persolvere perpetuo debemus.

[m] Rom. i. 8, 10. 2 Cor. i. 11. Eph. i. 15. Phil. i. 3, 4.

[n] Psal. li. 1.

[o] Rom. i. 18.
[p] Rom. iii. 3, 4.
[q] Psal. lxv. 9, &c. et lxviii. 5, &c.
[r] Psal. xix. 1, 2.

[s] Psal. xxxiv. 1, 2. et l. 14, 15, 23. 1 Thess. i. 2. et v. 18. 2 Thess. i. 3.

[t] Psal. xcii. 1. et xciii. et ciii. totis.

M. Perge.

A. Præterea vero Divinam bonitatem, justitiam, sapientiam, potentiam [u]laudibus prosequi et celebrare, illique nostro, ac totius humani generis nomine, grates agere, est cultus Dei pars, ad ejus majestatem æque ac invocatio proprie pertinens; qua nisi eum rite colamus, non solum indigni ejus [v]tot tantisque beneficiis, ut ingrati, sed et æternis suppliciis, ut in Deum impii, dignissimi profecto erimus.

[u] Psal. xxix. 1, 2. et l. 14, 15, 23. Rom. xv. 6.

[v] Luc. xvii. 18. Joan. v. 44. Rom. i. 21, 24. 1 Pet. iv. 11.

M. Quum ab hominibus etiam beneficia accipiamus, an non et illis gratias agere fas erit?

A. Quæcunque nobis beneficia homines deferunt, ˣea
Deo accepta referre debemus; quod unus ille revera
hominum ea ministerio largiatur. Ob quam etiam causam,
tametsi homines benefici et liberales esse non debent, ut
gratiam exigant, sed ut ʸDei gloriam illustrent, illis tamen,
qui ᶻbenignitate adducti, per beneficium et gratiam aliquid
nobis concedant, gratias agere quid ni licebit, quum et ipsa
id postulet ᵃæquitas, et ita humanitatis Lege astringamur?
Sed et Deus ipse, hac nos illis ratione devinciens, nos id
ipsum vult agnoscere.

M. Gratum ergo animum etiam in homines probas?

A. Maxime; quum gratitudo, ut ita loquar, erga
homines nostra, ad Deum ipsum redeat, quod a liberalitatis
Divinæ fonte, quasi quadam rivulorum deductione, ᵇbona sua
per manus hominum Deus in nos derivet. Itaque ni hominibus nos gratos præbeamus, in ipsum etiam Deum ingrati
erimus. Tantum hoc curemus, ut ad Deum ipsum, tanquam
ad bonorum omnium authorem atque fontem unicum, ᶜsolida
sua gloria redeat, atque redundet.

M. Ecqua est norma atque præscriptio, quam, dum Deum
gloria et honore afficimus, aut illi grates agimus, certo sequi
possumus?

A. Innumeræ Dei laudes passim in ejus verbo descriptæ
extant, a quarum regula si non aberrabimus, habebimus quod
in sua Deo gloria et honore deferendo, atque in gratiarum
actione perpetuo sequamur. In summa vero, quum Deum
ᵈnon Dominum solum, sed patrem etiam ac servatorem nostrum
esse, nosque vicissim ejus esse filios, atque servos Scripturæ
Sacræ doceant, æquissimum est, ᵉvitam nos omnem amplificandæ illius gloriæ addicere, debitum ipsi honorem reddere,
eum colere, precari, venerari, gratias illi perpetuo et habere
et agere; quum in hunc ᶠfinem ab eo conditi simus, et in hoc
mundo collocati, ut immortalis ipsius gloria splendorem inter
mortales maximum obtinere, et ad summam amplitudinem
pervenire posset.

QUARTA PARS, DE SACRAMENTIS.

M. Absoluta jam Legis Divinæ, Symbolique, id est,
confessionis Christianæ, precationis item, et gratiarum actionis
tractatione, superest jam, ut de Sacramentis, mysteriisque

Divinis, quæ precationem et gratiarum actionem semper conjunctam habent, ultimo loco dicatur. Dic igitur mihi, quid est Sacramentum?

A. ^gEst externa Divinæ erga nos per Christum benevolentiæ beneficentiæque testificatio, signo aspectabili arcanam, spiritualemque gratiam repræsentans, qua ^hDei promissiones de remissione peccatorum, et æterna salute per Christum data, quasi consignantur, et earum veritas in cordibus nostris certius confirmatur.

M. Sacramentum quot partibus constat?

A. Duabus; externo ⁱelemento, seu signo aspectabili, et invisibili gratia.

M. Cur Deus ita externis signis nos uti voluit?

A. Nos quidem mente, atque intelligentia adeo cœlesti Divinaque præditi non sumus, ut nobis Angelorum instar Divinæ gratiæ pure per se appareant; hac ergo ratione infirmitati nostræ consuluit Deus, ut, qui terreni sumus atque cœci, in externis elementis et figuris, quasi speculis quibusdam, cœlestes gratias, quas alioqui non cerneremus, intueremur; et id nostra maxime refert, ut sensibus etiam nostris Dei promissiones ingerantur, quo mentibus nostris sine ulla dubitatione confirmentur.

M. At promissionibus Divinis certam fidem non adjungere, nisi ejusmodi subsidiis fulciamur, an non infidelitatis in nobis manifestum est argumentum?

A. ^kExigua quidem atque imperfecta Fide, quoad in hoc mundo versamur, præditi sumus, neque tamen fideles esse desinimus; reliquiæ enim diffidentiæ, quæ semper in carne nostra hærent, imbecillitatem Fidei indicant, ^lsed eam tamen non prorsus extinguunt. Has quum omnino excutere non possimus, est tamen continuo profectu, usque ad vitæ finem, ad Fidei ^mperfectionem contendendum, in quo nos conatu Sacramentorum usus plurimum sublevat.

M. Ecqua alia causa subest, quare Dominus externorum etiam signorum usum adhiberi voluerit?

A. Dominus mysteria sua in hunc præterea usum instituit, ut ⁿprofessionis nostræ notæ, atque indicia quædam essent, quibus de Fide nostra quasi testimonium coram hominibus diceremus, patefaceremusque nos cum aliis piis Divinorum beneficiorum participes esse, et unum cum illis Religionis quasi concentum, atque consensum habere, Christianique °nominis, atque appellationis discipulorum Christi nos minime pudere palam testificaremur.

M. Quid ergo de illis judicas, qui mysteriis Divinis tanquam minus necessariis, carere se posse censent?

A. Primum, huic in Deum Patrem, ac Servatorem nostrum Jesum Christum, atque ejus etiam Ecclesiam officio tam pio atque debito deesse sine ᵖsummo scelere non possunt. Nam quid hoc aliud esset, quam Christum oblique abnegare? Et qui se Christianum ᑫprofiteri non dignatur, indignus est, qui in Christianorum numero habeatur. Deinde, si qui Sacramentorum usum, ac si opus iis ʳnon haberent, aspernarentur, non modo arrogantiæ summæ, sed et impietatis etiam in Deum merito damnari debere existimo; quum non suæ tantum infirmitatis subsidia, sed et Deum ipsorum authorem contemnant, ipsius ˢgratiam respuant, et Spiritum, quantum in ipsis est, extinguant.

M. De visibilibus quidem signis, et externo Sacramentorum usu rationem intelligis; sed quod secundo loco vim atque efficaciam consignandi confirmandique in cordibus nostris promissiones divinas Sacramentis tribuis, videris officia Spiritus Sancti propria illis assignare.

A. ᵗMentes quidem atque animos humanos illustrare, atque illuminare, conscientias item tranquillas atque securas reddere, ut revera sunt, ita et censeri debent solius Spiritus Dei proprium opus, illique accepta referri, ne laus hæc alio transferatur. Verum hoc nihil obstat, quin mysteriis suis secundas partes in animis atque conscientiis nostris tranquillandis atque stabiliendis Deus tribuat; sed ita tamen, ut Spiritus sui virtuti nihil detrahatur. Quare statuamus oportet, externum elementum neque ᵘex seipso, neque in seipso vim atque efficacitatem Sacramenti inclusam habere, sed totam a Spiritu Dei, ut e fonte manare, et per Divina mysteria, quæ in hunc usum a Domino sunt instituta, ad nos derivari.

M. Quot in Ecclesia sua Sacramenta instituit Dominus?

A. Duo.

M. Quæ?

A. ˣBaptismum, et sacram Cœnam; quorum communis est inter omnes fideles usus. Altero enim renascimur, altero sustentamur ad vitam æternam.

M. De Baptismo ergo primum dic quid censeas.

A. Quum natura ^yFilii iræ, id est, alieni ab Ecclesia, quæ Dei familia est, simus, baptismus veluti ^zaditus quidam nobis est, per quem in eam admittimur; unde et testimonium etiam amplissimum accipimus, ^ain numero domesticorum, adeoque Filiorum Dei nos jam esse; imo in Christi ^bcorpus quasi cooptari, atque inseri, ejusque membra fieri, et in unum cum ipso corpus coalescere.

M. Sacramentum antea dicebas duabus constare partibus, signo externo, et arcana gratia. Quod est in Baptismo signum externum?

A. ^cAqua, in quam baptizatus intingitur, vel ea aspergitur IN NOMINE PATRIS, ET FILII, ET SPIRITUS SANCTI.

M. Quæ est arcana et spiritualis gratia?

A. Ea duplex est; remissio ^dvidelicet peccatorum, et regeneratio, quæ utraque in externo illo signo, solidam et expressam effigiem suam tenent.

M. Quomodo?

A. Primum, quemadmodum sordes corporis aqua, ita animæ ^emaculæ per remissionem peccatorum eluuntur; ^fdeinde regenerationis initium, id est naturæ nostræ mortificatio, vel immersione in aquam, vel ejus aspersione exprimitur. Postremo vero, quum ab aqua, quam ad momentum subimus, statim emergimus, nova vita, quæ est regeneratonis nostræ pars altera, atque finis repræsentatur.

M. Videris aquam effigiem tantum quandam rerum Divinarum efficere.

A. ^gEffigies quidem est sed minime inanis, aut fallax; ut cui rerum ipsarum veritas adjuncta sit atque annexa. Nam sicuti Deus peccatorum condonationem, et vitæ novitatem nobis vere in baptismo offert, ita a nobis certo recipiuntur. ^hAbsit enim ut Deum vanis nos imaginibus ludere atque frustrari putemus.

M. Non ergo remissionem peccatorum externa aquæ lavatione aut aspersione consequimur?

A. Minime: Nam solus Christus ⁱsanguine suo animarum nostrarum maculas luit atque eluit. Hunc ergo honorem externo elemento tribuere nefas est. Verum Spiritus Sanctus ^kconscientias nostras sacro illo sanguine quasi aspergens, abstersis omnibus peccati sordibus, puros nos coram Deo reddit. Hujus vero peccatorum nostrorum expiationis obsignationem atque pignus in Sacramento habemus.

M. Regenerationem vero unde habemus?

A. Non aliunde quam a morte et resurrectione Christi; nam per mortis suæ vim vetus homo noster quodammodo crucifigitur et mortificatur, et naturæ nostræ vitiositas quasi sepelitur, ne amplius in nobis vivat et vigeat. Resurrectionis vero suæ beneficio nobis largitur, ut in novam vitam ad obediendum Dei justitiæ reformemur.

[1] Rom. vi. 3, &c. toto.

M. An gratiam hanc omnes communiter et promiscue consequuntur?

A. [m]Soli fideles hunc fructum percipiunt: increduli vero oblatas illic a Deo promissiones respuendo, aditum sibi præcludentes, inanes abeunt, non tamen ideo efficiunt, ut suam Sacramenta vim et naturam amittant.

[m] Marc. xvi. 16. Joan. i. 12. et iii. 16, 18.

M. Rectus ergo baptismi usus quibus in rebus sit situs, breviter edissere.

A. In Fide et Pœnitentia. [n]Primum enim Christi nos sanguine a cunctis purgatos sordibus Deo gratos esse, spiritumque ejus in nobis habitare certa fiducia cum animis nostris statutum habere oportet. Deinde in carne nostra [o]mortificanda, obediendoque justitiæ Divinæ, assidue omni ope et opera est enitendum, et pia vita apud omnes declarandum nos in Baptismo Christum ipsum quasi [p]induisse, et ejus spiritu donatos esse.

[n] Matt. xxvi. 28. Marc. xvi. 16. Rom. viii. 9, 11, 15, 16, 17. Eph. i. 7. et v. 25, 26. Col. i. 14, 20.
[o] Rom. vi. 3, &c. 6, 11, &c. 13, 19. et viii. 13. Eph. iv. 24. Col. iii. 5.
[p] Rom. xiii. 14. Gal. iii. 26, 27.

M. Quum infantes hæc quæ commemoras hactenus per ætatem præstare non possint, qui fit ut illi baptizentur?

A. Ut Fides et Pœnitentia baptismo præcedant, tantum in adultis, [q]qui per ætatem sunt utriusque capaces, exigitur; infantibus vero promissio [r]Ecclesiæ facta per Christum, in cujus Fide baptizantur, in præsens satis erit, deinde postquam adoleverint, Baptismi sui veritatem ipsos agnoscere, ejusque vim in animis eorum vigere, atque ipsorum vita et moribus repræsentari omnino oportet.

[q] Marc. xvi. 16. Joan. iii. 16, 18.
[r] Rom. iii. 3. et iv. 21, 22, 24. Heb. x. 23.
[s] Matt. xxviii. 19.

M. Unde nobis constabit, infantes a baptismo arcendos non esse?

A. Quum Deus, [t]qui nunquam a veritate deflectit, neque a recta via usquam declinat, infantes [u]in Ecclesia Judaica a Circumcisione non excluserit, neque nostri infantes a Baptismo repellendi sunt.

[t] Rom. iii. 4. et iv. 21.
Heb. x. 23.
[u] Gen. xvii. 10, 11, 12, &c. Luc. i. 59. et ii. 21. Act. vii. 8. Phil. iii. 5.

M. Itane similia ista, eandemque utrisque causam atque rationem subesse putas?

A. Omnino. Nam Circumcisionem Pœnitentiæ signum fuisse, ut Moses [x]et Prophetæ omnes testantur, ita divus

[x] Deut. x. 16. et xxx. 6. Jer. iv. 4.

Paulus eam Fidei Sacramentum esse docet. Nihilo minus tamen pueri ʸJudaici, Fidei adhuc et Pœnitentiæ per ætatem minime capaces, circumcidebantur; quo aspectabili signo Deus patrem se parvulorum, et seminis populi sui esse, in veteri Testamento ostendebat. Quum vero constet Dei gratiam ᶻet abundantius in nos effusam, et luculentius declaratam in Evangelio per Christum esse, quam olim in veteri Testamento per Mosen fuerat, indignum foret, si ea vel obscurior, vel aliqua ex parte imminuta videretur.

ʸ Rom. ii.28, 29. et iv. 11. Gen. xvii. 7, 10, 11, 12, &c.

ᶻ Act. ii. 17, 18. et x. 4, 5. 2 Cor. iii. 6, 7, 8, 9, &c. Gal. iii. 23, 24. Tit. iii. 5, 6.

M. Perge adhuc.

A. Cum infantes nostros vim, ᵃet quasi substantiam Baptismi communem nobiscum habere certum sit, illis injuria fieret, si signum, quod veritate est inferius, ipsis negaretur; eoque, quod ad testandam Dei misericordiam, confirmandasque ejus promissiones plurimum valet, sublato, eximia consolatione, qua veteres fruebantur, Christiani fraudarentur; duriusque cum nostris parvulis in novo Testamento sub Christo ageretur, quam in veteri cum Judæorum infantibus sub Mose actum fuerat. Itaque æquissimum est, ut parvulis nostris, ᵇDivinæ gratiæ atque salutis fidelium semini promissæ hæredes se esse, Baptismo, impresso quasi sigillo testatum fiat.

ᵃ Matt. xviii. 3, 4, 10. et xix. 14. Luc. xviii. 15, 16, 17. Rom. iv. 16, 23, 24. 1 Pet. ii. 2.

ᵇ Rom. iv. 16, 23, 24.

M. Ecquid est amplius, quod de hac re velis dicere?

A. ᶜQuum Christus Dominus infantes ad se vocet, edicat etiam ne quis eos accessu prohibeat, ad se venientes amplectatur, ad eos regnum cœleste pertinere testetur; quos cœlesti palatio Deus dignatur, eos ab hominibus primo aditu vestibuloque prohiberi, et a Christiana Repub. quodammodo excludi, summa videtur esse iniquitas.

ᶜ Matt. xviii. 3, 4, 10. et xix. 14. Marc. x. 13, 14, 15.

M. Ita est; verum quum antea parvulos postquam adoleverint, Baptismi sui veritatem agnoscere debere dixeris, de eo te velim paulo explicatius nunc dicere.

A. Parentes et Pædagogi pueros olim cum primum per ætatem sapere, et intelligere cœpissent, primis Christianæ religionis rudimentis diligenter instituebant, ut pietatem una pene cum lacte nutricis imbiberent, et a primis statim cunis, virtutis incunabulis ad vitam illam beatam alerentur. Quem etiam ad usum breves libri, quos Catechismos nostri appellant, conscribebantur; in quibus eadem fere ista, de quibus nunc inter nos agitur, aut istis certe similia tractabantur. Postquam vero primis nostræ pietatis elementis pueri satis jam initiati videbantur, eos Episcopo sistebant atque offerebant.

M. Quorsum nam istuc?

A. Ut idem hoc ipsum pueri post Baptismum præstarent, quod adulti olim, qui et Catechumeni appellabantur, ante Baptismum, vel in ipso potius Baptismo præstare sunt soliti. Episcopus enim rationem Religionis a pueris exquirebat; pueri Fidei suæ rationem Episcopo reddebant; quos vero in Religionis scientia progressus jam satis magnos fecisse Episcopus putabat, eos approbabat; et imposita illis manu, bene precatus dimittebat. Hanc Episcopi approbationem benedictionemque, nostri Confirmationem appellant.

M. At alia nuper usitata erat Confirmationis ratio.

A. In locum hujus utilissimæ et antiquissimæ Confirmationis suum commentum supposuerant, ut Episcopi videlicet non de pueris, an religionis præceptis imbuti essent, cognoscerent, sed ut infantes adhuc fari nescios, nedum ad rationem Fidei reddendum idoneos, oleo ungerent; additis aliis etiam cæremoniis sacræ Scripturæ et veteri Ecclesiæ incognitis. Hoc suum inventum Sacramentum esse voluerunt, et dignitate cum Baptismo tantum non exæquabant, prætulerunt etiam illi eorum aliqui. Omnino voluerunt Confirmationem hanc suam Baptismi quasi supplementum quoddam esse, ut ea absolveretur, atque ad exitum perduceretur; quasi alioqui imperfectus esset Baptismus, puerique, qui Christum cum suis donis in Baptismo jam induissent, sine ea semichristiani essent; qua injuria Divino Sacramento, Deoque adeo ipsi, ac Christo servatori sacri Baptismi authori, nulla major fieri unquam potuit.

M. Optandum ergo, ut vetus ille inquirendi in pueros mos atque ratio revocaretur.

A. Maxime; sic enim Parentes cogerentur ad satisfaciendum suo in liberis pie instituendis officio, quod hodie plerique plane prætermittunt atque repudiant; quas officii sui partes si vel Parentes, vel Præceptores hodie susciperent, præstarent atque persolverent, mirus esset Religionis Fideique Christianæ consensus atque concentus, qui nunc miserandum in modum divulsus est; certe non sic aut ignorantiæ tenebris offusa, obductaque jacerent, aut variarum dissidentiumque opinionum dissentionibus disturbarentur, dissolverentur, atque dissiparentur universa, ita ut hodie fieri videmus; de quo miserabili casu, omnibus bonis maxime dolendum est.

M. Verissimum quidem est, quod dicis. Jam, quæ Cœnæ Dominicæ sit ratio, edissere.

Cœna Dominica.

^d 1 Cor. xi. 23, 24, &c.
Matt. xxvi. 26. Marc. xiv. 22, &c.
Luc. xxii. 19, &c.

A. Eadem nimirum, ^dquam Christus Dominus instituit; qui ea, qua traditus est nocte, ACCEPIT PANEM, ET POSTQUAM GRATIAS EGISSET, FREGIT, ET DEDIT DISCIPULIS SUIS, DICENS; ACCIPITE, ET EDITE; HOC EST CORPUS MEUM, QUOD PRO VOBIS FRANGITUR; HOC FACITE IN MEI COMMEMORATIONEM. AD EUNDEM MODUM ET POCULUM, PERACTA CŒNA, ACCEPIT, ET QUUM GRATIAS EGISSET, DEDIT EIS DICENS; BIBITE EX HOC OMNES; HIC EST ENIM SANGUIS MEUS NOVI TESTAMENTI, QUI PRO VOBIS, ET PRO MULTIS EFFUNDITUR IN REMISSIONEM PECCATORUM: HOC FACITE, QUOTIESCUNQUE BIBERITIS, IN MEI COMMEMORATIONEM. QUOTIESCUNQUE ENIM COMEDERITIS HUNC PANEM, ET DE POCULO BIBERITIS, MORTEM DOMINI ANNUNCIABITIS, DONEC VENERIT. Hæc est Cœnæ Dominicæ forma atque ratio, quam quoad ipse venerit, tenere et sancte observare oportet.

M. In quem usum?

^e Luc. xxii. 19. 1 Cor. xi. 24, 26.

A. ^eUt mortis Domini, summique beneficii illius, quo per eam affecti sumus, gratam perpetuo memoriam celebremus et retineamus; et sicuti in Baptismo semel renati sumus, ita Cœna Dominica ad vitam spiritualem atque sempiternam jugiter alamur, atque sustentemur.

M. Baptismo ergo semel tantum initiari, ut et semel nasci, satis esse dicis; at Cœnæ Dominicæ perinde atque alimenti usum, identidem esse repetendum affirmas.

A. Sane, Præceptor.

M. Duasne etiam in hoc Sacramento, ut in Baptismo, partes esse dicis?

^f Matt. xxvi. 26, 27, 29.
Luc. xxii. 19. 1 Cor. xi. 23, 24, 25, 26, 27, 28.
^g Joan. vi. 35, 48, 50, 51, 53, &c.

A. Ita. Panem nempe, ^fet vinum, externa signa, quæ oculis cernuntur, attrectantur manibus, gustu percipiuntur; et ^gChristum ipsum, quo animæ nostræ, ut proprio alimento interius nutriuntur.

M. Et omnes peræque utraque Sacramenti parte uti debere dicis?

A. Certe, Præceptor; nam cum Dominus ita diserte ^hpræceperit, de ejus mandato ulla ex parte derogare summum esset nefas.

^h Matt. xxvi. 27. Marc. xiv. 23.

M. Cur duo signa adhiberi hic Dominus voluit?

ⁱ Joan. xix. 34.

A. Primum, quo mortis suæ, quam lacero corpore, ⁱet perfosso latere, ac toto sanguine effuso perpessus est, expressior esset imago; et ut ejus memoria animis nostris infixa, altius hæreret, utriusque corporis pariter atque sanguinis signum separatim exhibuit. Deinde, ut infirmitati nostræ consuleret Dominus, atque mederetur, manifesteque declararet, [k]sicuti panis ad corpora nutrienda, ita et corpus suum ad animas nostras spiritualiter alendas, vim atque efficacitatem summam habere; et sicut vino hominum corda exhilarantur, et roborantur vires, ita sanguine suo animas nostras refici atque recreari; ut non [l]cibum modo se, sed et potum etiam nostrum esse, certo statuentes, nusquam, nisi in ipso solo nutrimenti spiritualis, atque sempiternæ vitæ partem ullam quæramus.

[k] Joan. vi. 50, 55, 56.

[l] Joan. vi. 35, 53, 54, 55, &c.

M. Beneficiorum ergo, quæ commemorasti, non imago tantum, sed et ipsa veritas in Cœna exhibetur?

A. Quid ni? Quum enim Christus ipsa sit [m]veritas, non dubium est, quin quod verbis testatur, et signis repræsentat, id revera etiam præstet, et nobis exhibeat; quodque sibi fidentes [n]tam certo faciat corporis atque sanguinis sui participes, quam certo se panem atque vinum ore et ventriculo recepisse sciunt.

[m] Joan. i. 17. et xiv. 6.

[n] Joan. vi. 54, 56, 64.

M. Quum nos in terris versemur, Christi vero corpus in cœlo sit, quomodo fieri potest, quod dicis?

A. Mentes atque animos humo excitare, [o]et in cœlum, ubi Christus est, per Fidem erigere debemus.

[o] Joan. vi. 62, 64. Col. iii. 1. Heb. iv. 14, 16.

M. Recipiendi ergo corporis et sanguinis Dominici rationem, Fide constare dicis?

A. Sane. Nam quum mortuum Christum [p]credimus, quo nos a morte liberaret; excitatum item, quo nobis vitam acquireret; redemptionis per mortem suam partæ, ac vitæ, omniumque adeo suorum bonorum participes nos habet, eaque conjunctione, qua caput et [q]sua membra inter se cohærent, arcana, mirificaque Spiritus sui virtute sibi copulat; ita ut nos corporis sui membra, et ex ejus carne atque ossibus simus, et in unum cum ipso corpus coalescamus.

[p] Joan. vi. 35. Act. iv. 10, 12. Rom. iv. 24, 25. et v. 8. et xiv. 9.

[q] 1 Cor. vi. 15. et xii. 27. Eph. iv. 15, 16. et v. 30.

M. An ergo ut ista conjunctio efficiatur, panem et vinum in substantiam carnis et sanguinis Christi mutari imaginaris?

A. Nihil opus est hujusmodi mutationem comminisci. Nam et sacræ literæ, et optimi atque antiquissimi etiam Interpretes docent per Baptismum [r]itidem membra nos corporis Christi, et ex ejus carne atque ossibus esse, et in unum cum ipso corpus coalescere; cum nulla interim mutatio ejusmodi in aqua ipsa efficiatur.

[r] Rom. vi. 3. 1 Cor. xii. 13. Eph. iv. 15, 16. et v. 30. Gal. iii. 27.

M. Perge.

A. In utroque Sacramento, rerum externarum naturis

non mutatis, sed accedente ˢDivino verbo, gratiaque cœlesti, ea est efficientia ut sicuti per Baptismum semel ᵗregeneramur in Christo, et in ejus corpus primum quasi cooptamur et inserimur; ita Cœnam Dominicam ᵘrite percipientes, corporis et sanguinis sui nutrimento plane Divino, et salutis atque immortalitatis plenissimo, Spiritus sancti opera nobis communicato, a nobis vero Fide, quasi animæ nostræ ore, excepto, ad æternam ˣvitam jugiter alamur atque sustentemur; utrobique in unum cum Christo corpus coalescentes.

M. Aliter ergo etiam quam per solam Cœnam sese nobis Christus exhibet, arctissimaque nos conjunctione sibi copulat.

A. Christus tum se nobis authorem salutis in primis exhibuit, quum morti ʸsese pro nobis objecit, ne nos merita morte periremus. Per ᶻEvangelium item sese fidelibus exhibet, et clare docet, se panem esse illum vivum, qui de cœlo ad nutriendas sibi fidentium animas descendit. Sed et ᵃin Baptismo, ut ante est explicatum, Christus se nobis efficienter exhibuit, quod nos tunc Christianos effecerit.

M. Neque minus arcta conjunctionis vincula in Cœna esse dicis?

A. In Cœna vero Dominica et illa, quam dixi, communicatio nobis confirmatur ᵇet augetur, etiam, dum quisque eam ad se pertinere, et peculiari quadam ratione sibi Christum exhiberi, ut eo quam plenissime, conjunctissimeque perfruatur, tum verbis, tum mysteriis divinis certior fit; ut non animæ solum nostræ, ᶜejus sacro corpore atque sanguine tanquam proprio suo alimento nutriantur; sed et corporibus etiam nostris, quod vitæ æternæ symbolis communicent, quasi dato pignore, resurrectionis atque immortalitatis certa spes confirmetur; quo tandem Christo ᵈhabitante in nobis, et nobis vicissim in Christo manentibus, non modo vitam æternam, sed et gloriam, quam ipsi dedit Pater, nos etiam per Christum in nobis manentem consequamur. Summa illa sit; sicuti non crassam aliquam conjunctionem imaginor, ita arcanam et mirificam illam corporis Christi in Cœna communicationem arctissimam, certissimam, verissimam, et plane summam esse statuo.

M. Ex iis quæ jam de Cœna Dominica commemorasti, videor mihi colligere, eam non in hunc finem institutam esse, ut Christi corpus Deo Patri pro peccatis in sacrificium offeratur.

A. Minime vero ita offertur; nam ipse, ut corpore suo

^e vescamur, non ut illud offeramus, cum Cœnam suam institueret, præcepit. ^f Offerendi vero pro peccatis prærogativa ad solum Christum, ut qui æternus ille sit sacerdos, pertinet, qui et unicum illud perpetuumque sacrificium, moriens in cruce pro salute nostra semel fecit, illique abunde in omne tempus satisfecit. Nobis vero nihil restat, nisi ut æterni illius sacrificii usumfructum, nobis ab ipso Domino legatum gratis animis capiamus; quod quidem in Cœna Dominica maxime facimus. e Matt. xxvi. 26. 1 Cor. xi. 24, &c. f Heb. v. 6.

M. Sacra igitur Cœna, ut video, ad mortem Christi, ejusque in cruce perpetratum semel sacrificium, quo solo placatus nobis Deus efficitur, nos remittit.

A. Planissime; nam panis et vini symbolis nobis confirmatur Christi corpus, ^g ut semel pro nobis, ad nos cum Deo in gratiam reconciliandos, hostia immolata fuit, sanguis ejus semel ad eluendas peccatorum nostrorum maculas effusus; ita nunc quoque Fidelibus in sacra ejus Cœna ^h utrumque exhiberi; ut reconciliationem gratiæ ad nos pertinere certo sciamus, fructumque redemptionis per mortem ejus partæ capiamus atque percipiamus. g Rom. v. 8. et vi. 10. 1 Cor. xv. 3. 2 Cor. v. 14, 15. 1 Pet. iii. 18. h Matt. xxvi. 26, 27, 28. Luc. xxii. 19. 1 Cor. xi. 24, 25, 26.

M. An ergo soli fideles corpore et sanguine Christi pascuntur?

A. Soli omnino; cum quibus enim corpus suum, ⁱ cum iisdem et vitam æternam, ut dixi, communicat. i Joan. vi. 52, 53, 54, 56, 57, &c.

M. Quamobrem corpus et sanguinem Christi in pane et calice includi, aut panem et vinum in substantiam corporis et sanguinis ejus mutari non fateris?

A. Quia illud esset ^k veritatem corporis Christi in dubium vocare; Christum ipsum contumelia afficere; eos etiam qui Sacramentum recipiunt, horrore perfundere, si vel corpus ejus tam angusto loco includi, ^l aut in multis simul locis esse, ^m vel carnem ejus in ore dentibus mandi, et perinde atque alium cibum, extenuari, atque manducari imaginaremur. k Luc. xxiv. 39. Joan. xx. 25, 27. l Matt. xxviii. 6. Luc. xxiv. 6. Joan. xii. 28. et xvi. 28. m Joan. vi. 52, 60, 61.

M. Cur ergo exitialis est impiis Sacramenti communicatio, si hujusmodi mutatio non fiat?

A. Quia ad Sancta et Divina mysteriaⁿ per hypocrisin et simulationem accedunt, eaque impie cum Domini ipsius, qui ea instituit, summa injuria contumeliaque profanant. n 1 Cor. xi. 27, 28, 29, &c.

M. Nostrum igitur quid sit officium, ut recte ad Cœnam Dominicam accedamus, edissere.

A. Illud ipsum quod Sacris Scripturis docemur; ut

videlicet nos ipsos °exploremus, num vera simus Christi membra.

M. Quibus id notis atque indiciis manifeste deprehendemus?

A. Primum, si ᴾex animo nos pœniteat peccatorum nostrorum, quæ Christum ᑫad mortem, cujus nunc mysteria nobis traduntur, adegerunt: deinde si ʳcerta spe de Dei per Christum misericordia nos sustineamus, atque nitamur, cum grata redemptionis per mortem ejus acquisitæ ˢmemoria: præterea, si de vita ᵗin futurum pie degenda seriam cogitationem et destinatum propositum suscipiamus: postremo, cum conjunctionis etiam, charitatisque inter homines mutuæ ᵘSymbolum in Cœna Dominica contineatur, si ˣproximos, id est mortales omnes, fraterno amore, sine ulla malevolentia odiove, prosequamur.

M. An quisquam ista quæ commemoras, omnia plene perfecteque præstare potest?

A. Absolutio omnibus numeris perfecta, in qua nihil desideretur, ʸin homine, quoad hunc mundum incolit, inveniri non potest; neque tamen imperfectio, qua laboramus, nos ab accessu ad Cœnam Dominicam, quam imperfectionis nostræ atque imbecillitatis subsidium esse Dominus voluit, arcere debet; imo si perfecti essemus, nullum inter nos amplius usum Cœna jam haberet. Huc tamen quæ dixi spectant, ut ᶻPœnitentiam quisque ᵃFidemque atque ᵇCharitatem, quoad ejus fieri potest, synceram et sine fuco, ad Cœnam accedens secum adferat.

M. Verum quum antea dicebas, ad Fidei confirmationem valere Sacramenta, quomodo jam Fidem ad ea adferendam esse dicis?

A. Minime ista pugnant; ᶜFidem enim in nobis inchoatam esse oportet; ad quam alendam et roborandam Dominus Sacramenta instituit, quæ ad ᵈconfirmandas et quasi obsignandas in cordibus nostris Dei promissiones, permagna momenta adferunt.

M. Superest adhuc ut dicas, ad quos proprie Sacramentorum pertineat administratio.

A. Quum pascendi verbo Dei gregis Dominici, ᵉSacramentaque administrandi officia atque munera sint inter se junctissima, non est dubium, quin eorum administratio ad eos pertineat proprie quibus publice docendi munus est demandatum. Nam ut in Cœna Dominus ^fipse publici ministri officio fungens, exemplum suum ad imitandum proposuit; ita baptizandi pariter atque docendi munus Apostolis suis peculiariter delegavit. f Matt. xxvi. Marc. xiv. Luc. xxii. 1 Cor. xi.

M. Suntne promiscue omnes nullo discrimine ad Sacramenta a Pastoribus admittendi?

A. Olim cum adulti, ^get natu grandiores ad Religionem nostram accederent, ne ad Baptismum quidem admittebantur, nisi prius de eorum Fide in præcipuis Christianæ Religionis articulis constaret. Nunc quia soli infantes baptizantur, nullus potest adhiberi delectus. Diversa est de Cœna ratio; ad quam cum non nisi adulta jam ætate accedant, si quem indignum esse palam constiterit, is ad Cœnam a pastore minime est admittendus, quia sine Sacramenti id profanatione fieri non potest. g Marc. xvi. 15, 16. Act. ii. 41. et viii. 12, 37. et xviii. 8.

M. Cur Dominus igitur Judam ^hproditorem a Cœnæ suæ communione non arcebat? h Matt. xxvi. 21, 22, &c. Marc. xiv. 18, 19, &c. Joan. xiii. 26, 27, &c.

A. Quia ejus impietas, utut erat Domino cognita, nondum erat palam nota.

M. Hypocritas ergo Ministri arcere non possunt?

A. ⁱNon, quoad occulta eorum nequitia fuerit. i 1 Cor. v. 2.

M. Quum ergo Sacramentis boni pariter ac mali promiscue et communiter utantur, quæ potest in illis certa esse atque stabilis conscientiarum fiducia, quod tu paulo antea affirmabas?

A. Quamvis ^kimpii, quantum ad ipsos spectat, Dei dona in Sacramentis oblata non recipiant, sed respuant, et seipsos frustrentur; ^lpii tamen, qui per Fidem Christum in illis ejusque gratiam quærunt, optima mentis conscientia et consolatione gratissima, ex salutis atque solidæ fœlicitatis certa spe, nunquam destituuntur, aut fraudantur. k Joan. xiii. 26, 27. Rom. iii. 3, 4. 1 Cor. x. 21, 22. l 1 Cor. x. 16. et xi. 28, 31.

M. At si quos Pastor indignos esse vel ipse cognoverit, vel clam admonitus fuerit, eos certe a communione licebit excludere?

A. Tales et concionibus publicis, modo ne nominatim eos proferat, aut infamiam illis maculamve inurat, sed suæ tantum conscientiæ suspicione, et conjectura eos perstringat atque coarguat, et admonere debet, et privatim graviter etiam deterrere potest; arcere vero a communione, nisi legitima Ecclesiæ cognitio, judiciumque intercesserit, non licebit.

M. Quod ergo remedium huic malo inveniendum est atque adhibendum?

A. In Ecclesiis bene institutis atque moratis, certa, ut ^mantea dixi, ratio atque ordo gubernationis instituebatur atque observabatur. Deligebantur seniores, id est Magistratus Ecclesiastici, qui disciplinam ecclesiasticam tenerent, atque colerent. Ad hos authoritas, animadversio, atque castigatio censoria pertinebant; ⁿhi adhibito etiam Pastore, si quos esse cognoverant, qui vel opinionibus falsis, vel turbulentis erroribus, vel anilibus superstitionibus, vel vita vitiosa flagitiosaque magnam publice offensionem Ecclesiæ Dei adferrent, quique sine Cœnæ Dominicæ profanatione accedere non possent, eos a communione repellebant, atque rejiciebant, neque rursum admittebant, donec Pœnitentia publica Ecclesiæ satisfecissent.

M. Quis debet esse Pœnitentiæ publicæ modus?

A. Qui falsarum opinionum commentis, pietatem veram ^olædere, et Religionem labefactare conantur; aut vitiosa atque flagitiosa vita graves et publicas offensiones concitarunt, eos æquum est, Ecclesiæ, cui ita facta est offensio, ^ppublice satisfacere, id est, suum coram tota congregatione peccatum ingenue agnoscere et confiteri, palamque testari, sibi ex animo dolere, quod Deum Opt. Max. tam graviter offenderint; Religionem Christianam quam sunt professi; Ecclesiam in qua censebantur, quantum in ipsis quidem fuerat, ignominia affecerint; quodque non peccato solum, sed pernicioso etiam exemplo aliis nocuerint; a Deo primum, deinde ab ejus Ecclesia veniam se petere atque precari.

M. Quid deinde fiet?

A. Postremo, ut in Ecclesiam, e qua suo merito ejecti sunt, et ad sancta ejus mysteria rursum admittantur, suppliciter postulare, atque orare debent. In summa, ^qeam adhiberi in pœnitentia publica moderationem oportet, ut neque severitate nimia, qui peccavit, animum despondeat; neque rursum facilitate nimia Ecclesiæ disciplina labatur, atque ejus imminuatur authoritas, cæterique ad similia audenda animentur atque incitentur. Sed ubi seniorum, ^rpastorisque judicio, et ejus, qui peccavit, castigationi, et exemplo aliorum satisfactum fuerit, rursum ad communionem Ecclesiæ, qui erat excommunicatus admittebatur.

M. Video te, Fili mi, Christianæ pietatis summam exacte tenere. Superest ut ad hanc cognitionis piæ regulam, vitam tuam ita dirigas, ne frustra ista didicisse videaris. Non enim qui audiunt ^stantum, intelliguntque verbum Dei, sed qui

Dei voluntati obsequuntur, atque imperio ejus obtemperant, beati erunt. Imo servus ille, qui Domini voluntatem noverit, neque obsecundarit, ᵗgravius vapulabit; adeo nihil prodest pietatis, Religionisque veræ intelligentia, nisi vitæ etiam integritas, innocentia, atque sanctitas accedant. Age igitur, mi Fili, omni cura et cogitatione in hoc incumbe, ut ne in officio labaris, aut ab hac piæ vitæ norma, atque præscriptione unquam aberres. ᵗ Luc. xii. 47. Jacob. iv. 17.

A. Dabo operam, venerande Præceptor, et nihil prætermittam, quantum quidem facere, et omni ope atque opera eniti possum, quo professioni nominique Christiano respondeam. Sed et a Deo optimo maximo supplex precibus et votis omnibus semper exposcam, ne cœlestis doctrinæ suæ semen, in animo meo quasi arido ᵘsterilique solo exceptum perire sinat; sed gratiæ suæ ˣDivino rore cordis mei siccitatem sterilitatemque ita irriget atque fœcundet, ut uberes pietatis fructus feram, in regni cœlestis ʸhorreum et cellam condendos, atque reponendos. ᵘ Matt. xiii. 4, 5, 6, 7, 19, 20, 21, 22. ˣ Psal. i. 3. et civ. 13. Matt. xiii. 8, 23. 1 Cor. iii. 6, 7. ʸ Matt. iii. 12. Luc. iii. 17.

M. Ita facito, mi Fili, neque dubita, quin uti hanc mentem voluntatemque ᶻDeo duce suscepisti, ita studii hujus tui, conatusque pii eventum et exitum, quem optas atque expectas, id est, optimum, fœlicissimumque reperturus sis, atque habiturus. ᶻ 2 Cor. iii. 5. Phil. ii. 12, 13.

VOCABULA NOSTRATIA,

ET

LOQUENDI FORMÆ CHRISTIANORUM PROPRIÆ,

IN QUIBUS

A COMMUNI MORE VERBORUM LATINORUM

DISCESSUM EST,

EX LITERARUM ORDINE SEQUUNTUR.

A

Angelus, Græca vox; Latine, nuntius, internuntius, legatus, index.

Angeli, id est, spiritus, vel mentes cœlestes; nostrum; veteres Græci Dæmonas, Latini genios, vel lares appellarunt.

Animalis homo; vide *Caro*.

Apostolus, Græc. Latine, legatus.

B

Benedicere; vide *Maledicere*.

C

Cœlum, in singulari numero, potius quam in plurali cœlos usurpare solet Cicero.

Caput, pro præcipua parte, MEMBRA, pro aliis partibus rei alicujus, ut et CORPUS, pro universitate aut societate populi usurpant Cicero et Livius; ut, totum corpus reipub. curare, unum corpus reipub. esse, civitatis corpus, unum corpus conciliumque totius Peloponnesi. Cicero. Cur non et ecclesiæ corpus, id est, piorum universitas, vel Respub. Christiana? Unius corporis esse, id est societatis. Livius. Christus ecclesiæ caput, nos ecclesiæ membra; Latinitas in his ferenda. At corpus Christi, pro Ecclesia, et piorum universitate; et nos membra Christi, aut membra corporis Christi, locutiones nostræ propriæ sunt.

Caro, pro genere humano; ut, omnis caro fœnum; nostrum.

Caro item pro vitiosa et corrupta natura; et carnalis vel animalis, vel vetus homo, pro tali natura prædito; carnem, membra terrestria mortificare, carnem crucifigere, veterem hominem deponere, exuere, crucifigere, expurgare vetus fermentum; nostra sunt propria. Et contra, spiritus, spiritualis, vel spiritalis, novitas spiritus, novus homo, nova creatura, renovari spiritu, ambulare secundum spiritum, nova conspersio, novum hominem induere, regenerari, regeneratio, regeneratus, renatus, apud nostrates usurpantur, quum naturæ vitiosæ reparationem, vel renovationem, aut hominem divina virtute, mente, vel divino consilio præditum, divino spiritu vel numine afflatum, aut instinctum cœlesti vel divino afflatu, inflatu, vel instinctu motum, vel actum, et vera pietate divinitus imbutum, significamus. Gratia Dei pro divino afflatu, instinctu, vel virtute; nostrum.

Catechismus, vel potius Catechesis, Græc. Latine, prima institutio; ut et Catechumeni, Catechizatio; nostratia.

Catholica; vide *Ecclesia.*

Certitudo, et incertitudo, vide *Credo.*

Claves, claudere, recludere, cœlumque ligare, solvere peccata, vel peccatores; metaphoræ nostræ; ut sunt etiam retinere, vel detinere peccata, pro, condonare; nostratia.

Concupiscentia, i. e. rerum malarum appetitus, vel appetitio; nostrum.

Contritio, vide *Pœnitentia.*

Corpus Christi, pro Ecclesia, et piorum universitate; nostrum. Vide *Caput.*

Credo, cum accusativo, et præpositione; nostrum; ut credere in Deum, i. e. Deum vere agnoscere, illi fidem habere, illi confidere, spem et fiduciam omnem in illo collocare; nam hæc omnia simul complectitur. Credo item, cum solo accusativo, ut Credo resurrectionem mortuorum, et vitam æternam, id est, certo expecto, vel spero; nostra sunt. Fides item cum non solum Dei cognitionem, et credulitatem, sed et fiduciam quoque in Deo significat, et fidelis pro tali fide prædito; et contraria, infidelitas, infidelis; nostra sunt propria. Propius accedunt ad latinitatem hoc sensu, diffidens, diffidentia, incredulus, incredulitas; sic suspensus, incertus, dubius, obscura spe pendens, pro infideli; Latina sunt. Certitudo et incertitudo, parum usitata Latinis. Fiducia, Fidentia, firma animi confisio; Ciceroniana sunt; verum ea fidem nostram plene non explicant, sed ejus duntaxat partem significant. Credo, fido, et spero, sæpe in nostra religione finitimæ sunt significationis, quam his fere formis Latini exprimunt. Est mihi fiducia, est firma animi confisio in Deo. Est mihi stabilis Divinæ per Christum benevolentiæ fiducia. Spes omnis residet, spem omnem colloco in Deo, in Christo. Spem certam concipio, sustineo me, et nitor spe veniæ, immortalitatis, vitæ sempiternæ, &c.

Creo, creatio, creator, conditor, effector, fabricator; Ciceroniana sunt. Creatura Latinis inauditum. Ex argilla, lutoque fictus homo. Hominem humo excitatum, celsum et erectum constituit. Hominem generavit, et exornavit Deus. Animum ex sua mente et divinitate genuit Deus. Deus parens hujus universitatis. Lucem qua fruimur, spiritum quem ducimus, commoda quibus utimur, a Deo nobis dari videmus; modi loquendi sunt apud Cic.

Crucifigo, crucifixus. Quintil. Plin. Suetonii sunt, non Ciceronis. Passio Christi, pro ejus supplicio, cruciatu, et morte; sic passus absolute, sine alia voce adjuncta; nostratia sunt. Multa gravia, horrenda passus; Latin. De Christo crucifixo, aut passo, sic Latine dici potest; Christus in crucem sublatus, vel actus, crucifixus, cruce affectus, innocens pro nocentibus pœnas luit; alieni peccati pœnas sustinuit, pertulit, persolvit; supplicium pro nobis pertulit; supplicio, cruciatu, cruce, morte affectus est, pro peccatis nostris pœnas pendit, dependit, tulit.

D

Dæmones Græce, lares Cicer. Ethnici in bonam partem accipiunt.

Dæmones; id est, mentes, vel spiritus impii et malitiosi; nostrum.
Deitas; nostrum; Divinitas, Numen divinum; Cicer.
Diabolus Græc. Adversarius, Budæo; Calumniator, Erasmo; deceptor, delator.
Dilectio, pro *amore,* vix audita Latinis.

E

Ecclesia, Græcum; Latin. congregatio. Ecclesia catholica; Latine, universa congregatio, universitas piorum hominum; universitas legitur lib. ad Herennium. Respub. Christiana, vel Christianorum.
Electi Dei, substantive, pro, electi a Deo; nostrum. Sic prædestinari, prædestinatio, prædestinatus, præscientia, præscitus, verba sunt nobis peculiaria. Cicero. Deus non ignorat ea, quæ ab ipso constituta et designata sunt; id est, Deus præscit prædestinata, ut nos loquimur. Præscisse oportuit. Terent.
Effectus, substantive, Plin. Propertii, non Cic.
Effectio, eventus, eventum, et eventa in plur. Cic.
Essentia, et substantia, Plauti, Quintiliani, Plinii, non Ciceronis.
Ethnici, Græc. Gentiles, Gentes, pro alienigenis, impiis, idolatris, aliis quam Christianis, aut Judæis; nostræ voces sunt.
Evangelium Græc. Latine bonum nuntium; apud nos sacras Novi Testamenti historias, et scripturas significat.
Evangelista, scriptor Evangelii, quales fuerunt illi quatuor, Matthæus, Marcus, Lucas, Joannes; vel qui de Evangelio concionatur apud populum; nostrum.
Excommunicare, pro, Ecclesia ejicere, expellere, vel arcere; nostrum. Sic Excommunicatio, pro expulsione vel ejectione.

F

Fides, vide *Credo.*

G

Gentiles, vide *Ethnicus.*
Glorificare, vide *Sanctificare.*
Gratitudo, Latinis hominibus inaudita; Ingratitudo, inusitata; Gratus et Ingratus, Latina sunt.

H

Hypocrisis Græc. Latine, simulatio, alienæ personæ simulatio; hypocrita, simulator alienæ personæ.

I

Jesus, Hebraice; Latine, servator.
Idolum, idololatra, idololatria, Græc. Lat. simulachrum, simulachrorum cultor, et cultus. Idololatria latius apud nos patet, omnem Divinum cultum cuiquam, præterquam soli Deo, habitum significans.
Imperfectio, et increatus, Latinis inusitata sunt.
Inferna absolute sine substantivo addito; nostrum; ut Descendit ad inferna; ad inferos Latine.
Infidelis, infidelitas; vide *Credo.*
Inobedientia, inobediens; nostra. Inobsequens; Senec. in Hippol. Minus obsequens, minus obediens, Lat.
Invisibilis, vide *Visibilis.*
Invoco, oro, precor; Latina. Invocatio, oratio, pro precatione, precibus, aut votis; intercedere item et intercessio; nostra. Divinum numen scelere violatum precibus placare. Cic.
Justificare, vide *Sanctificare.*
Jusjurandum Latina vox est, juramentum Latinis inusitatum.

Lavacrum apud Claud. et Gell. Lavatio apud Ciceronem legitur.

M

Malitia, κακία, quam vitiositatem Cicero mavult appellare, quam Malitiam. Malitiam enim certi cujusdam vitii, vitiositatem omnium nomen esse. Sic κακίας, vitia mavult, quam malitias nominare.

Maledicere, una vox; nostrum; pro, execrari, devovere, diris devovere, diras obnuntiare; Cicer. Maledictus item pro execrando, execrabili et detestabili, et maledictio pro execratione; nostra sunt. Sic benedicere. i. e. fausta precari, vel bene ominari. Benedictus item, et benedictio; nostratia.

Mandere, et Mandi, Cic. Manducare rarum, Manducari vix invenitur.

Mediator, pro advocato, aut patrono, nostrum. Intercessor apud Senecam pro mediatore; sed aliud Ciceroni significant Intercessor, et Intercedere.

Membra Christi, aut Membra corporis Christi, locutiones nostræ sunt. Vide *Caput*.

Minister Dei, minister Ecclesiæ, vel minister Ecclesiasticus, pro eo quem Sacerdotem dicimus, usurpari possunt. Sic enim Cicero loquitur; Ministri publici Martis, atque ei Deo consecrati.

Mortifico, Mortificatio; vide *Caro*.

Mundani, pro impiis, Mundus pro impiorum universitate, Seculum pro Mundo; nostratia. Res mundanæ, res incertæ, lubricæ, fluxæ, fugaces, caducæ. Cic.

O

Observare leges, Cicer. Observator legis, vix legitur apud Latinos.

Omnipotens, Plautus et Cicero, ex veteri poeta. Omnipotentia; nostrum. Præpotens, omnium rerum præpotens Deus. Cicer. Immensa, infinita, interminata magnitudo, potentia, &c.

Oratio, vide *Invoco*.

P

Peccator, pro nocente, sonte, impio, nefario; nostrum.

Peccatum originis, originale peccatum; nostratia. Origo peccati, Ovidius. Origo boni, Cicer. Nativum malum, insitum in natura malum. Cic. Naturale malum. Ovid. Cur non et naturale peccatum? Natura corrupta. Quintil. Natura mendosa. Hor. Natura depravata, Natura improbi, contra naturam depravati. Cic.

Passio, passus, vide *Crucifigo*.

Personæ in Trinitate; nostrum.

Pœnitentia, Livius, Plinius. Ex conscientia peccatorum timor. Cic. Pro quo nostri quidam contritionis nomine usi sunt. Resipisco usitatum, resipiscentia inusitatum Latinis.

Prædestinatio, præscientia. Vide *Electi*.

Profano, profanatio; Livius, Plinius, non Cicero. Violare sacra; Cicero. Violatio templi; Livius. Violator templi; Ovidius.

Propheta, et prophetia, Græc. Lat. Vates, vaticinatio, prædictio divina. Propheta, pro sacrarum literarum interprete; nostrum.

Proximus, vicinus, frater, charitatis vocabula, nobis sunt peculiaria. Frater, eum, qui eandem nobiscum religionem profitetur, significat. Proximus et vicinus, universitatem humani generis complectuntur. Fraternus amor, pro mutuo amore Christianorum; nostrum.

R

Remissio pœnæ, apud Cic. sic et culpæ remissio dici potest.

Resipiscentia, vide *Pœnitentia*.

Resurgo, Livius, et Ovidius. Revivisco, redivivus. Cic. Resurrectio, carnis resurrectio; nostra. Excitare aliquem a mortuis, Excitatio corporum a mortuis, pro conditione vitæ mortalis, immortalitatem consequi, Cic.

S

Salvare, salvator, salvatio, Latinis inaudita. Servare, servator, servatrix, liberator, liberatio, Latina sunt. Redemptor, id est, servator aut liberator; nostrum.

Sacramentum, pro mysteriis Divinis; nostrum. Baptismus Græc. Lat. immersio vel intinctio, lavatio salutaris, expiatio aqua salutari. Cœna Domini, vel Dominica, Communio, Eucharistia Græce, Latine gratiarum actio.

Sancti, sanctorum, sine substantivo addito, inusitatum Latinis. Sanctificare, sanctificatio; glorificare, glorificatio; justificare, justificatio, nostratia sunt. Sanctitas, sanctimonia, sanctitudo, Latina.

Sanctificare, et glorificare ad Deum relata, ut, sanctificetur nomen tuum; nostra. Sancte colatur, gloria, honore afficiatur; gloria Dei, vel nomen Dei amplificetur, celebretur, laudibus celebretur, amplitudo ejus illustretur, Ciceronis et Livii sunt.

Sanctificare et justificare, ad homines relata; ut Deus suos justificat, sanctificat; nostra; sanctos atque integros facit, efficit, reddit, sanctitati, innocentiæ atque integritati, vel in sanctitatem, atque innocentiam restituit, sanctorum atque innocentium loco habet, ponit, collocat, damnatos in integrum restituit, &c. Latina. Fide, vel per fidem justificamur; nostrum. Justitiæ fundamentum fides; virtutum omnium fundamentum fides. Cicero. Justificus, qui justa facit. Catullus; Poeticum est.

Spiritus, spiritualis, vide *Caro.*

Scriptura, apud Ciceronem, non nisi pro stylo usurpatur. In Rhetorica ad Herennium, et Terent. propius ad nostrum sensum accedit. Sacræ literæ; profana pagina, Claud. cur non et sacra pagina? Verbum Dei pro sacris literis; nostrum; verbum veritatis pro sacra scriptura quid ni? ut verbum voluptatis apud Ciceronem.

Sensibilis, vide *Visibilis.*

T

Tentatio, pro sollicitatione ad vitia; et inducere in tentationem, usurpantur a nostris. Novi morborum tentationes. Cic.

Tractatio usitatior apud Cicer. quam tractatus; et Artis, philosophiæ, &c. tractatio vel tractatus; potius quam tractatio vel tractatus de arte, philosophia, &c.

Traditiones, pro doctrinis aut inventis humanis, pro opinionum commentis futilibus, et commentitiis sententiis, fabulis, nugis: nostrum.

Trinitas; nostrum. Trinus, ternus, vel terni potius: Triplex, triplus, Latina sunt; verum hic, ut alibi sæpe, pietatis potius, quam Latinitatis rationem habere oportet.

V

Venerandus ad Deum, et religionem fere semper; honorandus ad homines refertur a Cic. Reverendus, reverendissimus, in titulis consuetudini condonantur.

Verbum Dei, vide *Scriptura.*

Vetus homo, vide *Caro.*

Vita nova, pro innocentia; nostrum. Latine, studium innocentiæ atque sanctitatis. Avocare animum a vitiis, a peccatis; pravos affectus et appetitus vitiosos frænare. Cic. Rarum est quoddam genus eorum, qui se a corpore avocant, et ad divinarum rerum cognitionem cura omni, studioque rapiuntur.

Visus raro, aspectus sæpe apud Cicer.

Visibilis, et sensibilis, Plinii, non Ciceronis; conspicuus, aspectabilis, spectabilis, sub oculos, sub aspectum cadens, vel veniens, sub oculorum sensum cadens, sub sensibus, in sensum cadens, in sensum credendi cadens, percipere sensibus, Ciceronis sunt. Invisibilis, ut gratia invisibilis, Latinum non est. Occultus, abditus, tectus, non conspicuus, Latina sunt.

Unitas, Col. Plin. non Cicero.

Z

Zelotypus, vel Zelotes potius, et Zelotypia, Græca sunt. Socii impatiens, socii impatientia, Plinii sunt potius quam Ciceronis. Zelotypia, inquit Cicero, est ægritudo ex eo, quod alter potiatur eo, quod ipse concupiverit.

A CATECHISME,

or first Instruction and Learning of Christian
Religion.

¶ *Translated out of Latine into
Englishe.*

¶ AT LONDON.

Printed by Iohn Daye
dwelling ouer Aldersgate.
¶ *Cum Priuilegio Regiæ Maiestatis
per Decennium.*
AN. 1570.

⁋ To the most reverend Fathers in God, my Lords, Matthew Archbishop of Canterbury, and Edmond archbishop of York, and to the reverend father in God, Edwin, my lord bishop of London, and to all the other reverend fathers, my lords the bishops of all the several dioceses in England.

MAY it please your good graces and fatherhoods to permit me, with all humility and reverence to render you in this preface an accompt of my purpose and doing in publishing this Catechism by me translated, and offered to the church of England under protection of your names.

Whereas there was very lately a Latin Catechism printed, wherein the sum of Christian religion was set forth in short questions and answers, yet not containing bare and naked affirmations only, but shewing also some causes and reasons to the same annexed, and well furnished with places of scripture noted in the margin for proof thereof: in which Catechism there hath also great labour and diligence been bestowed about the purity of the Latin tongue, that such as were studious of that language, specially the youth, might at once with one labour learn the truth of religion and the pureness of the Latin tongue together. That Catechism I have thought good to translate into English, as well for the use of such as understand no Latin at all, as also for their commodity, who, having a little sight in that language, desire some more perfection therein. For which cause I have not used that liberty in rendering the sense at large which the order of translation doth permit unto me, but have willingly, for the benefit of the meaner learned, tied myself very much to observing of the words themselves, but so yet that I had alway regard to the natural property and easiness of our native tongue.

This book as it will be profitable to such as do understand English only, so will it bring double profit to those, who, being somewhat skilled in the Latin tongue and desiring more skill, will compare the Latin book with the English, whereby they may at once learn, as I said, the truth of religion and the purity of the Latin tongue. And, lest the reader desirous to compare any the parts or sentences of the Latin and English books might be hindered, I have procured that the English print answereth the Latin, page for page, throughout the whole books, so that any sentence may at the first easily be found in both the books. This exercise in my opinion is most meet for the use of such ecclesiastical ministers and studious youth as have not yet the perfect knowledge either of religion or of the Latin speech, who by experience may find (as I think) more profit hereby than they would suppose upon the first view. Neither is this conference of translations by them who be very well learned judged unprofitable for such as are competently learned.

The book hath also one further use of very good exercise for those that desire to see more at large how the doctrine herein taught is confirmed by the word of God, the only rule of true religion; that is, if such as shall read it to learn truth, but specially ecclesiastical ministers whose charge is to teach truth, shall resort to the places of scripture noted in the margin, and read them in the Bible at large, and then mark how each thing here affirmed is there well confirmed, and how the doctrine here delivered is not only in all parts fully approved by God's holy word, but also for the most part uttered in the very words of the text, so far as may be with respect of pureness of the Latin phrase; by which mean they shall also be occasioned to be better acquainted with the scriptures themselves and with the true and natural understanding of them. And therein be it remembered that the last numbers in the quotations, shewing the divisions within the chapters, are gathered according to the great Bible last printed. This exercise whoso shall assay shall find it of marvellous great profit, both for conceiving truth to the satisfying of conscience, and for delivering truth to the discharge of duty.

It may perhaps be marvelled of some, why throughout the book, as well in the Latin as in this translated, the master asketh, the scholar answereth, and ever the declaration of the matter is put in the scholar's mouth, so as some may muse why the scholar may seem to be made wiser than the master. This objection hath easy answer; and such answer as it hath I thought meet to disclose. It may not be thought that the master here inquireth of the scholar as desirous to learn of him, nor that the scholar informeth the master as presuming to teach him. But the master opposeth the scholar to see how he hath profited, and the scholar rendereth to the master to give accompt of his memory and diligence. And that it may appear that this order of opposing by the master and rendering by the scholar for good reason might seem to the author more convenient than the other form which some other writers of catechisms have used, that is, of inquiring by the scholar and teaching by the master, (without prejudice alway or condemning the other) it may be remembered that the end and purpose of catechism is in good and natural order fitly applied to serve the good use of confirmation by the bishop, at which time the bishop which confirmeth doth not teach but examine, and in his whole manner of opposing useth such form as here in like sort the *Catechumenus* or child is prepared unto; which is also not done without example, for the same manner is in the short catechism now used in the Church of England at confirmation.

Now surely there are no greater means of advancing true religion and rooting out of errors than these two, that is to say, catechism or good instruction of youth, and good information of ecclesiastical ministers in sound truth, and the proofs thereof, howsoever perhaps they may lack some full furniture of other learnings. And therewith for my part I have long thought it a much better way toward removing of heresies and superstitions (whereof Rome hath brought us and left us plenty) to deal first with plain setting out of truth as not in controversy, without dealing at the beginning with the strife of confutation. For so both discretion and charity in the teacher is easilier kept, and truth once being settled, error will fall of itself, so that he which hath once thus with conference of God's word conceived a certain and stayed judgment of truth, shall either wonder how absurd errors have been received, or shall with less peril hear them talked of.

These things all considered, and how this book serveth to all these good ends, and therewithal remembered how it hath pleased almighty God of his great goodness and love, and to the singular benefit of this his church of England, under the queen's most excellent majesty the most honourable instrument of advancing his religion and glory in her dominions and of bringing truth and peace to the consciences of her subjects, to ordain your graces and fatherhoods the chief pastors and governors of his flock for doctrine and all ecclesiastical duties: the first author of this book in Latin had very good reason to offer his work unto you, that as the people of God's flock in England are under your charge, so they might receive so great a benefit as this is under your name, and thereby you our governors on the one part might be the rather moved to further so good intention, and we all under your governance on the other part be made more ready to receive it with better assurance of good allowance, and to thank God, the giver of all good things and guider of all good doings and purposes, and (as meet is) that we and our posterity, so long as an English child or other shall in this Catechism learn Christianity, may keep in thankful remembrance the happiness of these good times, the blessed memory of her majesty, and the good names of you God's good ministers, now chief pastors of this his flock, in whose time (to your and our comfortable consideration be it spoken) God hath so liberally spread among us the light of his gospel, and (praised be he, and happy be ye therefore) hath made you his faithful dispensers of so great a grace.

The same reasons that so moved the first author have also moved me to offer my translation unto you, comprising herein as patrons all the fathers and lords of the clergy, but specially and by name your graces my lords the archbishops, to whose provinces the whole realm pertaineth, and your fatherhood my lord of London, to whose diocese London a light to the rest of England belongeth, and to whom myself dwelling within your charge do owe particular duty.

This my intent and labour being to do good to as many and largely as I possibly could, if I shall understand to be with the readers taken in good part and used to their benefit (as the rather by your good means, and names it may be), I shall think my travail very well bestowed, holding myself in the meantime contented with the conscience of a good meaning bent to do good so far as my skill and power would extend.

The success hereof I commit to God, the judgment I
submit to you, for whom and whose zeal
I praise God, and pray to him for
your preservation to the
benefit of his
Church.
(∴)

Your most humble.   *T. Norton.*

NOWELL'S CATECHISM.

THE MASTER. THE SCHOLAR.

Master. FORASMUCH as the master ought to be to his scholars a second parent and father, not of their bodies, but of their minds, I see it belongeth to the order of my duty, my dear child, not so much to instruct thee civilly in learning and good manners, as to furnish thy mind, and that in thy tender years, with good opinions and true religion. [a]For this age of childhood ought no less, yea, also much more, to be trained with good lessons to godliness, than with good arts to humanity: wherefore I thought meet to examine thee by certain short questions, that I may surely know whether thou have well bestowed thy study and labour therein, or no.

Scholar. And I for my part, right worshipful master, shall willingly answer your demands, so far as I have been able with wit to conceive or keep in memory, and can at this present call to mind and remember, what I have heard you teach me out of the holy scriptures.

M. Go to therefore, and tell me what religion it is that thou professest.

S. The religion that I profess, right worshipful master, is the same whereof the Lord Christ is the Author and Teacher, and which is therefore properly and truly called the Christian religion, like as the professors thereof are also [b]named Christians.

M. Dost thou then acknowledge thyself to be a follower of Christian godliness and religion, and a scholar of our Lord and schoolmaster Christ?

S. I do so acknowledge indeed, [c]and do unfeignedly and freely profess it: yea, I do settle therein the sum of all [d]my felicity, as in that which is the chiefest good that can come to man, and such as without it our state should be far more miserable than the state of any brute creatures.

M. Well then, I would have the substance and nature

The Master's duty.

Godliness in childhood.
a Deut. iv. 9, 10. & xxxi. 12, 13.
Ps. lxxviii. 3, 4, &c. Matt. xix. 13.
2 Tim. iii. 15.

Christian religion.

Christian, named of Christ.
b Acts xi. 26.

c Rom. x. 9, 10.

d Ps. i. & xxxiii. 12.
John iii. 13, 36.

of Christian religion and godliness, the name whereof is most honourable and holy, to be briefly expressed, with some definition of it.

S. Christian religion is the ᵉtrue and godly worshipping of God and keeping of his commandments.

M. Of whom dost thou think it is to be learned?

S. Of none other surely but of the heavenly ᶠword of God himself, which he hath left unto us written in the holy scriptures.

M. What writings be those which thou callest the word of God and the holy scriptures?

S. None other but those that have been published, first, by ᵍMoses and the holy prophets, the friends of Almighty God, by the instinct of the Holy Ghost in the old Testament; and afterward more plainly in the new Testament by our ʰLord Jesus Christ, the Son of God, and by his holy ⁱapostles inspired with the Spirit of God, and have been ᵏpreserved unto our time whole and uncorrupted.

M. Why was it God's will so to open unto us his word in writing?

S. Because we of ourselves (such is the ˡdarkness of our hearts) are not able to understand the will of Almighty God, in the ᵐknowledge of whom, and in obedience towards him, true godliness consisteth. God having pity upon us, hath ⁿopened and clearly set it out unto us; and the same so clearly set out he hath left in the book of the two ᵒTestaments, which are called the holy ᵖscriptures, to the end that we should not be uncertainly ᵠcarried hither and thither, but that by his heavenly doctrine there should be made us, as it were, a certain entry into heaven.

M. Why dost thou call God's word a Testament?

S. Because it is evident that in conceiving of religion, it is the chief point to understand what is the ʳwill of the everliving God. And since by the name of Testament is signified not only a will, but also a ˢlast and unchangeable will, we are hereby admonished that in religion we ᵗfollow nothing, nor seek for any thing further than we are therein taught by God; but that as there is one only true God, so there be but one godly worshipping and pure religion of one only God. Otherwise we should daily ᵘforge ourselves new-feigned religions; and every nation, every city, and every man would have his own several religion; yea, we should in our doings follow for our guide, not religion and true godliness, the beginning and foundation of virtues, but superstition, a deceitful shadow of godliness, which is most plain to see by the sundry and innumerable, not religions, but worse than doting superstitions of the ˣold gentile nations, who otherwise in worldly matters were very wise men.

M. Dost thou then affirm that all things necessary to godliness and salvation are contained in the written word of God?

S. ʸYea: for it were a point of intolerable ungodliness and madness to think, either that God hath left an imperfect doctrine, or that men were able to make that perfect, which God left imperfect. Therefore the Lord hath most straitly forbidden men, that they neither ᶻadd anything to, nor take anything from, his word, nor turn any way from it, either to the right hand or the left.

M. If this be true that thou sayest, to what purpose then are so many things so oft in councils and ecclesiastical assemblies, decreed, and by learned men taught in preaching, or left in writing?

S. All these things serve either to expounding of dark places of the word of God, and to take away controversies that rise among men, or to the orderly stablishing of the outward governance of the Church, and not to make new articles of religion. ᵃFor all things necessary to salvation, that is to say, how godliness, holiness, and religion are to be purely and uncorruptedly yielded to God: what obedience is to be given to God, by which alone the order of a godly life is to be framed; what affiance we ought to put in God; how God is to be called upon, and all good things to be imputed to him; what form is to be kept in celebrating the divine mysteries; all these things, I say, are to be learned of the word of God, without the knowledge whereof all these things are either utterly unknown, or most absurdly done; so that it were far better that they were not done at all, as the Lord himself witnesseth that ᵇignorance of the scripture is the mother of all errors; and he himself in his teaching, doth commonly allege the ᶜwritten word of God, and to it he sendeth us to learn of it. For this cause therefore, in old times also, the ᵈword of God was openly read in churches, and the help of

8—2

expounders used when they might have them, as appeareth by the histories of the church. And the Lord himself, immediately before his ascending to heaven, gave principally in charge to his apostles whom he had chosen, [e]that they should instruct all men throughout the world with his word. And Paul following his example, ordained that some should be appointed [f]in every church to teach the people, for that he well knew that faith and all things pertaining to godliness do hang upon the reading and [g]hearing of the word of God, and that therefore, [h]apostles, teachers, prophets, and expounders, are most necessary in the church of God.

[e] Matt. xxviii. 20. Mark xvi. 15. John xxi. 15.
[f] Acts xiv. 23.
[g] Rom. x. 14, 17.
[h] 1 Cor. xii. 28. Eph. iv. 11, 12.

M. Dost thou then think that we are bound to hear such teachers and expounders?

S. Even as the Lord himself if he were present, so far as they teach only those things which they have received of the Lord; which himself witnesseth, saying, "[i]He that heareth you, heareth me; he that despiseth you, despiseth me;" yea, and moreover, to these preachers of his word he hath given the power to [k]bind and loose, that whose sins soever they by the word of God shall pardon or detain in earth, the same shall be pardoned or detained in heaven.

[i] Matt. x. 20, 40. & xxviii. 19, 20. Luke x. 16. John xiii. 20.
[k] Matt. xvi. 19. & xviii. 18. John xx. 22, 23.

M. Is it enough to hear them once treat of religion?

S. [l]We ought to be the scholars of Christ to the end, or rather, without end. It is not therefore enough for a man to begin, unless he continue: and such is our [m]dulness and forgetfulness, that we must oft be taught and put in remembrance, oft pricked forward, and, as it were pulled by the ear. For things but once or seldom heard are more likely to slip out of mind. And for this cause (as is afore said) [n]every sabbath-day (as appeareth by the ecclesiastical histories) the people assembling together, the word of God was openly read, and the expounders thereof if any were present, were heard; which custom is also at this day received in our churches by the ordinance of the apostles, and so of God himself.

[l] Matt. x. 22. & xxiv. 13. Luke ix. 62. Rom. xi. 22. 1 Cor. ix. 24. 2 Tim. iii. 14.
[m] Jud. iii. 7. Ps. cvi. 7. 14. Jer. ii. 32. Luke xxiv. 25.
[n] Acts xiii. 15, 27. & xv. 21.

M. Dost thou then think that the word of God is to be read in a strange tongue, and such as the people understandeth not?

S. That were grossly to mock God and his people, and shamelessly to abuse them both. For whereas God commandeth that his word be plainly read to young and old,

°men and women, namely, to the intent that all may understand and learn to fear the Lord their God as he himself in his own word expressly witnesseth, it were a very mockery that the word of God, which is appointed by God himself to teach his people, should be read to the people in a tongue unknown to them, and whereof they can learn nothing. Also St Paul doth treat of this matter, ᴾand thereupon concludeth that the unlearned people cannot answer Amen to the thanksgiving which they understand not, but that the readers and hearers should be ᑫstrangers the one to the other, if anything be spoken in the congregation that is not understood of them that be present; ʳand that he had rather to speak in the church of God five words understood, than ten thousand words not understood.

M. Shall we then have sufficiently discharged our duties, if we so endeavour ourselves that we hear and understand the word of God?

S. No. For we must not only hear and understand the word of God, but also ˢwith stedfast assent of mind embrace it as the truth of God descended from heaven, and heartily love it, ᵗyield ourselves to it desirous and apt to learn, and to frame our minds to obey it, that, being once planted in our hearts, it may take deep roots therein, and bring forth the fruits of a godly life, ordered according to the rule thereof, that so it may turn to our salvation as it is ordained. ᵘIt is therefore certain that we must, with all our travail, endeavour that in reading it, in studying upon it, and in hearing it both privately and publicly, we may profit; but profit in any wise we cannot, if it be set forth to us in a tongue that we know not.

M. But shall we attain to such perfection as thou speakest of by only reading the word of God, and diligently hearing it, and the teachers of it?

S. Forasmuch as it is the wisdom of God, men should vainly labour in either teaching or learning it, unless God would vouchsafe with the ˣteaching of his Spirit to instruct our hearts, as Paul teacheth, ʸthat in vain is the planting and the watering, unless God give the increase; therefore, that we may attain the wisdom of God hidden in his word, we must ᶻwith fervent prayer crave of God that with his Spirit he lighten our minds, being darkened ᵃwith extreme darkness.

For him the Lord hath promised to us to be our ^bteacher sent from heaven, that shall guide us into all truth.

M. Into what chief parts dost thou divide all this word of God?

S. Into the law and the gospel.

M. How be these two known the one from the other?

S. The law setteth out our duties both of godliness toward God, that is, the true worshipping of God, and of ^ccharity toward our neighbour, and severely requireth and exacteth ^dour precise obedience, and to the obedient promiseth everlasting life, but to the disobedient pronounceth threatenings and pains, yea, and eternal death. The gospel ^econtaineth the promises of God; and to the offenders of the law, so that they repent them of their offence, it promiseth that God will be merciful through faith in Christ.

M. Hitherto then thou hast declared that the word of God doth teach us his will, and containeth all things needful to salvation, and that we ought earnestly to study upon it, and diligently to hear the teachers and expounders of it; but, above all things, that we must by prayer obtain us a teacher from heaven; and what is the word of God, and of what parts it consisteth.

S. It is true.

M. Since then Christian religion floweth out of God's word as out of a spring-head, as thou hast before done with God's word, so now divide me also religion itself, which is to be drawn out of God's word into her parts and members, that we may plainly determine whereunto each part ought to be applied, and, as it were, to certain marks to be directed.

S. As of the word of God, so of religion also, there are principally two parts; ^fobedience, which the law, the perfect rule of righteousness commandeth, and faith, ^gwhich the gospel, that embraceth the promises concerning the mercy of God, requireth.

M. It seemeth yet, that there are either more or other parts of religion; for sometime, in dividing it, the holy scriptures do use other names.

S. That is true. For sometime they divide whole religion into faith ^hand charity, and sometime into ⁱrepentance and faith. For sometime for obedience they set ^kcharity, which by the law is required to be perfect toward God and men; and sometime because we perform neither obedience nor charity such as we ought, they put in place thereof ^l repentance most necessary for sinners to the obtaining of the mercy of God. Some, which like to have more parts, do set forth first out of the law, ^n the knowledge of our due duty, and damnation by the law for forsaking and rejecting our duty; secondly, out of the gospel, the ^o knowledge and affiance of our deliverance; thirdly, ^p prayer and craving of the mercy and help of God; fourthly, ^q thanksgiving for deliverance and other benefits of God. But howsoever they differ in names, they be the same things; and to those two principal parts, obedience and faith, in which is contained all the sum and substance of our religion, all the rest are referred. For whereas many do add, as parts, invocation and thanksgiving, and the divine mysteries most nearly conjoined to the same, which are commonly called sacraments, these, in very deed, are comprised within those two former parts. For no man can truly perform the duty toward God, either of affiance or of obedience, which will not, when any necessity distresseth him, flee to God, and account all things to come from him, and, when occasion and time serveth, rightly use his holy mysteries.

M. I agree with thee, that all may be drawn to these two parts, if a man will precisely and somewhat narrowly treat of them. But forasmuch as the most precise manner of dividing is not to be required of children, I had rather that somewhat in plainer sort thou divide religion into more parts, that the whole matter may be made the clearer. Therefore let us handle these things more grossly, so it be more openly.

S. Where you like best to deal with me in plainer sort, I may conveniently of two parts make four, and divide whole religion into obedience, faith, invocation, and sacraments.

M. Go to, then. Since I desire to have this treating of religion to be as plain as may be, let us keep this order; *first,* to inquire of obedience, which the law requireth; *secondly,* of faith, which looketh to, and embraceth the promises of the gospel; *thirdly,* of invocation and thanksgiving, which two are most nearly joined together; *fourthly* and lastly of the sacraments and mysteries of God.

S. And I, worshipful master, shall willingly, according

to my slender capacity, answer your questions, as I am taught by the holy scriptures.

The First Part. Of the Law and Obedience.

^r Lev. xxvi. 3, 14. Deut. x. 12. & xxviii. Ps. cxix. 4. Luke x. 25. John xiv. 15, 21, 23, 24. James ii. 10.

M. Forasmuch as ^rour obedience whereof we have first to speak, is to be tried by the rule of the law of God, it is necessary that we first search out the whole substance and nature of the law, which being found and known, it cannot be unknown, what and of what sort our obedience ought to be. Therefore, begin to tell what thou thinkest of the law.

^s Deut. iv. 2. & v. 32. & xxxii. 4. Ps. xix. 6, 7.
^t Exod. xx. & Deut. v. Isai. xxx. 21.
^u Deut. vi. 17, 18. & xiii. 18. Rom. xii. 2. Eph. v. 17. & vi. 7. Col. i. 9.

S. I think that the law of God is the ^sfull and in all points perfect rule of the righteousness that is required of man, which ^tcommandeth those things that are to be done, and forbiddeth the contraries. In this law God hath ^urestrained all things to his own will and judgment, so as no godliness toward him, nor dutifulness toward men can be allowed of him, but that only which doth in all things agree with the straitness of this rule. Vainly, therefore, do mortal

^w 1 Sam. xv. 22. Isai. xxix. 13. Matt. xv. 3, 9.
^x Matt. xxii. 36, 40. 1 John iii. 23.
^y Exod. xxxi. 18. & xxxiv. 28, 29. Deut. iv. 13.
^z Deut. v. 32. & x. 12. & xi. 26. Matt. xix. 16. 1 John iii. 24.
^a Deut. vi. 5. Matt. xxii. 36, 37.

men invent to themselves forms of ^wgodliness and duty after their own fancy; for God hath set forth to us his law, ^xwritten in two tables, as a most sure rule both of our worshipping of God, and ^yof our duties to men, and therewith also hath declared that there is nothing on earth more pleasant ^zand acceptable to him than our obedience.

M. Whereof treateth the first table?

S. It treateth of our ^agodliness toward God, and containeth the first four commandments of the law.

M. Whereof treateth the second?

^b Matt. xxii. 39. Rom. xiii. 8, 9. Gal. v. 14.
^c Exod. xxxiv. 28. Deut. iv. 13.

S. Of the duties of ^bmutual charity or love among men, which containeth six commandments. And so, in a sum, ^cten commandments make up the whole law, for which cause the law is called the Ten Commandments.

M. Rehearse me the first commandment of the first table.

^d Exod. xx. 1, 2, 3. Deut. v. 6, 7. Ps. lxxxi. 8, 9. Mich. vi. 4.

S. God spake thus: "^dHear, O Israel: I am the Lord thy God, which have brought thee out of the land of Egypt, out of the house of bondage. Thou shalt have none other gods before me."

M. Why doth God first speak somewhat of himself and of his benefit?

S. He had principally care that the ᵉestimation of the laws ordained by him should not be shortly abated by contempt: and therefore that they might have the greater authority, he useth this, as it were, an entry, "I am the Lord thy God." In which words he teacheth that he is ᶠour Maker, Lord, and Saviour, and the Author of all good. And so, with good right by his dignity of a law-maker, he challengeth to himself the authority of commanding, and by his goodness he procureth favour to his law, and by them both together, burdeneth us with necessity to obey it, unless we will be both ᵍrebels against him that is most mighty, and unthankful toward him that is most bountiful.

M. But whereas he speaketh of Israel by name, and maketh expressly mention of breaking the yoke of the bondage of Egypt, doth not this belong only to the people of Israel?

S. God, indeed, rescued the Israelites by his servant Moses from bodily ʰbondage; but he hath delivered all them that be his, by his Son Jesus Christ, from the spiritual ⁱthraldom of sin, and the tyranny of the devil, wherein else they had lain pressed and oppressed. This kind of deliverance pertaineth indifferently to ʲall men which put their trust in God their deliverer, and do ᵏto their power obey his laws; which if they do not, he doth by this rehearsal of his most great benefit pronounce that they shall be ˡguilty of most great unthankfulness. For let every man imagine the ᵐdevil, that hellish Pharaoh, ready to oppress him, and how ⁿsin is that most foul mire wherein he most filthily walloweth; let him set before the eyes of his mind, hell, ᵒthe most wretched Egyptian bondage, and then shall he easily perceive that this freedom, whereof I speak, is the thing that he ought principally ᵖto desire, as the thing of most great importance to him, whereof yet he shall be most unworthy, unless he honour the ᑫAuthor of his deliverance with all service and obedience.

M. Say on.

S. After that he hath thus stablished the authority of his law, now followeth the commandment, "Thou shalt have none other gods before me."

M. Tell me what this meaneth.

S. This commandment condemneth and forbiddeth idolatry, ʳwhich God throughly hateth.

ᵉ Lev. xxvi.
Deut. vi. 6.

ᶠ Deut. x. 12.
Ps. cxxxv. 3.
& cxxxvi. 1.
Isai. viii. 13.
& xliii. 1.
Mal. ii. 10.
1 Tim. vi. 14,
15, 16.

ᵍ Mal. i. 5, 6.

ʰ Exod. xii. xiv.

ⁱ John viii. 34, 36. Rom. vi. 20. Col. i. 13. Heb. ii. 14, 15. Acts x. 38.
ʲ Rom. iii. 22.
ᵏ John viii. 51. 1 John iii. 21.
ˡ Ps. lxxviii. 13, 14. & ciii. 1. Jer. ii. 6.
ᵐ Luke xiii. 16. 2 Tim. ii. 26. 1 Pet. v. 8.
ⁿ Ps. xl. 2. Isai. lix. 3. 2 Pet. ii. 20, 22. Rev. xvi. 15.
ᵒ Matt. xiii. 40. Luke xvi. 23. 2 Pet. ii. 4.
ᵖ Matt. xvi. 26. Acts xxvi. 18. Rom. xvi. 20.
ᑫ Isai. xvii. 10. John xiv. 15. Rom. vi. 13. 1 Cor. vi. 19.

ʳ Lev. xxvi. 1, 13. Deut. xii. 3. Jud. xi. 6, 16.

M. What is idolatry, or to have strange gods?

S. It is in the place of the one only ^atrue God, which hath openly and manifestly shewed and disclosed himself unto us in the holy scriptures, to set other persons or things, and of them ^tto frame and make to ourselves as it were certain gods, to worship them as gods, and to set and repose our trust in them. For God commandeth us to ^uacknowledge him alone for our only God, that is, that of those things that wholly belong to his majesty, and ^xwhich we owe to him alone, we transfer not any part, be it never so little, to any other, but that to him alone and entirely we give his whole honour and service, whereof to yield any whit to any other, were a most heinous offence.

M. What be the things that we properly owe to God alone, wherein thou sayest that his proper and peculiar worshipping consisteth?

S. Innumerable are the things that we owe to God; but they all may be well reduced to four chief points.

M. Which be they?

S. That we give unto his majesty ^ythe sovereign honour, and to his goodness the greatest ^zlove and affiance; that we flee to him, ^aand crave his help; that with thankfulness we yield, ^bas due to him, ourselves and all that we have. These things are to be given, as to none other, so to him alone, if we desire to have him alone our ^cGod, and to be his peculiar people.

M. What mean those last words, "before me," or "in my sight"?

S. That we cannot once so much as tend to revolting from God, but that God is ^dwitness of it; for there is nothing so close nor so secret that can be hid from him. Moreover, he thereby declareth that he requireth not only the ^ehonour of open confession, but also inward and sincere godliness of heart, for that he is the understander and judge of secret thoughts.

M. Well then, let this be enough said of the first commandment. Now let us go on to the second.

S. "^fThou shalt not make to thyself any graven image, nor the likeness of anything that is in heaven above, or in the earth beneath, nor in the water under the earth: thou shalt not bow down to them, nor worship them; for I the

Lord thy God am a [g]jealous God, and visit the sins of the fathers upon the children unto the third and fourth generation of them that hate me, and shew mercy unto thousands in them that love me, and keep my commandments."

[g] Exod. xxxiv. 7, 14. Deut. vii. 9.

M. What is the meaning of these words?

S. As in the first commandment he commandeth that himself alone be honoured and worshipped, so in this commandment he restraineth us from all superstition, and from all wrongful and bodily inventions, forasmuch as the worshipping of him ought to be [h]spiritual and pure; and chiefly he [i]frayeth us from the most gross fault of outward idolatry.

[h] Isai. ii. 18. John iv. 23, 24.
[i] Ps. lxxviii. 64. Isai. xlii. 8, 17. & xliv. 9. Jer. x. 14.

M. It may seem then that this law wholly condemneth the arts of painting and portraiture, so that it is not lawful to have any images made at all.

S. Not so. But he first forbiddeth us to make any images, to [k]express or counterfeit God or to worship him withal; and secondly he [l]chargeth us not to worship the images themselves.

[k] Lev. xxvi. 1.
[l] Deut. iv. 15. Isai. xl. 18. 12; & xlvi. 5, 6.

M. Why is it not lawful to express God with a bodily and visible form?

S. Because there can be no likeness or agreeing between God, which [m]is a Spirit eternal, unmeasurable, infinite, incomprehensible, severed from all mortal composition—and a frail, bodily, silly, spiritless, and [n]vain shape. Therefore they do most injuriously abate the majesty of the most good and most great God, when they go about in such sort to make resemblance of him.

Ps. lxxviii. 64. Acts xvii. 29.
[l] Deut. v. 8, 9. Ps. xcvii. 7. & cvi. 34. Isai. xliv. 17, 19.
[m] Ps. cxv. 3, 4. Isai. xl. 10, &c. John iv. 24. Rom. i. 20, 23.
[n] Isai. ii. 18, 19. xl. 18, 19. & xlvi. 5, 6. Jer. x. 14. Acts xvii. 29.

M. Have not they then said well, which affirm that images are unlearned men's books?

S. I know not what manner of books they be; but surely, concerning God, they can teach us nothing but errors.

M. What manner of worshipping is that which is here condemned?

S. When we, intending to pray, do [o]turn ourselves to portraitures or images; when we do fall down and kneel before them with uncovering our heads, or with other signs shewing any honour unto them, as if God were represented unto us by them; briefly, we are in this law forbidden, that we neither seek nor worship God in images, or, which is all one, that we worship not the images themselves in honour of

[o] Ps. xcvii. 7. & cvi. 34. Isai. xliv. 17, 19. Dan. iii. 5, 7. Hos. xi. 2. Mich. v. 12. Acts vii. 41.

God, nor in any wise by idolatry or superstition abuse them with injury to his majesty. Otherwise the lawful use [p]of making portraitures and of painting is not forbidden.

[p 1 Kings vii. 24, 25. Ezek. xli. 19. Matt. xxii. 20.]

M. By this that thou tellest me, it may easily be gathered, that it is very perilous to set any images or pictures in churches, which are [q]properly appointed for the only worshipping of God.

[q Deut. vii. 5. & xxvii. 15. 2 Chron. xxxi. 1. Isai. x. 10, 11. & xxx. 22. Ezek. vi. 4. Matt. xxi. 13.]

S. That that is true we have had already too much experience, by the decay in a manner of whole religion.

M. Yet there remaineth a certain, as it were, addition or appendant of this law.

S. "For I," saith he, "I the Lord your God [r]am a jealous God, and visit the sins of the fathers upon the children unto the third and fourth generation of them that hate me."

[r Exod. xx. 5. Deut. v. 9. & vi. 15. Ps. lxxviii. 58. Nah. i. 2.]

M. To what end, or wherefore, were these things spoken?

S. These serve to this end, to stablish and confirm this law, by adding as it were a certain special decree. For in naming himself our Lord and our God, he doth by two reasons, that is, in respect [s]of his authority and of his bountifulness, urge us to obey him in all things. And by this word "[t]jealousy," he declareth that he can abide no partner or equal.

[s Deut. x. 12. 1 Kings xviii. 39. 1 Tim. vi. 15.
t Exod. xxxiv. 14. Josh. xxiv. 19. Isai. xlii. 8.]

M. What is the reason of this jealousy that thou speakest of?

S. A most just reason. For since that to us, which have [u]nothing deserved, only of his own infinite goodness, he hath given himself; by most good right it is that he will have us, to be [x]wholly, altogether, and entirely his own. For this is that [y]bond, as it were, of a holy marriage, wherein to God, the faithful husband, our souls, as chaste spouses, are coupled; whose chastity standeth in this, to be dedicated to God alone, and to cleave wholly to him, like as on the other side our souls are said to be [z]defiled with adultery, when they swerve from God to idolatry or superstition. And how much more heartily the husband loveth his wife, and the chaster he is himself, so much is he more grievously displeased with his wife when she breaketh her faith.

[u Ps. xliv. 4, 5. Isai. xlviii. 9. Rom. v. 8. & xi. 35. 2 Tim. i. 9.
x Matt. iv. 10. & xxii. 37.
y Jer. ii. 2. 2 Cor. xi. 2. Eph. v. 24.
z Jer. ii. 20. & iii. 1, &c. Ezek. vi. 9. & xvi. 15.]

M. Go on.

S. Now to the intent to shew more vehemently how he

hateth idolatry, and with greater fear to restrain us from offending therein, he threateneth that he will take vengeance not only of them that shall so offend, but also ᵃof their children and posterity.

M. But how doth this agree with the righteousness of God, that any one should be punished for another's offence?

S. The very state of mankind doth sufficiently assoil¹ this question. ᵇFor by nature we are all subject to damnation, in which state, if God do leave us, we have no cause to complain of him. And as toward the godly he sheweth his love and mercy, ᶜin defending and cherishing their posterity with giving them their preservation which he owed them not; so toward the ungodly he executeth his vengeance in ᵈwithholding that his goodness from their children, and yet in the meantime, he doeth them no wrong, in that he giveth them not the grace which ᵉhe oweth them not, but as he found them, so leaveth them to their own disposition and nature.

M. Go forward to the rest.

S. That he should not seem to enforce us with only threatenings, now followeth the other part, wherein God, with gentle and liberal promising, entreateth and allureth us to obey him. For he promiseth that ᶠhe will shew most great mercifulness both toward all themselves that love him and obey his commandments, and also toward their posterity.

M. By what reason dost thou think this to be righteous?

S. Some reason it is because of the godly education ᵍwherein godly parents do so instruct their children, that they commonly use to succeed them as their heirs in the true fear and love of God; also ʰnature itself draweth us to a good will toward our friend's children. But the surest reason is, that God so promiseth, ⁱwhich neither can swerve from righteousness, nor at any time break his promise.

M. But it appeareth that this is not continually certain, and ever falleth so. For sometime godly parents beget ᵏungodly children, and such as go out of kind from their parents' goodness whom God, notwithstanding this promise, hath grievously punished.

S. This indeed cannot be denied. For as God, when he will, ˡsheweth himself merciful to the children of the wicked, so is he by no such necessity bounden to the children

¹ solve.

of the godly, but that he ^mis at liberty to reject such of them as he will. But therein he always useth such moderation, that the truth of his promise ever remaineth stedfast.

M. Where afore we speaking of revenging, he nameth but three or four generations at the most; why doth he here, in speaking of mercy, contain a thousand?

S. To shew that he is much more inclined to ⁿmercifulness and to liberality, than he is to severity; like as also in another place he professeth that he is very slow to wrath, and most ready to forgive.

M. By all this that thou hast said, I see thou understandest that God made special provision that the worshipping of him, which ought to be spiritual and most pure, should not be defiled with any gross idolatry or superstition.

S. Yea, he most earnestly provideth for it. For he hath, not only plainly °and largely reckoning by all forms of images, decreed it in a manner in the first part of his law, as a thing that principally concerneth his majesty, but also hath confirmed this law with terrible ^pthreatenings to the offender, and on the other side offering most great rewards to the observer of it. So that it may well seem more than wonderful that this commandment either was not understood, as being obscure, or not espied, as lying hid in the multitude; or not regarded, as light or of small charge: yea, that it hath lien as it were wholly neglected of all men, as if it had been no commandment, with no threatenings, no promises, adjoined unto it.

M. It is true as thou sayest. But now rehearse me the third commandment.

S. "^qThou shalt not take the name of thy Lord God in vain, for the Lord will not hold him guiltless that taketh his name in vain."

M. Tell me what is it to take the name of God in vain.

S. To abuse it either ^rwith forswearing, or with swearing rashly, unadvisedly, and without ^snecessity, or with once naming it without a weighty cause. For since the majesty of God's ^tname is most holy, we ought by all means to beware that we seem not either to despise it ourselves, or to give other any occasion to despise it; yea and so to see that we never once ^uutter the name of God without most great reverence, that it may ever appear honourable and glorious both to ourselves, and to all other. For it is not lawful once ˣto think, much less to speak, of God and of his works, otherwise than to his honour. Briefly, whosoever useth the name of God otherwise than for most weighty causes, and for most holy matters, abuseth it.

M. What thinkest thou then of them that blaspheme God, and of sorcerers, and such other kinds of ungodly men?

S. If they do great injury to God, which ʸ use his name only of a certain lewd custom, and intemperate readiness of speech, much more do they make themselves guilty of a most heinous and outrageous offence, which abuse the name of God ᶻ in bannings, in cursings, in enchantments, in forespeakings¹, or in any other manner of superstition.

M. Is there any lawful using of the name of God in swearing?

S. Yea, forsooth. When ᵃ an oath is taken for a just cause, either to affirm a truth, specially if the magistrate require or command it, or for any other matter of great importance, wherein we are either to maintain unviolate the honour of God, or to preserve mutual agreement and charity among men.

M. May we therefore lawfully, whensoever we say truth, use an oath with it?

S. I have already said, that this is not lawful; for so the estimation and reverence of the name of God should be abated, and should become of no price, and contemned as common. But when in a weighty matter the truth should otherwise not be believed, we may lawfully confirm it with an oath.

M. What followeth next?

S. "For the Lord will not hold him guiltless that taketh his name in vain."

M. Since God doth in other places pronounce that he will punish generally ᶜall the breakers of his law, why doth he here particularly threaten them that abuse his name?

S. His meaning was to shew how highly he esteemeth the ᵈglory of his name, to the end that seeing punishment ready for us, we should so much the more heedfully beware of profanely abusing it.

¹ fortune-tellings.

M. Dost thou think it lawful to swear by the names of saints, or by the names of other men or creatures?

S. No. For since a lawful oath is nothing else but the swearer's religious affirming that he calleth and useth God, ⁿthe knower and judge of all things, for witness that he sweareth a true oath, and that he calleth upon and wisheth the same God to be the punisher and avenger of his lying and offence if he swear falsely; it were a most heinous sin to part or communicate among other persons or creatures this honour of God's wisdom and majesty, which is his own proper and ᶠpeculiar honour.

<small>ᵉ Exod. xxii. 11. Heb. vi. 16.</small>

<small>ᶠ Deut. vi. 13; x. 20. Josh. xxiii. 7. Isai. lxv. 16.</small>

M. Now remaineth the fourth commandment, which is the last commandment of the first table.

<small>ᵍ Exod. xvi. 23. & xx. 8. & xxxi. 13. Lev. xxiii. 3. Deut. v. 12. Ezek. xx. 12.</small>

S. "Remember that thou ᵍkeep holy the Sabbath-day. Six days shalt thou labour, and do all that thou hast to do. But the seventh day is the Sabbath of the Lord thy God. In it thou shalt do no manner of work: thou, and thy son, and thy daughter, thy man-servant, and thy maid-servant; thy cattle, and the stranger that is within thy gates. For in six days the Lord ʰmade heaven and earth, the sea, and all that in them is, and rested the seventh day. Wherefore the Lord blessed the seventh day, and hallowed it."

<small>ʰ Gen. ii. 1, 2, 3. Heb. iv. 3, 10.</small>

M. What meaneth this word "Sabbath"?

<small>ⁱ Exod. xvi. 23. Lev. xvi. 31. ᵏ Jer. xvii. 21, 24, 27. Ezek. xlvi. 3. Mark vi. 2. Luke xxiii. 56.</small>

S. Sabbath, by interpretation, signifieth ⁱrest. That day, for that it is ᵏappointed only for the worshipping God, the godly must lay aside all worldly business, that they may the more diligently attend to religion and godliness.

M. Why hath God set herein before us an example of himself for us to follow?

<small>ˡ John xiii. 13, 15. 1 Cor. iv. 16. & xi. 1.</small>

S. Because notable and noble ˡexamples do more throughly stir up and sharpen men's minds. For servants do willingly follow their master, and children their parent. And nothing is more to be desired of men than to frame themselves to the ᵐexample and imitation of God.

<small>ᵐ Heb. iv. 3, 4, 10. & xii 2. 1 Pet. ii. 21.</small>

M. Sayest thou then that we must every seventh day abstain from all labour?

<small>ⁿ 1 Cor. x. 1. Gal. iv. 2, 3, 4, 10, & 12. Col. ii. 16, 17. Heb. viii. 5. & x. 1. ᵒ 2 Cor. iii. 14. Col. ii. 16. Heb. x. 1.</small>

S. This commandment hath a double consideration. For insomuch as it containeth a ceremony, and requireth only outward rest, it ⁿbelonged peculiarly to the Jews, and hath not the force of a continuing and eternal law. But now, by the ᵒcoming of Christ, as the other shadows of Jewish ceremonies are abrogated, so is this law also in this behalf abridged.

M. What then, beside the ceremony, is there remaining, whereunto we are still perpetually bound?

S. This law was ordained for these causes; first to stablish and maintain an ᵖecclesiastical discipline, and a certain order of the christian commonweal; secondly, to provide for the ᑫstate of servants, that it be made tolerable; thirdly, to express a certain form and ʳfigure of the spiritual rest.

M. What is that ecclesiastical discipline that thou speakest of?

S. That the people assemble together to ˢhear the doctrine of Christ, to yield ᵗconfession of their faith, to ᵘmake openly public prayers to God, to celebrate and retain the ˣmemory of God's works and benefits, and to use the ʸmysteries that he hath left us.

M. Shall it be enough to have done these every seventh day?

S. These things indeed every man privately ought to ᶻrecord and think upon every day; but for our negligence and weakness' sake, one certain special day is, by public order, appointed for this matter.

M. Why was there in this commandment provision made for relieving of servants?

S. It was reason that they which be ᵃunder other men's power should have some time to rest from labour. For else their state should be too grievous and too hard to bear. And surely meet it was that servants should, together ᵇwith us, sometimes serve him that is the common master of them and us; yea, and father too, since he hath, by Christ, adopted them to himself as well as us. It is also profitable for the masters themselves that servants should sometimes ᶜrest between their workings, that, after respiting their work awhile, they may return more fresh and lusty to it again.

M. Now remaineth for thee to tell of the spiritual rest.

S. That is, when, resting from worldly business ᵈand from our own works and studies, and as it were having a certain holy vacation, we yield ourselves wholly to God's governance, that he may do his works in us; and when (as the scripture termeth it) ᵉwe crucify our flesh, we bridle the froward desires and motions of our heart, restraining our own

ᵖ Mark i. 21. Acts xiii. 14. & xv. 21.
ᑫ Exod. xxi. 2. Deut. v. 14. Gal. iii. 26, 28.
ʳ Isai. lviii. 13. Rom. xiii. 12. Heb. iv. 9, 10.
ˢ Mark vi. 4. Luke iv. 16, 27.
ᵗ Ps. xcv. 2.
ᵘ Isai. lvi. 7.
ˣ Matt. x. 32. Matt. xxi. 13. Eph. iii. 21. Heb. ii. 12.
ʸ Ps. xxii. 23. & xxxv. 21. 1 Cor. xiv. 26.
ᶻ Ps. i. 2. & lxxxiv. 4. Luke xviii. 1. Eph. v. 20.
ᵃ Deut. v. 14. & xv. 12, 15. Jer. xxxiv. 12.
ᵇ Ps. cxxxiv. 1. Gal. iii. 26, 28. Eph. vi. 9. Col. iii. 11.
ᶜ Deut. v. 14. Isai. xxviii. 12.
ᵈ Isai. i. 14, 16. & lviii. 13. Heb. iv. 9.
ᵉ Gal. v. 24. Col. iii. 5.

[NOEL. CATEC.]

nature, that we may obey the will of God. For so shall we most aptly reduce and bring the figure and image of eternal rest to the very thing and truth itself.

M. May we then cast away this care on the other days?

S. No; for when we have once begun, we must go forward to the end, ᶠthroughout the whole race of our life. And the number of ᵍseven, forasmuch as in the scripture it signifieth perfection, putteth us in remembrance that we ought with all our force and endeavour, continually to labour and ʰtravail toward perfection: and yet therewithal is it shewed us, that so long as we live in this world, we are ⁱfar from the perfection and full attaining of this spiritual rest, and that here is given us but a certain taste of that rest which we shall enjoy, ᵏperfectly, fully, and most blessedly in the kingdom of God.

M. Hitherto thou hast well rehearsed me the laws of the first table, wherein the true worshipping of God, which is the fountain of all good things, is briefly comprehended. Now, therefore, I would have thee tell me what be the duties of our charity and love towards men, which duties do spring and are drawn out of the same fountain, and which are contained in the second table.

S. The second table beginneth thus: "¹Honour thy father and thy mother, that thy days may be long in the land which the Lord thy God giveth thee."

M. What is meant in this place by this word "honour"?

S. The honour of parents containeth love, ᵐfear, and reverence, and consisteth as in the proper work and duty of it, in obeying them, in saving, helping, and defending them, and also finding and relieving them if ever they be in need.

M. Doth the law extend only to parents by nature?

S. Although the very words seem to express no more; yet we must understand that all those to whom any authority is given, as ⁿmagistrates, ᵒministers of the church, ᵖschoolmasters; finally, all they that have any ornament, either of ᑫreverent age, or of wit, wisdom, or learning, worship, or wealthy state, or otherwise be our superiors, are contained under the name of fathers; because the authority both of them and of fathers come out of one fountain.

M. Out of what fountain?

S. The ʳholy decree of the laws of God, by which they are become worshipful and honourable, as well as natural parents. For from thence they all, whether they be parents, princes, magistrates, or other superiors, whatsoever they be, have all their power and authority; because by these it has pleased God to rule and govern the world.

M. What is meant by this, that he calleth magistrates, and other superiors, by the name of parents?

S. To teach us that they are given us of God, both for our own and ˢpublic benefit, and also by example of that authority, which of all other is naturally ᵗleast grudged at, to train and inure the mind of man, which of itself ᵘis puffed with pride, and loth to be under other's commandment, to the duty and obedience towards magistrates. For by the name of parents, we are charged not only to yield and obey to magistrates, but also to honour and love them. And likewise, on the other part, superiors are taught so to govern their inferiors, as a just parent useth to rule over good children.

M. What meaneth that promise which is added to the commandment?

S. That they shall ˣenjoy long life, and shall long continue in sure and stedfast possession of wealth, that give just and due honour to their parents and magistrates.

M. But this promise seemeth to belong peculiarly to such Jews as be kind to their parents.

S. It is no doubt, that which is by name spoken of the land of ʸCanaan, pertaineth only to the Jews. But forasmuch as God is ᶻLord of the whole world, what place soever he giveth us to dwell in, the same he promiseth and assureth us in this law that we shall keep still in our possession.

M. But why doth God reckon for a benefit long-continued age in such a miserable and wicked life?

S. Because when he relieveth the miseries ᵃand calamities of them that be his, or preserveth them in so many perils that beset them round about, and calleth them back from vices and sins, he sheweth to them a fatherly mind and good-will, as to his children.

M. Doth it follow, on the contrary side, that God hateth them whose life is taken away quickly, or before their ordinary race of years is expired, or that be distressed with miseries and adversities of this world?

S. Nothing less; but rather the [b]dearlier that any man is beloved of God, he is commonly the more burdened with adversities, or is wont the sooner to remove out of this life, as he were delivered and let by God out of prison.

M. Doth not this in the mean time seem to abate the truth and credit of God's promise?

S. No. For when God doth promise us worldly good things, he always addeth this exception, either expressly uttered [c]or secretly implied; that is, that the same be not unprofitable or hurtful to our souls. For it were against order and reason, [d]if chief regard should not be had of the soul, that we may so either attain or [e]lack worldly commodities as we may with blessedness enjoy eternal life for ever.

M. What shall we then say of them that be disobedient to parents or magistrates, or do misuse them, yea, or kill them?

S. Commonly all such do either [f]continue a most vile and miserable life, or lose it most shamefully, being taken out of it with untimely and cruel death, or infamous execution. And not only in this life, but also in the [g]world to come, they shall for ever suffer the everlasting punishment of their ungodliness. For if we be forbidden by the commandment of God, as here next followeth, to hurt any men, be they never so much estranged from us, yea, [h]even our edversaries and deadly enemies, much more to kill them; surely it is easy to perceive how much we ought to forbear and beware of all doing of any injury to our parents, of whom we receive our life, inheritance, liberty, and country. And since it is notably well said by the wise men in old time, that natural duty may be broken with a look, and that it is a most heinous wickedness once to offend his parents with word or speech; what punishment can be found sharp enough for him that shall offer death to his parent, for whom himself ought to have been content to die by the law of God and man, if need so required?

M. But it is much more heinous for a man to offend or kill the parent of his country than his own parent.

S. Yea, surely. For if it be for every private man a heinous offence to offend his private parents, and parricide to kill them; what shall we say of them that have conspired and borne wicked armour against the commonweal, against their country, the most ancient, sacred, and common mother of us all, which ought to be dearer unto us than ourselves, and for whom no honest man will stick to die to do it good, and against the prince, the father of the country itself, and parent of the commonweal; yea, and to imagine the overthrow, death, and destruction of them whom it is high-treason once to forsake or shrink from? So outrageous a thing can in no wise be expressed with fit name.

M. Now rehearse the sixth commandment.

S. "¹Thou shalt not kill." ^{l Exod. xx. 13. Matt. v. 21. James ii. 11.}

M. Shall we sufficiently fulfil this law if we keep our hands clean from slaughter and blood?

S. God made his law not only for outward works, but also and chiefly for the ᵏaffections of the heart. For ˡanger and hatred, and every desire to hurt, is, before God, adjudged manslaughter. Therefore these also God by this law forbiddeth us. ^{k Deut. xxx. 6. Ps. xxiv. 4. Matt. ix. 4. Heb. iii. 12. ˡ Matt. v. 21, 22, 23. Gal. v. 20. 1 John ii. 11.}

M. Shall we then fully satisfy the law if we hate no man?

S. God in condemning hatred requireth love ᵐtowards all men, even our enemies, yea, so far as to wish health, safety, and all good things to them that wish us evil, and do bear us a hateful and cruel mind, and as much as in us lieth, to do them good. ^{m Matt. v. 23, 24, 25. Luke vi. 27. Rom. xii. 18.}

M. What is the seventh commandment?

S. "ⁿThou shalt not commit adultery." ^{n Exod. xx. 14. Deut. v. 18. Matt. xix. 18.}

M. What dost thou think to be contained therein?

S. By this commandment is forbidden all kind of filthy and wandering lust; and all uncleanness that riseth of such lust, as fondness in handling, °unchasteness of speech, and all wantonness of countenance and gesture, all outward show of unchastity whatsoever it be. And not only filthiness of words and uncleanness of doings is forbidden by God, but also forasmuch as both our bodies and our souls are ᵖthe temples of the Holy Ghost, that honesty may be kept undefiled in them both, shamefacedness and chastity is commanded, that neither our bodies be defiled with uncleanness of lust, nor our minds with unhonest thoughts ᑫor desires, but be always preserved chaste and pure. ^{o Rom. xiii. 13. Eph. v. 3, 4. James ii. 11. p 1 Cor. iii. 16, 17. & vi. 15, 19. 2 Cor. vi. 16. q John xxxi. 9. Prov. vi. 25. Matt. v. 27, 28.}

M. Go on to the rest.

S. The eighth commandment is, "ʳThou shalt not steal." ^{r Exod. xx. 15. Matt. xix. 18. 1 Cor. vi. 8, 9, 10.}

By which commandment are condemned not only those thefts which are punished by men's laws, but also all frauds ˢand deceivings. But none doth offend more heinously against this law, than they that are wont by means of trust to beguile them toward whom they pretend friendship. For they that break faith labour to overthrow the common succour of all men. We are therefore commanded that we deceive no man; that we undermine no man; that we suffer not ourselves to be allured with advantage or gain of buying or selling, to do any wrong; that in trading of buying or selling we seek not wealth unjustly, nor make our profit by untrue and uneven ᵗmeasures and weights, nor increase our riches with sale of slight and deceitful ware.

M. Thinkest thou there is any more to be said of this commandment?

S. Yea, forsooth; for not only outward thefts and frauds are forbidden, and we are commanded to use bargaining without guile and deceits, and to do all things else without subtle undermining; but also we are charged to be altogether so minded, that though we were sure to escape unpunished and unespied, yet we would of ourselves forbear from wrong. For that which is wrong before man to do, is evil before God to have will to do. Therefore all counsels and devices, and especially ᵘthe very desire to make our gain of other's loss, is forbidden by this law. Finally, we are by this law commanded to endeavour all the ways we may that every man may most speedily come to his own, and safely keep that which he possesseth.

M. What is the ninth commandment?

S. "ˣThou shalt bear no false witness against thy neighbour."

M. What is the meaning of this commandment?

S. That we ʸbreak not our oath or faith. And in this law we are forbidden, not only open and manifest perjuries, but also wholly all lying, slanders, ᶻbackbitings, and evil speakings, whereby our neighbour may take loss or harm, or lose his good name and estimation. For one example containeth a general doctrine. Yea, and we ought neither ourselves, at any time, to speak any false or untrue thing, nor with our words, writing, silence, presence, or secret assent in holding our peace, once allow the same in other. But we ought always to be ^alovers and followers of simple truth, ever to rest upon truth, to bring forth all things diligently into the light of truth, as place, time, or necessity shall require; finally, ever readily to take upon us the defence of truth, and by all means to maintain and uphold it. a Prov. xii. 17, 19. 2 Cor. xiii. 8. Eph. iv. 25.

M. For satisfying of this law, is it not enough to bridle our tongue and pen?

S. By the same reason that I have before said, when he forbiddeth evil speaking, he therewith also forbiddeth sinister ^bsuspicions and wrongful misdeemings. For this lawmaker hath ever chief respect to the affections of the heart. This law, therefore, forbiddeth us to be inclined so much as to think evil of our neighbours, much less to ^cdefame them. Yea, it commandeth us to be of such gentle sincerity and indifference toward them, as to endeavour, so far as truth may suffer, to think well of them, and to our uttermost power to preserve their estimation untouched. b Matt. vii. 1, 2. Rom. xiv. 3, 4. 1 Cor. xiii. 5, 7. c Prov. xxv. 17. 1 Pet. ii. 1, 2.

M. What is the reason why the Lord in his law doth term the corrupt affections of the heart by the names of the most heinous offences? For he comprehendeth wrath and hatred under the name of manslaughter; all wantonness and unclean thoughts under the name of adultery, and unjust coveting under the name of theft.

S. Lest we (as the nature of man is) should wink at the ungodly ^daffections of the heart, as things of small weight, therefore the Lord setteth them out by their true names, according as he measureth them by the rule of his own righteousness. For our Saviour, the best interpreter of his Father's meaning, doth so expound the same: "^eWhoso," saith he, "is angry with his brother, he is a manslayer; whoso lusteth after a woman, he hath committed adultery." d Rom. vii. 7. 1 Cor. x. 6. James iv. 1. e Matt. v. 22, 28. & xv. 19. 1 John iii. 15.

M. But whereas only vices and sins are forbidden in these commandments, why dost thou, in expounding them, say that the contrary virtues are also commanded therein? For thou sayest that, in forbidding of adultery, chastity is enjoined; and in forbidding manslaughter and theft, most entire good-will and liberality is commanded. And so of the rest.

S. Because the same our Saviour doth so expound it, which setteth the sum of the law not in abstaining only from injury and evil doing, but in ^flove and charity; like as the f Matt. xxii. 39. Rom. xiii. 8, 9. Gal. v. 14.

^g Ps. xxxvii. 27.

^h Exod. xx. 17. Mich. ii. 2. Rom. vii. 7. 1 Cor. x. 6.

ⁱ Isai. i. 16. Rom. xiii. 14. Gal. v. 24.

^k Gen. vi. 5. & viii. 21. Ps. xciv. 11. Prov. xx. 9. Matt. xv. 18, 19.

^l Isai. i. 16. & xxix. 13, 15. Jer. iv. 14. Ezek. xviii. 31. Matt. v. 8. ^m Ps. v. 4, 5. 2 Cor. vi. 14.

ⁿ Matt. xxii. 37. Mark xii. 30. Luke x. 27.

kingly prophet had also before taught, saying, "^g Depart from evil, and do good."

M. Now remaineth the last commandment.

S. "Thou shalt not covet ^hthy neighbour's house, thou shalt not covet thy neighbour's wife, nor his servant, nor his maid, nor his ox, nor his ass, nor any thing that is his."

M. Seeing that, as thou hast oft said already, the whole law is spiritual, and ordained not only to restrain outward evil doings, but also to bridle the inward affections of the heart; what is there herein commanded more than was before omitted?

S. God hath before forbidden evil doings and corrupt affections of the mind; but now he requireth of us a ⁱmost precise pureness, that we suffer not any desire, be it never so light, nor any thought, be it never so small, in any wise swerving from right, once to creep into our heart.

M. How then? Dost thou say that unadvised and sudden desires, and short thoughts that come upon the very godly, are sins, although they strive against such, rather than yield to them?

S. Surely it is plain that all corupt ^kthoughts, although our consent be not added to them, do proceed of our corrupted nature. And it is no doubt that sudden desires that tempt the hearts of men, although they prevail not so far as to win a stedfast assent of mind and allowance, are in this commandment condemned by God as sins. For it is meet that even in our ^lvery hearts and minds should shine before God their most perfect pureness and cleanness. For no innocency and righteousness ^mbut the most perfect can please him, whereof he hath also set before us this his law a most perfect rule.

M. Hitherto thou hast shortly and plainly opened the law of the ten commandments: but cannot all these things that thou hast severally and particularly declared, be in few words gathered as it were into one sum?

S. Why not? seeing that Christ, our heavenly schoolmaster, hath comprised the whole pith and substance of the law in a sum and short abridgment, in this manner, saying, "ⁿThou shalt love the Lord thy God with all thy heart, with all thy soul, with all thy mind, and with all thy strength. And this is the greatest commandment in the law. And the second is like unto this,—Thou shalt love thy neighbour as thyself. For in these two commandments are contained the whole law and the prophets."

M. What manner of love of God dost thou take to be here required?

S. Such as is meet for God; that is, that we acknowledge °him, both for our most mighty Lord, and our most loving ᴾFather, and most merciful Saviour. Wherefore, to this love is to be adjoined both ᑫreverence to his majesty, and obedience to ʳhis will, and ˢaffiance in his goodness.

°Deut. x. 17. 1 Kings xviii. 39. 1 Tim. vi. 15.
ᴾIsai. lxiii. 16. Matt. vi. 8. 1 Tim. i. 1.
ᑫDeut. x. 12. Ps. xcvi. 7.
ʳ1 Cor. x. 31. Deut. vi. 17. Rom. xii. 2.

M. What is meant by all the heart, all the soul, all the strength?

S. Such fervency and such unfeignedness of love, that there be no room for any ᵗthoughts, for any desires, for any meanings or doings, that disagree with the love of God. Dear (as one saith) are our parents, dear are our children, our kinsfolks, our friends, and dearer yet is our country; but all the dear ᵘloves of them all, entire zeal toward God, and the most perfect love of him, not only containeth, but also much and far surmounteth, for whom what good man will stick to die? For every godly man loveth God not only more dearly than all his, but also more dearly than himself.

ˢPs. ii. 12, & xxv. 1. & xxxi. 1. & cxviii. 8.
ᵗDeut. xxx. 6. Josh. xxiii. 11. Matt. x. 37. Luke xiv. 26.
ᵘJohn xiv. 15, 21, 23, 24. & xv. 10.

M. Now what sayest thou of the love of our neighbour?

S. Christ's will was, that there should be most strait bonds of love among his Christians. And as we be by nature most ˣinclined to the love of ourselves, so can there not be devised a plainer nor shorter, nor more pithy, nor more indifferent rule of brotherly love than that which the Lord hath gathered out of our own nature and set before us; that is, that every man should bear to his neighbour the same good-will that he beareth to himself. Whereof it followeth that we should ʸnot do anything to our neighbour, nor say nor think anything of him which we would not have others to do to ourselves, or to say or think of ourselves. Within the compass of which only law, which is indeed as it were the soul of all other laws, if we could be holden, surely there were no need of so many bars of laws as men do daily devise, to hold men in from doing wrong one to another, and to maintain civil society, and all well near in vain, if among men this one law be not regarded.

ˣ1 Cor. xiii. 5. Eph. v. 29. Phil. ii. 21.
ʸMatt. vii. 12. & xxii. 39. Luke vi. 31. Rom. xiii. 9, 10.

M. How far extendeth the name of neighbour?

S. The name of neighbour containeth not only those that be of our kin and alliance, or friends, or such as be knit to us in any civil bond of love, but also those whom we ᶻknow not, yea, and our enemies.

M. Why, what have those to do with us?

S. Surely they are knit to us with the same bond wherewith God hath coupled together all mankind; which bond his will is to have inviolable and ᵃstedfast, and therefore it cannot be taken away by any man's frowardness, hatred, or malice. For though any man hate us, yet that notwithstanding, he remaineth still our neighbour, and so must alway be accounted, because the same order by which this fellowship and conjoining among men is knit together ought alway to remain stedfast and inviolable. And hereby it may be easily perceived why the holy scripture hath appointed charity or ᵇlove to be one of the principal parts of religion.

M. But what meaneth that addition in the end, that therein are contained the whole law and the prophets?

S. Because in very deed the sum of them all belongeth thereunto. For all the warnings, commandments, exhortations, promises, and threatenings, which the law itself and the prophets and apostles do everywhere use, are directed to nothing else, but to the end of this law, as it were to a mark. And ᶜall things in the holy scriptures are so applied to charity, that they seem as it were to lead us by the hand unto it.

M. Now I would have thee to tell me what law that is, that thou speakest of—whether is it the same that we call the law of nature, or some other besides it?

S. I remember, master, that I have long ago learned this of you, that is, that the law, as the highest reason, was by God grafted in the nature of man, while man's nature was yet ᵈsound and uncorrupted, being created after the image of God; and so this law is indeed, and is called, the law of nature. But since the nature of man became stained with sin, although the ᵉminds of wise men have been in some sort lightened with the brightness of this natural light, yet in the most part of men this light is so put out, that scarce any sparkles thereof are to be seen; and in many men's minds is deeply grafted ᶠa sharp hatred of God and men, against the ordinances of God and his commandments written in this law, which command most hearty love to God and men.

And hereof cometh so great ungodliness toward God, and so deadly cruelty toward men.

M. How cometh it to pass that God would have these commandments written in tables?

S. I will tell you. ^gThe image of God in man is, since the fall of Adam, by original sin and by evil custom, so darkened, and natural judgment so corrupted, that man doth not sufficiently understand what difference is between honest and dishonest, right and wrong. Merciful God therefore, minding to renew the same image in us, hath by his law, written in tables, set forth the rule of ^hperfect righteousness, and that so lively and fully, that God requireth no more of us but to follow the same rule. For he accepteth none other sacrifice but ⁱobedience, and therefore he hateth all, whatsoever it be, that we admit in religion, or in the case of worshipping God without the warrant of his prescribed ordinance.

^g Luke i. 79.
1 Cor. ii. 14.
Eph. iv. 17, 18.

^h Ps. xix. 8.
& cxix. 1.
Baruc. iv. 1.

ⁱ 1 Sam. xv. 22. Hos. vi. 6. Mark xii. 33.

M. But where, in this law, there are no commandments set out of every man's private vocation, how can this be a perfect rule of life?

S. Though here be no commandments expressly set out concerning the duties of every several man, yet forasmuch as the law commandeth to ^kgive to every man his own, it doth in a sum comprise all the parts and duties of every man privately in his degree and trade of life. And in these tables the Lord hath briefly and summarily comprehended all those things which in the scriptures are eachwhere most largely set out concerning the several commandments and duties of every several man.

^k Exod. xx. 12, 15, *et toto capite.*

M. Seeing then the law doth shew a perfect manner of worshipping God aright, ought we not to live wholly according to the rule thereof?

S. Yea, and so much that God ^lpromiseth life to them that live according to the rule of the law, and, on the other side, ^mthreateneth death to them that break his law, as is aforesaid. And for this cause, in my division, I have named obedience as one of the principal parts of religion.

^l Deut. viii. 1.
& xxx. 15
Matt. xix. 17.
John xii. 50.

^m Deut. xi. 28. & xxx. 17. Rom. i. 18. & vi. 23.

M. Dost thou then think them to be justified that do in all things obey the law of God?

S. Yea, surely, if any were able to perform it, they should be justified by the law; but we ⁿare all of such weak-

ⁿ Gen. vi. 5. & viii. 11. Prov. xx. 9. Rom. vii. 14, 15. Gal. ii. 16.

ness, that no man in all points fulfilleth his duty. For though we put case, that there be one found that performeth the law in some point, yet shall he not thereby be justified before God; for he pronounceth them all to be °accursed and abominable that do not fulfil all things that are contained in the law.

M. Dost thou then determine that no mortal man is justified before God by the law?

S. No man. For the ᴾscriptures do also pronounce the same.

M. Why then did God make such a law as requireth a perfection above our ability?

S. In making the law, God respected not so much what we were able to perform, which by our own fault ᑫare very weak, as what was meet for his own righteousness. And forasmuch as none but the highest ʳrighteousness could please God, it behoved that the rule of life which he set out should be throughly perfect. Moreover, the law requireth nothing of us but that we are bound to perform. But since we are far from due ˢobeying the law, men can have no sufficient or lawful excuse to defend themselves before God; and so the law accuseth all men for guilty, yea, ᵗand condemneth them before the judgment-seat of God: and that is the cause why Paul calleth the law the ministry of death and damnation.

M. Doth then the law set all men in this most remediless estate?

S. The unbelieving ᵘand the ungodly the law doth both set and leave in such case as I have spoken, who, as they are not able to fulfil the least jot of the law, so have they no affiance at all in God through Christ. But among the godly the law hath other uses.

M. What uses?

S. First, the law, in requiring so ˣprecise perfectness of life, doth shew to the godly as it were a mark for them to level at, and a goal to run unto, that, daily profiting, they may with earnest endeavour travel toward the highest uprightness. This purpose and desire the godly, by the guiding of God, do conceive. But principally they take heed, so much as they are able to do and attain to, that it may not be said that there is any notorious fault in them. Secondly, whereas the law requireth things far above ʸman's power, and where they find themselves too weak for so great a burden, the law doth raise them up to crave strength at the Lord's hand. Moreover, when the law doth continually ᶻaccuse them, it striketh their heart with a wholesome sorrow, and driveth them to the repentance that I spake of, and to beg and obtain pardon of God through Christ, and therewithal restraineth them, that they trust not upon their own innocency, nor presume to be proud in the sight of God, and is always to them as a bridle to withhold them in the fear of God. Finally, when beholding by the law, ᵃas it were in a glass, the spots and uncleanness of their souls, they learn thereby that they are not able to attain perfect righteousness ᵇby their works: by this mean they are trained to humility, and so the law prepareth them and sendeth them to seek righteousness in Christ.

[z Deut. xxvii 27. Rom. iii. 10, 11, 12. 2 Cor. iii. 9.]

[a Rom. iii. 20. & vii. 7.]

[b Prov. xx. 9. Rom. i. 20, 21. Gal. ii. 16.]

M. Then, as far as I perceive, thou sayest that ᶜthe law is as it were a certain schoolmaster to Christ, to lead us the right way to Christ, by knowing of ourselves, and by repentance and faith.

[c Rom. x. 4. Gal. iii. 10, &c. 24.]

S. Yea, forsooth.

THE SECOND PART. OF THE GOSPEL AND FAITH.

M. Since now, my dear child, thou hast so much as may be, in a short abridgment, largely answered this matter of the law and obedience, good order requireth that we speak next of the gospel, which containeth the promises of God, and promiseth the mercy of God through Christ to them that have broken God's law, and to the which gospel faith hath specially respect. For this was the second point in our division: and this also, the very orderly course of those matters that we have treated of hath as it were brought us by the hand unto. What is now the sum of the gospel and of our faith?

S. Even the same wherein the chief articles of the christian faith have been in old time briefly knit up and contained, and which is commonly called the Creed or Symbol of the Apostles.

M. Why is the sum of our faith called a symbol?

S. A symbol by interpretation is a badge, mark, watchword, or token, whereby the soldiers of one side are known from the enemies. For which cause the short sum of our faith, by which the Christians are severally known from them that be not Christians, is rightly called a symbol.

M. But why is it called the symbol of the apostles?

S. Because it was first received from the apostles' own mouth, or most faithfully gathered out of their writings, and allowed from the very beginning of the church, and so hath continually remained among all the godly, firm, stedfast, and unmoved, as a sure and staid rule of christian faith.

M. Go to. I would have thee now rehearse to me the symbol itself?

S. I will. "I believe in God the Father Almighty, maker of heaven and earth; and in Jesus Christ, his only Son, our Lord; which was conceived by the Holy Ghost; born of the Virgin Mary; suffered under Pontius Pilate; was crucified, dead, and buried; he descended into hell: the third day he rose again from the dead; he ascended into heaven; sitteth at the right hand of God the Father Almighty; from thence shall he come to judge the quick and the dead. I believe in the Holy Ghost; the holy catholic church; the communion of saints; the forgiveness of sins; the resurrection of the body; and the life everlasting. Amen."

M. These things, my child, thou hast briefly and in short sum set forth. Wherefore it is good that thou declare more plainly and at large what thou thinkest of every particular. And first, into how many parts dost thou divide this whole confession of faith?

S. Into four principal parts: in the first whereof is entreated of God the Father, and the creation of all things: in the second, of his Son Jesus Christ, which part also containeth the whole sum of the redemption of man: in the third, of the Holy Ghost: in the fourth, of the church, and of the benefits of God towards the church.

M. Go forward then to declare me those four parts in order. And first, in the very beginning of the Creed, what meanest thou by this word "believe"?

S. I mean thereby that I have a true and a lively faith, that is to say, [d]a christian man's faith in God the Father, the Son, and the Holy Ghost, and that I do by this form of confession [e]testify and approve the same faith.

M. Is there any faith which is not a true and a lively faith?

[d] Matt. xxviii. 19. Rom. i. 17. John i. 12, 13. Gal. iii. 26.
[e] Matt. x. 32. Rom. x. 9. Heb. iv. 14.

S. There is indeed a certain general faith, as I may so call it, and there is a ᶠdead faith.

M. Since then it is a matter of no small weight what thou comprehendest under the name of believing and of a christian faith, that is to say, a true and lively faith, go to and tell me what faith that same is, and how it differeth from the general faith, and also from the dead faith.

S. The general faith is that which ᵍcrediteth the word of God; that is, which believeth all those things to be true that are contained in the scriptures concerning God, his incomprehensibleness, power, righteousness, wisdom, mercy towards the faithful and godly, and most earnest severity toward the unbelieving and ungodly, and likewise all other things taught in the scriptures.

M. Doth not the true faith that thou speakest of believe also all these same things?

S. Yea, forsooth. But the true faith goeth further, as I shall shew by and by. ʰFor thus far not only ungodly men, but also the very devils, do believe; and therefore neither are they ⁱindeed faithful, nor are so called. But the true faith, as it nothing doubteth that all things taught in the word of God are most certainly true, ᵏso doth it also embrace the promises made concerning the mercy of God the Father, and the forgiveness of sins to the faithful through Jesus Christ; which promises are properly called ˡthe gospel, which faith whosoever have, they do not only fear ᵐGod as the most mighty Lord of all, and the most righteous Judge (which we already said that the most part of the ungodly and the ⁿdevils themselves do), but also they love him as their most bountiful and merciful ᵒFather; whom as they travail in all things to please (as becometh obedient children) with godly endeavours and works, which are called the fruits of faith, so have they a good and sure hope of ᵖobtaining pardon through Christ, when, as men, they swerve from his will. For they know that Christ (whom they trust upon), ᵠappeasing the wrath of his Father, their sins shall never be imputed any more unto them, than if the same had never been committed. And though themselves have not satisfied the law, and their duty towards God and men, yet believe they that Christ, with his most full observing of the law, hath abundantly satisfied God for them, and are persuaded that by

ᶠ Rom. i. 32. Tit. ii. 16. James ii. 26.

ᵍ Matt. vii. 22. Luke xii. 47. 1 Cor. xiii. 2.

ʰ Rom. i. 32. Tit. i. 16. James ii. 19.
ⁱ John i. 12. Gal. iii. 25, 26.
ᵏ Luke xxiv. 47. Rom. iv. 16.

ˡ Isai. lxi. 2. Luke ii. 10, 11. & iv. 18.
ᵐ Deut. x. 20. Ps. cxi. 10.

ⁿ James ii. 19.
ᵒ Deut. x. 12. Ps. i. 2, 3. Col. ii. 6. Eph. v. 1, 2, 8.

ᵖ Matt. i. 21. Rom. ii. 24. & v. 1.

ᵠ Eph. ii. 15, 16. Col. ii. 14. Heb. x. 17. 1 John ii. 1, 2.

this his ʳrighteousness and observing of the law of God, themselves are accounted in the number and state of the righteous, and that they are beloved of God even as if themselves had fulfilled the law. And this is the ˢjustification which the holy scriptures do declare that we obtain by faith.

M. Cannot these things also be in the devils, or in wicked men?

S. Nothing less. For ᵗthough they fear or rather with horror do dread God as most mighty and righteous, for that they know he will take vengeance of their ungodliness, yet can they neither have any trust in his goodness and mercy toward them, nor any recourse to his grace, nor enter into any endeavour to obey his will. Therefore their faith, although they doubt not of the truth of the word of God, is called ᵘa dead faith, for that like a dry and dead stock it never bringeth forth any fruits of godly life, that is, of love to God and charity toward men.

M. Give me then, out of that which thou hast hitherto said, a definition of that same lively, true, and christian faith.

S. ˣFaith is an assured knowledge of the fatherly goodwill of God toward us through Christ, and an affiance in the same goodness, as it is witnessed in the gospel; which faith hath coupled with it an ʸendeavour of godly life, that is, to obey the will of God the Father.

M. Thou hast sufficiently declared what thou meanest by the terms of "faith" and "believing." Now go forward, and tell me in as apt words as thou canst, what thou understandest by the name of God, which followeth next in the Creed.

S. I will do the best I can, good master, as my wit and ability will serve me. I understand that there is ᶻone nature, or ᵃsubstance, or soul, or mind, or rather ᵇdivine Spirit (for diversely have wise men, both heathen and christian, termed God, where indeed by no words he can be properly termed) ᶜeternal, without beginning and end, ᵈimmeasurable, ᵉuncorporal, invisible with the eyes of men, of ᶠmost excellent majesty, which we call God, whom all peoples of the world ᵍmust reverence and worship with highest honour; and in him, as in the best and greatest, ʰto settle their hope and affiance.

M. Seeing there is but one God, tell me why, in the confession of the christian faith, thou rehearsest three, the Father, the Son, and the Holy Ghost.

S. Those be not the names of ⁱsundry gods, but of three distinct persons in one Godhead. For in ᵏone substance of God we must consider, the ˡ*Father*, which of himself begat the Son even from eternity, the beginning and first author of all things; the ᵐ*Son*, even from eternity begotten of the Father, which is the eternal wisdom of God the Father; the ⁿ*Holy Ghost*, proceeding from them both, as the power of God spread abroad through all things, but yet so as it also continually abideth in itself; and ᵒyet that God is not therefore divided. For of these three persons, none goeth before the other ᵖin time, in greatness, nor in dignity: but the Father, the Son, and the Holy Ghost, three distinct persons,ᑫ in eternity of like continuance, in power, even in dignity equal, and in Godhead one. There is therefore ʳone eternal, immortal, almighty, glorious, the best, the greatest, God the Father, the Son, and the Holy Ghost. For so hath the universal number of Christians, which is called the catholic church, taught us by the holy scriptures concerning God the Father, the Son, and the Holy Ghost; where otherwise the infinite depth of this mystery is so great that it cannot with mind be conceived, much less with words be expressed; wherein therefore is required a simplicity of Christian faith ready to believe, rather ˢthan sharpness of wit to search, or the office of the tongue to express so secret and hidden a mystery.

ⁱ Matt. xxviii. 19.
1 John v. 7.
ᵏ John x. 30.
Gal. iii. 20.
ˡ Gen. i. 1.
1 Cor. viii. 6.
ᵐ John i. 1; xvii. 5. Col. i. 15. Heb. i. 2, 3, 5.
ⁿ Luke i. 35. John xiv. 26. Acts v. 3, 4. 1 Cor. xii. 4.
ᵒ John x. 30. 1 Cor. viii. 6. Gal. iii. 20.
ᵖ John i. 1. & v. 17, 18, 21, 23. Phil. ii. 6.
ᑫ 1 John v. 7.
ʳ Deut. iv. 35, 39. Ps. lxxxvi. 9, 10. & civ. 30, 31. 1 Tim. i. 17.
ˢ Prov. xxv. 26.

M. Thou sayest true. Go forward therefore. Why dost thou call God Father?

S. Beside the same principal cause which I have already rehearsed, which is, for that he is the ᵗnatural Father of his only Son begotten of himself from before all beginning, there be two other causes why he both is indeed and is called our Father. ᵘThe one is, for that he first created us, and gave life unto us all. ˣThe other cause is of greater value, namely, for that he hath heavenly begotten us again through the Holy Ghost, and ʸby faith in his true and natural Son Jesus Christ he hath adopted us his children, and through the same Christ hath given us his kingdom, and the inheritance of everlasting life.

The first part of the Creed. God the Father.
ᵗ Matt. iii. 17. John i. 14.
Rom. xv. 6. 2 Cor. i. 3. & xi. 31.
ᵘ Gen. i. 27. Mal. i. 6; ii. 10.
ˣ John iii. 3, 5. 1 Pet. i. 3, 23.
ʸ John i. 12. Rom. viii. 15, 17, 23, & ix. 4.
Gal. iv. 5, 6. Eph. i. 5, 6. Tit. iii. 7.

M. In what sense dost thou give him the name of "Almighty"?

S. For that ᶻas he hath created the world and all things, so he hath the same in his power, governeth them by

ᶻ Isai. xl. 21. Matt. v. 45. & x. 29. Eph. i. 11.

his providence, ordereth them after his own will, and commandeth all as it pleaseth him; so as there is nothing done but by his appointment or sufferance, and nothing is there which he is not able to do: for I do not imagine God to have a certain idle power which he putteth not in use.

M. Dost thou then make ungodly men also and wicked spirits subject to the power of God?

S. ^aWhy not? For else were we in most miserable case, for that we should never be out of fear if they might have any power over us without the will of God. But God, as it were with a bridle of his power, so restraineth them, that they cannot once stir but at his beck and sufferance. And we for our parts are upholden with this comfort, that we are so in the power of our Almighty Father, that not so much as ^bone hair of ours can perish, but by his will, that beareth us so good will.

^a Job i. 10. Luke xxii. 31, 32. John x. 28, 29. Acts ii. 23. & iv. 27, 28. & xii. 11.

^b Luke xii. 7. & xxi. 18.

M. Go forward.

S. ^cForasmuch as the mind of man is not able of itself to conceive the goodness and incomprehensibleness of the most good and most great God, we add further, that he is the Creator of heaven and earth, and of all things contained in them. By which words we signify that God is as it were in a glass to be beholden, and (so far as behoveth us) to be known in his works, and in the orderly ^dcourse of the world. For when we see that same unmeasurable greatness of the world, and all the parts thereof, to be so framed as they could not possibly in beauty be fairer, nor for profit be better, we forthwith thereby understand the infinite power, wisdom, and goodness of the workman and builder thereof. For who is so brutish, that in looking up to heaven doth not perceive that there is a God? Yea, for this cause specially it seemeth that God hath fashioned men out of the earth, tall and upright, that they should be beholders of things above, and heavenly matters, and in beholding heaven might conceive the knowledge of him.

^c John i. 18. 1 Tim. i. 17.

^d Psal. xix. 1. & l. 7. Rom. i. 19, 20.

M. How dost thou say that God created all things?

S. ^eThat God, the most good and mighty Father, at the beginning and of nothing, ^fby the power of his Word, that is, of Jesus Christ his Son, framed and made this whole visible world, and all things, whatsoever they be that are contained therein, and ^galso the uncorporal spirits whom we call angels.

^e Gen. i. 1. Ps. xxxiii. 6. Acts xiv. 15. ^f John i. 3. 1 Cor. viii. 6. Heb. i. 2.

^g Col. i. 16.

M. But dost thou think it godly to affirm that God created all spirits, even those wicked spirits, whom we call devils?

S. God did not ^hcreate them such: but they, by their own evilness, fell from their first creation, without hope of recovery, and so are they become evil, not by creation and nature, but by corruption of nature. <small>h Gen. i. 31. John viii. 44. Col. i. 16. Jude 6.</small>

M. Did God think it enough to have once created all things, and then to cast away all further care of things from thenceforth?

S. I have already briefly touched this point. Whereas it is much more excellent to maintain and preserve things created, than to have once created them; we must certainly believe, ⁱthat when he had so framed the world and all creatures, he from thenceforth hath preserved and yet preserveth them. For all things would run to ruin, and fall to nothing, unless by his virtue, and, as it were, by his hand they were upholden. We also assuredly believe, ^kthat the whole order of nature and changes of things, which are falsely reputed the alterations of fortune, do hang all upon God: ^lthat God guideth the course of the heaven, upholdeth the earth, tempereth the seas, and ruleth this whole world, and that all things obey his divine power, and by his divine power all things are governed: that he is the ^mauthor of fair weather and of tempest, of rain and of drought, of fruitfulness and of barrenness, of health and of sickness: that of ⁿall things that belong to the sustentation and preserving of our life, and which are desired either for necessary use or honest pleasure; finally, of all things that nature needeth, he hath ever given, and yet most largely giveth abundance and plenty with most liberal hand; to this end, verily, that we should so use them as becometh mindful and kind children. <small>i Ps. lxxv. 3. & civ. 10. & cxlv. 15. Heb. i. 3.
k Matt. x. 29, 30.
l Exod. xiv. 21. Ps. lxxxix. 10. & cxlvii. 8, 9.
m Lev. xxvi. 4, &c.
n Ps. cxliv. 12. & cxlv. 16, 17. Isai. li. 3. Matt. v. 45. Rom. xiv. 6. 1 Cor. x. 31. Eph. v. 4. 1 Tim. iv. 3, 4. 1 Pet. v. 7.</small>

M. To what end dost thou think that Almighty God hath created all these things?

S. The world itself ^owas made for man, and all things that are therein were provided for the use and profit of men. And as God made all other things for man, ^pso made he man himself for his own glory. <small>The final cause.
o Gen. i. 26, 29, 30. Ps. viii. 7, &c.
p Prov. xvi. 4. Isai. xliii. 7. Rom. xi. 36. Col. i. 16.</small>

M. What hast thou then to say of the first beginning and creation of man?

S. That which Moses wrote; that is, that God ^qfashioned <small>q Gen. ii. 7, 21, 22.</small>

the first man of clay, and breathed into him soul and life; and afterward, out of the side of man, being cast in a sleep, he took out woman, and brought her into the world, to join her to man for a companion of his life. And therefore was ^rman called Adam, because he took his beginning of the earth; and ^swoman was called Eve, because she was ordained to be the mother of all living persons.

^r Gen. ii. 7. & iii. 19.
^s Gen. iii. 20.

M. Where at this day there is to be seen in both sorts, both men and women, so great corruption, wickedness, and perverseness, did God create them such from the beginning?

S. Nothing less. For God being most perfectly good, can make nothing ^tbut good. God therefore, at the first, made man according to his own ^uimage and likeness.

^t Gen. i. 31.
^u Gen. i. 26. Col. iii. 10.

M. What is that image, according to the which thou sayest that man was fashioned?

S. It is most absolute righteousness and most perfect holiness, which most properly belongeth to the very nature of God; and which hath been most evidently shewed ^xin Christ our new Adam, and whereof in us there now scarcely appear any sparkles.

^x Rom. viii. 29. 1 Cor. xv. 49. 2 Cor. iii. 18. & iv 4. Col. i. 15. & iii. 10.

M. Yea, do there scarcely appear any?

S. Yea, truly; for they do not now so shine, as at the beginning before the fall of man, because man, ^ywith darkness of sins and mist of errors, hath extinguished the brightness of that image.

^y Rom. i. 22. 1 Cor. i. 18, 23. & ii. 14. & iii. 19. Eph. iv. 17.

M. But tell me how this came to pass.

S. I will tell you. When the Lord God had made this world, ^zhe prepared a most finely trimmed garden, and most full of delight and pleasantness, everywhere abounding with all delightful things that might be wished. Herein the Lord God, for a certain singular good-will placed man, and allowed him the use of all things, only ^ahe forbad him the fruit of the tree of knowledge of good and evil, threatening him with death, if he once tasted of it. For reason it was, that man ^bhaving received so many benefits, should, in so far obeying, shew himself willingly obedient to the commandment of God, and that being contented with his own estate, he should not, being himself a creature, advance himself higher against the will of his Creator.

^z Gen. ii. 8.
^a Gen. ii. 17.
^b Gen. iii. 11. Ps. viii. 4, 5, 6, &c.

M. What then followed?

S. The woman, ^cdeceived by the devil, persuaded the

^c Gen. iii. 1, 6, 7.

man to taste the forbidden fruit, which thing made them both forthwith subject to death. And that heavenly image, according to which he was first created, being defaced, in place of wisdom, strength, holiness, truth, and righteousness, the jewels wherewith God had adorned him, there succeeded the most horrible plagues, ^dblindness, weakness, vain lying, and unrighteousness, in which evils and miseries he also wrapped and overwhelmed his issue and all his posterity.

^d Acts xiv. 12, 13. & xvii. 22. Rom. i. 22. & viii. 7, 8. 1 Cor. ii. 14. Eph. iv. 17, 18, 22.

M. But may it not seem that God did too rigorously punish the tasting of one apple?

S. Let no man extenuate the most heinous offence of man as a small trespass, ^eand weigh the deed by the apple and the only excess of gluttony. For he with his wife, catched and snared with the guileful ^fallurements of Satan, by infidelity, revolted from the truth of God to a lie: he gave credit to the false suggestions of the serpent, wherein he accused God of untruth, of envy, and of malicious withdrawing of some goodness: having received so many benefits, ^ghe became most unthankful toward the giver of them: he, the issue of the earth, not contented that he was made according to the image of God, with ^hintolerable ambition and pride sought to make himself equal with the majesty of God. Finally, ⁱhe withdrew himself from allegiance to his Creator, yea, and malapertly shook off his yoke. Vain, therefore, it is to extenuate the sin of Adam.

^e Gen. iii. 6.

^f Gen. iii. 4, 5.

^g Ps. viii. 4, 5, 6.

^h Gen. iii. 22.

ⁱ Gen. iii. 11. Hos. vi. 7. Rom. v. 19.

M. But how can it seem but unrighteous, that for the parents' fault all the posterity should be deprived of sovereign felicity, and burdened with extreme evils and miseries?

S. Adam was the first parent of mankind: therefore God endued him with those ornaments, to have them or lose them for him and his, that is, for all mankind. So soon as he therefore was spoiled of them, his whole nature was left naked, in penury, and destitute of all good things. So soon as he was defiled with that spot of sin, ^kout of the root and stock corrupted, there sprung forth corrupted branches, that conveyed also their corruption into the other twigs springing out of them. Thence it came that so short, ^lsmall, and uncertain race of life is limited unto us. Thence came the infirmity of our flesh, ^mthe feebleness of our bodies, the weakness and frailness of mankind. Thence came the horrible ⁿblindness of our minds and perverseness of our hearts.

^k Rom. v. 12, 14, 17, 18, 19. 1 Cor. xv. 22, 48.

^l Psal. cii. 3, 6, 7, 9, 10, 11. & ciii. 15, 16. & cix. 23, &c.

^m Job xiv. 1, &c.

ⁿ Rom. i. 22. 1 Cor. iii. 18, 19. Eph. iv. 17. 18, 19.

Thence came that crookedness and corruptness of all our affections and desires. Thence came that °seed-plot, as it were, a sink of all sins, with the faults whereof mankind is infected and tormented. Of which evil, learned Christians that have sought the proper and true name, have called it original sin.

^o Rom. v. 12, &c.

M. Doth mankind suffer the punishments of this sin in this life only?

S. No: but man's nature hath been so corrupted and destroyed with this native mischief, that if the goodness and ᵖmercy of Almighty God had not, with applying a remedy, holpen and relieved us in affliction, like as we fell in our wealth into all calamities, and in our bodies into all ᑫmiseries of diseases and of death, so should we of necessity fall headlong ʳinto darkness and everlasting night, and into fire unquenchable, there, with all kind of punishment, to be perpetually tormented. And no marvel it is, that ˢother creatures also incurred that pain which man deserved, for whose use they were created. And the whole order of nature being troubled, both ᵗin heaven and in earth, harmful tempests, barrenness, diseases, and infinite other evils, brake into the world, ᵘinto which miseries and woes, besides the said native mischief, we by our own many and great sins are most deservedly fallen.

ᵖ Gen. iii. 14, 15. Matt. i. 21. Col. i. 13.

ᑫ Gen. iii. 17, 18, 19.

ʳ Matt. viii. 12. & xxii. 13.

ˢ Gen. iii. 17.

ᵗ Gen. iii. 17, 18, 19.

ᵘ Hos. vi. 7. 2 Cor. xi. 3.

M. Oh deadly and horrible plague and calamity by sin! But what remedy is that which thou sayest that God hath provided for us, wherein our forefathers, and from thenceforth all their posterity, have set and settled their hope?

The second part of the Creed. God the Son. ᵛ Gen. iii. 14, 15.

S. Forsooth, they were comfortably raised to that hope of salvation, which they have conceived of faith in Jesus Christ, the deliverer and Saviour ᵛpromised them of God. For that is it which now followeth next in the Creed: "I believe in Jesus Christ," &c.

M. Did God give also to our first parents, by and by, hope of deliverance by Jesus Christ?

ˣ Gen. iii. 11, 12, 13, 17, 23, 24.

ʸ Gen. iii. 14.

S. Yea; for as he thrust ˣAdam and Eve out of the garden, after that he had first sharply chastised them with words, so he cursed the serpent, and threatened him ʸthat the time should one day come, when the seed of the woman should bruise his head.

M. What seed is that whereof God speaketh?

S. That same seed [z]is (as St Paul plainly teacheth us,) Jesus Christ the Son of God, very God, and the son of the Virgin, very man, in whom we profess, in the second part of the Creed, that we settle our hope and confidence: which was [a]conceived of the Holy Ghost, and born of the nature of the holy, chaste, and undefiled Virgin Mary; and of the same mother he was so born and nourished as other infants be, [b]saving that he was altogether pure and free from all contagion of sin.

[z] Gal. iii. 16, 19.
[a] Matt. i. 20, 21. Luke i. 31, 35.
[b] John i. 29. Heb. iv. 15. & ix. 14.

M. Did God think it sufficient once in the old Testament to have made promise of this seed?

S. No: but this most joyful promise to mankind, [c]which was first made to our parents, the Lord God did often confirm to their posterity, to the end that men should have the greater expectation of the performance of it. For after he had [d]entered into covenant by circumcision with Abraham and his seed, he confirmed his promise, first to Abraham himself, and then to Isaac his son, and after to Jacob his son's son. Last of all, with most evident oracles uttered [e]by Moses and his other prophets, he continued and maintained the assuredness of his promises.

[c] Gen. iii. 14, 15.
[d] Gen. xvii. 10. & xxii. 18. & xxvi. 4. & xxviii. 14.
[e] Deut. x. 15. & xxxiv. 4. Ps. lxxxix. 4, 35. Isai. liii. & liv. 3. & lxv. 9.

M. What mean these words, "to bruise the serpent's head"?

S. In [f]the head of the serpent his poison is contained, and the substance of his life and strength consisteth. Therefore the serpent's head signifieth the whole strength, power, and kingdom, or rather the tyranny of the devil the old serpent; [g]all which Jesus Christ, that same seed of the woman, in whom God hath performed the full sum of his promise, hath subdued by the virtue of his death. And so in breaking the serpent's head, he hath rescued and made free from tyranny all them that trust in him. For this is it which we here profess in the Creed, that we "believe in Jesus Christ the Son of God;" that is, that Jesus Christ is the deliverer and Saviour of us which were holden bond, and fast tied with impiety and wickedness, and wrapped in the snares of eternal death, and holden thrall in foul bondage of the serpent the devil.

[f] Ps. lxxiv. 13. & cxl. 3, 4. Eccles. x. 10. Amos ix. 3.
[g] Matt. i. 21. Acts x. 38. Col. i. 13. 2 Tim. ii. 26. Heb. ii. 14, 15. 1 John iii. 8.

M. It seemeth me that thou hast expounded the name of Jesus with a very plain declaration.

S. It is true. For JESUS in Hebrew signifieth none

other than in Greek, SOTER, in Latin, SERVATOR, and in English, a SAVIOUR. For they have no fitter name to express the force and signification thereof. And by this that we have said, it cannot now be unknown why he had this name. For he alone hath delivered and saved them that be his from eternal damnation, whereunto otherwise they were appointed. Some others indeed have taken upon them this name, because it was thought that they had saved some men's bodies; [h]but Jesus Christ alone is able to save both souls and bodies of them that trust in him.

[h] Matt. i. 21. Acts iv. 10, 12. Rom. v. 9, 10. Phil. ii. 9.

M. Who gave him this name?

S. The angel by the commandment of God himself. And [i]also it was of necessity that he should indeed answer and perform the name that God had given him.

[i] Matt. i. 21. Luke i. 31. & ii. 21.

M. Now tell me what meaneth the name of Christ.

S. It is as much to say, as [k]"Anointed;" whereby is meant that he is the sovereign King, Priest, and Prophet.

[k] Ps. ii. 6. & cix. 5. Dan. ix. 24, 25. Luke vii. 16. Acts vii. 37.

M. How shall that appear?

S. By the holy scripture, [l]which both doth apply anointing to these three offices, and doth also oft attribute the same offices to Christ.

[l] Lev. iv. 3. 1 Sam. xvi. 1, 12, 13. 1 Kings xix. 15, 16.

M. Was then Christ anointed with oil, such as they used at creation of kings, priests, and prophets in old time?

S. No: but with much more excellent oil; namely, [m]with the most plentiful grace of the Holy Ghost, wherewith he was filled and [n]most abundantly endued with his divine riches. Of which heavenly anointing that outward anointing was but a shadow.

[m] Luke iv. 18. Acts iv. 27. & x. 38. Heb. i. 9.
[n] John i. 14, 16.

M. Obtained he these things for himself alone, or doth he also give us any commodities thereby?

S. Yea, Christ received these things of his Father, to the intent that he should communicate the same unto us, in such measure and manner as he knew to be most meet for every one of us. For [o]out of his fulness, as out of the only holy and ever-increasing noble fountain, we all do draw all the heavenly good things that we have.

[o] Luke xxii. 29. John i. 14, 16. 2 Cor. i. 21. Col. i. 13. 2 Tim. iv. 8.

M. Dost thou not then say that Christ's kingdom is a worldly kingdom?

S. No: but [p]a spiritual and eternal kingdom, that is governed and ordered by the word and spirit of God, which bring with them righteousness and life.

[p] Luke i. 32. John xviii. 36. Col. i. 13. 14. 2 Tim. iv. 1.

M. What fruit take we of this kingdom?

S. It furnisheth us with ᑫstrength and spiritual armour to vanquish the flesh, the world, sin, and the devil, the outrageous and deadly enemies of our souls: it giveth us blessed freedom of conscience; finally, it endoweth us with heavenly riches, and comforteth and strengtheneth us to live godlily and holily. ^q Rom. xiii. 12. & xvi. 20. 2 Cor. vi. 7. & x. 4. Eph. iv. 8. & vi. 11.

M. What manner of priest is Christ?

S. The ʳgreatest and an everlasting priest, which alone is able to appear before God, only able to make the sacrifice which God will allow and accept, and only able to appease the wrath of God. ^r Ps. cx. 4. Heb. iv. 14, 15. & v. 6. & vii. 3, 11, 15, 16, 21, 26, &c. & ix. 14.

M. To what commodity of ours doth he this?

S. For ˢus he craveth and prayeth peace and pardon of God, for us he appeaseth the wrath of God, and us he reconcileth to his Father. For Christ alone is our mediator, by whom we are made at one with God. Yea, he maketh us as it were ᵗfellow-priests with him in his priesthood, giving us also an entry to his Father, that we may with assuredness come into his presence, and be bold by him to offer us and all ours to God the Father in sacrifice. ^s Luke ii. 14. John xiv. 27. Acts x. 36. Eph. ii. 14, 17. Col. i. 20. 1 Tim. ii. 5. Heb. ix. 14, 15. ^t Rom. viii. 14, 15. & xii. 1. Gal. iv. 5, 6. Eph. iii. 12.

M. What manner of prophet is Christ?

S. Whereas men did ᵘdespise and reject the prophets, the servants of Almighty God, sent before by himself, to teach mortal men his will, and had with their own dreams and inventions darkened and drowned his holy word, he himself, the Son of God, the Lord of all prophets, came down into this world, that fully declaring the will of his Father, he might make an end of all prophecies and foretellings. He therefore came, ˣhis Father's ambassador and messenger to men, that by his declaration they might be brought into the right knowledge of God, and into all truth. So, in the name of Christ are contained those three offices which the Son of God received of his Father, and fulfilled to make us partners with him of all the fruit thereof. ^u Matt. xv. 3, 8, 9. & xxi. 34, 37. Luke xi. 47, 50. Acts vii. 51, 52. Heb. i. 1, 2. ^x John i. 4, 5. & viii. 26, 40. & xv. 15. & xvii. 6, &c.

M. It seemeth then, that in a sum thou sayest thus, that the Son of God is not only called, and is indeed Jesus Christ, that is, the Saviour, King, Priest, and Prophet, but also that he is so for us, and to our benefit and salvation.

S. It is true.

M. But since this honour is given to ʸall the godly to ^y John i. 12, 13. & xi. 52. Rom. ix. 26.

be called the children of God, how dost thou call Christ the only Son of God?

S. God is ^zthe natural Father of Christ alone, and Christ alone is naturally the Son of God, being begotten of the substance of the Father, and being of one substance with the Father. But us hath God, freely through Christ, made and adopted his children. Therefore we rightly acknowledge Christ the only Son of God since this honour is by his own and most just right due unto him: yet the ^aname of children by right of adoption is also freely imparted to us through Christ.

M. Now how dost thou understand that he is our Lord?

S. For that the Father hath given him ^bdominion over men, angels, and all things, and for that he governeth the kingdom of God both in heaven and in earth, with his own will and power. And hereby are all the godly put in mind, that they are not ^cat their own liberty, but that both in their bodies and souls, and in their life and death, they are wholly subject to their Lord, to whom they ought to be obedient and serviceable in all things, as most faithful servants.

M. What followeth next?

S. Next is declared how he took upon him man's nature, and hath performed all things needful to our salvation.

M. Was it then necessary that the Son of God should be made man?

S. Yea; for ^dnecessary it was that what man had offended against God, man should atone and satisfy it; which most heavy burden, none but ^ethe man Jesus Christ was able to take up and bear. And other ^fmediator could there not be to set men at one with God, and to make peace between them, but Jesus Christ both God and man. Therefore being made man, he did as it were put upon him our person, that he might therein take upon him, bear, perform, and fulfil the parts of our salvation.

M. But why was he conceived of the Holy Ghost, and born of the Virgin Mary, rather than begotten after the usual and natural manner?

S. It behoved that he that should and could satisfy for sins, and entirely restore wicked and damned persons, should not himself ^gbe defiled or blemished with any stain or spot of sin, but be endued with singular and perfect uprightness and innocency. Therefore when the seed of man was wholly ʰcorrupt and defiled, it behoved that in conception of the Son of God, there should be the marvellous and secret working of the Holy Ghost, whereby he might be fashioned ⁱin the womb of the most chaste and pure Virgin, and of her substance that he should not be defiled with the common stain and infection of mankind. Christ, therefore, that ᵏmost pure Lamb, was begotten and born by the Holy Ghost and the conception of the Virgin without sin, that he might cleanse, wash, and put away our spots, who, as we were first conceived and born in sin and uncleanness, so do still from thenceforth continue in unclean life. ʰ Gen. vi. 5, 6. Ps. xiv. 2, 3. & li. 5. Rom. iii. 10. ⁱ Isai. vii. 14. Matt. i. 20, 23. Luke i. 31, 34, 35. ᵏ Exod. xii. 5. John i. 29, 36. 1 Pet. i. 19. Rev. xiv. 4.

M. But why is there, in this Christian confession, mention made by name of the Virgin Mary?

S. That he may be known to be that ˡtrue seed of Abraham and David, of whom it was from God foretold and foreshewed by the prophecies of the prophets. ˡ Gen. xxii. 18. Isai. xi. 1. Matt. i. 1. & xxii. 42. Rom. i. 2.

M. By this that hath been said, I perceive that Jesus Christ the Son of God did put on man's nature for salvation of men. Now go forward. What was done next?

S. That same most joyful and altogether heavenly doctrine of restoring salvation by Christ, (which doctrine is in Greek called *Evangelion*, the Gospel or glad tidings,) ᵐwhich in old time was disclosed by the holy prophets, the servants of God; ⁿhe himself, at length, the Lord of prophets, Jesus Christ the Son of God, and also of the Virgin, even the same promised seed, hath most clearly taught all men, and ᵒcommanded his apostles whom he chose for that purpose, to teach the same throughout the whole world. ᵐ Isai. liii. & lxi. 1. Jer. xxxiii. 14. ⁿ Luke iv. 18. Acts iii. 22, 23. & vii. 37. ᵒ Matt. xxviii. 18, 19. Mark xvi. 15.

M. Did he think it enough to have simply and plainly taught this doctrine in words?

S. No: but to the end that men should with more willing minds embrace it, he confirmed and approved the same ᵖwith healing of diseases, ᑫchasing away devils, and with infinite other good deeds, miracles and signs, whereof ʳboth his own life and the life of his apostles, most innocently and holily led, was most plentiful. ᵖ Matt. iv. 24. & viii. 2, 13, 15. ᑫ Mark ix. 18. Acts x. 38. ʳ Acts ii. 22, 43. & iii. 6. & v. 5, 12, 15, 16, 19.

M. But why doth the Creed omit the story of his life, and passeth straight from his birth to his death?

S. Because in the Creed are rehearsed only the ˢchief ˢ Isai. liii. Acts xiii. 23, 27, &c.

points of our redemption, and such things as so properly belong to it that they contain as it were the substance thereof.

M. Now tell me the order and manner of his death.

S. He was ᵗwickedly betrayed and forsaken of his own disciples, falsely and maliciously accused of the Jews, condemned by Pontius Pilate the judge, cruelly beaten with sore stripes, vilely handled and scorned, nailed up to the cross and fastened upon it; and so, tormented with all extreme pains, he suffered shameful and most painful death.

M. Is this the thank and recompense they gave him for that heavenly doctrine, and for these most great and infinite benefits?

S. These things verily they did to him for their parts cruelly, maliciously, and wickedly. But he ᵘof his own accord and willingly suffered and performed all these things, to the intent, with this most sweet sacrifice, to appease his Father toward mankind, and ˣto pay and suffer the pains due to us, and by this mean to deliver us from the same. Neither is it unused among men, one to promise and to be surety, yea sometimes to suffer for another. ʸBut with Christ as our surety so suffering for us, God dealt as it were with extremity of law: but, to us whose sins, deservings, punishments, and due pains he laid upon Christ, he used singular lenity, gentleness, clemency, and mercy. Christ therefore suffered, and in suffering overcame death, the pain appointed by the everliving God for men's offence. Yea, and by his death he overcame, subdued, overthrew, and vanquished him that had the dominion of death; that is, ᶻthe devil, from whose tyranny and thraldom he rescued us, and set us at liberty.

M. But since we are nevertheless punished with death, which daily hangeth over us, and do still suffer the penalty of our sin, what fruit receive we of this victory?

S. Surely most large fruit. For by Christ's death it is come to pass, that to ᵃthe faithful, death is now not a destruction, but as it were a removing and changing of life, and a very short and sure passage into heaven, whither we ought to follow our guide without fear, which as he was not destroyed by death, so will he also not suffer us to perish. Wherefore the godly ought now no more to shrink or quake ᵇfor fear of death, which is to them the refuge from all the labours, cares, and evils of this life, and their leader to heaven.

M. Cometh there any other profit to us by the death of Christ?

S. In them that through faith are of one body with Christ, crooked ᶜaffections and corrupt desires, which we call the lusts of the flesh, are as it were crucified with him, and die, so as they have no more dominion in our souls.

^c Rom vi. 4, 7, 11, 12, 13, 22. & viii. 1, 2, 3, 10, 11, 13. Col. ii. 13.

M. Why is the Roman governor, under whom he suffered, expressly named?

S. First, the certain expressing of the persons and times bringeth credit to the matter: secondly, the very thing itself declareth that Christ took our nature upon him at his due time, the very time limited and appointed by God, that is, when the ᵈsceptre was transferred from the issue of Judah to the Romans, and ᵉto foreign kings that held the kingdom of sufferance under the Roman empire. Moreover, it had been long before foreshewn by God, that Christ should be ᶠdelivered to the Gentiles to execution, and should suffer death by the judge's sentence.

^d Gen. xlix. 10. Dan. ix. 25.
^e Luke ii. 1. & iii. 1.
^f Ps. ii. 2. Luke xviii. 31, 32. & xxiv. 26.

M. Why so?

S. He being guiltless, was condemned by the judge's sentence, that he might ᵍbefore the heavenly judgment-seat acquit and entirely restore us that were guilty, whose cause was convicted and condemned by the judgment of God. For if he had been murdered by thieves, or slain with sword by private men in an uproar or sedition, such death could have had no form of satisfaction and recompense.

^g Isai. liii. 3, 8. Rom. v. 1, 6, 8. & viii. 1. 2 Cor. v. 18, 21. 1 Pet. iii. 18.

M. But Pilate ʰdid bear witness of his innocency.

S. Pilate did well to bear such witness of him, ⁱsince he evidently knew him innocent. For if he had been guilty, he had not been fit nor meet to bear and pay the pains of the sins of others, and to appease God toward sinners. But the same Pilate, accumbered with the continual and agreeable crying out of the Jews, ᵏand wearied and overcome with their importunate outcries, did afterward, according to the people's mind and request, condemn innocent Christ; whereby it is plain that he was not punished for his own sins, ˡwhich were none at all in him, nor suffer pains due to himself, but did bear and pay the pains due to men's wickedness, not due to himself, which of his own will he took upon him, suffering

^h Matt. xxvii. 18, 23. Mark xv. 10. Luke xxiii. 14. John xviii. 38.
ⁱ Isai. liii. 5. John i. 29, 36. 1 Pet. iii. 18.
^k Matt. xxvii. 22. Luke xxiii. 18, 21, 23, 24.
^l Isai. liii. 4, 5. 1 Pet. ii. 24. & iii. 18.

for them by his willing death, and with his own guiltless blood washing away the spots of our offences.

M. But for what cause did the people so bitterly and throughly hate a man of so great and singular uprightness and innocency?

S. The ^mpriests, Pharisees, and scribes, burning with the fire of envy, when they could ⁿnot abide the face and light of the truth, ^oincensed the hatred of the unwise multitude against the rescuer and defender of the truth.

<small>m Matt. xxvii. 18. Mark xv. 10.
n Matt. xv. 12. Luke xx. 19. John viii. 40, 45. & xi. 47.
o Matt. xxvii. 20. Mark xv. 11.</small>

M. Since he was condemned by the judge's sentence, why dost thou say that he died of his own will?

S. If the Pharisees, scribes, or other Jews, or they all together, had had power of life and death upon Christ, they had long before hastened his death, ^pfor they oftentimes before had conspired his death and destruction; yea, and also where they had determined to defer the execution till another time, because the feast of ^qsweet-bread was now at hand, (which feast the Jews were accustomed yearly to keep holy with most great religiousness and solemnity), they could not bring that intent to pass, but that he suffered even hard before the feast-day, in a time most unseasonable for them, but appointed by God for this purpose; whereby sufficiently appeareth, that no governance of these things and times was in their hand and power, but that ^rof his own will, not compelled by any force, he suffered this death for our salvation.

<small>p Luke xi. 53. & xx. 19. John viii. 59. & xi. 53, 57.
q Matt. xxvi. 4. Mark xiv. 1.
r Isai. liii. 7, 12. Matt. xx. 28. & xxvi. 53. John x. 17.</small>

M. Why did God specially appoint that day for his death?

S. That by the very time also it might be perceived that Christ is that ^sPaschal Lamb, that is to say, the truly chaste and pure Lamb that should be slain, and yield himself the most acceptable sacrifice to his Father for us.

<small>s Matt. xxvi. 2. Luke xxii. 1, 7. Mark xiv. 1. 1 Cor. v. 7. Heb. vii. 27.</small>

M. Since he had the power to choose his own death, why would he be crucified rather than suffer any other kind of death?

S. First, for his Father's will, whereunto he ^tconformed himself, and which had been long afore in old time uttered and declared by God, by so many prophecies and oracles, signs and tokens. Moreover, his will was to suffer all extremity for us that had deserved all extremity; for that kind of death was of all other ^umost accursed and abominable, which death yet he chiefly chose to die for us, to the intent

<small>t Isai. liii. 12. Matt. xxvi. 39, 42. Mark xv. 28. Luke xxii. 37. John iii. 14.
u Deut. xxi. 23. Gal. iii. 13.</small>

to take upon himself the grievous curse, wherein our sins had bound us, and thereby to deliver us from the same curse. For all ˣspiteful handlings, all reproaches and torments for our salvation, he counted light, and as things of nought, and so was contented to be despised, an abject, and to be accounted the basest of all men, that he might restore us which were utterly undone, to the hope of salvation that we had lost. x Isai. liii.
Ps. xxii. 6, 7,
12, 13, &c.
Matt. xxvi.
67. & xxvii.
21, 26, 28, 34,
38, 44, 48.
Phil. ii. 7, 8.

M. Hast thou any more to say of the death of Christ?

S. That Christ ʸsuffered not only a common death in the sight of men, but also was touched with the horror of eternal death: he fought and wrestled as it were hand to hand, with the whole army of hell: before the judgment-seat of God he put himself under the heavy judgment and grievous severity of God's punishment: he was driven into most hard distress: he for us suffered and went through horrible fears, and most bitter griefs of mind, to satisfy God's just judgment in all things, and to appease his wrath. For ᶻto sinners whose person Christ did here bear, not only the sorrows and pains of present death are due, but also of death to come and everlasting: so when he did take upon him and bear both the guiltiness and just judgment of mankind, which was undone, and already condemned, he was tormented with so great trouble and sorrow of mind, that ᵃhe cried out, "My God, my God, why hast thou forsaken me?"

M. Is not the Son of God hereby dishonoured and touched with some note of desperation?

S. He suffered all these things ᵇwithout any sin, much less did any desperation possess his soul. For he never ceased in the mean time ᶜto trust in his Father, and to have good hope of his safety. And being beset round about with fear, he was never dismayed or overwhelmed with sorrow; and ᵈwrestling with the whole power of hell, he subdued and overcame all the force that stood against him, and all the furious and violent assaults; and all these he took upon him, and utterly destroyed them; and himself remained nevertheless most blessed, and imparted his blessedness to us that put our trust in him: ᵉfor if we had not by this his blessed death obtained salvation and life, we had all perished for ever in everlasting death.

M. But how could Christ, being God, have so great sorrow of mind and fearfulness?

S. This came to pass according to the ᶠstate of his human nature; his Godhead in the mean time not putting forth the force of his power.

M. Now rehearse me briefly and in a sum these most large benefits which the faithful receive of the death of Christ, and his most grievous pain.

S. Briefly, with the ᵍone only sacrifice of his death he satisfied for our sins before God, and appeasing the wrath of God, made us at one with him. With his blood, as with ʰmost pure washing, he hath washed and cleansed away all the filth and spots of our souls; and defacing with everlasting ⁱforgetfulness the memory of our sins, that they shall no more come in the sight of God, he hath cancelled, made void, and done away the ᵏhand-writing whereby we were bound and convicted, and also the decree by the sentence whereof we were condemned. All these things hath he done by his death, both for the living and for the dead ˡthat trusted in him while they lived. Finally, by the strength of his death he so ᵐbridleth and subdueth in them that cleave wholly to him by faith, the lusts which otherwise are unbridled and untamed, and so quencheth the burning heat of them, that they more easily obey and yield to the Spirit.

M. Why dost thou also add, that he was buried?

S. His ⁿdead and spiritless body was laid in the grave, that his death should be the more evident, and that all men might certainly know it. For if he had by and by revived, many would have brought his death in debate and question, and so might it seem that it was likely to prove doubtful.

M. What meaneth that which followeth, of his descending into hell?

S. That as Christ in his body descended into the bowels of the earth, so, in his soul severed from the body, he descended into hell: and that therewith also the virtue and efficacy of his death, so pierced ᵒthrough to the dead, and to very hell itself, that both the souls of the unbelieving felt their most painful and just ᵖdamnation for infidelity, and Satan himself, the ᑫprince of hell, felt that all the power of his tyranny and darkness was weakened, vanquished, and fallen to ruin. On the other side, ʳthe dead, which, while they lived, believed in Christ, understood that the work of their redemption was now finished, and understood and perceived the effect and strength thereof with most sweet and assured comfort.

M. Now let us go forward to the rest.

S. The third day after ªhe rose again; and by the space of forty days oftentimes shewed himself alive to them that were his, and was conversant among his disciples, eating and drinking with them. ^{a Matt. xxviii. 6, 9. Mark xvi. 6, 9. Luke xxiv. 6, 7, 14, 15. John xx. 14, 19, 20, 26. & ii. 1, 4. Acts i. 3, 4. & ii. 24, 32.}

M. Was it not enough that by his death we obtain deliverance from sin, and pardon?

S. That was not enough, if ye consider either him or ourselves. For if he had not risen again, he could not be thought to be ᵗthe Son of God; yea, and the same did they that saw it, when he hung on the cross, reproach him with and object against him. "He ᵘsaved others" (said they); "himself he cannot save. Let him now come down from the cross, and we will believe him." But now, rising from the dead to eternity of life, he declared a greater ˣpower of his Godhead, than if in descending from the cross he had fled from the terrors of death. To die, ʸcertainly, is common to all; and though some for a time have avoided death intended against them, yet to loose or break the bonds of death once suffered, and by his own power to rise alive again, that is the proper doing of the only Son of God, Jesus Christ, the Author of life, by which ᶻhe hath shewed himself the conqueror of sin and death, yea, and of the devil himself. ^{t Rom. i. 4. u Matt. xxvii. 40, 41, 42. Mark xv. 30. Luke xxiii. 35, 37. x Rom. i. 4. y Heb. ix. 27. z Rom. i. 4. & vi. 4, 9. & xiv. 9. 1 Cor. xv. 54, 55, 57. Eph. i. 20. Col. i. 17, 18. 1 John iii. 8. Heb. ii. 14.}

M. For what other cause rose he again?

S. That the prophecies of ªDavid and of other holy prophets might be fulfilled, which told before, that neither his body should be touched with corruption, nor his soul be left in hell. ^{a Ps. xvi. 10. Matt. xii. 40. Acts ii. 26, 31.}

M. But what profits bringeth it unto us that Christ rose again?

S. Manifold and divers. For thereof cometh to us ᵇrighteousness, which before we lacked: thence cometh to us endeavour of ᶜinnocency, which we call newness of life: thence cometh to us power, virtue, and strength to live well and holily: thence have we hope that ᵈour mortal bodies also shall one day be restored from death, and rise whole again. For if Christ himself had been ᵉdestroyed by death, he had not been our deliverer; for what hope of safety should we have had left by him that had not saved himself? It was ^{b Rom. iv. 25. c Rom. vi. 4, 5, 11, 12, 13. Col. iii. 1, 2. d John xi. 25. Rom. viii. 11. 1 Cor. xv. 20, 21, 22. e 1 Cor. xv. 13, 14, 16, 17.}

therefore meet for the person which the Lord did bear, and a necessary help for us to salvation, that Christ should [f]first deliver himself from death, and afterward that he should break and pull in sunder the bands of death for us, and so that we might set the hope of our salvation in his resurrection. For it cannot be [g]that Christ our head, rising again, should suffer us, the members of his body, to be consumed and utterly destroyed by death.

[f] Rom. viii. 11. 1 Cor. xv. 11, 12, 20, 21. 1 Pet. i. 3.

[g] Eph. i. 22. & iv. 15, 16. & v. 23. Col. i. 18.

M. Thou hast touched, my child, the principal causes of the resurrection of Christ. Now would I hear what thou thinkest of his ascending into heaven.

S. He being covered with a cloud spread about him, in sight of his apostles [h]ascended into heaven, or rather, above all heavens, where he sitteth on the right hand of God the Father.

[h] Mark xvi. 19. Luke xxiv. 51. Acts i. 9, 10.

M. Tell me how this is to be understood.

S. Plainly, that Christ [i]in his body ascended into heaven, where he had not afore been in his body, and left the earth, where he had afore been in his body. For in his nature of Godhead, which filleth all things, both he ever was in heaven; and also with the same, and with his Spirit, [k]he is alway present in earth with his church, and shall be present till the end of the world.

[i] John xiv. 19. & xvi. 10, 16, 28.

[k] Matt. xviii. 20. & xxviii. 20.

M. Then thou sayest, that there is one manner of his Godhead and another of his manhood?

S. Yea, forsooth, master. For we neither make of his Godhead a body, nor of his body God; for his manhood is [l]a creature, his Godhead not created. And the holy scriptures witness that his [m]manhood was taken up into heaven, and abideth in heaven; but [n]his Godhead is so everywhere that it filleth both heaven and earth.

[l] Isai. vii. 14. Matt. i. 2, 23. Luke ii. 7, 40, 52, 53. John i. 3, 14. Gal. iv. 4.

[m] Mark xvi. 19. Luke xxiv. 51. Acts i. 9, 10. & iii. 21. Eph. iv. 10.

[n] John i. 3. & xvi. 15. 1 Cor. xv. 28. Eph. i. 23. Col. i. 16, 17.

M. But dost thou say that Christ is in any wise present with us in body?

S. If we may liken great things to small, Christ's body is so present to our faith, as the sun when we see it is present to our eye. For no one thing, subject to our senses, cometh more near to the likeness of Christ than the sun, which, though it still abide in the heaven, and therefore in very deed toucheth not the eye, yet the body of the sun is present to the sight, notwithstanding so great a distance of place between. So the body of Christ, which by his ascending is taken up from us, °and hath left the world, and is gone to his Father, is indeed absent from our senses; yet our faith is ᴾconversant in heaven, and beholdeth that Sun of Righteousness, and is verily in presence with it there present, like as our sight is present with the body of the sun in the heaven, or as the sun is present with our sight in earth. Moreover, as the sun is with his light present to all things, so is also Christ, with his Godhead, Spirit, and power, ᑫpresent to all, and filleth all.

° John xiv. 19. & xvi. 10, 28.
ᴾ Acts vii. 55. Col. iii. 1. Heb. iv. 16. & x. 22. & xi. 1, 3.
ᑫ Matt. xxviii. 20. 1 Cor. xv. 28. Eph. i. 23. Col. i. 17, 18.

M. Now as touching Christ, what dost thou chiefly consider in his ascending and sitting at the right hand of his Father.

S. It was meet that Christ, ʳwhich from the highest degree of honour and dignity had descended to the basest estate of a servant, and to the reproach of condemnation and shameful death, should on the other side obtain most noble glory and excellent estate; even the same which he had before, that his glory and majesty might in proportion answer to his baseness and shame; which thing St Paul also, writing to the Philippians, doth most plainly teach. "ˢHe became (saith he) obedient unto the death, even the death of the cross; and therefore God made him the head of the Church, advanced him above all principalities, endowed him with the dominion of heaven and earth, to govern all things; exalted him to the highest height, and gave him a name that is above all names, that at the name of Jesus every knee should bow, both of things in heaven, earth, and hell."

ʳ Phil. ii. 6, 7, 8.
ˢ Phil. ii. 8, 9, 10. Eph. i. 20, 21, 22, 23. Col. i. 18. Heb. ii. 9.

M. When thou namest the right hand of God, and sitting, dost thou suppose and imagine that God hath the shape or form of a man?

S. No, forsooth, master. But because we speak of God among men, we do in some sort, after the manner of men, express thereby how Christ hath received the kingdom given him of his Father. For ᵗkings use to set them on their right hands to whom they vouchsafe to do highest honour, and make lieutenants of their dominion. Therefore in these words is meant that God the Father ᵘmade Christ his Son the head of the Church, and that by him his pleasure is to preserve them that be his, and to govern all things universally.

ᵗ 1 Kings ii. 19. Ps. cx. 1. Matt. xx. 21.
ᵘ Eph. i. 22. & iv. 15, 16. & v. 23. Col. i. 18.

M. Well said. Now what profit take we of his ascending into heaven, and sitting on the right hand of his Father?

S. First, Christ, as he had descended to the earth, as into banishment for our sake; so when he went up into heaven, his Father's inheritance, he entered in our name, ˣmaking us a way and entry thither; and opening us the gate of heaven, which was before shut against us for sin: for since Christ, our head, hath carried with him our flesh into heaven, ʸhe, so mighty and loving a head, will not leave us for ever in earth that are members of his body. Moreover, ᶻhe being present in the sight of God and commending us unto him, and making intercession for us, is the patron of our cause, who being our advocate, our matter shall not quail.

M. But why did he not rather tarry with us here in earth?

S. When he had fully performed ᵃall things that were appointed him of his Father, and which belonged to our salvation, he needed not to tarry any longer in earth. Yea, also, all those things he doth, being absent in body, which he should do if he were bodily present; he preserveth, comforteth, and strengtheneth, correcteth, restraineth, and chasteneth. Moreover, as he promised, ᵇhe sendeth down his holy Spirit from heaven into our hearts, as a most sure pledge of his good will, by which Spirit he bringeth us out of darkness and mist into open light; he giveth sight to the blindness of our minds; he chaseth sorrow out of our hearts, and healeth the wounds thereof; and with the ᶜdivine motion of his Spirit he causeth, that, looking up to heaven, we raise up our minds and hearts from the ground, from corrupt affections and from earthly things, upward to the place where Christ is at the right hand of his Father; that we, thinking upon and beholding things above and heavenly, and so raised up and of upright mind, we contemn these our base things, life, death, riches, poverty; and with lofty and high courage despise all worldly things. Finally, this may be the sum, that Christ, sitting on the right hand of God, doth with his ᵈpower, wisdom, and providence rule and dispose the world; move, govern, and order all things, and so shall do, till the frame of the world be dissolved.

M. Since then Christ, being in his body taken up into heaven, doth yet not forsake his here in earth, they judge very grossly that measure his presence or absence by his body only?

S. Yea, truly; for things that are not bodily cannot be subject to sense. Who ever saw his own soul? No man. But what is presenter, what nearer, what closer joined than every man's soul to himself? ᵉSpiritual things are not seen but with the eye of the Spirit. Therefore, whoso will see Christ in earth, let him open his eyes, not of his body but of his soul, and of faith, and he shall see him present, whom the eye seeth not. ^e John viii. 47. & xiv. 21. Gal. iii. 1. Eph. i. 17, 18.

M. But with whom doth faith acknowledge that he is peculiarly and most effectually present?

S. The eyesight of faith shall espy him present, yea, and in the midst, wheresoever ᶠtwo or three are gathered together in his name: it shall see him present with them, that be his, that is, with all the true godly, even to the end of all worlds. What said I? It shall see Christ present; yea, every godly person shall both see and feel him dwelling in himself even as his own soul. For he ᵍdwelleth and abideth in that man's soul that setteth all his trust and hope in him. ^f Matt. xviii. 19, 20. & xxviii. 20. John xiv. 18, 21. ^g John xiv. 23. Eph. iii. 16, 17. Col. iii. 11.

M. Hast thou yet any more to say hereof?

S. Christ, by ascending and sitting on the right hand of his Father, hath removed and throughly rooted up out of men's hearts, ʰthat false opinion which sometimes his ⁱapostles themselves had conceived, namely, that Christ should reign visible here in earth, as other kings of the earth and worldly princes do. The Lord would ᵏpull this error out of our minds, and have us to think more highly of his kingdom. Therefore his will was to be absent from our eyes and from all bodily sense, that by this mean our ˡfaith may be both stirred up and exercised to behold his governance and providence that is not perceived by bodily sense. ^h Luke ii. 23. & xvii. 20, 21. John vi. 15. ⁱ Matt. xx. 21. Luke xxiv. 21. Acts i. 6. ^k John xviii. 36. ^l Eph. i. 18. Col. iii. 1, 2.

M. Is there any other reason why he withdrew himself from the earth into heaven?

S. Since he is prince not of some one land, ᵐbut of all lands of the world, yea, and of ⁿheaven also, and Lord both of quick and dead, meet it was that he should govern his kingdom in order unknown to our senses. For if he should be within the reach of sight, then must he needs change place and seat, and ᵒbe drawn now hither and now thither, and now and then remove into sundry countries to do his ^m Matt. xxviii. 18. 1 Cor. xv. 24, 25, 27, 28. ⁿ Rom. xiv. 9. Phil. ii. 9, 10. ^o Luke xvii. 20, 21.

affairs. For if in one moment of time he were everywhere present with all men, then should he seem not to be a man, but some ghost; and not to have a very body, but imaginative, or (as Eutyches thought) that his body was turned into his Godhead, that it might be thought to be everywhere; whereof would by and by arise infinite false opinions, all which he hath driven away with carrying his body up whole into heaven, and hath delivered men's minds from most foul errors. Yet in the meantime, though he be not seen of us, he wonderously ^pruleth and governeth the world, with most high power and wisdom. It is for men to govern and order their commonweals after a certain order of men, but for Christ, that is, the Son of God, to do it after the manner of God.

^p Matt. xxviii. 18. Phil. ii. 9, 10. Rev. xi. 15.

M. Thou hast touched certain of the chief of the infinite and unmeasurable benefits, the fruit whereof we receive by the death, resurrection, and ascension of Christ: for the whole cannot be conceived by the mind and heart of man, much less in anywise be expressed with words and utterance. But yet thus far will I try thy cunning in this matter, to have thee set me out briefly and in a sum the chief principal points whereunto all the rest are referred.

S. Then, I say, that both of these and of the other doings of Christ we take two kinds of profit: the one, that whatsoever things he hath done, he hath done them all for our benefit, even so far as that they be ^qas much our own, so that with stedfast and lively faith we cleave unto them as if we ourselves had done them. He was crucified; and we also are crucified with him, and our sins punished in him. He died and was buried; we also, together with our sins, are dead and buried, and that so as all the remembrance of our sins is for ever forgotten. He rose from death; and we also are risen again with him, being so made partakers of his resurrection and life, that from thenceforth death hath no more dominion over us. ^rFor in us is the same spirit which raised Jesus Christ from the dead. Finally, beside that, since his ascension, we have most abundantly received the ^sgifts of the Holy Ghost; he hath also lifted and carried us up into heaven with him, that we might, as it were with our head, take possession thereof. These things indeed are not yet seen, ^tbut then shall they be brought abroad into light, when Christ

^q Isai. ix. 6. 1 Cor. xv. 48, 49. Rom. vi. 6, 7, &c. & viii. 32. & xiii. 14. Gal. ii. 20. & iii. 27. Heb. iii. 14. & x. 17.

^r Rom. viii. 11.

^s Eph. iv. 8.

^t John viii. 12. Rom. viii. 24. 1 Cor. i. 30. Col. i. 5. & ii. 3. & iii. 4, 11. 1 Pet. i. 4.

which is the light of the world, in whom all our hope and wealth is set and settled, shining with immortal glory, shall shew himself openly to all men.

M. What manner of profit is the other which we receive of the doings of Christ?

S. That Christ hath set himself for [u]an exemplar for us to follow, to frame our life according thereunto. Where Christ died for sin and was buried, he but once suffered the same. Where he rose again and ascended into heaven, he but once rose again and but once ascended, he now dieth no more, but enjoyeth eternal life, and reigneth in most high and everlasting glory. So [v]if we be once dead and buried to sin, how shall we hereafter live in the same? If we be risen again with Christ, if by assured faith and stedfast hope we be conversant with him in heaven, then ought we from henceforth to bend all our cares and thoughts upon heavenly, divine, and eternal things, not earthly, worldly, and transitory. And as we have [x]heretofore borne the image of the earthly man, we ought from henceforth to put on the image of the heavenly man, quietly and patiently bearing, after his example, all sorrows and wrongs, and following and expressing his other divine virtues so far as mortal man be able. And whereas Christ our Lord never ceaseth to do us good, continually to intreat for and to crave his Father's mercy for us, to give us his holy Spirit, and wonderfully and continually to garnish his church with most liberal gifts; it is meet that [y]we in like manner, with our whole endeavour, should help our neighbour, and that we be bound to all men in most strait bonds of love, concord, and most near friendship, so much as shall lie in us, and so to be [z]wholly framed after the manners of Christ, as our only exemplar.

[u] John xiii. 15. 1 Pet. ii. 21. 1 John ii. 6.

[v] Rom. vi. 2, 3, 10. Gal. ii. 19. Col. ii. 20. & iii. 1. 2 Tim. ii. 11.

[x] Rom. viii. 20. 1 Cor. xv. 47, 48, 49.

[y] John xiii. 13, 14. & xv. 12. Eph. v. 2. Heb. xii. 14.

[z] Gal. ii. 20. 1 Pet. ii. 21. 1 John ii. 6.

M. Are we not hereby also put in mind of our duty toward Christ?

S. We are indeed admonished that we [a]obey and follow the will of Christ, whose we are wholly, and whom we profess to be our Lord: that we so again on our part, and with all our affection, love, esteem, and embrace Christ our Saviour, which shewed us such dear love while we were yet his enemies, as his most entire love toward us could not possibly be increased: that we hold Christ dearer unto us than ourselves: that to Christ which hath so given himself wholly to us, [b]we

[a] Rom. v. 8, 10. 2 Cor. v. 15. 1 Thess. v. 10.

[b] Matt. x. 19, 37. & xvi. 25. Luke ix. 23, 24. & xiv. 26.

again yield ourselves wholly and all that is ours: that we esteem riches, honours, glory, our country, parents, children, wives, and all dear, pleasant, and delightful things, of no value in comparison of Christ; and account light, and despise all dangers for Christ: finally, that we lose our life and our very soul, rather than forsake Christ, and our love and duty toward him. For happy is the death, that, being due to nature, is chiefly yielded for Christ: for Christ, I say, which offered and yielded himself to willing death for us, and which, being the author of life, both will and is able to ^cdeliver us, being dead, from death, and to restore us to life.

e Mark viii. 35.

M. Go forward.

S. We are furthermore taught purely and sincerely to worship Christ the Lord now reigning in heaven, not with any ^dearthly worship, wicked traditions, and cold inventions of men, but with heavenly and ^every spiritual worship, such as may best beseem both us that give it, and him that receiveth it, even as he honoured and honoureth his Father, seeing that all in one we give the same honour to his Father. For he that ^fhonoureth Christ, honoureth also his Father; whereof he himself is a most sure and substantial witness.

d Matt. xv. 3, 6, 8, 9.
e John iv. 23, 24.

f John v. 23.

M. Now I would hear thee tell me shortly what thou thinkest of the last judgment, and of the end of the world.

S. Christ shall come ^gin the clouds of the heaven with most high glory, and with most honourable and reverend majesty, waited on and beset with the company and multitude of holy angels. And at the horrible sound and dreadful blast of trumpet all the dead that have lived from the creation of the world to that day, shall rise again with their souls and bodies whole and perfect, and shall ^happear before his throne to be judged, every one for himself, to give account of their life, which shall be examined by the uncorrupted and severe Judge according to the truth.

g Matt. xxiv. 29, 30. & xxv. 31.
1 Cor. xv. 52.
1 Thess. iv. 16.

h Rom. xiv. 10, 12. 1 Cor. iv. 4, 5.
2 Cor. v. 10.

M. But seeing the day of judgment shall be in the end of the world, and death is limited and certainly appointed for all, how dost thou in the Creed say that some shall then be quick or alive?

S. St Paul teacheth ⁱthat they which then shall remain alive shall suddenly be changed and made new, so that the ^kcorruption of their bodies being taken away, and mortality removed, they shall put on immortality; and this change shall

i 1 Cor. xv. 51. 1 Thess. iv. 17.

k 1 Cor. xv. 42, 43, 53, 54.
Phil. iii. 21.

be to them instead of a death, because the ending of corrupted nature shall be the beginning of a nature uncorrupted.

M. Ought the godly at thinking upon this judgment be stricken and abashed with fear, and to dread it and shrink from it?

S. No. For He shall give the sentence, which was once by the Judge's sentence condemned for us, to the end that we, coming under the grievous judgment of God, should not be condemned but acquitted in judgment. He, I say, shall pronounce the judgment in whose faith and protection we are, and which hath taken upon him the defence of our cause. Yea, ¹our consciences are cheerfully stayed with a most singular comfort, and in the midst of the miseries and woes of this life, do leap for joy that Christ shall one day be the Judge of the world; for upon this hope we chiefly rest ourselves, that then at last we shall, with unchangeable eternity, possess that same kingdom of immortality and everlasting life, in all parts fully and abundantly perfect, which hitherto ᵐhath been but begun, and which was ordained and appointed for the children of God before the foundations of the world were laid. But the ⁿungodly, which either have not feared the justice and wrath of God, or have not trusted in his clemency and mercy by Christ, and which have persecuted the godly by land and sea, and done them all kinds of wrong, and slain them with all sorts of torments and most cruel deaths, shall, with Satan and all the devils, be cast into the prison of hell appointed for them, the revenger of their wickedness and offences, and into everlasting darkness, where, being tormented with conscience of their own sins, with eternal fire, and with all and most extreme execution, they shall pay and suffer eternal pains. For that offence which mortal men have done against the unmeasurable and infinite majesty of the immortal God, is worthy also of infinite and ever-during punishment.

¹ Rom. viii. 9, 23, 38, 39. 1 Cor. i. 7. Phil. iii. 20. Tit. ii. 13. 2 Pet. iii. 12.

ᵐ Matt. xxv. 34. 1 Cor. xiii. 9, 10. & xv. 42, 43, 53, 54.
ⁿ Matt. viii. 12. & xxii. 13. & xxv. 30, 41. Heb. x. 26, 27. Jude 6, 7, 8. Rev. xiv. 10, 11. & xix. 20. & xx. 10, 14. & xxi. 18.

M. To the last judgment is adjoined the end of the world, whereof I would have thee speak yet more plainly.

S. The apostle declareth that the end of the world shall be thus. The °heaven shall pass away like a storm, the elements with heat shall be molten, the earth and all things in it shall be inflamed with fire; as if he should say, The time shall come when this world burning with heat, all the corruption thereof (as we see in gold) tried out by fire, shall be

° Matt. xxiv. 29, 30, 35. 2 Pet. iii. 10, 11, &c.

wholly fined and renewed to most absolute and high perfection, and shall put on a most beautiful face, which in everlasting ages of worlds shall never be changed. For this is it that St Peter saith, ᵖwe look for, according to the promise of God, a new heaven and a new earth, wherein righteousness shall inhabit. Neither is it uncredible, that as sin, so the ᑫcorruption of things and changeableness and other evils grown of sin, shall once at the last have an end. And this is the sum of the second part of the christian faith, wherein is contained the whole story of our redemption by Jesus Christ.

M. Since then thou hast now spoken of God the Father, the Creator, and of his Son Jesus Christ, the Saviour, and so hast ended two parts of the christian confession, now I would hear thee speak of the third part, what thou believest of the *Holy Ghost?*

S. I confess that he is the ʳthird Person of the most Holy Trinity, proceeding from the Father and the Son before all beginning, equal with them both, and of the very same substance, and together with them both to be honoured and called upon.

M. Why is he called holy?

S. Not only for his own holiness, which yet is the highest holiness, but also for that by him the elect of God and ˢthe members of Christ are made holy. For which cause the holy scriptures have called him "the Spirit of sanctification."

M. In what things dost thou think that this sanctification consisteth?

S. First, we are by his instinct and breathing ᵗnewly begotten, and therefore Christ said that we must be born again of water and of the Spirit. Also by his heavenly breathing on us, God the Father doth ᵘadopt us his children, and therefore he is worthily called the Spirit of Adoption. By his expounding, the ˣdivine mysteries are opened unto us: by his light, the eyes of our souls are made clear to understand them; by his judgment, sins ʸare either pardoned or reserved; by his strength, ᶻsinful flesh is subdued and tamed, and corrupt desires are bridled and restrained. At his will ᵃmanifold gifts are distributed among the godly. ¹In the manifold and divers discommodities, molestations, and miseries

[¹ The paragraph beginning "In the manifold, &c.," and ending "Paraclete, or the Comforter," does not occur in the Translation by Norton, printed in 1570, but is found in the Edition printed in 1571.]

of this life, the Holy Ghost with his secret consolation, and with good hope, doth assuage, ease, and comfort the griefs and mourning of the godly, which commonly are in this world most afflicted, and whose sorrows do pass all human consolation: whereof he hath the true and proper name of ᵇParaclete, or the Comforter. Finally, by his power our mortal bodies ᶜshall rise alive again. Briefly, whatsoever benefits are given us in Christ, all these ᵈwe understand, feel, and receive by the work of the Holy Ghost. Not unworthily, therefore, we put confidence and trust in the Author of so great gifts, and do worship and call upon him.

^b John xiv. 16, 26. & xv. 26. xvi. 7.
^c Rom. viii. 11.
^d 1 Cor. xii. 4, 7, &c.

M. Now remaineth the fourth part, of the *Holy Catholic Church*, of the which I would hear what thou thinkest?

The fourth part of the Creed. The Church.

S. I will bring into few words that which the holy Scriptures do hereof largely and plentifully declare. Before that the Lord God made heaven and earth, he determined to have to himself a certain most beautiful kingdom and most holy commonweal. This the Apostles that wrote in Greek called ᵉ*Ecclesia*, which by interpreting the word may fitly be called a *Congregation*. Into this, as into his own city, God did incorporate an ᶠinfinite multitude of men, which must all be subject, serviceable, and obedient to Christ their only king, and which have all committed themselves to his protection, and of whom he hath taken upon him to be defender, and doth continually maintain and preserve them. To this commonweal do all they properly belong, ᵍas many as truly fear, honour, and call upon God, altogether applying their minds to live holily and godly, and which putting all their trust and hope in God do most assuredly look for the blessedness of eternal life. They that be stedfast, stable, and constant in this faith, ʰwere chosen and appointed, and (as we term it) predestinated to this so great felicity, before the foundations of the world were laid; whereof they have a ⁱwitness within them in their souls, the Spirit of Christ the the author, and therewith also the most sure pledge of this confidence. By the instinct of which divine Spirit I do also most surely persuade myself that I am also, by God's good gift through Christ, freely made one of this blessed city.

^e Matt. xvi. 18.
^f Matt. xxviii. 19. Acts ii. 5, 9. 1 Cor. xii. 13. Eph. v. 23, 24.
^g Acts x. 34, 35. Rom. ii. 11. Gal. vi. 15, 16. Col. iii. 11, 12, &c.
^h Matt. xvi. 18. Rom. viii. 29, 30. Eph. i. 4, 5. Col. iii. 12. Tit. i. 1.
ⁱ Rom. viii. 9, 15, 16. 2 Cor. i. 22. & v. 5. Eph. i. 13, 14. & v. 30.

M. It is sure a godly and very necessary persuasion. Now, therefore, give me the definition of the Church that thou speakest of.

S. I may most briefly and truly say, that ᵏ*the Church is the body of Christ.*

M. Yea; but I would have it somewhat more plainly and at large.

S. The Church is ˡthe body of the Christian commonweal; that is, the universal number and fellowship of all the faithful, whom God through Christ hath before all beginning of time ᵐappointed to everlasting life.

M. Why is this point put into the Creed?

S. Because if the Church were not, both Christ had died without cause, and all the things that have been hitherto spoken of, should be in vain and come to nothing.

M. How so?

S. Because hitherto we have spoken of the causes of salvation, and have considered the foundations thereof, namely, how God by the deserving of Christ loveth us and dearly esteemeth us, how also by the work of the Holy Ghost we receive this grace of God whereunto we are restored. But of these this is the only effect, ⁿthat there be a Church, that is, a company of the godly, upon whom these benefits of God may be bestowed; that there be a certain blessed city and commonweal, in which we ought to lay up, and, as it were, to consecrate all that we have, and to give ourselves wholly unto it, and for which we ought not to stick to die.

M. Why dost thou call this church holy?

S. That by this mark it may be ᵒdiscerned from the wicked company of the ungodly. For all those whom God hath chosen he hath restored unto holiness of life and innocency.

M. Is this holiness which thou dost attribute to the church already upright and in all points perfect?

S. Not yet. For so long as we live a mortal life in this world, such is the ᵖfeebleness and frailty of mankind we are of too weak strength wholly to shun all kinds of vices. Therefore the holiness of the church is not yet full and perfectly finished, but yet very well begun. But when it shall be fully joined to Christ, from ᑫwhom she hath all her cleanness and pureness, then shall she be clothed with innocency and holiness in all points full and perfectly finished, as with a certain snowy white and most pure garment.

M. To what purpose dost thou call this church catholic?

S. It is as much as if I called it universal. For this company, or assembly of the godly, is not pent up in any certain place or time, but it containeth and compriseth the universal number of the ʳfaithful, that have lived, and shall live in all places and ages, since the beginning of the world, that there may be one body of the church, ˢas there is one Christ, the only head of the body. For whereas the Jews claimed and challenged to themselves the church of God as peculiar and by lineal right due to their nation, and said that it was theirs and held it to be only theirs, the Christian faith professeth that a ᵗgreat number and infinite multitude of godly persons, gathered together out of all countries of the world, out of all parts of all nations everywhere, and all ages of all times, by the strength and power of his holy word and voice, and by the divine motion of his heavenly Spirit, is by God incorporated into this church as into his own city: which all agreeing together in one ᵘtrue faith, one mind and voice, may be in all things obedient to Christ their only King, as members ˣto their head.

ʳ Matt. xxviii. 19. Acts ii. 5, 9. & x. 34, 35.
ˢ 1 Cor. xii. 13, 14.
* Matt. viii. 11. Eph. ii. 12, 13, 14, &c. & iv. 4, 5, &c.
ᵗ Acts i. 8. & ii. 5, 8, 9. & x. 35. Col. iii. 11, &c.
ᵘ Eph. iv. 4, 5. & v. 23.
ˣ 1 Cor. vi. 15. Eph. iv. 15, 16. & v. 30. Col. i. 18.

M. Dost thou think that they do well that join to this part of the Christian belief, that they believe the holy catholic church of Rome?

S. I do not only think that they join a wrong forged sense to this place, while they will have no man to be counted in the church of Christ but him that esteemeth for holy all the decrees and ordinances of the bishop of Rome; but also I judge, that when, by adding afterward the name of one nation, they abridge and draw into narrow room the universal extent of the church, which themselves do first confess to be far and wide spread abroad everywhere, among all lands and peoples, they are herein far madder than the Jews, joining and pronouncing with one breath mere contrary sayings. But into this madness are they driven by a blind greediness, and desire to shift and foist in the bishop of Rome to be head of the church in earth, in the stead of Christ.

M. Now would I hear thee tell, why, after the holy church, thou immediately addest, that we believe "the communion of saints."

S. Because these two belong all to one thing, and are very fitly matched and agreeing together. For this parcel doth somewhat more plainly express the conjoining and society that is among the members of the church, than which there can none be nearer. For, whereas God hath as well in all coasts and countries, as in all times and ages, them that worship him purely and sincerely, ʸall they, though they be severed and sundered by divers and far distant times and places, in what nation soever, or in what land soever they be, are yet members most nearly conjoined and knit together, of one and of the selfsame body, whereof Christ is the head; such is the communion that the godly have with God and among themselves. ᶻFor they are most nearly knit together in community of spirit, of faith, of sacraments, of prayers, of forgiveness of sins, of eternal felicity, and, finally, of all the benefits that God giveth his church through Christ. Yea, they are so joined together with most strait bonds of concord ᵃand love, they have so all one mind, that the profit of any one and of them all is all one; and to this endeavour they do most bend themselves, how they may with interchange of beneficial doings, with counsel and help, further each other in all things, and specially to attaining of that blessed and eternal life. But because this communion of saints cannot be perceived by our senses, nor by any ᵇnatural kind of knowledge or force of understanding, as other civil communities and fellowships of men may be, therefore it is here rightly placed among these things that lie in belief.

M. I like very well this brief discourse of the church, and of the benefits of God bestowed upon her through Christ: for the same is most plainly taught in the holy scriptures. But may the church be otherwise known than by believing—by faith?

S. Here in the Creed is properly entreated of the congregation of those whom God by his secret ᶜelection hath adopted to himself through Christ: which church can neither be seen with eyes, nor can continually be known by signs. Yet there is a church of God visible, or that may be seen, the tokens or marks whereof he doth shew and open unto us.

M. Then, that this whole matter of the church may be made plainer, so describe and paint me out that same visible church with her marks and signs, that it may be discerned from any other fellowship of men.

S. I will assay to do it as well as I can. The visible church is nothing else but a certain multitude of men, which,

---

y 1 Cor. xii. 12, 13, &c. 20, 26. Eph. iv. 15, 16. & v. 30. Col. i. 18. & ii. 19.

z Eph. iv. 3, 4, 5, &c. 15, 16. Col. ii. 19.

a Matt. vii. 12. & xix. 14. & xxii. 39. Rom. xii. 5. 1 Cor. x. 24. & xiii. 5. 2 Cor. xi. 28. Gal. vi. 2. Phil. ii. 1, 2, 3, 4, 5.

b 1 Cor. ii. 14, 15.

c Rom. viii. 29, 30, 33. Eph. i. 4, 5, 11. Col. iii. 12.

in what place soever they be, ᵈdo profess the doctrine of Christ, pure and sincere, even the same which the evangelists and apostles have, in the everlasting monuments of holy scriptures, faithfully disclosed to memory, and which do truly call upon God the Father ᵉin the name of Christ, and moreover do use his ᶠmysteries, commonly called sacraments, with the same pureness and simplicity (as touching their substance) which the apostles of Christ used and have put in writing.

M. Thou sayest then that the marks of the visible church are, the sincere preaching of the gospel, that is to say of the benefits of Christ, invocation and administration of the sacraments.

S. These are indeed the chief and the necessary marks of the visible church, such as without the which it cannot be indeed, nor rightly be called, the church of Christ. But yet also in the same church, if it be well ordered, there shall be seen to be observed a certain ᵍorder and manner of governance, and such a form of ecclesiastical discipline, that it shall not be free for any that abideth in that flock publicly to speak or do anything wickedly or in heinous sort without punishment, yea, and so that in that congregation of men all offences (so far as is possible) be avoided. But this discipline since long time past by little and little decaying, as the manners of men be corrupt and out of right course, specially of the rich and men of power, which will needs have impunity and most free liberty to sin and do wickedly, this grave manner of looking to them and of chastisement can hardly be maintained in churches. But in whatsoever assembly the word of God, the calling upon him, and his sacraments, are purely and sincerely retained, it is no doubt that there is also the church of Christ.

M. Are not, then, all they that be in this visible church of the number of the elect to everlasting life?

S. Many, by hypocrisy and counterfeiting of godliness, do join themselves to this fellowship, which are nothing less than true members of the church. But, forasmuch as wheresoever the word of God is sincerely taught, and his sacraments rightly ministered, there are ever some appointed to ʰsalvation by Christ, we count all that whole company to be the church of God, seeing that Christ also promiseth that himself will be present with two ⁱor three that be gathered together in his name.

M. Why doest thou, by and by, after the church, make mention of the forgiveness of sins?

S. First, because the ᵏkeys, wherewith heaven is to be shut and opened, that is, that power of binding and loosing, of reserving and forgiving sins, which standeth in the ministry of the word of God, is by Christ given and committed to the church, and properly belongeth unto the church. Secondly, because no man obtaineth forgiveness of sins that is not a true member of the body ˡof Christ, that is, such a one as doth not earnestly, godlily, holily, yea, and continuingly ᵐand to the end embrace and maintain the common fellowship of the church.

M. Is there then no hope of salvation out of the Church?

S. Out of it can be nothing but damnation, death, and destruction. For what hope of life can remain ⁿto the members when they are pulled asunder and cut off from the head and body? They therefore that seditiously stir up discord °in the Church of God, and make division and strife in it, and trouble it with sects, have all hope of safety by forgiveness of sins cut off from them, till they be reconciled and return to agreement and favour with the Church.

M. What meanest thou by this word "forgiveness"?

S. That the faithful do obtain at God's hand discharge of their fault and pardon of their offence: for God, ᵖfor Christ's sake, freely forgiveth them their sins, and rescueth and delivereth them from judgment and damnation, and from punishments just and due for their ill-doing.

M. Cannot we then, with godly, dutiful doings, and works, satisfy God, and by ourselves merit pardon of our sins?

S. There is no mercy due to our merits, but God doth yield and remit to Christ his correction and punishment that he would have done upon us. For Christ alone, with sufferance of his pains, ᵍand with his death, wherewith he hath paid and performed the penalty of our sins, hath satisfied God. Therefore by Christ alone we have access to the grace of God. We, receiving this benefit of ʳhis free liberality and goodness, have nothing at all to offer or render again to him by way of reward or recompence.

M. Is there nothing at all to be done on our behalf, that we may obtain forgiveness of sins?

S. Although among men, the fault once granted, it is hard to obtain forgiveness of him that ought to be the punisher of offences, yet even they ˢthat are strangers to our religion, have not been ignorant that confession is a certain remedy to him that hath done amiss. And I have already said, how sinners for obtaining of pardon have need of repentance, which some like better to call resipiscence or amendment, and of change of mind; and the Lord promiseth that he will pardon sinners if they repent, ᵗif they amend and turn their hearts from their naughty lives unto him. ˢ Cic.
ᵗ Jer. xviii. 8.
Ezek. xviii. 21, 30, 31, 32. & xxxiii. 14.
Matt. iv. 17. Luke v. 32.

M. How many parts be there of repentance?

S. Two chief parts: the mortifying of the old man, or the flesh; and the quickening of the new man or the spirit.

M. I would have these more largely and plainly set out.

S. The mortifying of the old man is unfeigned and sincere acknowledging and ᵘconfession of sin, and therewith, a shame and sorrow of mind, with the feeling whereof the person is sore grieved for that he hath swerved from righteousness, and not been obedient to the will of God. For every man ought, in remembering the sins of his life past, wholly to ˣmislike himself, to be angry with himself, and to be a severe judge of his own faults, and to give sentence and pronounce judgment of himself, to the intent he abide not the grievous judgment of God in his wrath. This sorrow some have called contrition, whereunto are joined in nearness and nature an earnest hatred of sin, and a love and desire of righteousness lost. ᵘ Ps. xxxii. 4, 5. & li. 3, 4. Prov. xxviii. 13. 1 John i. 8, 9.
ˣ Ps. vi. 6, 7. & xxxi. 9, 10. & xxxviii. 3, 4, 6, 8, 9, 10, 17, 18. & li. 17. & cii. 4, 5. 1 Cor. xi 31. 2 Cor. vii. 9, 10, 11.

M. But the conscience of heinous offences, and the force of repentance, may be so great, that the mind of man, on each side compassed with fear, may be possessed with despair of salvation.

S. ʸThat is true, unless God bring comfort to the greatness of sorrow. But to the godly there remaineth yet one other part of repentance, which is called ᶻrenewing of the Spirit, or quickening of the new man. That is, when faith cometh, and ᵃrefresheth and lifteth up the mind so troubled, assuageth sorrow, and comforteth the person, and doth revoke and raise him up again from desperation, to hope of obtaining ʸ Gen. iv. 13. Matt. xxvii. 3, 4. 2 Cor. ii. 7, 8.
ᶻ Eph. iv. 23, 24. 1 Pet. iv. 6.
ᵃ Matt. iv. 17. Luke vii. 38, 47, 48, 50. & xv. 18, 21. xviii. 13. & xxiv. 47. Acts ii. 37. & iii. 19. & xvi. 30, 31. 1 Tim. i. 15.

pardon of God through Christ, and from the gate of death, yea, from hell itself, unto life. And this is it that we profess that we believe the forgiveness of sins.

M. Is man able in this fear and these hard distresses to deliver himself by his own strength?

S. Nothing less. For it is only God [b]which strengtheneth man despairing of his own estate, raiseth him up in affliction, restoreth him in utter misery, and by whose guiding the sinner conceiveth this hope, mind, and will, that I spake of.

[b] Matt. xviii. 12. Luke xv. 22. 2 Cor. i. 3, 4. 2 Thess. ii. 16, 17.

M. Now rehearse the rest of the Creed.

S. I believe "[c]the resurrection of the flesh, and life everlasting."

[c] Matt. xxii. 31, 32. John xi. 25. 1 Cor. xv. toto.

M. Because thou hast touched somewhat of this before in speaking of the last judgment, I will ask thee but a few questions. Whereto or why do we believe these things?

S. Although we believe that the souls of men are immortal and everlasting, yet if we should think that our bodies should by death be utterly destroyed for ever, then must we needs be [d]wholly discouraged; for that, wanting the one part of ourselves, we should never entirely possess perfect joy and immortality. We do therefore certainly believe not only that our souls, when we depart out of this life, being delivered from the company of our bodies, do by and by fly up pure and whole [e]into heaven to Christ, but also that our bodies shall at length be restored [f]to a better state of life, and joined again to their souls, and so we shall wholly be made perfectly and fully blessed; that is to say, we doubt not that both in our bodies and souls we shall enjoy eternity, immortality, and most blessed life, that shall never in everlasting continuance of time be changed. This hope [g]comforteth us in miseries. Endued with this hope, we not only patiently suffer and bear the incommodities and cumbrances that light upon us in this life, but also very departure from life and the sorrows of death. For we are throughly persuaded that death is not a destruction that endeth and consumeth all things, but a guide for us to [h]heaven, that setteth us in a way of a quiet, easy, blessed, and everlasting life. And therefore gladly and cheerfully we run, yea, we fly out, from the bonds of our bodies, as from a prison, to heaven, as to the common town and city of God and men.

[d] 1 Cor. xv. 14, 17, 18, 19.

[e] Luke xvi. 22. & xxiii. 43.
[f] Rom. viii. 11. 1 Cor. xv. 42, 43, 44, 53, 54. Phil. iii. 21. 1 Thess. iv. 13, 14, 15, 16, 17.

[g] John xi. 25. 1 Cor. xv. 58. 1 Thess. iv. 13, 14, 18. Rev. xiii. 18.

[h] 2 Cor. v. 1, 2. Eph. ii. 19.

M. Doth the believing of these things avail us to any other end?

S. We are put in mind that we cumber not nor entangle ourselves with uncertain, transitory, and frail things; that we bend not our eye to earthly glory and felicity, but inhabit this world ¹as strangers, and ever minding our removing; that we long upward for heaven and heavenly things, where we shall in bliss enjoy eternal life. ^{l Heb. xiii. 13, 14. 1 Pet. ii. 11.}

M. Sith thou hast before said, that the wicked shall rise again in sort most far ᵏdiffering from the godly, that is to say, to eternal misery and everlasting death, why doth the Creed make mention only of life everlasting, and of hell no mention at all? ^{k Matt. xxv. 34, 41, 46.}

S. This is a confession of the Christian faith, which pertaineth to none but to the godly, and therefore rehearseth only those things that are ˡfit for to comfort, namely, the most large gifts which God will give to them that be his. And therefore here is not recited what punishments are provided for them that be out of the kingdom of God. ^{l Mark xvi. 16. Luke xxiv. 47. John iii. 15, 16. Rom. iv. 16.}

M. Now thou hast declared the Creed, that is the sum of the Christian faith, tell me, what profit get we of this faith?

S. Righteousness ᵐbefore God, by which we are made heirs of eternal life. ^{m Rom. iii. 21, 22. Gal. ii. 16.}

M. Doth not then our own godliness toward God, and leading of our life honestly and holily among men, justify us before God?

S. Of this we have said somewhat already after the declaring of the law, and in other places, to this effect. If any man were able to live uprightly according to the precise rule ⁿof the law of God, he should worthily be counted justified by his good works. But seeing we are ᵒall most far from that perfection of life, yea, and be so oppressed with conscience of our sins, we ᵖmust take another course, and find another way, how God may receive us into favour, than by our own deserving. ^{n Rom. x. 5. Gal. iii. 12 o Gen. vi. 5. & viii. 11. Luke xviii. 11, 12, 14. Rom. vii. 14, 15. Gal. ii. 16. p Rom. xi. 6.}

M. What way?

S. We must flee to the ᑫmercy of God, whereby he freely embraceth us with love and good-will in Christ, without any our deserving, or respect of works, both forgiving us our sins, and so giving us the righteousness of Christ by faith in him, that for the same Christ's righteousness he so accepteth ^{q Rom. iii. 24. & iv. 4, 7, 16. Eph. ii. 4, 5. 2 Tim. i. 9. Tit. iii. 4, 5. 1 Pet. i. 3. & ii. 10.}

us, as if it were our own. To God's mercy therefore through Christ we ought to impute all our justification.

M. How do we know it to be thus?

S. By the gospel, which containeth the promises of God by Christ, ʳto the which when we adjoin faith, that is to say, an assured persuasion of mind and stedfast confidence of God's good-will, such as hath been set out in the whole Creed, we do, as it were, take state and possession of this justification that I speak of.

M. Dost not thou then say that faith is the principal cause of this justification, so as by the merit of faith we are counted righteous before God?

S. No; for that were to set faith in the place of Christ. But the spring-head of this justification ˢis the mercy of God, which is conveyed to us by Christ, and is offered to us by the gospel, ᵗand received of us by faith as with a hand.

M. Thou sayest then that faith is not the cause but the instrument of justification; for that it embraceth Christ, ᵘwhich is our justification; coupling us with so strait bond to him, that it maketh us partakers of all his good things?

S. Yea forsooth.

M. But can this justification be so severed from good works, that he that hath it can want them?

S. No: for by faith we receive Christ such as he delivereth himself unto us. But he doth not only set us at liberty from sins and death, and make us at one with God, but also with the divine inspiration and virtue of the ˣHoly Ghost doth regenerate and newly form us to the endeavour of innocency and holiness, which we call ʸnewness of life.

M. Thou sayest then that ᶻjustice, faith, and good works, do naturally cleave together, and therefore ought no more to be severed, than Christ, the author of them in us, can be severed from himself.

S. It is true.

M. Then this doctrine of faith doth not withdraw men's minds from godly works and duties?

S. Nothing less. For good works do stand upon faith as ᵃupon their root. So far, therefore, is faith from withdrawing our hearts from living uprightly, that, contrariwise, it doth most vehemently stir us up to the endeavour of good life; yea and so far, that he is not truly faithful that doth not also to his power both ᵇshun vices and embrace virtues, so living always as one that looketh to give an account. ᵇ Rom. vi. 1, 2, 3, 4.

M. Therefore tell me plainly how our works be acceptable to God, and what rewards be given to them?

S. In good works, two things are principally required. First, that we do those works ᶜthat are prescribed by the law of God; secondly, that they be done with that mind and ᵈfaith which God requireth. For no doings or thoughts enterprised or ᵉconceived without faith can please God.

ᶜ Deut. iv. 1, 2. & xii. 32.
ᵈ Mark vii. 6, 7, 8, 9. & x. 17, 19. John xv. 10.
ᵉ Rom. ix. 31, 32. & xiv. 23. Heb. xi. 6.

M. Go forward.

S. It is evident, therefore, that all works whatsoever we do, before that we ᶠbe born again and renewed by the Spirit of God, such as may properly be called our own works, are faulty. For whatsoever shew of gayness and worthiness they represent and give to the eyes of men, since they spring and proceed from a faulty and corrupted ᵍheart, which God chiefly considereth, they cannot but be defiled and corrupted, and so grievously offend God. Such works, therefore, as evil fruits, ʰgrowing out of an evil tree, God despiseth and rejecteth from him.

ᶠ John iii. 3, 4, 5, 6. Rom. ix. 31, 32. Eph. ii. 3. 1 Pet. i. 22, 23.
ᵍ Rom. viii. 5, 6, 7. 1 Cor. i. 19, 20. & iii. 19. 2 Cor. i. 12.
ʰ Matt. vii. 18, 19. & xii. 33, 35.

M. Can we not, therefore, prevent God with any works or deservings, whereby we may first provoke him to love us, and be good unto us?

S. Surely, with none. For God loved and chose us in Christ, not only when we were his enemies, ⁱthat is, sinners, but also before the foundations of the world were laid. And this is the same spring-head and original of our justification, whereof I spake before.

ⁱ Rom. v. 8, 10. & xi. 35. 1 John iv. 9, 10, 19. Eph. i. 4.

M. What thinkest thou of those works which we, after that we be reconciled to God's favour, do by the instinct of the Holy Ghost?

S. The dutiful works of godliness, which proceedeth out of faith, working ᵏby charity, are indeed acceptable to God, yet not by their own deserving; ˡbut for that he, of his liberality, vouchsafeth them his favour. For though they be derived from the Spirit of God, as little streams from the spring-head, yet of our flesh, that mingleth itself with them, in the doing by the way, they receive corruption, as it were by infection, like as a river, otherwise pure and clear, is troubled and mudded with mire and slime, wherethrough it runneth.

ᵏ Rom. xii. 1. Gal. v. 6.
ˡ Luke xvii. 10. & xviii. 11, 12, 14.

M. How then dost thou say that they please God?

S. ⁿIt is faith that procureth God's favour to our works, while it is assured that he will not deal with us after extremity of °law, nor call our doings to exact account, nor try them as it were by the square: that is, he will not, in valuing and weighing them, use severity, but remitting and pardoning all their corruptness, for Christ's sake and his deservings, will account them for fully perfect.

ⁿ Rom. ix. 31, 32. Gal. v. 6. Heb. xi. 6
^o Ps. cxxx. 3. & cxliii. 2.

M. Then thou standest still in this, that we cannot by merit of works obtain to be justified before God, seeing thou thinkest that all doings of men, even the perfectest, do need pardon?

S. God himself hath so decreed in his word; and his Holy Spirit doth teach us to pray that he ^pbring us not into judgment. For where righteousness, such as God the Judge shall allow, ought to be throughly ^qabsolute, and in all parts and points fully perfect, such as is to be directed and tried by the most precise rule, and, as it were, by the plumb-line of God's law and judgment; and sith our works, even ^rthe best of them, for that they swerve and differ most far from the rule ^sand prescription of God's law and justice, are many ways to be blamed ^tand condemned; we can in no wise be justified before God by works.

^p Luke xviii. 11, 12, 14. Rom. iv. 2. Gal. ii. 16.
^q Rom. iii. 20.

^r Ps. cxliii. 2.

^s Job iv 18. & xv. 14, 15, 16. & xxv. 4, 5. Ps. cxxx. 3.
^t Job xv. 14, 15, 16. & xxv. 6. Isai. lxiv. 6. 1 Cor. iv. 4.

M. Doth not this doctrine withdraw men's minds from the duties of godliness, and make them slacker and slower to good works, or at least less cheerful and ready to godly endeavours?

S. No: for we may not therefore say that good works are unprofitable or done in vain and without cause, for that we obtain not justification by them. For they serve both to the profit of our neighbour ^uand to the glory of God; and they do, as by certain testimonies, ^xassure us of God's good-will toward us, and of our love again to God-ward, and of our faith, and so consequently of our salvation. And reason it is, that we being redeemed with the blood of Christ the Son of God, and having beside received innumerable and infinite benefits of God, should live and wholly frame ourselves after the ^ywill and appointment of our Redeemer, and so shew ourselves mindful and thankful to the Author of our salvation, and ^zby our example procure and win other unto him. The man that calleth these thoughts to mind may sufficiently rejoice in his good endeavours and works.

^u Matt. v. 16. 1 Pet. ii. 12.
^x Matt. xii. 33. Phil. ii. 12. 1 Pet. i. 10.

^y Rom. xiv. 7, 8. 1 Cor. vi. 20. 2 Cor. v. 15. 1 Thess. v. 10.
^z Matt. v. 16. 1 Pet. ii. 12.

M. But God doth allure us to good doing with certain rewards, both in this life and in the life to come, and doth covenant with us as it were for certain wages.

S. ^aThat reward, as I have said, is not given to works for their worthiness, and rendered to them as recompence for deservings, but by the bountifulness of God is freely bestowed upon us without deserving. And justification God doth give us as a gift of his own dear love toward us, and of his liberality ^bthrough Christ. When I speak of God's gift and liberality, I mean it ^cfree and bountiful, without any our desert or merit: that it be God's mere and sincere liberality, which he applieth to our salvation only whom he loveth and which trust in him, not hired or procured for wages, as it were a merchandise of his commodities and benefits used by him for some profit to himself, requiring again of us some recompence or price, which once to think were to abate both the liberality and majesty of God.

^a Matt. v. 12. & x. 41, 42. & xxv. 34, 35. Eph. iii. 20. 2 Tim. i. 9.

^b Rom. iii. 24. 1 Cor. i. 1.
^c Rom. iii. 24. & xi. 6. Gal. v. 4. 2 Tim. i. Tit. iii. 4, 9. Rev. xxi. 6.

M. Whereas then God doth by faith both give us justification, and by the same faith alloweth and accepteth our works, tell me, dost thou think that this faith is a quality of nature, or the gift of God?

S. Faith is the gift ^dof God, and a singular and excellent gift. For both our wits are too gross ^eand dull to conceive and understand the wisdom of God, whose fountains are opened by faith, and our hearts are more apt either ^fto distrust, or to wrongful and corrupt trust in ourselves, or in other creatures, than to true trust in God. But God, instructing us with his word and ^glightening our minds with his Holy Spirit, maketh us apt to learn those things that otherwise would be far from entering into the dull capacity of our wits; and sealing the promises of salvation in our souls, he so informeth us that we are most surely persuaded of the truth of them. These things the apostles understanding, do pray to the Lord to ^hincrease their faith.

^d Mark ix. 23, 24. John xi. 40. 1 Pet. i. 20, 21.
^e Matt. xvi. 7, 8, 9, 11. Luke xviii. 34. Rom. viii. 6, 7. 1 Cor. ii. 14.
^f Matt. vi. 30. & viii. 26. & xvi. 8. & xiv. 31.
^g Matt. xvi. 17. Luke xxiv. 45. Col. i. 9. 2 Tim. ii. 7.

^h Luke xvii. 5.

The Third Part. Of Prayer and Thanksgiving.

M. Thou hast in good time made mention of prayer. For now thou hast ended the declaration of the law of God, and of the Creed, that is to say, the Christian confession, it followeth next to speak of prayer, and of thanksgiving, which is nearly conjoined to it: for these are in order knit, and fitly hanging together with the rest.

S. They be indeed most nearly joined, for they belong to the first table of God's law, and do contain the principal duties of ⁱgodliness toward God.

M. In declaring of prayer what order shall we follow?

S. This order, master, if it so please you: first, to shew who is to be prayed unto: secondly, with what affiance: thirdly, with what affection of heart: and, fourthly, what is to be prayed for.

M. First, then, tell me who thou thinkest is to be called upon?

S. Surely, none but God alone.

M. Why so?

S. Because ᵏour life and salvation standeth in the hand of God alone, in whose power are all things. Sith then God doth give us all that is good and that a Christian man ought to wish and desire; and sith he alone is able, in every ˡdanger, to give help and succour, and to drive away all perils, it is meet that of him we ask all things; and in all distresses flee to him alone, and crave his help. For this he himself in ᵐhis word asketh and requireth, as the peculiar and proper worshipping of his majesty.

M. Shall we not then do well to call upon holy men that are departed out of this life, or upon angels?

S. No. For that were to give to them an infiniteness to be present everywhere, or to give them, being absent, an understanding of our secret meanings, that is, as much as a certain godhead, and therewithal partly to convey to them our confidence and trust, ⁿthat ought to be set wholly in God alone, and so to slide into idolatry. But forasmuch as God calleth us to himself alone, and doth also, with adding an oath, promise that ᵒhe will both hear and help us; to flee to the help of other were an evident token of distrust and infidelity. And as touching the holy men that are departed out of this life, what manner of thing, I pray you, were this, forsaking the ᵖliving God, that ᑫheareth our prayers, that is most mighty, ʳmost ready to help us, that ˢcalleth us unto him, that in the word of truth promiseth ᵗand sweareth, that, with his divine power and succour, he will defend us; forsaking him, I say, to flee to men dead, deaf, and weak, which neither have promised help, nor are able to relieve us, to whom God never gave the office to help us, to whom we are by no scriptures directed, whereupon our ^ufaith may surely rest, but are unadvisedly carried away, trusting only upon the dreams, or rather dotages of our own head. [u Rom. x. 8, 14, 17.]

M. But God doth to our salvation use the service of angels, that wait upon us, and therefore do hear us.

S. ^xThat is true. But yet it appeareth nowhere in the word of God that God would have us pray to angels, or to godly men deceased. And sith faith resteth upon ^ythe word of God, and what is not of faith ^zis sin, I said rightly that it is a sure token of infidelity to forsake God, ^ato whom alone the scriptures do send us, and to pray to and crave help of angels, or godly men departed this life, for calling upon whom there is not one word in the holy scriptures. [x Ps. xci. 11, 11, 12. Heb. i. 14.] [y Rom. x. 17.] [z Rom. xiv. 23.] [a Matt. vi. 6, 9.]

M. But seeing charity never ^bfalleth out of the hearts of the godly, even while they be in heaven they are careful for us, and do desire our salvation. [b 1 Cor. xiii. 8.]

S. That cannot be denied; yet it doth not follow that we must therefore call upon them, unless we think that we must call for the help and succour of our friends, be they never so far from us, only because they bear us good-will.

M. But we oft crave help of men that be alive, and with whom we are presently conversant.

S. I grant. For men, as they have ^cmutually need one of another's help, so hath God granted them power, one mutually to help another; yea, and he hath expressly commanded every man ^dto relieve his neighbour with such help as he can. We do therefore call upon men, as ministers of God's goodness, according to the will of God, looking for help and succour of them: but yet so that all our trust be settled in God alone, and that we reckon received from him, as the spring-head of all liberality, whatsoever is delivered us ^eby the hands of men. Therefore this is well and orderly done, and no impediment to the calling upon of God alone, so that we confess that we do not from elsewhere look for any good thing, nor settle our whole succour in any other. [c 1 Cor. xii. 11, 21, 25. 1 Pet. iv. 10.] [d Matt. vii. 12. 1 Cor. x. 24. Gal. vi. 2.] [e 1 Pet. i. 10.]

M. Dost thou then say that we must use prayer and supplication, like as all other duties of godliness, according to the prescription of God's word, or else we cannot please God?

S. Yea, verily; [f]for all offence in religion is committed by changing the order and manner appointed by God.

M. Hitherto then thou hast said that God alone is to be called upon, putting all our trust in him, and that to him all things, as to the spring-head of all good things, are to be imputed; now followeth next to declare with what confidence we wretched mortal men, that are so many ways unworthy, ought to call upon the immortal God.

S. We are indeed every way most unworthy. But we thrust not ourselves in, proudly and arrogantly, as if we were worthy, but we come to him in the name, and upon trust of [g]Christ our Mediator, by whom the door being opened to us, though we be most base silly wretches, made of clay and slime, oppressed with conscience of our own sins, we shall not be forbidden to enter, nor shall have hard access to the majesty of God, and to the obtaining of his favour.

M. We need not then, for access to God, some man to be our mean or interpreter, to commend and declare our suit unto him, as it were unto some worldly prince.

S. Nothing less; unless we will think that God is [h]as men be, bound to one place; that he cannot understand many things but by his servants; that he sometime sleepeth, or hath not leisure to hear. For, as touching our unworthiness, we have already said, that our prayers stand in confidence, not upon anything in us, but upon the only worthiness of [i]Christ, in whose name we pray.

M. Dost thou then think that God the Father is to be called upon in the name, and upon trust of Christ alone?

S. Yea, forsooth, master; for he alone, above all other, most singularly [k]loveth us, so far that he will do all things for our sakes: he alone is with God his Father, at whose right hand he sitteth, [l]in most high favour, that he may obtain what he will of him: he therefore alone is the Mediator of God and men, the man Jesus Christ; he alone, I say, is the Mediator of redemption, and also of invocation, in whose [m]name alone the holy scriptures do expressly bid us to go unto God the Father, adding also promises that he by his intercession will bring to pass that we shall obtain all that we pray for: otherwise [n]without Christ the ear and heart of God abhorreth men.

M. But we do yet with mutual °prayers one help another, so long as we abide in this world. ^o 1 Thess. i. 2. Col. iv. 2, 3. Eph. vi. 18, 19.

S. That is true. But we do not therefore set other mediators in place of Christ; but with conjoined hearts and prayers, according to the rule of charity and the word of God, we do by one ^pMediator call upon our common Father. ^p 1 Tim. ii. 5. Heb. ix. 15.

M. Thou sayest then, that to appoint other mediators to God, or patrons for our cause, but Christ alone, is both against the holy Scriptures, and therefore against faith, and also containeth great injury to Christ himself.

S. Yea forsooth, master.

M. Go on then.

S. The sum is this, that we must come to call upon God the Father, resting upon affiance of the promises made ^qto us by Christ, and trusting upon his intercession, leaving all respect of our own worthiness, and framing our prayers, as it were, out of the mouth ^rof Christ; which doing, as it is most agreeable to the truth of the Scriptures, so is it most far from the fault of ^sarrogancy and presumption. ^q Rom. i. 2, 5. & iv. 21, 24. 2 Cor. i. 20. & iii. 4, 5. Gal. iii. 22. Tit. i. 2. ^r Matt. ix. 10. John xiv. 15, 26. & xv. 16, 21. & xvi. 23, 24, 26. ^s Ps. xxix. 1, 2. Acts iii. 12, 16.

M. Thinkest thou that they which so pray to God as thou sayest, ought to have a good hope to obtain what they ask?

S. The Lord himself doth also command us to ask with sure ^tfaith, making therewith a promise, and adding an oath, that it shall be given us whatsoever we ask with faith. And likewise his apostles do teach that right prayer proceedeth from faith. Therefore we must alway lay this most assured foundation of prayer; that, resting ^uupon sure trust of his fatherly goodness, we must determine that God will hear our prayers and petitions, and that we shall obtain so far as it is expedient for us. Therefore they that come rashly ^xand unconsiderately to prayer, and such as pray doubting and uncertain of their speeding, they do without fruit pour out vain and bootless words. ^t Matt. xxi. 21. Mark xi. 22, 23, 24. John xvi. 23. James i. 6. & v. 15, 16. ^u Matt. vii. 10. Heb. iv. 16. & x. 22. 1 John v. 14. ^x Matt. xx. 22. & xxi. 21. John xvi. 24. James i. 6. & iv. 3.

M. I see with what confidence thou sayest we must call upon God. Now tell me with what affection of heart we must come unto him.

S. ^yOur hearts must be sore grieved with feeling of our need and poverty, and miseries that oppress us, so far forth that we must burn with great desire of deliverance from that grief, and of God's help which we pray for. Being thus ^y Ps. l. 15. & xciv. 7. & cxxiv. 1, 2. & cxxvii. 1, 2. Rom vii. 18. & viii. 23. 2 Cor. iii. 4, 5.

disposed in heart, it cannot be but that we shall most attentively and with ᶻmost fervent affection, with all manner of prayers and petitions, crave that we desire.

M. I see then it is not enough to pray with tongue and voice alone.

S. To pray, not applying thereto our mind ᵃand attentiveness, without which our prayers can never be effectual, is not only to take fruitless labour in vain (for how shall God hear us when we heed not ᵇnor hear not ourselves?), and not only to pour out vain and fruitless, but ᶜalso hurtful words, with offending God's majesty; so far off is it that such prayers can appease the majesty of God that is displeased with our offence.

M. How know we that it is thus?

S. ᵈSith God is a Spirit, and (as I may so call him) a most pure mind; he both in all other things, and specially in prayer, whereby men, as it were, talk and commune with God, requireth the soul and mind. And he also testifieth that he will be near to them only that call upon him ᵉtruly; that is with their heart, and that their prayers please him. On the other side, God doth worthily abhor and detest their prayers that ᶠfeignedly and unadvisedly utter with their tongue that which they conceive not with their heart and thought; and deal ᵍmore negligently with immortal God, than they are wont to do with a mortal man. Therefore in prayer the mind is ever needful, but the tongue is not alway necessary.

M. But there is some use of the tongue in prayer?

S. Yea forsooth. For meet it is that ʰthe tongue do also diligently and earnestly employ all her strength and ability to set forth the honour of God, sith it is above all other parts of the body properly created by God to that use. Moreover, as from a mind earnestly bent with study and care, sometime words break out of us ere we be aware; so oftentimes the very sound of utterance, and the hearing of our own words, quickeneth and sharpeneth our mind, and helpeth the heedfulness thereof, and keepeth off and driveth away slackness wherewith the heart is continually tempted.

M. Sith it is so, what thinkest thou of them that pray in a strange tongue, and such as they understand not?

S. I think that they not only lose their labour, but therewith also mock God himself. For if *loqui*, to speak, be wittingly to bestow each word in his right place, they that utter words ¹which they understand not, chatter rather than speak, so far be they from praying. For they play the parrots rather than men, much less Christian men. Therefore far be from godly men such hypocrisy and mockery; for if ᵏSt Paul think it an absurdity for a man to speak to other that speech which they understand not, because words move no man but him that hath the same language, and affirmeth that both he that speaketh and he that heareth shall either of them be an alien to the other, how much greater absurdity is it that we ourselves be aliens to ourselves, while we use that speech that we know not, and go about to utter our meanings and prayers in that tongue wherein ourselves are deaf? Wise men in old time thought that such men, as most fond, were most worthy to be laughed at.

¹ 1 Cor. xiv. 7, 9, 11.
ᵏ 1 Cor. xiv. 11.
Cic. de Offic. Tusc. Quæst. lib. v. et de Oratore.

M. I see how heedful a mind and fervent affection is required in prayer. But tell me, dost thou think this ferventness to be natural, and by kind planted in our hearts, or that it is a raising up of our minds by God?

S. The holy scriptures do testify that the Spirit of God raiseth up unspeakable ˡgroanings, whereby our prayers are made effectual. He therefore, without doubt, with his inspiration stirreth up our minds, and whetteth and helpeth us to pray.

ˡ Rom. viii. 26. Eph. ii. 18.

M. How then, when this ferventness of mind, that cannot alway be present, is slacked, or wholly quenched, shall we, as it were drowsy with sloth and sleeping, idly look for the stirring and moving of the Spirit?

S. Nothing less. But rather, when we be faint and slack in mind, we must ᵐby and by crave the help of God, that he will give us cheerfulness, and stir up our hearts to prayer. For this mind and will we conceive by the guiding of God.

ᵐ Ps. li. 17. Matt. xxvi. 40, 41.

M. Now remaineth that I hear of thee what we ought to ask of God by prayer. Is it lawful to ask of God whatsoever cometh in our mind and mouth?

S. When men that were strangers to true godliness had such an honest opinion of the majesty and mind of their gods, that they thought they ought not to ask of them any-

Cicero pro domo sua.

thing unjust or unhonest, God forbid that we Christians should ever ask anything of God in prayer that may ⁿmislike the mind and will of God. For this were to do God's majesty most high injury and dishonour; so much less may such a prayer please him, or obtain anything of him. And sith both the wits of men are °too dull to understand what is expedient for them, and the desires of their hearts are so blind and wild, that they not only need a guide whom they may follow, but also bridles to restrain them, it were too great an absurdity that we should in prayer be carried rashly and headlong by our own affections. By a certain rule therefore and prescribed form our prayers ought wholly to be directed.

ⁿ Matt. vii. 11. John xvi. 24. James iv. 3. 1 John v. 14.

° Matt. xx. 22. Rom. viii. 26, 27. James iv. 3.

M. What rule and form?

S. Even the same form of prayer verily ᵖwhich the heavenly Schoolmaster appointed to his disciples, and by them to us all; wherein he hath couched in very few points all those things that are lawful to be asked of God, and behoveful for us to obtain; which prayer is after the Author thereof called the Lord's Prayer. If therefore we will follow the heavenly teacher with his divine voice, saying before us, truly we shall never swerve from the right rule of praying.

ᵖ Matt. vi. 9, 10. Luke xi. 1, 2, &c.

M. Rehearse me then the Lord's Prayer.

S. When ye will pray (saith ᵍthe Lord) say thus:—"Our Father which art in heaven, hallowed be thy name. Thy kingdom come. Thy will be done in earth as it is in heaven. Give us this day our daily bread. And forgive us our trespasses, as we forgive them that trespass against us. And lead us not into temptation: But deliver us from evil. For thine is the kingdom, and the power, and the glory, for ever. Amen."

ᵍ Matt. vi. 9, &c. Luke xi. 1, 2, &c.

M. Dost thou think that we are bound ever so to render these very words that it is not lawful in one word to vary from them?

S. It is no doubt that we may use other words in praying, so that we swerve not from the meaning of this prayer. For in it the Lord hath set out certain special and principal points, to the which, unless all our prayers be referred, they cannot please God. Yet, let every man ask of God as the present ʳtime and his need shall require; and let him tarry upon which part of this prayer he will, and so long

De hoc constat ex Psal. libro, et aliis S. Scripturæ locis pene infinitis.

ʳ Ps. cvii. 5, 12, 18, 28, &c.

as he list, and dilate it in sundry sorts as he will; for there is no impediment to the contrary, so that he pray to God with such affiance and affection as I have before spoken of, and to the same meaning that is set out in this prayer.

M. How many parts hath the Lord's Prayer?

S. It containeth indeed six petitions, but in the whole sum there are but two parts; whereof the first belongeth only to the glory of God, and containeth the three former petitions; the second, which containeth the three latter petitions, belongeth properly to our commodity.

The division.

M. Dost thou so sever and divide our profit from God's glory, that thou also makest equal partition between them?

S. I do not sever things conjoined, but for plainness of the whole declaration I distinguish things to be severally discerned, for understanding whereunto each thing belongeth. Otherwise those things that do properly belong to the glory of God, do also bring most great profits to us; and likewise those things that serve our profit, are all referred to the glory of God. ^sFor this ought to be the end whereunto all things must be applied; this ought to be our mark, that God's glory be most amply enlarged. Yet in the meantime, I think that this division in parts shall not be inconvenient, and is made not without reason, but according to the property of the things themselves: because, while we ask those things that belong properly to the advancing of God's glory, we must for that time omit our own profits, when yet in the later petitions we may well intend our own commodities.

s 1 Cor. x. 30, 31. Col. iii. 17. The end of all things, God's glory.

M. Now let us somewhat diligently examine the weight of every word. Why dost thou call God, "Father"?

S. There is great pith in the use of this one name "Father." For it containeth two things which we have before said to be specially necessary in praying.

M. What be those?

S. First, I speak not as to one absent ^tor deaf, but I call upon and pray to God as to one that is present and heareth me, being surely persuaded that he heareth me when I pray, for else in vain should I crave his help. And this surely without all doubting I cannot so affirm of ^uany angel or any man deceased.

t Ps. xxxiii. 13, 14. & xxxiv. 15, 17. & xciv. 9, 10, 11. & cxxxix. 1, 2, &c.

u Isai. lxiii. 16.

Secondly, we have before said, that sure trust of obtaining

is the foundation of right praying. And dear is the name of Father, and of fatherly love, and most full of good hope and confidence. It was God's will therefore to be called by the ˣsweetest name in earth, by that mean alluring us to himself, that we should without fear come to him, taking away all doubting of his fatherly heart and good will. For when we determine that he is our Father, then being ʸencouraged with his Spirit, we go to him as children use to go to their father. God therefore in this place liked better to be called "Father," by name of dear affection and ᶻlove, rather than "King" or "Lord," by terms of dignity and majesty; and so therewithal to leave to us, as to his ᵃchildren, a most rich inheritance of his fatherly name.

M. Shall we then come to God with such sure trust of obtaining, as children use to come to their parents?

S. That far more sure and stedfast is the trust of the goodwill of God than of men, Christ ᵇthe natural Son of God, best acquainted with his Father's mind, doth assure us, saying "ᶜIf ye," saith he, "being evil, suffer not your children to crave in vain, but grant their requests, how much more shall your heavenly Father, who is self-goodness and liberality, be bountiful to you?" But ᵈChrist, as is aforesaid, bringeth us all this confidence. For God doth not adopt us, or acknowledge us to be his children, who by nature are the children of wrath, but by Christ.

M. What else doth the name of Father teach us?

S. That we come to prayer with that love, ᵉreverence, and obedience, which is due to the heavenly Father from his children, and that we have such mind as becometh the children of God.

M. Why dost thou call God "our Father" in common, rather than severally thine own Father?

S. Every godly man may, I grant, lawfully call God ᶠhis own; but such ought to be the community and fellowship of Christian men together, and such dear love and goodwill ought every one to bear to all, that no one of them, neglecting the rest, care for himself alone, but have regard to the public profit of all. And therefore in all this prayer nothing is privately asked, but all the petitions are made in the common name of all. Moreover, when they that be of smallest wealth and basest state do call upon their common ᵍheavenly

Father, as well as the wealthy and such as have attained degrees of highest dignity, we are taught not to disdain them to be our brethren that are accepted with God to the honour of his children. On the other side, ʰthe most despised, and they that in this world are vilest, may yet in the mean-time ease and relieve themselves with this comfort, that in heaven they have all one most mighty and most loving Father. Furthermore, we that ⁱtrust in God do rightly profess him to be our Father. For the wicked and unbelieving, howsoever they dread God's power and justice, yet can they not have trust in his fatherly goodness toward them.

ʰ Deut. x. 17, 18. Ps. x. 18. & lxviii. 5, 6. & cxlvi. 6, 7, &c.

ⁱ Ps. xi. 5, 6, 7. & xxv. 1, 2, &c. & lxxiii. 25, 26, &c. Rom. i. 18. & ii. 6, 7, 8.

M. Why dost thou say that God is in heaven?

S. As heaven with round and endless circuit containeth all things, compasseth the earth, hemmeth in the seas, neither is there anything or place that is not environed and enclosed with the roominess of heaven; and it is on every side wide and open, and alway so present to all things, that all things universally are placed, as it were, in sight thereof: so we thereby understand that God, possessing ʲthe tower of heaven, therewith also holdeth the governance of all things, is each-where present, seeth, heareth, and ruleth all things.

ʲ Ps. xi. 4, 5. & xx. 6. & xxxiii. 13. & cxiii. 4, 5, 6. & cxv. 3.

M. Go forward.

S. God is also therefore said to be in heaven, because that same highest and ᵏheavenly region doth most royally shine, and is garnished with his divine and excellent works. Moreover by ˡGod reigning in heaven is declared that he is in eternal and highest felicity, while we as yet in earth, expulsed from our country, like children disherited from their father's goods, live miserably and wretchedly in banishment. It is as much therefore to say, that ᵐGod is in heaven, as if I should call him heavenly and altogether divine; that is to say, incomprehensible, most high, most mighty, most blessed, most good, most great.

ᵏ Ps. viii. 3. & xix. 1.

ˡ Ps. viii. 1, 2, 3, 4. & xi. 4, 5.

ᵐ Ps. l. 3, 4, 6. & lvii. 5, 10, 11. & lxviii. 32, 33. & cxiii. 4, 5.

M. What profit takest thou of these things?

S. These things do pull out of our hearts base and corrupt opinions concerning God, and do instruct our minds to conceive a far other thinking of our heavenly ⁿFather, than we use to have of earthly parents; to use most great reverence towards his holy majesty, and in worshipping manner to look up to it, and have it in admiration, and certainly to believe that he doth hearken to and ᵒhear our prayers and

ⁿ Ps. l. 4, 5. & lxxxix. 5, 6, 7. Matt. xxiii. 9.

ᵒ Ps. xx. 6. & cii. 15, 17. & cxiii. 4, 5.

[NOEL. CATEC.]

desires; to put our whole trust in him, that is both governor and keeper of heaven and earth. And therewith also we are by these words admonished not to ask anything unmeet for God; but, as speaking to our heavenly Father, to have our hearts ᵖraised from earth, high and looking upward, despising earthly things, thinking upon things above and heavenly, and continually to aspire to that most blessed felicity of our Father, and to heaven as our ᵠinheritance by our Father.

ᵖ Col. iii. 1.

ᵠ Rom. viii. 17. Eph. i. 14, 18. Heb. ix. 15. 1 Pet. i. 3, 4.

M. This then so happy a beginning and entry of prayer, being now opened unto us, go to rehearse me the first petition.

S. First we pray that God's name be hallowed.

M. What meaneth that?

S. Nothing else but that his glory be ʳeverywhere magnified.

ʳ Ps. lxxxix. 5, 6, &c. Rom. xi. 36. & xvi. 27. 1 Cor. x. 31.

M. Why do we ask this first?

S. Because it is most meet that the children should principally desire and wish the glory of their father, the ˢservants of their master, and the creatures of the Creator to be increased.

ˢ Mal. i. 6.

M. Can God's glory be anything increased or decreased?

S. The glory of God, forasmuch as it is continually ᵗmost ample, cannot indeed in itself be made either greater by increase, or lesser by decrease. For it is not changed with any addition or diminishing, as our earthly things be. But our prayer is, that the ᵘname of God be made renowned and known to mortal men, and his praise and glory be celebrated here in earth, as it is meet to be. And as the infinite power, wisdom, righteousness, and goodness of God, and all his divine works, do truly set forth the glory and majesty of God, so we wish that they may appear noble and glorious ˣto us, that the magnificence of the author of them, as it is in itself most large, so it may also in all sorts shine honourable and excellent among us, and be both privately and publicly praised and honoured.

ᵗ Ps. lvi. 5, 11. & civ. 31.

ᵘ Ps. xcvi. 1, 3, &c.

ˣ Ps. cxiii. 2, 3, &c. & cxiv. 1. & cxlv. toto. Rom. xi. 36.

M. Go forward.

S. Moreover, we pray that the holy name of God be not ʸevil spoken of for our faults, and as it were dishonoured thereby; but rather that his glory be, by our godliness to-

ʸ Isai. liii. 5, 6. Ezek. xxxvi. 20. Rom. ii. 24.

ward God, and goodness towards men, everywhere magnified. Finally, we wish that the names of all other that in heaven, earth, sea, or elsewhere, have attained the names and honours ᶻof gods, and be worshipped in temples in sundry forms and with sundry ceremonies; or to whom men, filled with error and false fond opinions, have dedicated their hearts, as it were churches; the names, I say, of all those imagined and feigned gods, once utterly destroyed, and drowned and defaced with eternal forgetfulness, the only divine name and majesty of God the heavenly Father be great and glorious, and that all men in all countries may acknowledge it, honourably and holily worship and reverence it, and with pure desires and hearts pray to it, call upon it, and crave help of it.

ᶻ Josh. xxiv. 14, 23. Ps. xcvi. 4. & xcvii. 7, 9. & cxv. 3, 4, &c. & cxxxv. 15. Rom. i. 23. 1 John v. 21.

M. Thou hast said well; I pray thee go forward.

S. Secondly, we pray that "God's kingdom come;" that is, that he suffer not the divine ᵃtruth of his word, which also Christ calleth the gospel of the kingdom, to lie hidden in darkness, but that he daily more and more bring it abroad, and with his succour maintain and defend it against the devices, craft, and policy of Satan ᵇand of wicked men, and against their feigned treasons, that labour to darken the truth, and to defame it, or spot it with lies; and against the violence ᶜand cruelty of tyrants, that travail by all means to extinguish and oppress the truth, and utterly to root it up; so as it may be made manifest and well known to all men that there is nothing able to resist the invincible strength of God's truth.

ᵃ Matt. iv. 23. & ix. 35. Mark i. 14. John viii. 31, 32.

ᵇ Matt. xiii. 25, 38, 39. & xv. 2, 3, 6. Luke xvi. 8. John iii. 19, 20.

ᶜ Luke x. 3. & xx. 12, &c. 17, 18. John xvi. 2, 3. & xvii. 14, 15.

M. Say on more of the kingdom of God.

S. We pray him to bring very many out of darkness into the light, instructed in the doctrine of ᵈthis holy word, and led by truth; and that, winning them to his number and holy company, that is to say, his church, in the which he reigneth specially, he will continually govern them ᵉwith his Spirit, and strengthen them with his aid as his soldiers; alway earnestly fighting ᶠwith their enemies, the band of sin and the army of Satan; that having strength and stedfastness by his divine power, restraining corrupt and ᵍcrooked affections, subduing and taming lusts, conquering, vanquishing, putting to flight, and chasing away all vices, they may increase and enlarge the heavenly common-weal and kingdom;

ᵈ Mark i. 14, 15. Luke iv. 18, 19. John xvii. 17, 19, 20, 21. 1 Pet. ii. 9, 10.

ᵉ John xvi. 13.

ᶠ Luke xxii. 31. Eph. vi. 10, 11, 17, 18. 1 Pet. v. 8, 9.

ᵍ Rom. i. 11, 12. & viii. 1, 5, &c. 10, 12, &c.

God in the meantime reigning and ruling imperially in their hearts ʰby his Spirit.

M. This we see daily done.

S. These things are indeed daily done, so as we sufficiently perceive that ⁱGod hath an eye both to the godly and to the wicked, and so as the kingdom of God may seem to be fair begun in this world; yet we pray that with continual increasing it may grow so far, that all the reprobate ᵏthat, by the motion of Satan, stubbornly and obstinately resist and strive against God's truth, and defiling themselves with all vices and heinous sins, refuse to submit themselves to the kingdom and dominion of God, being once subdued and destroyed, and the tyranny of ˡSatan himself utterly rooted out, and all the enemies slain, oppressed, and trodden down, so as nothing may once breathe against the beck and power of God, he alone may everywhere gloriously reign, imperially rule, and triumph. And as, while God reigneth ᵐby his Spirit in us, men have a certain community with God in this world, so we pray and wish that he will also by Christ communicate with us in heaven the joy of the most blessed ⁿkingdom, and the glory that in everlasting ages of worlds shall never be changed; that we may be not only children, ᵒbut also heirs of our heavenly Father; which desire also we verily nothing mistrust or doubt that our heavenly Father will one day grant us to enjoy.

M. What followeth next?

S. That "God's will be done." For it is the duty ᵖof children to frame their life according to the will of their fathers; and not, contrariwise, the parents to conform themselves to the will of their children.

M. Dost thou then think that men are able to do anything against the will of God?

S. Surely it is evident and plainly known among all, that many sins and foul deeds are daily done and committed by mortal men, to the grievous ᵠoffending of his will, yet so as God cannot by any force or necessity be compelled, but that he can most easily bring to effect whatsoever he hath ʳpurposed to do. We do therefore pray, not only that that may come to pass which he hath decreed, which must needs come to pass, because the will of God doth ever carry with it a necessity of performing; but forasmuch as our minds, ᵃburning with lusts, are commonly carried to desire and to do those things that most displease God, we pray that he will, with the ᵗmoving of his Holy Spirit, so change and fashion all the wills of us all to the meaning and will of his majesty, that we may will or wish nothing, much less do anything that his divine will misliketh; and that whatsoever we perceive ᵘto betide by his will, we may receive and suffer it, not only with contented, but also with gladsome hearts.

^a Rom. viii. 7, &c. Gal. v. 16, 17.
^t Rom. viii. 2, 4, 5, &c. 14, 15, 16. 1 Cor. ii. 12. & iii. 16.
^u Acts xxi. 14. 1 Pet. iii. 17. & iv. 13.

M. Whereto dost thou add, that God's will be done "in earth as it is in heaven?"

S. Forsooth, that we be in all things serviceable and obedient to God's majesty, after the example of ˣthose heavenly spirits whom we call angels; and as in heaven there is no rebellion, so in earth also there be none anywhere found that will or dare resist and strive against the holy will of God. Yea, and when we behold the ʸsun and moon, and other stars which we see in the heaven, to be carried with continual motion and perpetual stirring, and with their beams to lighten the earth by the will of God, we behold an example of obedience set forth for us to follow. Moreover, whereas ᶻGod hath in the holy scriptures expressly declared his will, which he hath plainly notified by giving them the ᵃname of his testament or last will, they that vary from the meaning of the scriptures surely do manifestly depart from the will of God.

^x Ps. xci. 11. & ciii. 20, 21. & civ. 4, 5. Heb. i. 6, 7. Rev. vii. 11. & xix. 10. & xxii. 9.
^y Ps. xix. 4, 5. & civ. 20, &c. & cxxxv. 7. & cxxxvi. 7, 8, 9.
^z Deut. v. 32. Matt. vii. 21. & xii. 50.
^a 2 Cor. iii. 6, 14. Gal. iv. 24.

M. Now I think thou hast sufficiently spoken of the first part of the Lord's Prayer, which part containeth these three points that belong only to the glory of God. Now it is good time for us to go forward to the second part, which properly concerneth things profitable for us, and meet for our commodities.

S. The first point of the second part is, "Give us this day our daily bread."

M. What dost thou mean by the name of daily bread?

S. Not only those ᵇthings that minister us food and apparel, but also all other things universally that are needful to the maintaining and preserving of our life, and leading it in quietness without fear.

^b Ps. civ. 15, 27, &c. & cv. toto, & cxliv. 10, 11, 12, &c. & cxlv. 14, 15, 16, &c.

M. Is there anything else whereof this word "bread" doth admonish us?

S. That we seek ᶜnot and gather together curiously

^c Ps. lxxviii. 18, 19, 20, 29, 30. & cvi. 14. Matt. vi. 25. Luke xvi. 19. 1 Tim. v. 8, 9.

dainty things for banqueting, or precious apparel, or sumptuous household stuff, for pleasure; but that we, despising delicacies and excess, and contented with little, be satisfied with temperate and healthful diet, and with mean and necessary apparel.

M. How dost thou call bread thine, which thou prayest to have given thee of God?

^d Ps. cxv. 16.
Matt. vii. 7, 8.
1 Cor. iv. 7.
James i. 17.

S. By God's ^dgift it becometh ours, when he liberally giveth it us for our daily uses, though by right it be not due to us.

M. Is there any other cause why thou callest it thy bread?

^e Gen. iii. 19.
Eph. iv. 28.
2 Thess. iii. 8, 10, 12.

S. By this word we are put in mind that we must get our living ^ewith our labour, or by other lawful mean, that, being therewith contented, we do never by covetise or fraud seek anything of other men's.

M. Seeing God biddeth us get our living by our own labour, why dost thou ask bread of him?

^f Ps. xxiv. 1.
& lxv. 9. &
lxviii. 9. &
civ. 13. &
lxxxv. 12. &
cxlvii. 8, &c.

S. It is God alone that giveth ^ffruitfulness to the ground, that maketh the land plentiful, and to bear fruit abundantly; and therefore it is certain that in vain shall we waste and spend out all the course of our life in toil of body and travail of mind, ^gunless it please God to prosper our endeavours. It is meet therefore that we daily crave in prayer things necessary for our food and life at the hands of Almighty God, which, according to the divine saying of David, as he created all things, ^hso doth also feed and preserve them, and that with thankful hearts we receive the same, as it were given and reached to us by God, and delivered by his own hand into our hands.

^g Ps. cxxvii. 1, 2.
1 Cor. iii. 7.

^h Ps. civ. &
cxxxvi. 25. &
cxlv. 15. &
cxlvii. &c.

M. Thinkest thou that rich men also, which have flowing plenty and store of all things, must daily crave bread of God?

ⁱ Ps. xxxiv. 9.
Luke i. 53. &
xii. 15.
1 Tim. vi. 17.
Rev. iii. 17.

S. In vain ⁱshall we heap together and lay up plenty, yea, such as may for many years suffice either our vain-glory, or our daily expences, or necessary use, unless God of his grace do make the use of them healthful to us for our life. Yea, in vain shall we cram meat ^kinto our stomach, unless God's power, by which we are rather fed and sustained, than by nourishments of meat, do give both to the meat power to nourish, and to the stomach ability to digest it. For which

^k Deut. viii. 3.
Ps. lxxviii. 29, 30.
Matt. iv. 4.

cause, even after supper, we pray to have the daily meat which we have already received, to be given us of God, that is to say, to be made lifeful and healthful to us.

M. Why be added these words, "daily," and "this day?"

S. To pull out of our hearts the stings of cares ¹for to-morrow, that we be not day and night tormented with them in vain, and that the unsatiable covetise, and, as it were, raging hunger of excessive wealth, ᵐbeing driven from our minds, we diligently doing our duty, should daily crave of our most liberal Father that which he is ready daily to give.

¹ Matt. vi. 25, 34. Luke x. 41. Phil. iv. 6. 1 Pet. v. 7.

ᵐ 1 Tim. vi. 9, 10.

M. Go forward to the rest.

S. Now followeth the fifth petition, wherein we pray our Father " to forgive us our trespasses."

M. What fruit shall we get by this forgiveness?

S. Most large fruit. For where God ⁿhath mercy on humble suitors, we shall be in like place and all one favour with him as if we were innocent, holy, and upright in all parts of our life.

ⁿ Ps. xxxii. 1, 2. Rom. v. 8, 10. 2 Cor. v. 18. Col. i. 20, 21, 22.

M. Is this asking of forgiveness necessary for all men?

S. Yea; forasmuch as there liveth no mortal man that doth not oft ᵒslip in doing his duty, and that doth not oft and grievously offend God; yea, and ᵖas the scripture beareth witness against us, he that offendeth in any one point is holden manifestly guilty of all, and that he who laboureth to purge himself of one sin to God, shall be convicted of a thousand heinous offences; that we may therefore obtain forgiveness of sins, ᑫone only hope remaineth, one only refuge for all men, the goodness and mercy of God through Christ. As for them that ʳdo not confess that they have sinned, nor do crave pardon of their defaults, but ˢwith that Pharisee do glory in their innocency and righteousness before God, or rather against God, they exclude themselves from the fellowship of the faithful, to whom this form of prayer is appointed for them to follow, and from the haven and refuge of safety. For this is it that Christ saith, "That he came into this world, ᵗnot to call the righteous, but sinners to repentance."

ᵒ Ps. xiv. 2, 3. & xliii. 2, 3.
ᵖ Rom. iii. 10, 11. 1 John i. 8, 10.
P Job ix. 1, 2. James ii. 10.

ᑫ 2 Cor. v. 18. 19, 20, &c. 1 John i. 7, 9. & ii. 1, 2, 12.

ʳ 1 John i. 8, 10.
ˢ Luke xviii. 9, &c.

ᵗ Matt. ix. 13. Luke v. 31, 32. & xv. 7. 1 Tim. i. 15.

M. Dost thou affirm that God doth freely forgive our sins?

S. ᵘYea, altogether; for else it could not seem forgiveness, but amends; but to make sufficient amends for one, yea, the very least fault, we are not by any power of ours in

ᵘ Rom. iii. 24, 25. & xi. 5, 6.

^x 2 Tim. 1. 9, 10. Tit. iii. 5.

any wise able. We cannot therefore with our ^xworks, as it were with a certain price, redeem both the offence past and the peace of God, and make recompense of like for like, but ought with all lowly prayers to crave of God pardon both of

^y Ps. xxxii. 5, 6. 1 John i. 9. & ii. 1.

our fault and punishment, which ^ypardon is not possible to be obtained but by only Christ, and most humbly to beseech him to forgive us.

M. But this, and the condition which is by and by after limited unto us, seem scant to agree fitly together. For we pray that God so forgive us as we forgive our debtors, or them "that trespass against us."

^z Matt. xviii. 32, 33. Luke vi. 36, 37, 38.

S. Surely God doth offer us ^zforgiveness upon a most reasonable condition, which yet is not so to be taken as if in forgiving men we should so deserve pardon of God, that the same should be as a certain recompense made to God.

^a Rom. iii. 24, 25. & xi. 5, 6. Gal. v. 4.

For then should not God's forgiveness ^abe freely given, neither had Christ alone, as the scriptures teach us, and as we have before declared, upon the cross fully paid the pains of our sin due to us. But unless other do find us ready to forgive

^b Matt. v. 7. Luke vi. 36. James ii. 13.

them, and unless we ^bin following the mercifulness and lenity of God our Father, do shew ourselves to be his children, he plainly warneth us to look for nothing else at his hand but extreme severity of punishment. He hath, therefore, appointed our easiness to forgive, not as a cause to deserve pardon of God, but to be a pledge to confirm our hearts with sure confidence of God's mercy.

M. Is there then no place of forgiveness with God left for them that shew themselves to other not intreatable to forgive and to lay away displeasures, and such as will not be appeased?

^c Matt. vi. 14, 15. & xviii. 24, 28, 29, 33, 34.

S. No place at all. Which both is confirmed and manifest by ^cmany other places of the holy scripture, and namely, by that parable in the gospel, of the servant, which, owing his lord ten thousand talents, refused at the same time to forgive his fellow-servant one hundred pence that he had lent him, he

^d Matt. vii. 2, 3. Luke vi. 37, 38. James ii. 13.

notably warneth us. For ^daccording to the same rule of rigour, and the same example, shall justice without mercy be done upon him that cannot find in his heart to shew lenity and mercy to other.

M. Thinkest thou that suits in law about right and wrong are here condemned?

S. ^eA wreakful mind and revengeful of injuries the word of God doth surely condemn. Let contenders at law, therefore, look well to it with what mind they sue any man. But ^fthe laws and ordinances of common right, and their lawful use, that is to say, such use as is directed by the rule of justice and charity, are not taken away or condemned by the gospel of Christ. But in this part of the Lord's Prayer our minds are bound to follow the rule of Christian lenity and love, ^gthat we suffer not ourselves to be overcome of evil, that is to say, to be drawn so far by other men's offence, as to have will to render evil for evil, but rather that we overcome evil with good; that is, recompense evil deeds with good deeds, and bear and keep good will toward our foes, yea, and our cruel and deadly enemies.

^e Rom. xii. 19, 20. Heb. x. 30.
^f Rom. xiii. 1, 4, 6, &c. Tit. iii. 1. 1 Pet. ii. 13, 15.
^g Matt. v. 39, 44. Luke vi. 27, 28. Rom. xii. 14, 17, 18, 19, 20.

M. Now go forward to the sixth petition.

S. Therein we pray that he "lead us not into tentation, but deliver us from evil." For as we before do ask forgiveness of sins past, so now we pray that ^hwe sin no more. A thousand fears are set afore us; ⁱa thousand perils threatened us; a thousand snares provided and laid for us. And we on our part are so ^kfeeble by nature, so unware to foresee them, so weak to resist them, that with most small force and occasions we are shoved down, and carried headlong into deceit.

^h John v. 14. & viii. 11.
2 Pet. ii. 20, 21, 22.
ⁱ Matt. x. 16, 17, &c. Eph. vi. 12, &c. 1 Pet. v. 8, 9.
^k Matt. xxvi. 41. 1 Cor. i. 27.

M. Go forward.

S. Sith, therefore, we be most sharply and continually assaulted both by ^lcrafty and violent men, and by concupiscence ^mand our own lusts, by the enticements of the flesh, this world and all means of corruption, but specially by that subtle, guileful, and old wily ⁿserpent, the devil, which like a ravening ^olion, seeking whom he may devour, together with infinite other malicious ^pspirits, armed with a thousand crafty means to hurt us, is ever ready to destroy us, and thereby, as our weakness is, we must needs by and by fall down and be utterly undone, we flee to the faithful protection of ^qour almighty most loving Father; and pray to him in these distresses and perils not to forsake us and leave us destitute, but ^rso to arm us with his strength, that we may be able not only to resist and fight against the lusts of our flesh, the enticements of this world, and the force and violent assault of Satan, but also to overcome and get the overhand of them;

^l Matt. x. 16, 17. Luke xvi. 8. 2 Cor. xi. 13, 15.
^m James i. 14. & iv. 1.
ⁿ 1 John ii. 16. Gen. iii. 1. &c. 2 Cor. xi. 3. Rev. xii. 4. & xx. 2.
^o 1 Pet. v. 8.
^p Eph. vi. 11.
^q John xvi. 33. 1 John iv. 4. & v. 4.
^r Rom. xvi. 20. Eph. vi. 10. 2 Tim. iv. 17, 18.

and that therefore he will withdraw our hearts ˢfrom vices and offences, that we fall not into them, nor at any time fail in our duty, but may ever lie safe and without fear in the ᵗprotection and defence of our most good and also most mighty Father.

M. Then thou meanest by the name of tentation the craft and violence of the devil, the snares and deceits of this world, and the corruptions and enticements of our flesh, by which our souls are moved to sin, and holden fast entangled.

S. Yea, forsooth, master.

M. Since, then, to catch and entangle men, as it were, in snares of tentation, is the propriety ᵘof Satan, why dost thou pray that God lead thee not into tentation?

S. God, as he defendeth and preserveth ʷthem that be his, that they be not snared with the guiles of Satan, and so fall into vices and foul sins; so from the wicked he ˣholdeth back and withdraweth his help and succour, whereof they being destitute, blinded with lust and running headlong, are catched in all sorts of deceitful traps, and carried unto all kind of wickedness; and at length with custom of ill-doings, as it were gathering ʸa thick tough skin, their hearts wax hard; and so they becoming bondmen, and yielding themselves to slavery to the tyrant Satan, they run in ruin to their undoing and everlasting destruction.

M. There remaineth yet a certain appendant of the Lord's Prayer.

S. "For thine is the kingdom, and the power, and the glory, for ever. Amen."

M. Why would Christ have this conclusion added?

S. First, to make us understand that our sure confidence of obtaining all those things that we have before prayed for standeth in his goodness and power, and ᶻnot in any deservings of our own or of others. For by these words is declared, that there is nothing that He which ruleth and governeth ᵃthe world, in whose dominion and power are all things which most nobly shining in most ample and immortal glory, infinitely excelleth above all other, either cannot or will not give us, ᵇwhen we pray for it, so that it be asked rightly and with assured faith; that now there be no more doubting left in our hearts; which is also declared and confirmed by this word, "ᶜAmen," added to the end of the prayer. Moreover,

forasmuch as God alone is able at his own will ^dto give what- ^d Ps. cxv. 3. 2 Cor. ix. 8.
soever he hath appointed, it most plainly appeareth, that of Eph. iii. 20. 1 Tim. vi. 15, 16.
him alone all these things ought to be asked, and may be obtained; and that there is ^eno peril or evil of ours so great, ^e 1 Cor. i. 8, 9, 10. 2 Tim. iv.
which he is not able most easily by his exceeding power, 17, 18. Jude, 24.
wisdom, and goodness, to overcome and drive from us, and
also to turn it to our safety.

M. Why is there in the latter end mention made of the glory of God?

S. To teach us to conclude all our prayers with praises of God's glory the end of all.
God: for that is ^fthe end whereunto all things ought to be ^f 1 Cor. x. 31. Eph. iii. 20,
referred, that issue ought always to be set before the eyes of 21. Phil. i. 11. 1 Tim. i.
us Christians, for all our doings and our thoughts to reach 17. Jude, 25.
unto, that God's honour be most largely amplified and gloriously set out to sight; howsoever yet among men, in whose
hearts Christian religion is not settled, there is scarce any one
found, that for his enterprises attempted and perils adventured
desireth ^gnot glory as a reward of his deeds and virtues, ^g Matt. vi. 1, 2, 3, 4, 5, 6,
which yet as not true and sound glory, but vain shew and &c. Gal. v. 26. Phil. ii. 3.
boasting, the Lord vehemently and earnestly commandeth & iii. 19.
them that be his to eschew.

M. Then after entreating of prayer, shall we fitly and in
good time add somewhat of the praises of God and thanksgiving?

S. Surely ^hmost fitly. For not only in the last end of ^h Rom. i. 8, 10. 2 Cor. i.
the Lord's Prayer God's glory is mentioned, but also the very 11. Eph. i. 15. Phil. i. 3, 4.
first entry of it beginneth with the glory and praises of God.
For when we pray that God's name be hallowed, what pray
we else than that of all his works his glory be stablished,
that is, that he be judged in forgiving sinners, ⁱmerciful; ^jin ⁱ Ps. li. 1. ^j Rom. i. 18.
punishing the wicked, righteous; in performing his promises,
^ktrue; in heaping daily benefits upon the unworthy, ^lmost ^k Rom. iii. 3, 4.
good and liberal; that whatsoever ^mof his works we see or ^l Ps. lxv. 9, &c. & lxviii.
understand, we be thereby stirred to advance his glory with 5, &c. ^m Ps. xix. 1,
praises. So was it God's will to have his glory most nearly 2.
joined with prayer to him. For meet it is that as, when we
are touched and troubled ⁿwith distresses, we flee as humble ⁿ Ps. xxxiv. 1, 2. & l. 14,
petitioners to God's help and mercy, so we unfeignedly acknowledge that by him we obtain deliverance from all evils 15, 23. 1 Thess. i. 2. & v. 18. 2 Thess. i. 3.
and griefs, and that he is to us the only author of all good
things. For of whom we crave pardon and all good things,

to him, when he giveth them, not in heart and speech to render thanks were surely most great unkindness. We ought therefore continually with mindful heart and due honours to yield deserved °thanks to the ever-living God.

M. Go forward.

S. Moreover, ᵖto praise and magnify God's goodness, justice, wisdom, and power, and to give him thanks in our own name and in the name of all mankind, is parcel of the worshipping of God, belonging as properly to his majesty as prayer; wherewith if we do not rightly worship him, surely we shall not only be unworthy of his ᑫso many and so great benefits as unthankful persons, but also shall be most worthy of eternal punishments, as wicked against God.

M. Sith we also receive benefits of men, shall it not also be lawful to give them thanks?

S. Whatsoever benefits men do to us, we ought ʳto account them received of God, because he alone indeed doth give us them by the ministry of men. For which cause also, though men ought not be beneficial and liberal of intent to get thanks, but to set forth ˢthe glory of God, yet to give thanks to them, that, ᵗmoved by kindness, grant us anything beneficially and friendly, why should it not be lawful, sith both ᵘequity requireth it, and by law of natural kindness we are bound unto it? Yea, and God himself by this mean binding us unto them, willeth us to acknowledge the same.

M. Dost thou then allow a thankful mind to men also?

S. Yea. Sith our thankfulness to men redoundeth to God himself, because from the spring-head of his divine liberality, as it were by certain guiding of water-courses, God conveyeth ʷhis benefits to us by the hands of men; therefore if we shew not ourselves thankful to men, we shall be also unthankful to God himself. Only this let us look well to, that ˣhis full glory return and redound to God alone, as to the author and fountain of all good things.

M. Is there any rule and prescribed form for us certainly to follow, when we glorify and honour God, or give him thanks?

S. Innumerable praises of God are commonly to be seen set out in his word, from the rule whereof if we vary not, we shall alway have a good pattern to follow, in giving to God his glory and honour, and in yielding him thanks. Finally, in a sum, seeing the holy scriptures do teach that God is ʸnot only our Lord, but also our Father and Saviour, and we likewise are his children and servants, it is most meet that we employ all ᶻour life to the setting out of his glory, render to him his due honour, worship, pray to and reverence him, and with heart and mouth continually thank him; sith we are to this ᵃend created by him, and placed in this world, that his immortal glory should be in most great honour among men, and rise to most high magnificence.

ʸ Deut. x. 17, 20. & xxviii. 58. Mal. i. 6, 7. & ii. 10.

ᶻ Ps. xxix. 1, 2. & xxxiv. 1, 2. & xcii. 1. & ciii. toto. Rom. xv. 6.

ᵃ Prov. xvi. 4. Isai. xliii. 7. Rom. xi. 36. Col. i. 16.

THE FOURTH PART. OF SACRAMENTS.

M. Now having ended our treating of the law of God, of the Creed, or Christian confession, and also of prayer and of thanksgiving, it resteth last of all to speak of the sacraments and divine mysteries, which alway have prayer and thanksgiving joined unto them. Tell me, therefore, what is a sacrament?

S. It is ᵇan outward testifying of God's good-will and bountifulness toward us, through Christ by a visible sign representing an invisible and spiritual grace, by which the promises of God touching forgiveness of sins and eternal salvation given through Christ, are, as it were sealed, and the truth of them is more certainly confirmed in our hearts.

ᵇ Matt. iii. 11. & xxvi. 26. & xxviii. 19. John iii. 5. Acts ii. 38. Rom. vi. 3, 4. 1 Cor. x. 16. & xi. 24, &c. Gal. iii. 27. 1 Pet. iii. 21.

M. Of how many parts consisteth a sacrament?

S. Of two parts: ᶜthe outward element, or visible sign, and invisible grace.

ᶜ Matt. xxvi. 26. John iii. 5. Acts ii. 38. Gal. iii. 26, 27.

M. Why would God so have us to use outward signs?

S. Surely we are not endued with mind and understanding so heavenly and divine, that the graces of God do appear clearly of themselves to us, as it were to angels. By this mean therefore God hath provided for our weakness, that we which are earthly and blind should in outward elements and figures, as it were in certain glasses, behold the heavenly graces which otherwise we were not able to see. And greatly for our behoof it is that God's promises should be also presented to our senses, that they may be confirmed to our minds without doubting.

M. But is it not a manifest proof of infidelity in us not to give sure faith to God's promises unless we be underpropped with such helps?

S. Surely we are endued ᵈwith slender and unperfect

ᵈ Matt. vi. 30. & viii. 26. & xvi. 8.

faith so long as we are in this world, and yet we cease not to be faithful. For the remnants of distrust, which always stick in our flesh, do shew the weakness of our faith, ^ebut yet do not utterly quench it. These remnants of distrust, though we cannot altogether shake off, yet we must with continual increasing even to the end of our life travail toward ^four perfection of faith, in which endeavour the use of sacraments doth much further us.

M. Is there any other cause why the Lord would also have the use of external signs practised?

S. The Lord did furthermore ordain his mysteries to this end: that they should be certain marks and tokens ^gof our profession, whereby we should, as it were, bear witness of our faith before men, and should plainly shew that we are partakers of God's benefits with the rest of the godly, and that we have all one concord and consent of religion with them, and should openly testify that we are not ashamed ^hof the name of Christians, and to be called the disciples of Christ.

M. What thinkest thou then of them that think they may spare the divine mysteries as things not of so great necessity?

S. First, they cannot fail this so godly and due a duty without ⁱmost heinous offence against God the Father, and our Saviour Jesus Christ, and also against his church. For what were that else than indirectly to deny Christ? And he that vouchsafeth not ^kto profess himself a Christian is not worthy to be counted in the number of Christians. Again, they that would refuse the use of sacraments as if ^lthey had no need of them, I think were worthy to be condemned, not only of most high presumption, but also of unkind wickedness against God; forasmuch as they do despise not only the helps of their own weakness, but also God himself, the author of them; refuse ^mhis grace, and (as much as in them lieth) extinguish his Spirit.

M. Thou conceivest well the right understanding concerning the visible signs and outward use of the sacraments. But whereas, secondly, thou givest to the sacraments the strength and efficacy to seal and confirm God's promises in our hearts, thou seemest to assign to them the proper offices of the Holy Ghost.

S. To lighten and give bright clearness to men's ⁿminds and souls, and to make their consciences quiet and in security, as they be indeed, so ought they to be accounted the proper work of the Holy Ghost alone, and to be imputed to him, and this praise not to be transferred to any other. But this is no impediment but that God may give to his mysteries the second place in quieting and stablishing our minds and consciences, but yet so that nothing be abated from the virtue of his Spirit. Wherefore we must determine that, the outward element hath neither °of itself nor in itself inclosed the force and efficacy of the sacrament, but that the same wholly floweth from the Spirit of God, as out of a spring-head, and is by the divine mysteries, which are ordained by the Lord for this end, conveyed unto us. ° John i. 33.
Acts i. 5. &
x. 47.

M. How many sacraments hath God ordained in his church?

S. Two.

M. Which be they?

S. ᵖBaptism and the Holy Supper, which are commonly used among all the faithful. For by the one we are born again, and by the other we are nourished to everlasting life. ᵖ Matt. xxvi. 26. & xxviii. 19. John iii. 5. & vi. 35. Tit. iii. 5.

M. Then tell me first what thou thinkest of baptism?

S. Whereas by nature we are ᑫthe children of wrath, that is, strangers from the church, which is God's household, baptism is, as it were, ʳa certain entry, by which we are received into the church; whereof we also receive a most substantial testimony, that we are now ˢin the number of the household, and also of the children of God; yea, and that we are joined and graffed into ᵗthe body of Christ, and become his members, and do grow into one body with him. The description of baptism.
ᑫ Eph. ii. 3.
ʳ Matt. xxviii. 19.
Mark xvi. 16.
John iii. 5.
Tit. iii. 5.
ˢ Rom. viii, 15, 16, 17.
Eph. ii. 19.
ᵗ 1 Cor. vi. 15. & xii. 27.
Gal. iii. 27.
Eph. iv. 15, 16. & v. 30.

M. Thou saidst before that a sacrament consisteth of two parts, the outward sign, and inward grace. What is the outward sign in baptism?

S. ᵘWater: wherein the person baptized is dipped or sprinkled with it, "in the name of the Father, and of the Son, and of the Holy Ghost." ᵘ Matt. iii. 16. & xxviii. 19. John iii. 5, 23. Acts viii. 36, 38.

M. What is the secret and spiritual grace?

S. It is of two sorts; that is, ˣforgiveness of sins, and regeneration; both of which in the same outward sign have their full and express resemblance. ˣ Mark i. 4
John iii. 5.
Acts ii. 38.
Tit. iii. 5.

M. How so?

S. First, as the uncleannesses of the body are washed

away with water, so the ʸspots of the soul are washed away by forgiveness of sins. Secondly, ᶻthe beginning of regeneration, that is, the mortifying of our nature, is expressed by dipping in the water, or by sprinkling of it. Finally, when we by and by rise up again out of the water, under which we be for a short time, the new life, which is the other part, and the end of our regeneration, is thereby represented.

M. Thou seemest to make the water but a certain figure of divine things.

S. ᵃIt is a figure indeed, but not empty or deceitful, but such as hath the truth of the things themselves joined and knit unto it. For as in baptism God truly delivereth us forgiveness of sins and newness of life, so do we certainly receive them. ᵇFor God forbid that we should think that God mocketh and deceiveth us with vain figures.

M. Do we not then obtain forgiveness of sins by the outward washing or sprinkling of water?

S. No. For only Christ hath ᶜwith his blood washed and clean washed away the spots of our souls. This honour therefore it is not lawful to give to the outward element. But the Holy Ghost, as it were sprinkling ᵈour consciences with that holy blood, wiping away all the spots of sin, maketh us clean before God. Of this cleansing of our sins we have a seal and pledge in the sacrament.

M. But whence have we regeneration?

S. None other ways but from the death and resurrection of Christ. ᵉFor by the force of Christ's death our old man is, after a certain manner crucified and mortified, and the corruptness of our nature is, as it were, buried, that it no more live and be strong in us. And by the beneficial mean of his resurrection he giveth us grace to be newly formed unto a new life, to obey the righteousness of God.

M. Do all generally, and without difference, receive this grace?

S. ᶠThe only faithful receive this fruit: but the unbelieving, in refusing the promises offered them by God, shut up the entry against themselves, and go away empty. Yet do they not thereby make that the sacraments lose their force and nature.

M. Tell me then briefly in what things the use of baptism consisteth?

S. In faith and repentance. For ᵍfirst we must with assured confidence hold it determined in our hearts, that we are cleansed by the blood of Christ from all filthiness of sin, and so be acceptable to God, and that his Spirit dwelleth within us. And then we must continually, with all our power and endeavour, travail in ʰmortifying our flesh, and obeying the righteousness of God, and must by godly life declare to all men that we have in baptism as it were ⁱput on Christ, and have his Spirit given us.

M. Sith infants cannot by age perform those things that thou speakest of, why are they baptized?

S. That faith and repentance go before baptism, is required only in persons so grown in years, ᵏthat by age they are capable of both. But to infants the promise ˡmade to the Church by Christ, in whose faith ᵐthey are baptized, shall for the present time be sufficient; and then afterward, when they are grown to years, they must needs themselves acknowledge the truth of their baptism, and have the force thereof to be lively in their souls, and to be represented in their life and behaviours.

M. How shall we know that infants ought not to be kept from baptism?

S. Seeing God, ⁿwhich never swerveth from truth, nor in anything strayeth from the right way, did not exclude infants ᵒin the Jewish church from circumcision, neither ought our infants to be put back from baptism.

M. Thinkest thou these so like, and that they both have one cause and order?

S. Altogether. For as Moses ᵖand all the prophets do testify that circumcision was a sign of repentance, so doth St Paul teach that it was a sacrament of faith. Yet the ᑫJews' children, being not yet by age capable of faith and repentance, were nevertheless circumcised; by which visible sign God shewed himself in the Old Testament to be the Father of young children and of the seed of his people. Now sith it is certain that the grace of God is both ʳmore plentifully poured and more clearly declared in the Gospel by Christ, than at that time it was in the Old Testament by Moses, it were a great indignity if the same grace should now be thought to be either obscurer or in any part abated.

M. Go on forward.

[NOEL. CATEC.]

ᵍ Matt. xxvi. 28. Mark xvi. 16. Rom. viii. 9, 11, 15, 16, 17. Eph. i. 7. & v. 25, 26. Col. i. 14, 20.
ʰ Rom. vi. 3, &c. 6, 11, &c. 13, 19. & viii. 13. Eph. iv. 24. Col. iii. 5. ⁱ Rom. xiii. 14. Gal. iii. 26, 27.
ᵏ Mark xvi. 16. John iii. 16, 18. ˡ Rom. iii. 3. & iv. 21, 22, 24. Heb. x. 23. ᵐ Matt. xxviii. 19.
ⁿ Rom. iii. 4. & iv. 21. Heb. x. 23. ᵒ Gen. xvii. 10, 11, 12. &c. Luke i. 59. & ii. 21. Acts vii. 8. Phil. iii. 5.
ᵖ Deut. x. 16. & xxx. 6. Jer. iv. 4. ᑫ Rom. ii. 28, 29. & iv. 11. Gen. xvii. 7, 10, 11, 12, &c.
ʳ Acts ii. 17, 18. & x. 45. 2 Cor. iii. 6, 7, 8, 9, &c. Gal. iii. 23, 24. Tit. iii. 5, 6.

S. Sith it is certain that our infants have the force, ⁸and as it were the substance of baptism common with us, they should have wrong done them if the sign, which is inferior to the truth itself, should be denied them; and the same, which greatly availeth to testifying of the mercy of God and confirming his promises, being taken away, Christians should be defrauded of a singular comfort which they that were in old time enjoyed, and so should our infants be more hardly dealt with in the New Testament under Christ, than was dealt with the Jews' infants in the Old Testament under Moses. Therefore most great reason it is that by baptism, as by the print of a seal, it be ᵗassured to our infants that they be heirs of God's grace, and of the salvation promised to the seed of the faithful.

M. Is there any more that thou wilt say of this matter?

S. ᵘSith the Lord Christ calleth infants unto him, and commandeth that no man forbid them to come, embraceth them when they come to him, and testifieth that to them the kingdom of heaven belongeth, whom God vouchsafeth to be in the heavenly palace, it seemeth a great wrong that men should forbid them the first entry and door thereof, and after a certain manner to shut them out of the Christian commonweal.

M. It is so. But whereas thou didst say before, that children, after they were grown more in years, ought to acknowledge the truth of their baptism, I would thou shouldest now speak somewhat more plainly thereof.

S. Parents and schoolmasters did in old time diligently instruct their children, as soon as by age they were able to perceive and understand, in the first principles of Christian religion, that they might suck in godliness almost together with the nurse's milk, and straightways after their cradle might be nourished with the tender food of virtue towards that blessed life. For the which purpose also little short books, which we name Catechisms, were written, wherein the same, or very like matters as we now are in hand with, were entreated upon. And after that the children seemed to be sufficiently trained in the principles of our religion, they brought and offered them unto the bishop.

M. For what purpose did they so?

S. That children might after baptism do the same which such as were older, who were also called *catechumeni*, that is, scholars of religion, did in old time before, or rather, at baptism itself. For the bishop did require and the children did render reason and account of their religion and faith: and such children as the bishop judged to have sufficiently profited in the understanding of religion he allowed, and laying his hands upon them, and blessing them, let them depart. This allowance and blessing of the bishop our men do call Confirmation.

M. But there was another confirmation used of late?

S. Instead of this most profitable and ancient confirmation, they conveyed a device of their own, that is, that the bishop should not examine children, whether they were skilled in the precepts of religion or no, but that they should anoint young infants unable yet to speak, much less to give any account of their faith; adjoining also other ceremonies unknown unto the Holy Scripture and the primitive church. This invention of theirs they would needs have to be a sacrament, and accounted it in manner equal in dignity with baptism; yea, some of them preferred it also before baptism. By all means they would that this their confirmation should be taken for a certain supplying of baptism, that it should thereby be finished and brought to perfection, as though baptism else were unperfect, and as though children who in baptism had put upon them Christ with his benefits, without their confirmation were but half Christians; than which injury no greater could be done against the divine sacrament, and against God himself, and Christ our Saviour, the author and founder of the holy sacrament of baptism.

M. It were to be wished therefore that the ancient manner and usage of examining children were restored again?

S. Very much to be wished, surely. For so should parents be brought to the satisfying of their duty in the godly bringing up of their children, which they now for the most part do leave undone, and quite reject from them; which part of their duty if parents or schoolmasters would at this time take in hand, do, and throughly perform, there would be a marvellous consent and agreement in religion and faith, which is now in miserable sort torn asunder; surely all should not either lie so shadowed and overwhelmed with the darkness of ignorance, or with dissensions of divers and contrary opinions be so disturbed, dissolved and dissipated, as it is at this day: the more pity it is, and most to be sorrowed of all good men for so miserable a case.

M. It is very true that thou sayest. Now tell me the order of the Lord's Supper.

S. It is even the same which the Lord Christ did institute, who "in the same night that he was betrayed ˣtook bread, and when he had given thanks, he brake it, and gave it to his disciples, saying, Take, eat: this is my body, which is given for you: do this in remembrance of me. Likewise after supper he took the cup, and when he had given thanks, he gave it to them, saying, Drink ye all of this; for this is my blood of the new Testament which is shed for you, and for many, for remission of sins. Do this, as oft as ye shall drink it, in remembrance of me. For so oft as ye shall eat this bread, and drink of this cup, ye shall shew the Lord's death till he come." This is the form and order of the Lord's Supper, which we ought to hold, and holily to keep till he come.

M. For what use?

S. ʸTo celebrate and retain continually a thankful remembrance of the Lord's death, and of that most singular benefit which we have received thereby; and that as in baptism we were once born again, so with the Lord's Supper we be alway fed and sustained to spiritual and everlasting life.

M. Thou sayest then that it is enough to be once baptized, as to be once born; but thou affirmest that the Lord's Supper, like as food, must be often used.

S. Yea forsooth, master.

M. Dost thou say that there are two parts in this sacrament also, as in baptism?

S. Yea. The one part, the bread ᶻand wine, the outward signs, which are seen with our eyes, handled with our hands, and felt with our taste; the other part, ᵃChrist himself, with whom our souls, as with their proper food, are inwardly nourished.

M. And dost thou say that all ought alike to receive both parts of the sacrament?

S. Yea verily, master. For sith the Lord hath expressly so ᵇcommanded, it were a most high offence in any part to abridge his commandment. ^{ᵇ Matt. xxvi. 27. Mark xiv. 23.}

M. Why would the Lord have here two signs to be used?

S. First, he severally gave the signs both of his body and blood, that it might be the more plain express image of his death which he suffered, his body being torn, ᶜhis side pierced, and all his blood shed, and that the memory thereof so printed in our hearts should stick the deeper. And moreover, that the Lord might so provide for and help our weakness, and thereby manifestly declare, that as the bread for nourishment of our bodies, ᵈso his body hath most singular force and efficacy spiritually to feed our souls: and as with wine men's hearts are cheered, and their strength confirmed, so with his blood our souls are relieved and refreshed; that certainly assuring ourselves that he is not only ᵉour meat, but also our drink, we do not anywhere else but in him alone seek any part of our spiritual nourishment and eternal life. ^{ᶜ John xix. 34.} ^{ᵈ John vi. 50, 55, 56.} ^{ᵉ John vi. 35, 53, 54, 55, &c.}

M. Is there then not an only figure, but the truth itself of the benefits that thou hast rehearsed, delivered in the snpper?

S. What else? For sith Christ is ᶠthe truth itself, it is no doubt but that the thing which he testifieth in words, and representeth in signs, he performeth also in deed, and delivereth it unto us; and that he as surely maketh them ᵍthat believe in him partakers of his body and blood, as they surely know that they have received the bread and wine with their mouth and stomach. ^{ᶠ John i. 17. & xiv. 6.} ^{ᵍ John vi. 54, 56, 64.}

M. Sith we be in the earth, and Christ's body in heaven, how can that be that thou sayest?

S. We must lift our souls and hearts from earth, ʰand raise them up by faith to heaven, where Christ is. ^{ʰ John vi. 62, 64. Col. iii. 1. Heb. iv. 14, 16.}

M. Sayest thou then the mean to receive the body and blood of Christ standeth upon faith?

S. Yea. For when ⁱwe believe that Christ died to deliver us from death, and that he rose again to procure us life, we are partakers of the redemption purchased by his death, and of his life, and all other his good things; and with the same conjoining wherewith the head and ᵏthe members are knit together, he coupleth us to himself by secret ^{ⁱ John vi. 35. Acts iv. 10, 12. Rom. iv. 24, 25. & v. 8. & xiv. 9.} ^{ᵏ 1 Cor. vi. 15. & xii. 27. Eph. iv. 15, 16. & v.}

and marvellous virtue of his Spirit, even so that we be members of his body, and be of his flesh and bones, and do grow into one body with him.

M. Dost thou then, that this conjoining may be made, imagine the bread and wine to be changed into the substance of the flesh and blood of Christ?

S. There is no need to invent any such change. For both the Holy Scriptures, and the best and most ancient expositors, do teach that by baptism we are [1]likewise the members of Christ, and are of his flesh and bones, and do grow into one body with him, when yet there is no such change made in the water.

M. Go on.

S. In both the sacraments the substances of the outward things are not changed; but [m]the word of God and heavenly grace coming to them, there is such efficacy, that as by baptism we are once [n]regenerate in Christ, and are first, as it were, joined and grafted into his body; so, when we [o]rightly receive the Lord's Supper, with the very divine nourishment of his body and blood, most full of health and immortality, given to us by the work of the Holy Ghost, and received of us by faith, as the mouth of our soul, we are continually fed and sustained to eternal [p]life, growing together in them both into one body with Christ.

M. Then Christ doth also otherwise than by his supper only give himself unto us, and knitteth us to himself with most strait conjoining.

S. Christ did then principally give himself to us to be the author of our salvation, when he gave [q]himself to death for us, that we should not perish with deserved death. By the [r]Gospel also he giveth himself to the faithful, and plainly teacheth that he is that lively bread that came down from heaven to nourish their souls that believe in him. And also [s]in baptism, as is before said, Christ gave himself to us effectually, for that he then made us Christians.

M. And sayest thou that there are no less strait bands of conjoining in the supper?

S. In the Lord's Supper both that communicating which I spake of is confirmed unto us, [t]and is also increased, for that each man is both by the words and mysteries of God ascertained that the same belongeth to himself, and that

Christ is by a certain peculiar manner given to him, that he may most fully and with most near conjunction enjoy him, insomuch that not only our souls are nourished ᵘwith his holy body and blood as with their proper food, but also our bodies, for that they partake of the sacraments of eternal life, have, as it were by a pledge given them, a certain hope assured them of resurrection and immortality, that at length Christ ˣabiding in us, and we again abiding in Christ, we also, by Christ abiding in us, may obtain not only everlasting life, but also the glory which his Father gave him. In a sum I say thus: as I imagine not any gross joining, so I affirm that same secret and marvellous communicating of Christ's body in his supper to be most near and strait, most assured, most true, and altogether most high and perfect. ᵘ John vi. 51, 53, 54, &c.
ˣ John vi. 54, 56, 57. & xvii. 22.

M. Of this that thou hast said of the Lord's Supper, meseems, I may gather that the same was not ordained to this end, that Christ's body should be offered in sacrifice to God the Father for sins.

S. It is not so offered. For he, when he did institute his supper, commanded us ʸto eat his body, not to offer it. As for the prerogative ᶻof offering for sins, it pertaineth to Christ alone, as to him which is the eternal Priest; which also when he died upon the cross, once made that only and everlasting sacrifice for our salvation, and fully performed the same for ever. For us there is nothing left to do, but to take the use and benefit of that eternal sacrifice bequeathed us by the Lord himself, which we chiefly do in the Lord's Supper. ʸ Matt. xxvi. 26. 1 Cor. xi. 24, &c.
ᶻ Heb. v. 6, 9. & vii. 27. & ix. 26, 27, 28. & x. 10, 12,14.

M. Then I perceive the holy supper sendeth us to the death of Christ, and to his sacrifice once done upon the cross, by which alone God is appeased toward us.

S. It is most true. For by bread and wine, the signs, is assured unto us, ᵃthat as the body of Christ was once offered a sacrifice for us to reconcile us to favour with God, and his blood once shed, to wash away the spots of our sins, so now also in his holy supper ᵇboth are given to the faithful, that we surely know that the reconciliation of favour pertaineth to us, and may take and receive the fruit of the redemption purchased by his death. ᵃ Rom. v. 8. & vi. 10. 1 Cor. xv. 3. 2 Cor. v. 14, 15. 1 Pet. iii. 18.
ᵇ Matt. xxvi. 26, 27, 28. Luke xxii. 19. 1 Cor. xi. 24, 25, 26.

M. Are then the only faithful fed with Christ's body and blood?

S. They only. For to whom he communicateth his body, °to them, as I said, he communicateth also everlasting life.

M. Why dost thou not grant that the body and blood of Christ are included in the bread and cup; or that the bread and wine are changed into the substance of his body and blood?

S. Because that were to bring in doubt ᵈthe truth of Christ's body; to do dishonour to Christ himself; and to fill them with abhorring that receive the sacrament, if we should imagine his body either to be enclosed in so narrow a room, ᵉor to be in many places at once, ᶠor his flesh to be chawed in our mouth with our teeth, and to be bitten small, and eaten as other meat.

M. Why then is the communicating of the sacrament damnable to the wicked, if there be no such change made?

S. Because they come to the holy and divine mysteries ᵍwith hypocrisy and counterfeiting; and do wickedly profane them, to the great injury and dishonour of the Lord himself that ordained them.

M. Declare then what is our duty, that we may come rightly to the Lord's Supper.

S. Even the same that we are taught in the Holy Scriptures, namely, ʰto examine ourselves whether we be true members of Christ.

M. By what marks and tokens shall we manifestly find it?

S. First, if ⁱwe heartily repent us of our sins, which drove Christ ᵏto death, whose mysteries are now delivered us; next, if we stay ourselves, and rest ˡupon a sure hope of God's mercy through Christ, with a thankful ᵐremembrance of our redemption purchased by his death. Moreover, if we conceive an earnest mind and determined purpose to lead our life godlily ⁿhereafter. Finally, if, seeing in the Lord's Supper is contained also °a tokening of friendship and love among men, we bear brotherly love to ᵖour neighbours, that is, to all men, without any evil will or hatred.

M. Is any man able fully and perfectly to perform all these things that thou speakest of?

S. Full perfection in all points, wherein nothing may be lacking, cannot be found ᑫin man so long as he abideth in this world. Yet ought not the imperfection that holdeth us keep us back from coming to the Lord's Supper, which the Lord willed to be a help to our imperfection and weakness. Yea, if we were perfect, there should be no more need of any use of the Lord's Supper among us. But hereto these things that I have spoken of do tend, that every man bring with him to the supper, ^rrepentance, ^sfaith, and ^tcharity, so near as possibly may be, sincere and unfeigned.

^r Jer. xxiv. 7. & xxix. 13. Joel ii. 12, 13.
^s Gal. v. 6. Col. i. 4, 23. & ii. 5. 1 Tim. i. 5. 2 Tim. i. 5.
^t Matt. xxii. 39. Rom. xiii. toto. 2 Cor. vi. 6.

M. But when thou saidst afore, that the sacraments avail to confirmation of faith, how dost thou now say that we must bring faith to them?

S. These sayings do not disagree. For there must be ^ufaith begun in us, to the nourishing and strengthening whereof the Lord hath ordained the sacraments, which bring great effectual helps to ^xthe confirming, and, as it were, sealing, the promises of God in our hearts.

^u Rom. i. 17. 1 Thess. iii. 10. 2 Thess. i. 3. Heb. vi. 1.
^x Acts ii. 42. Rom. iv. 11. & xv. 8. & vi. 4. Gal. iii.

M. There remaineth yet for thee to tell to whom the ministration of the sacraments properly belongeth.

27. Eph. ii. 11, 19. & iv. 5. Col. ii. 11, 12. 1 Pet. iii. 21.

S. Sith the duties and offices of feeding the Lord's flock with God's word and the ministering of ^ysacraments, are most nearly joined together, there is no doubt that the ministration thereof properly belongeth to them to whom the office of public teaching is committed. For as the Lord ^zhimself at his supper, exercising the office of the public minister, did set forth his own example to be followed, so did he commit the offices of baptizing and teaching peculiarly to his apostles.

^y Matt. xxviii. 19. Mark xvi. 15. Acts ii. 38, 41. & viii. 12, 35, 36, 37.
^z Matt. xxvi. Mark xiv. Luke xxii. 1 Cor. xi.

M. Ought the pastors to receive all indifferently, without choice, to the sacraments?

S. In old time when men, grown ^aand of full years, came to our religion, they were not admitted so much as to baptism, unless there were first assurance had of their faith in the chief articles of Christian religion. Now because only infants are baptized, there can be no choice made. Otherwise it is of the Lord's Supper, whereunto sith none come but they that are grown in years, if any be openly known to be unworthy, the pastor ought not to admit him to the supper, because it cannot be done without profane abuse of the sacrament.

^a Mark xvi. 15, 16. Acts ii. 41. & viii. 12, 37. & xviii. 8.

M. Why did the Lord then not exclude the ^btraitor Judas from communicating of his supper?

^b Matt. xxvi. 21, 22, &c. Mark xiv. 18, 19, &c. John xiii. 26, 27, &c.

S. Because his wickedness, howsoever it was known to the Lord, was not yet at that time openly known.

M. May not ministers then put back hypocrites?

S. ᵉNo so long as their wickedness is secret.

ᵉ 1 Cor. v. 2.

M. Sith then both good and bad do indifferently and in common use the sacraments, what sure and stedfast trust of consciences can be in them, which thou even now didst affirm?

ᵈ John xiii. 26, 27. Rom. iii. 3, 4. 1 Cor. x. 21, 22.
ᵉ 1 Cor. x. 16. & xi. 28, 31.

S. Though ᵈthe ungodly, so much as concerneth themselves, do not receive the gifts of God offered in the sacraments, but do refuse and disappoint themselves; yet ᵉthe godly, which by faith seek Christ, and his grace in them, are never disappointed or defrauded of a most good conscience of mind, and most sweet comfort, by an assured hope of salvation and of perfect felicity.

M. But if any pastor do either himself know, or be privily informed that they be unworthy, may he not exclude them from the communion?

S. Such he may both in public sermons admonish, so he utter them not by name, or blot them with stain or infamy, but pinch them and reprove them only with suspicion of their own conscience, and with conjecture; and he may also privately grievously threaten them; but put them back from the communion he may not, unless the lawful examination and judgment of the church be first had.

M. What remedy is then to be found and used for this mischief?

ᶠ Matt. xviii. 15, 16, 17. Acts xiv. 23. & xv. 4, 6, 22, 24. & xx. 17, 28. 1 Cor. vi. 1, 2. & xii. 28. & xiv. 26, 30. 1 Tim. v. 17. Tit. i. 5.
ᵍ 1 Cor. v. 1, 4, 5. & xi. 16, 18, &c.

S. In churches well ordered and well mannered there was, as I said before, ᶠordained and kept a certain form and order of governance. There were chosen elders, that is, ecclesiastical magistrates, to hold and keep the discipline of the church. To these belonged the authority, looking to, and correction like censors. ᵍThese calling to them also the pastor, if they knew any that either with false opinions, or troublesome errors, or vain superstitions, or with corrupt and wicked life, brought publicly any great offence to the church of God, and which might not come without profaning the Lord's Supper, did put back such from the communion; and rejected them, and did not admit them again till they had with public penance satisfied the church.

M. What measure ought there to be of public penance?

S. Such as go about, with devices of false opinions, ʰto hurt true godliness, and shake religion, or with corrupt and wicked life have raised grievous and public offences, it is meet that they make ⁱpublic satisfaction to the church whom they have so offended, that is, sincerely to acknowledge and confess their sin before the whole congregation, and openly to declare that they be heartily sorry that they have so grievously offended Almighty God, and, as much as in them lay, have dishonoured the Christian religion which they have professed, and the church wherein they were accounted; and that not by their sin only, but also by pernicious example they have hurt other; and therefore they crave and pray pardon first of God, and then of his church.

M. What shall then be done?

S. Then they must humbly require and pray that they may be again received into the church, which by their deserving they were cast out of, and to the holy mysteries thereof. In short sum, ᵏthere must in public penance be such moderation used, that, neither by too much severity, he that hath sinned do despair, nor, on the other side, by too much softness the discipline of the church decay, and the authority thereof be abated, and other be encouraged and boldened to attempt the like. But when by the ˡjudgment of the elders and the pastor, both the punishment of him that sinned, and the example of other is satisfied, then he that had been excommunicate was wont to be received again to the communion of the church.

M. I see, my child, that thou well understandest the sum of Christian godliness. Now it resteth that thou so direct thy life by the rule of this godly knowledge, that thou seem not to have learned these things in vain. For not they that ᵐonly hear and understand God's word, but they that follow God's will, and obey his commandment, shall be blessed. Yea, that servant that knoweth his master's will, and followeth it not, shall be ⁿmore grievously beaten. So little profiteth the understanding of godliness and true religion, unless there be joined to it uprightness of life, innocency, and holiness. Go to therefore, my child, bend all thy care and thought hereunto, that thou fail not in thy duty, or swerve at any time from this rule and prescribed form of godly life.

S. I will do my diligence, worshipful master, and omit

nothing, so much as I am able to do; and with all my strength and power will endeavour that I may answer the profession and name of a Christian. And also I will humbly, with all prayers and desires, alway crave of Almighty God, that he suffer not the seed of his doctrine to perish in my heart, as sown in a dry °and barren soil, but that he will, with the ᵖdivine dew of his grace, so water and make fruitful the dryness and barrenness of my heart, that I may bring forth plentiful fruits of godliness to be bestowed and laid up in the ᑫbarn and granary of the kingdom of heaven.

M. Do so, my child; and doubt not, but as thou hast, by ʳGod's guiding, conceived this mind and will, so thou shalt find and have the issue and end of this thy godly study and endeavour, such as thou desirest and lookest for, that is, most good and happy.

° Matt. xiii. 4, 5, 6, 7, 19, 20, 21, 22.
ᵖ Psal. i. 3. & civ. 13. Matt. xiii. 8, 23. 1 Cor. iii. 6, 7.
ᑫ Matt. iii. 12. Luke iii. 17.
ʳ 2 Cor. iii. 5. Phil. ii. 12, 13.

APPENDIX.

[Caius College MSS. 64, pp. 71—74.]

APPENDIX.

M^R. NOEL'S SERMON AT THE PARLIAM^T. BEFORE THE QUEEN'S MA^{TIE}

[The Parliament met on 11th January, 1563.]

DAVID being troubled with the insurrection of his own son Absolom, who, although he were of so goodly personage and beauty as none was in all Israel, as appeareth in the 2 Kings xiv.; meet (as the common saying is) for a kingdom; yet, he being greedy of honour, wholly given to ambition, by sundry ways, and false subtle crafty and politic persuasions, attempts, and means, as appeareth 2 Kings v.; ungodlily stirred up the subjects against their godly prince, yea, most unnaturally against his own father: which said Absolom, although in years young, yet got unto him, for the better accomplishment of his enterprise, grave, sage, and politic counsellors, as Achithophel one of his own father's old sage counsellors; by which means, and others, he encouraged himself, thinking his enterprise to be half achieved; but, on the other side, although David saw his own servants, subjects, and counsellors, to depart from him, and therefore forced to fly over Jordan for fear of falling into the hands of his ambitious son, yet he despaired not, but encouraged himself, not only saying, "Offer ye the sacrifice of righteousness, and put your trust in the Lord," and so forth, as in the 4th Psalm, but also prayed that God would destroy the counsel of Achithophel: as 2 Kings xv. which former words, as they were spoken by him being a prince, yet a remembrance to princes and nobles that as they do excel other in nobility, even so ought they to excel other in wisdom and virtue. For as the "beginning of wisdom is the fear of the Lord," so is the trusting in him the finishing thereof; who is the only giver of all goodness and wisdom. And this Absolom is ungrate both to the Lord for his manifold benefits and mercies shewed unto him, and so ungrate to his own father, having obtained such an army and wise counsellors, thinking all the same to come of himself, and to be so noble that no hands durst lay hold on him, yet all being without the Lord, was but a puddle of mischief. For notwithstanding that he was so ungrate by subtil means to win away the hearts of the people from their prince, and made this unnatural rebellion; yet his godly father, David, so dearly loved him, that at such time as his army went forth to battle against him, commanded them to use and intreat him gently for his sake. Whereupon, after the battle, considering the love the king, his father, bare him, no man durst scarce lay hands upon him. Yet God clean overthrew him, and turned all upside down, and hanged him up without man's aid; yea, even by the yellow locks, as appeareth 2 Kings xviii. And his chief counsellor Achitophel, seeing his counsel took no effect, hanged himself, as in 2 Kings xvii. And thus, by them may be seen that, not trusting in the Lord, but in themselves, they came to ruin; and so shall all the like do. And, on the contrary side, David, trusting only in God, prospered; and so shall all other the like do. And although David did only so trust, yet he refused not to do his endeavour, but used the ordinary and reasonable means which God hath ordained by the wisdom of man given of God for that purpose. And they that will not so do, neither fear nor trust aright in God, but contemn and tempt him who made means to be used, although not to be trusted in, but in God; for that there is nothing good without the Lord.

Sacrifices of thanksgiving have been from the beginning, as in Gen. iv. appeareth by Cain and Abel. But all offerings of sacrifices be ungodly if the author have not a godly mind, and forsake sin, as in Ecclus. xxxv. And so, having a godly mind, "offer the sacrifice of righteousness" to repentance, penance, alms, thanksgiving, cleanness of heart, and all other virtues; subduing all vices, as in the 51. Psalm. For innocence of life is a chief sacrifice, and pertaineth to all ages and sexes, as well nobles, gentles, soldiers, as others; what ought first to be in heart, and after in life by works: which the nobles and others in authority, as they excel in honour and authority above others, so ought they specially to excel in good works. For in them the fault is more than a fault, because that as well their subjects, servants, curry-favourers, and others, will follow and practise who can go nearest to observe their order, and follow best their mind, (as in doing as they do) the inferior by the example of the superior will follow their step; for the young cock croweth as he heareth the old. And therefore they in authority ought chiefly to look unto it, because they are presidents of good life and justice; and give judgment, and therefore ought specially to " offer sacrifice of righteousness," and specially those which be now of this high House of Parliament assembled for making of laws for service of God and the realm. And then by their ensample other will follow. But this great pride of apparel which sheweth a troubled mind, and this excess in diet, and breaches of promises, and open crimes, do declare our unthankful sacrifices. Howbeit, as in Joshua xxiii., who saith to the people, if you have determined to trouble the commonwealth, and to anger the Lord (as in serving strange gods, and wallowing in other vices with such sacrifice of unrighteousness), yet " I and my house will serve the Lord," and "offer the sacrifice of righteousness" to him which giveth all: and seek first his kingdom, and then all things shall prosper. And in like manner let us say and do. For by the miserable estate of our neighbours of France we may see our own happiness; for which if we be unthankful, it will fall on us. And therefore let us serve only the Lord.

Furthermore, where the Queen's majesty of her own nature is wholly given to clemency and mercy, as full well appeareth hitherto. For in this realm was never seen a change so quiet; or so long time reigning without blood (God be praised for it). Howbeit those which hitherto will not be reformed, but obstinate, and can skill of no clemency or courtesy, ought otherwise to be used. But now will some say, Oh bloody man! that calleth this the house of right, and now would have it made a house of blood. But the Scripture teacheth us that divers faults ought to be punished by death: and therefore following God's precepts it cannot be accounted cruel. And it is not against this house, but the part thereof, to see justice ministered to them who will abuse clemency. Therefore the goodness of the Queen's majesty's clemency may well and ought now therefore to be changed to justice, seeing it will not help. But now to explicate myself, I say if any man keeping his opinion, will, and mind close within himself, and so not open the same, then he ought not to be punished. But when he openeth it abroad, then it hurteth, and ought to be cut off. And specially if in any thing it touch the Queen's majesty. For such errors or heresy ought not, as well for God's quarrel as the realm's, to be unlooked unto. For clemency ought not to be given to the wolves to kill and devour, as they do the lambs. For which cause it ought to be foreseen; for that the prince shall answer for all that so perish, it lying in her power to redress it. For by the scriptures, murderers, breakers of the holy day, and maintainers of false religion ought to die by the sword. But first are to be persuaded by the clergy by the sword of the Spirit, to win them from their errors (if it may be). Also the Lord's day, which now is so diversly abused, is to be looked unto: for on that day, taverns, alehouses, and other unruly places be full, but the Lord's house empty; which crime before this hath been punished with death. And therefore discipline ought now speedily to be restored with a law for redress of the same. For we having six days to our own use, the seventh to be dedicated to the Lord; and seeing it is abused, it ought to be punished. For we, "to whom much is given, shall be of much required." And therefore let us again to God offer much; and so ought the nobility to do, and the clergy also, by good example, or else the punishment will follow. Also some other sharper laws for adultery; and also for murder more straiter than for felony; which in France is well used: as the wheel for the one, the halter for the other; which if we had here I doubt not within few years would save many a man's life.

And where the Queen's majesty, to her great praise and no small charge, aided her neighbours of Scotland, (yea, although before her enemies) without any ambition or desire of their possessions, as by the same appeareth; but only, both for conscience' sake to save them which otherwise would have been destroyed (for he that saveth not him which he may is a murderer), as also for the surety of this our realm; by which her means the purpose of that her known and bent enemy was broken. And now again likewise hath entred wars in France clear without ambition, but to disappoint the same her enemy of his devilish pretensed purpose. And by that means to preserve numbers which otherwise he meaneth to destroy[1]. And therefore now seeing it is so honourably begun, both for conscience' sake and surety of the realm, let it be foreseen to go through withal. For it is not good to anger an enemy; well remembering that he that would be a bent enemy without cause, now being stirred, judge what he will do. For it is better to look to the banks before the water breaketh in, than after when the water is out, and therefore good to work apace in the ebb tides before the spring come. For that penny is ill spared which after will cost a pound: and better to give somewhat, and have the rest in quiet, than by sparing that somewhat to lose all: wherefore every man ought to lay to his hand, giving unto Cæsar that what is Cæsar's: which seeing Christ did so command to an infidel, how much more we to a Christian our right sovereign for maintenance of their most holy wars, and defence and surety of our own realm. Whereunto for the bishops of the spiritualty and the rest of the clergy, I dare boldly say will both largely and willingly give to their powers: lamenting their ability to be such that they are no abler to give larger. And even in time of peace it were good for younger brethren and others to join with some being in wars for experience' sake: unto whom and the rest of the soldiers I wish there might be some reward provided without the Queen's charge; and that now not to be forgotten which before at the suppression of abbeys had been foreseen:—that but two houses in every shire might have been maintained, the one for the reward of the soldiers, and the other for scholars. Then surely we should have had learned scholars and good soldiers.

And whereas things be scarce, is no marvel of dearth; as for example by corn at this present. But whereas plenty is and yet dearth, is great marvel; as now of sheep, and yet never so many, and yet never so dear. And now so many that they do not only eat up such void and waste grounds as be meet, and were accustomed for them, but the good ground which should be tilled and sown with corn; and also men. For that where there hath been accustomed to be twenty several houses for the Queen's subjects to inhabit in, now

[1] The preacher here alludes to the assistance afforded by Queen Elizabeth to the Protestants in Scotland, and in France.]

there remaineth only a shepherd and his dog[1]. And therefore as for payments, such persons as eat up men would be looked unto, for they may well pay. Yet notwithstanding there are good laws made for maintenance of tillage, but not executed. The cause thereof is (as men say) that those which should see the same executed be faulty therein themselves, and so not amended. For they cannot pluck forth the mote of another's eye, by reason of the beam in their own eye.

Furthermore, to have provision to avoid vagabonds, as the martial law, if it were put in execution, doth full well. For he that liveth idly, having not any ways whereon to live, is a thief, and robbeth the poor of their duty and living: which poor and impotent I wish not to lie so abroad in the streets; but order to be taken for them, that such which with any kind of art can get their own living, or somewhat towards their maintenance, may be put to be so occupied; and then the other will be the more easier and better provided for: which I wish were seen unto.

And whereas the Queen's majesty's most noble ancestors have commonly had some issue to succeed them, but her majesty yet none; which want is for our sins to be a plague unto us. For as the marriage of Queen Mary was a terrible plague to all England, and like in continuance to have proved greater; so now for the want of your marriage and issue is like to prove as great a plague. For if your parents had been of your mind, where had you been then? Or what had become of us now? When your majesty was troubled with sickness[2], then I heard continual voices and lamentations, saying, "Alas, what trouble shall we be in, even as great or greater than France! For the succession is so uncertain, and such division for religion! Alack! what shall become of us?" For as a man which doth afore he hath made his will, or get all things in a good order, is much troubled in his conscience for the care thereof, even so no doubt of it was and is the Queen's majesty much troubled for the succession of this crown. And of late as I chanced to walk up and down here in this church, I espied a ruinous

[1 See Latimer's Works, I. 99; and Pilkington's Works, p. 86. Park. Soc. Edd.]

[2 Alluding to an attack of the small-pox, from which the Queen had very recently recovered.]

monument or tomb of one of your ancestors, the longest reign that ever was, and yet his crown in the dust[3]. And passing a little further espied another like monument of one other of them, who reigned not half so long, and yet twice more noble, and his crown in like manner[4]. And yet not so staying, a little off saw the funeral place of that most virtuous imp your most noble brother of famous memory King Edward the 6th, and your sister Queen Mary. And now of later times for your and our better example the end and death of the Lady Jane[5], your almoner[6], and other even near or here about your court: which be worthy monuments and admonitions for us to remember the same, being the most certain thing that can be; and again the uncertain when the hour shall be, or how soon. Which I for my part weighing and foreseeing in my judgment, the ruin of this my most natural country to be at hand, thought to take to my meditation (but not such as old men have used to meditate on their beds), but to meditate myself in the Lamentations of Jeremy, and in the same to pass away these my old years. But then again when I heard of the calling of this Parliament I was thereby encouraged, hoping and not doubting, but there should be such order taken, and good laws established, which should again erect up the decay of the same. And thus beseeching God that this assembly of the two Houses may wholly together offer up a "sacrifice of righteousness and thanksgiving," and proceed forward with making of good laws; then I doubt not but your Majesty shall to our comfort long reign over us, and the nobles with their issues continue.

[3 Alluding probably to Henry III.]
[4 Meaning probably Edward IV.]
[5 Lady Jane Grey.]
[6 Dr May, Archbishop of York elect.]

INDEX.

N.B. The figures within parentheses refer to the pages of the Latin Catechism.

A.

Abbeys, Nowell says one house in each shire should have been reserved for soldiers, and one for scholars, 227.
Absolom, his rebellion, 223; his end, 224.
Absolution, on the power of the keys, (57) 100, 176.
Adam, his creation, (32) 148; his fall, (33, 34) 148, 149; God's promise of a Saviour, (34) 150.
Admonition to the Parliament, ix.
Adultery, to what the commandment extends, (19) 133.
Adversity, peculiarly the lot of those who are beloved of God, (18) 132.
Ahithophel, takes part in Absolom's rebellion, 223; hangs himself, 224.
Amen, its meaning, (81) 202.
Angels, some of them fell, (31) 147; their ministry, (65) 185.
Angelus, angeli, 99.
Anger, it is murder in God's sight, (19) 133.
Animalis homo, 99.
Apostles, v. *Creed*.
Apostolus, 99.
Articles, (XXXIX.) revised, 1562, iii.
Arts, not forbidden by the second commandment, (10) 123.
Assoil, to solve, 125.

B.

Baptism, what it is, (85) 207; the grace thereof, (86) 207, 208; received only by the faithful, (87) 208; proofs that infants ought to be baptized, (87) 209; there is no change in the water, (91) 214.

Benedicere, 99.
Bible, v. *Scriptures*.
Bread, (daily) what, (77) 197.
Buckhurst, (Thos. Lord) v. *Sackville*.

C.

Calvin, (Jo.) his Catechism followed to some extent by Nowell, vii.
Campion, (Edm.) the conference with him, vii, viii.
Caput, 99.
Carlisle, (Nich.) Grammar Schools, i.
Caro, carnalis, 99.
Carte, (Tho.) Hist. of England, i.
Catechisms, their use, 109.
Catechismus, catechesis, catechumeni, 100.
Catholic, meaning of the term, (54) 100, 173.
Cecil, (Sir William) afterwards Lord Burghley, letter to him, vi.
Certitudo, 100.
Charity, a principal part of Christian religion, (6) 118.
Children, punished for the sin of their fathers, (11) 125; what is promised to the children of the godly, (12) 125.
Christ, eternal God, (29) 145; the seed of the woman, (34) 151; promised to the fathers, (35) 151; meaning of the name Jesus, (35) 151; meaning of the name Christ, (35) 152; it denotes that he is a king, (36) 152; a priest, (36) 153; a prophet, (36) 153; he is the only Son of God, (37) 154; our Lord, (37) 154; his incarnation, (34, 38) 151, 154; his betrayal, condemnation, and death, (39) 156; crucifixion, 100; he voluntarily suffered as our surety, (39) 156; and overcame death, (39)

156; the day of his death specially foreordained, (41) 158; he was touched with the horror of eternal death, (42) 159; the benefits which the faithful receive by his death, (42) 160; his burial, (43) 160; his descent into hell, (43) 160; his resurrection, (43) 161; the profits thereof, (44) 161; his ascension and session at the right hand of the Father, (45) 163; the profits thereof, (46) 164; why he did not tarry with us bodily on earth, (46—48) 164, 165; his second coming, and the day of judgment, (50, 51) 168, 169; he is our mediator, (66) 186; and head of the Church, 99.

Christian, religion, what it is, (1, 2) 113, 114; its principal parts, (6, 7) 118, 119.

Christians, named of Christ, (1) 113; crucified, dead, buried, risen, and ascended with Christ, (48, 49) 166, 167.

Church, (The Holy Catholic) the company of the elect, (53, 54) 171, 172; the body of Christ, (53) 99, 172; why called holy, (54) 172; why catholic, (54) 101, 173; the holy catholic church of the elect is not visible, (56) 174; there is no hope of salvation out of it, (57) 176.

Church, (The Visible) what it is, (56) 174; its marks, (56) 175; all its members are not of the number of the elect, (57) 175.

Church of Rome, not the catholic church, (54) 173.

Churton, (Ralph), Life of Nowell, viii.

Cicero, (M. T.) referred to, (69) 189; his Latinity, i*, ii*, 97, &c.

Circumcision, a sacrament, (87, 88) 209, 210.

Claves, 100.

Cœlum, 99.

Commandments, (X.) contents of the two tables, (7) 120; the first commandment, (8) 120; the second, (9) 122: the third, (13) 126; the fourth, (14) 128; the fifth, (16) 130; the sixth, (19) 133; the seventh, (19) 133; the eighth, (19) 133; the ninth, (20) 134; the tenth, (21) 136; the sum of the Ten Commandments, (22) 136.

Communion, v. *Supper*.

Communion of Saints, what it is, (55) 173.

Concupiscentia, 100.

Confirmation, why appointed, (89) 210; popish confirmation, (89) 211; preparatory catechizing, 109.

Contritio, 100.

Convocation, i; that of 1562, Nowell prolocutor, iii.

Corpus Christi, the church, 100.

Councils, the use of their decrees, (3) 115.

Courtenay, (Edw.) Earl of Devon, i.

Covetousness, forbidden, (21) 136.

Creation, of all things, (30) 146; its end, (31) 147; of man, (32) 147.

Credo, 100.

Creed of the Apostles, why called a symbol, (26) 141; why the symbol of the Apostles, (26) 142; expounded, (27) 142.

Creo, creatio, creator, 100.

Crucifigo crucifixus, 100.

D.

Dæmones, 100, 101.

David, his conduct during Absolom's rebellion, 223.

Daye, (Jo.) prints Nowell's Catechism in English, 105.

Death, overcome by Christ, (39) 156; all will not die, (50) 168.

Deïtas, 101.

Devil, v. *Satan*.

Devils, (diaboli) not created wicked, (31) 147.

Devon, (Edw. Earl of) v. *Courtenay*.

Diabolus, 101.

Dilectio, 101.

Discipline, much decayed in the church, (56) 175.

Dorman, (Tho.) his controversy with Nowell, iii, iv.

Dorset, (Thos. Earl of) v. *Sackville*.

Doxology, in the Lord's prayer, (81) 202.

E.

Ecclesia, 101.
Edward VI., his tomb, 229.
Effectus, effectio, 101.
Egypt, represents man's state by nature, (8) 121.
Elders (seniores), their office in ecclesiastical government, (96) 218.
Electi Dei, 101.
Election, v. *Predestination*.
Elizabeth, queen, assists the protestants of Scotland and France, 226, 227; advised to marry, 228.
Essentia, substantia, 101.
Ethnici, 101.
Eucharist, v. *Supper*.
Eutyches, his heresy, (48) 166.
Evangelium, evangelista, 101.
Eve, her creation, (32) 148; deceived by Satan, (33) 148.
Evil, what the word means in the Lord's Prayer, (80) 201.
Excommunicare, excommunicatio, 101.
Excommunication, should be by the lawful judgment of the church, (95) 218.

F.

Faith, a principal part of christian religion, (6) 118; true faith and false, (27, 28) 142—144; not the cause of justification, but the instrument, (61) 180; good works necessarily follow it, (61) 180; it is the gift of God, (63) 183; needful in prayer, (67) 187; meaning of the word *credo*, 100.
False-witness, forbidden, (19) 134.
Fathers, v. *Parents*.
Fides, fiducia, 101.
Flesh and Spirit, 99.
Forespeaking, fortune-telling, 127.
Forgiveness, v. *Sin*.
France, its miserable state, 223, 228; capital punishments used there, 226; the protestants there assisted by queen Elizabeth, 226, 227.
Frankfort, troubles amongst the exiles there, ii.

G.

Gentiles, 101.
Glorificare, 101.
God, v. *Worship*.
Our Maker, Lord, and Saviour, (8) 121; what we owe to him, (9) 122; it is not lawful to represent him by a visible form, (10) 123; he is a jealous God, (11) 124; slow to anger, ready to forgive, (12) 126; his name to be reverenced, (13) 126; how he is to be loved, (22) 137; his nature cannot be expressed by words, (29) 144; the Trinity in Unity, (29) 145; God the Father, (29) 145; God created all things by his Word, (31) 146; his providence, (31) 147; our Father, (71, 72) 191, 192; in heaven, (73) 193; his name to be hallowed, (73) 194; his kingdom, (74) 195; his will, (76) 196; his glory, (81) 203.
Gospel, distinguished from the law, (5) 118; foretold by the prophets, and taught by Christ, (38) 155.
Grace, God is not unrighteous in giving it to some and withholding it from others, (11) 125; excludes the merit of works, (57) 176.
Gratitudo, 101.
Grey (Lady Jane), 229.
Grindal (Edm.), Abp of York, dedications to him, i*, 107.

H.

Habits, v. *Vestments*.
Harding (Tho.), writes against Jewell, iv.
Heaven, (59) 178; God's dwelling-place, (73) 193; God's will done there, (76) 197.
Hell, (inferi), how Christ descended thither, (43) 160; why not mentioned in the creed as the abode of the wicked, (60) 179.
Henry III., his tomb, 229.
Heresy, it should be suppressed, 226.
Holy Ghost, eternal God, (29) 145; his work in the elect, (52) 170.
Homily, Nowell composes one on the plague, iii.

Homo, animalis homo, vetus homo, novus homo, 99.
Humphry (Lau.) refuses the habits, ii.
Hypocrisis, hypocrita, 101.

I.

Idolatry, forbidden, (9, 10) 121, 123.
Idolum idololatria, 101.
Images, how far lawful, (10) 123; called by some the books of the unlearned, (10) 123.
Imp, Edward VI. styled a virtuous imp, 229.
Imperfectio, 101.
Inferna, 101.
Infidelis, 101.
Inobedientia, 101.
Invisibilis, 101.
Invoco, invocatio, 101.
Israel, v. *Jews*.

J.

Jesus, v. *Christ*.
Jewell (Jo.), Bp of Salisbury, his Apology attacked by Dorman, defended by Nowell, iii. iv.
Jews, how the precepts given to them belong to us, (8) 121.
Judgment, of the quick and the dead (50) 168.
Jusjurandum, juramentum, 101.
Justificare, 101.
Justification, the law would justify if it were perfectly kept, (24) 139; but no man is justified in this way, (25) 140; justification, but by faith, (28) 144; or rather by the righteousness of Christ through faith, (60) 179; for faith is not the cause but the instrument of justification, (61) 180; good works necessarily follow it, (61) 180; it does not discourage good works, (63) 182.

K.

Keys, v. *Absolution*.

L.

Lavacrum, lavatio, 102.
Law of God, distinguished from the gospel, (5) 118; the full and perfect rule of righteousness, (7) 120, (24) 139; having respect to the affections of the heart, (21) 135, 136; why written in tables, (24) 139; would justify if it were perfectly kept, (24) 139; but no man is so justified, (25) 140; for the law requires what man cannot perform, (25) 140: what it is to the unbelieving and what to the godly, (25) 140.
Law of Nature, (23) 138.
Law of England, on law-suits, (79, 80) 201; suggestions for legislators, 226.
Life, the promise of long life annexed to the fifth commandment, (17) 131; new life, 103.
Looe, Cornwall, Nowell elected member, i.
Lord's Supper, v. *Supper*.
Love, to God and our neighbour, (22) 137.

M.

Magistrates, to be honoured, (16, 17) 130, 131; rebellion against them worse than against parents (18) 132.
Maledicere, 102.
Malitia, 102.
Man, made for God's glory, (32) 147.
Mandere, mandi, 102.
Mary (B. V.), the mother of our Lord, (34, 38) 151, 154, 155.
Mary, queen, her marriage a plague to England, 228; her tomb, 229.
Master, or teacher, his duty, (1) 113.
May (Will.) Abp of York elect, and queen Elizabeth's almoner, 229.
Mediator, 102.
Membra Christi, 102.
Merit, disclaimed, (57) 176, (62) 182.
Middleton, Lanc., Nowell went to school at Middleton, i.; and afterwards founded a free school there, viii.
Minister Dei, seu ecclesiæ, 102.
Ministers, the ministration of sacraments properly belongs to those to whom public teaching is committed (94) 217.
Mortifico mortificatio, 102.
Mothers, v. *Parents*.
Mundani, mundus, seculum, 102.
Murder, forbidden (19) 133; its proper punishment, 226.

N.

Neighbour, how far the name extendeth, (23) 102, 137, 138.
Norton, (Tho.), a lawyer, notice of him and his works, viii.; translates Nowell's Catechism, *ib.*; his dedication thereof to the archbishops and bishops, 107.
Norton, (Tho.) called by Strype a minister, but probably identical with the last, viii.
Novus homo, 99.
Nowell, (Alex.) memoir, i.—ix.; birth, and early education, i.; sent to Oxford, *ib.*; master of Westminster school, and prebendary there, *ib.*; returned member for Looe, but displaced, *ib.*; goes into exile, ii.; the troubles at Frankfort, *ib.*; on queen Mary's death Nowell returns to England, and is appointed a royal visitor, archdeacon of Middlesex, &c., *ib.*; made dean of St Paul's, iii.; his preaching, *ib.*; prolocutor of the convocation, *ib.*; his controversy with Dorman, *ib.*; and Saunders, iv.; notice of his Catechism, iv.—vii.; sanctioned by convocation, v.; letter from Nowell to Sir William Cecil, on its being printed, vi.; editions and abridgments of it, vii.; Nowell and others confer with Campion, *ib.*; president of Brasenose, i.; and a benefactor to that college, viii.; his death, *ib.*; his Catechism, Latin, 1; Norton's translation thereof, 105; sermon before the queen and parliament, 1563, 223.
Nowell, (Jo.) the dean's father, i.

O.

Obedience, a principal part of christian religion, (6, 7) 118, 120.
Observare leges, 102.
Omnipotens 102.
Oratio, 102.
Oxford, Nowell a benefactor to Brasenose college, viii.

P

Pardon, v. *Sin.*
Parents, to be honoured, (16) 130; the commandment extends to all superiors, (16.) 130.
Parker, (Matth.) Abp. of Canterbury, dedications to him, i*, 107.
Parliament, a sermon before it. 223.
Passio, passus, 102.
Passover, the time of Christ's death, (41) 158.
Peccator, peccatum originis, 102.
Penance, on its public use, (96) 219.
Perjury, forbidden, (13) 126.
Personæ, 102.
Pharaoh, represents the devil, (8) 121.
Pictures, their lawful use, (10) 123, 124.
Pilate, (Pontius) why named in the Creed, (40) 157; bore witness of Christ's innocency, yet condemned him, (40.) 157.
Pœnitentia, 102.
Poor, they should be provided for, 228.
Poinet, (Jo.) bishop of Rochester, afterwards of Winchester, his catechism followed to some extent by Nowell, vii.
Prædestinatio, 102.
Prayer, of prayer and thanksgiving, (64) 183; must be to God alone, not to saints or angels, (64) 184; must be offered through Christ alone, (66) 186; with true faith, (67) 187; not with the voice alone, (68) 188; nor in a strange tongue, (69) 188; on fervent affection in prayer, (69) 189; the rule and form of prayer, (70) 190.
Prayer, (the Lord's) expounded, (70) 190.
Preachers, preachers and teachers most necessary, (3) 116.
Predestination and election asserted, (53, 54, 56) 171, 172, 174; those whom God has chosen he makes holy, (54) 172; all that are in the visible church are not of the number of the elect, (57) 175; election is the spring-head of justification, (62) 181.
Profano, profanatio, 102.
Propheta, prophetia, 102.
Providence, (31) 147.
Proximus, 102.
Psalms, Norton's share in the Old Version, viii.

R.

Rebellion, a grievous sin, (18) 132.
Redmayn, (Jo.) master of Trin. Coll. Cambridge, his death, i.
Regeneration, ascribed to the Spirit of God, (61) 181; connection with baptism, (85, 86) 207, 208; (91, 92) 214; use of the term, 99.
Religion, v. *Christian Religion.*
Remissio, pœnæ, 102.
Repentance, principal part of christian religion, (6) 119; what it is, (58), 177.
Recipiscentia, 102.
Resurgo, resurrectio, 103.
Resurrection, necessary to perfect joy and immortality, (59) 178.
Reverendus, v. *Venerandus.*
Rewards, freely bestowed by God without our deserving them, (63) 183.
Rome, v. *Church of Rome.*
Rulers, v. *Magistrates.*

S.

Sabbath, what of the precept was temporary, and what continues, (15) 128, 129; the spiritual rest, (16) 129, 130.
Sackville, (Tho.) lord Buckhurst, afterwards earl of Dorset, his writings, viii.
Sacraments, what sacraments are, and why they are given, (83, 84) 205; they are not to be thought unnecessary, (85) 206; their number, (85) 207; they strengthen faith, (94) 217; to whom their ministration properly belongeth, (94) 217; who should be admitted to them, (95) 217.
Sacramentum, 103.
Sacrifices of thanksgiving, 224.
Saints, (v. *Communion*,) not to be prayed to, (65) 184.
Salvare, salvator, salvatio, 103.
Salvation, no hope of it out of the church, (57) 176.
Sampson, (Tho.) refuses the habits, ii.
Sancti, sanctificare, 103.
Sandys, (Edwin) dedication to him as bishop of London, 107.
Satan, figured by Pharaoh, (8) 121; beguiled Eve, (33) 148; the bruising of the serpent's head, (35) 151; meaning of the word *diabolus*, 101.
Saunders, (Nich.) iv.
Scotland, the protestants there assisted by queen Elizabeth, 226, 227.
Scriptura, 103.
Scriptures, (the holy) christian religion only to be learned from them, (2) 114; what they are, *ib.*; why given to us, *ib.*; why called a testament, *ib.*; contain all things necessary for salvation and godliness, (2) 115; ought to be expounded, (3) 116; not to be read to the people in an unknown tongue, (4) 116; not only to be heard, but to be embraced as the truth of God, (4) 117; with prayer for divine illumination, (5) 117; divided into the law and the gospel, (5) 118.
Seculum, v. *Mundani.*
Sensibilis, 103.
Serpent, v. *Satan.*
Seven, meaning of this number in scripture, (16) 130.
Sin, the forgiveness of sins, (57) 176; on the petition for forgiveness of our trespasses, (78) 199; God forgives freely, (79) 199; yet we cannot be forgiven unless we forgive others, (79) 200.
Sin, (original) (33, 34) 102, 149, 150.
Soldiers, provision for them, 227.
Sorcery, a grievous sin, (13) 127.
Spiritus, spiritualis, 103.
Stealing, v. *Theft.*
Strype, (Jo.) ii, iii, v.
Substantia, v. *Essentia.*
Sun, a figure of Christ, (45) 162.
Sunday, the Lord's day, much abused, 226.
Supper of the Lord, what it is, and why ordained, (90) 212; Christ's body and blood present therein to faith, (91) 213; no change in the substance of the elements, (91) 214; it is not a sacrifice for sins, but a memorial of the sacrifice of Christ, (92) 215; only the faithful receive Christ's body and blood, (93) 215; it is damnable to the wicked,

(93) 216; there is no carnal presence, (93) 216; how we may come to it rightly, (93) 216; the openly wicked should not be admitted to it, (95) 217.

Swearing, its lawful use, (13) 127; we may not swear by the saints, or any creatures, (14) 128.

Symbol, v. *Creed*.

T.

Temptation, on the petition against it, (80) 201.

Tentatio, 103.

Testament, why God's word is so called, (2) 114.

Thanksgiving, (82, 83) 203, 204.

Theft, forbidden, (19) 133.

Tillage, its decay, 27, 228.

Tractatio, 103.

Traditiones, 103.

Tregonwell, (Jo.) prebendary of Westminster, and member of parliament, i.

Trespasses, v. *Sin*.

Trinitas, 103.

Trinity, (the Holy) v. *God*.

U.

Unitas, 104.

V.

Vagabonds, they should be punished, 228.

Venerandus, honorandus, reverendus, 103.

Verbum Dei, 103.

Vestments, controversy about them, ii.

Vetus homo, 103.

Visus, visibilis, 104.

Vita nova, 103.

W.

Warton, (Tho.) History of English Poetry, viii.

Westminster abbey, tombs of the kings, 229.

Whalley, Lancashire, the birthplace of Nowell, i.

Wicked, subject to the power of God, (30) 146.

Witness, v. *False witness*.

Wolfe, (Reg.) prints Nowell's Catechism, xi.

Word of God, v. *Scriptures*.

Works, (good) they are not meritorious, (57) 176; follow justification, (61) 180; are acceptable to God, (61, 62) 181, 182; there can be none before we are born again and renewed, (61) 181; not discouraged by the doctrine of justification through faith, (63) 182.

World, its end, (51) 169.

Worship, in what it consists, (9) 122; what sort is forbidden, (10) 123.

Z.

Zelotypus, Zelotes Zelotypia 104.

www.ingramcontent.com/pod-product-compliance
Lightning Source LLC
Chambersburg PA
CBHW062012220426
43662CB00010B/1298